American Queer, Now and Then

And you shall not lie with a male as with a woman. It is an abomination.
—Leviticus 18:20

When we say the Pledge of Allegiance, we say "with liberty and justice for all." Well, what part of "all" don't people understand?
—Former U.S. Representative Patricia Schroeder

Never be bullied into silence. Never allow yourself to be made a victim. Accept no one's definition of your life. Define yourself.
—Harvey Fierstein

If you are trying to transform a brutalized society into one where people can live in dignity and hope, you begin with the empowering of the most powerless. You build from the ground up.
—Adrienne Rich

American Queer, Now and Then

Edited by
DAVID SHNEER
AND CARYN AVIV

Paradigm Publishers
Boulder • London

Copyright © 2006 Paradigm Publishers

Published in the United States by Paradigm Publishers, 3360 Mitchell Lane, Suite E, Boulder, CO 80305 USA.

Paradigm Publishers is the trade name of Birkenkamp & Company, LLC,
Dean Birkenkamp, President and Publisher.

Library of Congress Cataloging-in-Publication Data
American queer, now and then / edited by David Shneer
and Caryn Aviv.
   p. cm.
 Includes bibliographical references and index.
 ISBN 13: 978-1-59451-171-4 (hc)—ISBN 978-1-59451-172-1 (pbk.)
 ISBN 1-59451-171-3 (hc)—ISBN 1-59451-172-1 (pbk.)
   1. Homosexuality—United States. 2. Gays—United States. 3. Gay rights—United States. 4. Gay liberation movement—United States. 5. Homophobia—United States. I. Shneer, David, 1972–
II. Aviv, Caryn, 1969–
 HQ76.3.U5A46 2006
 306.76'60973—dc22

                                                  2005030857

Designed and Typeset by Hoffman-Paulson Associates

10 09 08 07 06   1 2 3 4 5

Contents

Introduction

queer [adj]: 1. differing from what is usual or ordinary; odd; singular; strange 2. slightly ill 3. doubtful; suspicious 4. mentally unbalanced 5. counterfeit; not genuine 6. homosexual: in general usage, still chiefly a slang term of contempt or derision, but lately used by some academics and homosexual activists as a descriptive term without negative connotations

On the publication of our first book that involved queers in America, *Queer Jews,* Caryn's very proper, seventy-something Aunt Barbara from Skokie, Illinois, harangued her publicly at a Thanksgiving dinner: "Caryn, I love the book, but did you have to use the word (in a slight whisper) *queer??!!*" David has heard similar complaints about the use of such a "naughty" word from people ranging from his family members to administrators at his university who had issues with "that word" in a course called "Queer in America." "Who would take such a course?" one perplexed administrator worried.

Words have power. How people have referred to queers over the past 100 years has depended on how people defined queerness. Think of the following images: "*Fucking faggot!*" hurled as an epithet by drunken men from a passing car; "*homo-sex-ual,*" spoken in a genteel Boston Brahmin accent by a 1920s sexologist; "GLBT . . . wait, are there more letters now?" earnestly spoken by a straight ally. None of these are unusual scenes to imagine. How queers have referred to themselves can be even more difficult to keep up with. "Do you identify as genderqueer, butch dyke, power bottom, flaming queen, or 'straight-acting'?"

Although the word makes some people shudder, especially those raised in the 1940s, 1950s, and 1960s, for whom the word has been used as a form of violence against them, "queer" was, once upon a time in America, the playful insider term for people who were "that way." Queers started using the word in the early twentieth century to talk about themselves, to define a group of people who had something in common that was different from the norm.

Since the late 1980s, the term has come back into vogue with a vengeance. For some scholars, activists, and writers, "queer" marks an area of theory and way of looking at the world. Queer theory encourages people to look at things differently, invites readers to pick up on subtle cues, unpack hidden messages, and make texts more complicated. Others have taken the word "queer" as an identity label and a politics, a way of making an epithet yelled at someone on the playground into a word that screams "We're different, that's good, and if you don't like it, that's your problem."

Some younger Americans use "queer" to mark themselves as different not just from "straights" around them, but also from earlier generations of gay men and lesbians. In fact, some queers do not even identify as "gay" or "lesbian," as they see these terms as too confining. Queerness has been about difference, about not being "normal," about exploding the very idea of "normal," of reading texts, people, and experiences more subtly, flexibly, and creatively. A colleague who teaches queer studies once asked the students to describe a world in which queerness was squelched, suppressed, or eliminated, and students responded, "It would be a gray world. . . . It would be a joyless world. . . . It would be a world without Oscar Wilde or Gertrude Stein. . . . It would be a world without pink and sequins. It would be a world without me."

Before we go too far in romanticizing queerness as the life force that animates our social world, a word of caution: in some quarters, the word "queer" has become so popular that it has become commercial, so commercial in fact that it has lost some of the edge it once had. The cable network Showtime aired a wildly popular show called *Queer Eye for the Straight Guy*, which showed how people who are "that way" could save straight men from their terrible sense of style. A 2005 *New York Times* Sunday Styles article lamented the success of *Queer Eye*. It seems that straight men have taken the fashion hint from gay men so far that it's now getting harder to distinguish between who is straight and who is gay.

But these various streams of queerness—queer as theoretical approach to the world, queer as a sense of difference, queer as a sense of style, queer as a branding gimmick, queer as individual and collective identity, queer as camp, queer as consumerism, queer as a subversive political stance, queer as epithet—have not come together in one place, in one book.

In this book, we bring together autobiographies, historical documents, laws, organizational mission statements, academic studies, and other texts to explore the meanings of and debates about the word "queer." By this we mean: queer as both a form of verbal violence and a call to political activism; queer as played by Robin Williams and Sharon Stone on screen and as lived by Matthew Shepard and Brandon Teena in rural America; queer as argued in the courthouses of Washington, D.C., and lived on the streets of hometown America. By combining contemporary stories with ones from the past, and using the analytic tools of feminist social criticism and history, we literally and figuratively map what it has meant to be a part of queer America in the past and present.

WHAT'S INSIDE?

Queer—it's a word that makes Caryn's older relatives uneasy, but a word that has come to mean so many things. Chapter 1 introduces the power that words, labels, and names have in shaping human experiences. We show how doctors, scientists, lawyers, psychiatrists, preachers, moralists, and others have tried to identify, classify, quantify, discourage, and reshape gender identities and sexual orientations that seemed to deviate from what science, religion, and other institutions of power said was "normal." According to traditional interpretations of the Bible, men sleeping with men is not only *not* normal, but a criminal act. According to the laws of pro-creation, women sleeping with women is not only *not* normal, but a threat to women's moral virtue and the stability of society. Men dressing in women's clothing is not only *not* normal, according to many of these institutions that codify mas-culinity and femininity for America, but also a sickness or perversion. Women who dress in men's clothing are not only *not* normal, but accused of wanting to be like men. Nonetheless, those who sleep with the wrong gender or the wrong sex, who dress in the wrong clothing, or who have the wrong biology have their own voices, identities, and labels that play with, challenge, adopt, and frequently ignore what those with power are saying about them.

In Chapter 2, we complicate the assumption that queerness is the same as sex-ual orientation or sexual identity. We introduce the concepts of sex, gender, and gender presentation, and complicate what it means to live in a body defined and shaped by culture and society. Although the United States seems to be stuck in a system of assigning people a sex (male/female) and a corresponding gender identity (masculine/feminine), the reality is that people invent and play with many genders, and queers continue to explore the frontiers of gender expression in creative ways.

With our terms defined (or made even more complicated) we ask in Chapter 3 how queer folks move through the world of real places and spaces. We explore how queers meet, socialize, "hook up," and create homes and neighborhoods in the American landscape. We show how and why a place—like a street, store, club, neighborhood, or whole city—becomes known as queer, and why other places do not, correspondingly, get marked as "straight."

American queers may be defined by places, spaces, clothing, ideas, or texts. But at the root of it all, queerness has something to do with sex, eroticism, and peo-ple falling in love. In Chapter 4 we talk about sex. What is queer sex? Is it different from nonqueer sex? Why have some kinds of sex been considered more "taboo" than others? What is it about queer sex, especially two men and their penises, that gets some people so upset? How do transgender people complicate the definition of queer sex? Why has queer sex been so morally and politically regulated, and why has it taken the United States so long to make it legal for Americans to have queer sex?

Sex and romance sometimes lead to relationships and family, and in Chapter 5, we explore the increasingly loud public discussion about queer marriage and fam-ilies. We show that the feminist revolution of the 1960s and 1970s not only pro-moted women's liberation but also allowed for the creation of new kinds of family units that, for the first time in history, allowed queers to build families *as queers*. In this chapter we provide readings that map the rise of queer marriage as a key issue in political organizing. We invite readers to consider what these conversations, debates, and legal struggles mean for Americans, both queer and not.

Not only are people's experiences shaped by how they have sex, fall in love, and create families, but everyone (queer or not) learns how to be a person and how to live in the world through the images they see (or don't see) and the words they hear (or don't hear) around them. Chapter 6 is dedicated to how queers have portrayed themselves and been portrayed by others. We examine film, literature, plays, and other forms of art and media to examine what it means and what it meant to "play queer" in America. Queerness as a performance—whether it be Robin Williams playing queer in the movie *Birdcage* or Brandon Teena, the transgender teenager whose life was fictionalized in the movie *Boys Don't Cry,* passing as a young man in order to be himself and try to survive in small-town Nebraska—is a central theme in this book. At the same time, we remind the reader that Williams and Teena were in fact doing different things. The representation of queerness in film and other forms of media is almost always connected to gender presentation, stereotypes, cultural perceptions, and perhaps most important, audience reception. So what might have been a funny, campy performance of drag in San Francisco in the 1970s might have been considered terribly dangerous and an invitation to violence in other parts of the country. In this chapter we examine the artistic and cultural representations of queerness (whereas in Chapter 2 we discussed the human performance of queerness). We encourage the reader to compare the two and ask what Williams and Teena have in common . . . if anything.

We mention Brandon Teena, who was murdered because he did not conform to people's expectations of what he should be, as a way of showing that queerness is sometimes about violating boundaries, or, put another way, overturning and challenging expected roles. Overturning the gender system, as Teena found out, has often meant terrible consequences for queer people, including getting killed for who you are or want to be. In Chapter 7, we show how queerness is "put in its place" through violence, intimidation, and harassment. We emphasize that violence comes in many forms, ranging from the mundane and deeply damaging, like being fired for being queer or being screamed at from a passing car, to the murderous, as in the case of Brandon Teena and Matthew Shepard. When we started working on this chapter, we had expected to show readers that "things have only been getting better." What we discovered was that as queerness became more visible and as queer places began to occupy "too much space" (according to some people), violence increased.

But queerness became visible for one reason and one reason alone: queers began taking up more space. Queers began speaking out, writing books, making movies, protesting bad legislation, defending themselves, forming organizations, demanding police protection, protesting police harassment, establishing foundations, and participating in U.S. politics. Chapter 8 is on activism—the words and actions that spark change in our world. We pay homage to Audre Lorde, who said that the deepest and most powerful form of activism is transforming silence into action through speaking out. So the fact that you are reading these words would make Audre Lorde happy.

We end by asking what happens next? With queers out of the closet, on television, and in the suburbs, and with statehouses debating whether queers can get married or inherit each other's property, what's left, and what's next? If queerness is defined by difference, and if being in love with someone of the same sex or gender no longer seems very different, then what's so queer about being queer?

As you read these classics of American queers, keep in mind that our editors made us cut out many wonderful pieces. Who wants a book so thick and heavy that it gives you a backache and sends you to the chiropractor? We heeded their advice, and therefore must give the obligatory disclaimer. This book is by no means exhaustive, nor can it be considered a "canon" of all queer writing and experience. Our aim is to show what some important writers, thinkers, and activists have answered when posed with the question, "What does it mean and what has it meant to be an American queer?"

ACKNOWLEDGMENTS

We'd like to thank the following people who have helped us in our work and in our thinking. We owe thanks to our colleagues Audrey Sprenger, Amie Levesque, Jennifer Reich, Dwight McBride, Sarah Pessin, Nancy Wadsworth, Susan Sterett, Ann Pellegrini, Laura Levitt, Andrea Jacobs, and to our anonymous readers who made fantastic suggestions. We both relied heavily on our friends: Bonnie Feinberg, Debbie Findling, Tim Gill, Sarah Friedmann, Alan Karras, Julie Trestman, and Reba Connell. This book was inspired by our students at the University of Denver, particularly Caryn's students in Human Sexualities and David's students in Queer in America, and students at the University of Wisconsin, who studied queer theory and history with David. Thank you to the Walter Rosenberry Fund at the University of Denver for supporting the production of this book. Thanks go also to the folks at Paradigm Publishing, especially Dean Birkenkamp, Melanie Stafford, and Beth Davis; and our families, chosen and biological; and a special thanks to Gregg, Roland, and Sasha Drinkwater.

1

Bulldykes, Faggots, and Fairies, Oh My!

CALLING AND BEING CALLED QUEER

IN AMERICA, NOW AND THEN

Queer \kwier\ adj [origin unknown] 1a: differing in some odd way from what is usual or normal b (1): eccentric, unconventional (2): mildly insane: touched c: obsessed, hipped d slang: sexually deviate: homosexual 2a. slang: worthless, counterfeit

—Webster's Seventh New Collegiate Dictionary, *1971*

Queer /kwie/ a. and n. A. adj. 1. Strange, odd, eccentric; of questionable character, suspicious. 2a. Bad; worthless. b. Of a coin or banknote: counterfeit, forged. 3. Out of sorts; giddy, faint, ill. 4. Esp. of a man: homosexual. slang. derog.

—New Shorter Oxford English Dictionary, *1993*

Queer: adj. a. Strange, odd, peculiar, eccentric, in appearance or character. Also, of questionable character, suspicious, dubious. queer fellow, an eccentric person; also used, esp. in Ireland and in nautical contexts, with varying contextual connotations b. Of a person (usu. a man): homosexual. Also in phr. as queer as a coot (cf. COOT n.¹ 2b). Hence, of things: pertaining to homosexuals or homosexuality. orig. U.S. c. In U.S. colloq. phr. to be queer for (someone or something): to be fond of or 'keen on'; to be in love with 2. Not in a normal condition; out of sorts; giddy, faint, or ill: esp. in phr. to feel (or look) queer. Also slang: Drunk. Noun: A (usu. male) homosexual. Also in Comb., as queer-bashing vbl. n., the attacking of homosexuals; hence queer-basher.

—Oxford English Dictionary, *1989*

At the first public talk for our book *Queer Jews*, an elderly man stood up slowly from one of the back rows, his face purple and contorted in anger. With shaking hands

1

and a trembling voice, he read from a piece of crumpled paper. "Here is what the dictionary says about that word you use all the time. *Queer: perverted, odd, peculiar. Often used as an epithet in association with homosexuality.*" He paused and glared at us. The room was silent and expectant. "How can you stand up there and call yourselves queer? Queer is what I was called by bullies on the playground. Queer is what I heard when people yelled at me from passing cars. Queer was something that was considered terrible. I want you to know that I'm *not* queer, and I am disgusted that you would even *think* to use this word as something to be proud of, let alone use it as the title of your book." Little did this man know that "queer" was proudly used by many gay men as their name of choice only a few decades prior to his undoubtedly traumatic harassment on the playground.

What's in a name, and why does it matter? What queer people have called themselves and been called by others has changed over the course of the past one hundred years. But one thing has remained consistent: the language we use to describe queer people, identities, and practices reflects who has the power to name and be named. The following readings explore how the act of naming ranges from subtle codes among insiders to institutional efforts to promote gender and sexual compliance, from flamboyant opportunities for creative expression to potent political statements of resistance.

Two things are quite clear from the growing historical record of queer history. First, in the past, queerness had more to do with gender roles than with who was sleeping with whom. People were identified as "that way" if they transgressed the boundaries of what it meant to be male or female, masculine or feminine. In addition, queer people named themselves based on disparate ideas about masculinity and femininity as much as by what queers were actually *doing* sexually. Second, elite groups and institutions have used law, medicine, psychiatry, and religion throughout much of U.S. history to shape public perceptions and fears.

In the late nineteenth century, physicians began to consider sexuality a serious topic worthy of scientific study and classification. Early sexologists such as Henry Havelock Ellis and Richard von Krafft-Ebing attempted to explain same-sex desires through the lenses of medicine and biology. Krafft-Ebing, in fact, coined the term "homosexuality" in 1892 to explain a person who had a "great diminution or complete absence of sexual feeling for the opposite sex, with substitution of sexual feeling and instinct for the same sex." These scientists shifted the conversation away from seeing same-sex acts through a Christian lens as "sodomy," or sins against God, toward seeing them as medical and psychiatric issues beyond a person's control. By doing this, Ellis and other primarily European sexologists advocated for tolerance of "homosexuals" because, in their psychiatric framework, same-sex love was no longer a sin, but instead, an illness.

Magnus Hirschfeld, a German sexologist and gay rights advocate in the early 1900s coined terms like "transvestite" and "third-sex" as a way of categorizing and at the same time validating queer sexualities, genders, and even queer biologies. The continuing medicalization of sexuality also had negative consequences as queer people could be deemed "sick" and in need of "curing," a trend that became dominant in the mid-twentieth-century United States. At the same time, others used sociological language to describe and categorize sexuality. Some researchers showed that "deviant" sexual practices were a threat to public law and order and signs of immorality, and perversions that could potentially disrupt society and families.

Those who fell into these new biological, social, and psychological categories played with, contested, resisted, and quite often ignored them, as George Chauncey shows in his classic analysis of early twentieth-century gay New York. By examining what queers said about themselves rather than simply looking at what others said about them, scholars are now discovering that American queers have not always been a silent minority. In major U.S. urban areas in the early twentieth century, the first traces of organized gay and lesbian subcultures began to emerge, and with them, an astonishing array of names for the people who congregated in these places. Among these were queers, fairies, trade (a term that said as much about a man's class status as about his gender presentation or sexual orientation), "normal" men, bulldaggers, mannish lesbians, and flaming faggots. Queers described themselves differently depending on their race, class, sex, gender, sexual preferences, and even sexual roles. Butch, femme, pansy, fairy, top, bottom, trade, wolf—the list of labels *within* queer communities was and is far more extensive than the labels social authorities have invented. In claiming their own names, queers exercised self-determination in situations where they had less power.

If the early twentieth century was a heyday for queers to name themselves within the linguistic confines of vocabularies available to them, by World War II the state had become more actively involved in identifying and defining queers. Just as queers were coming together in ways unimaginable fifty years earlier, the military was asking questions as never before about people's identities. As Allan Berube shows in his classic work, *Coming Out under Fire,* both queer men and women were forming communities on navy ships, on military bases, and on leave in major ports while the U.S. government was simultaneously "outing queers" and discharging them. It was also one of the first times queerness was defined primarily by sexual desire and sexual act rather than by gender presentation. A formerly "straight" guy or "trade" might now be characterized as homosexual and discharged because of it.

By the 1950s, "queer" had moved from being an insider term of identity to an epithet of derision, a word with which no one wanted to be associated. "Homosexual"—that medicalized word from psychiatric literature—became the term to define people who expressed same-sex desire. It took radical queer activism to take power over naming away from institutions. The word "homosexual" began once again to be seen for what it was—a medicalized term that transformed personal, intimate identities into fixed categories—and the words "gay," "lesbian," "bisexual," and "transgender" began to take hold. Other groups reclaimed older terms and self-identified as "radical fairies" or "butch dykes," terms that had once been identity labels but which had become negative terms of social opprobrium. In this vein, a group of homosexuals in 1990 reclaimed a potent epithet by calling their activist group Queer Nation. In doing so, they returned the word to its former meaning as an insider badge of pride.

As the following excerpts demonstrate, the act of naming has been a series of struggles from inside out, and outside in, throughout the history of American queers over the past two centuries. On the one hand, queer people have tried to define for themselves who they are, what they do, and what their identities mean to them and the larger world. On the other hand, others have tried to define queers using medicine, religion, and the law. Sometimes that dialogue has been marked by constraint and repression. At other times, the conversation has reflected outright resistance to stigmatization and oppression. As Audre Lorde's essay demonstrates, to name oneself is an act of love and power. Naming, in the face of hostility and outright hatred, is no easy task and requires enormous courage. The following pieces ought to stimulate thought and discussion about who gets to name, how and why we call ourselves what we do, and how these ways of naming change over time. Thinking about the relationships between power and naming heightens our sensitivity to how language shapes our realities, our imagination, and our possibilities for living full and meaningful lives.

AUDRE LORDE

The Transformation of Silence into Language and Action (1978)

The work of Audre Lorde (1934–1992), one of the most important voices of second-wave feminism, is synonymous with the power of activism through poetry and literature. Born in New York to Caribbean immigrant parents, Audre Lorde began writing at an early age and published widely read prose and poetry. An outspoken advocate for feminism, lesbian and gay liberation, and civil rights, she was a featured speaker at the historic first march on Washington, D.C., for lesbian and gay liberation in 1979, and was poet laureate of New York State from 1991 to 1993. This speech was originally given at the Modern Language Association conference in 1977.

I have come to believe over and over again that what is most important to me must be spoken, made verbal and shared, even at the risk of having it bruised or misunderstood. That the speaking profits me, beyond any other effect. I am standing here as a Black lesbian poet, and the meaning of all that waits upon the fact that I am still alive, and might not have been. Less than two months ago I was told by two doctors, one female and one male, that I would have to have breast surgery, and that there was a 60 to 80 percent chance that the tumor was malignant. Between that telling and the actual surgery, there was a three-week period of the agony of an involuntary reorganization of my entire life. The surgery was completed, and the growth was benign.

But within those three weeks, I was forced to look upon myself and my living with a harsh and urgent clarity that has left me still shaken but much stronger. This is a situation faced by many women, by some of you here today. Some of what I experienced during that time has helped elucidate for me much of what I feel concerning the transformation of silence into language and action.

In becoming forcibly and essentially aware of my mortality, and of what I wished and wanted for my life, however short it might be, priorities and omissions became strongly etched in a merciless light, and what I most regretted were my silences. Of what had I *ever* been afraid? To question or to speak as I believed could have meant pain, or death. But we all hurt in so many different ways, all the time, and pain will either change or end. Death, on the other hand, is the final silence. And that might be coming quickly, now, without regard for whether I had ever spoken what needed to be said, or had only betrayed myself into small silences, while I planned someday to speak, or waited for someone else's words. And I began to recognize a source of power within myself that comes from the knowledge that while it is most desirable not to be afraid, learning to put fear into a perspective gave me great strength.

I was going to die, if not sooner then later, whether or not I had ever spoken myself. My silences had not protected me. Your silence will not protect you. But for every real word spoken, for every attempt I had ever made to speak those truths for which I am still seeking, I had made contact with other women while we examined the words to fit a world in which we all believed, bridging our differences. And it was the concern and caring of all those women which gave me strength and enabled me to scrutinize the essentials of my living.

The women who sustained me through that period were Black and white, old and young, lesbian, bisexual, and heterosexual, and we all shared a war against the tyrannies of silence. They all gave me a strength and concern without which I could not have survived intact. Within those weeks of acute fear came the knowledge—within the war we are all waging with the forces of death, subtle and otherwise, conscious or not—I am not only a casualty, I am also a warrior.

What are the words you do not yet have? What do you need to say? What are the tyrannies you swallow day by day and attempt to make your own, until you will sicken and die of them, still in silence? Perhaps for some of you here today, I am the face of one of your fears. Because I am woman, because I am Black, because I am lesbian, because I am myself—a Black woman warrior poet doing my work—come to ask you, are you doing yours?

And of course I am afraid, because the transformation of silence into language and action is an act of self-revelation, and that always seems fraught with danger. But my daughter, when I told her of our topic and my difficulty with it, said, "Tell them about how you're never really a whole person if you remain silent, because there's always that one little piece inside you that wants to be spoken out, and if you keep ignoring it, it gets madder and madder and hotter and hotter, and if you don't speak it out one day it will just up and punch you in the mouth from the inside."

In the cause of silence, each of us draws the face of her own fear—fear of contempt, of censure, or some judgment, or recognition, of challenge, of annihilation. But most of all, I think, we fear the visibility without which we cannot truly live. Within this country where racial difference creates a constant, if unspoken, distortion of vision, Black women have on one hand always been highly visible, and so, on the other hand, have been rendered invisible through the depersonalization of racism. Even within the women's movement, we have had to fight, and still do, for that very visibility which also renders us most vulnerable, our Blackness. For to survive in the mouth of this dragon we call America, we have had to learn this first and most vital lesson—that we were never meant to survive. Not as human beings. And neither were most of you here today, Black or not. And that visibility which makes us most vulnerable is that which also is the source of our greatest strength. Because the machine will try to grind you into dust anyway, whether or not we speak. We can sit in our corners mute forever while our sisters and our selves are wasted, while our children are distorted and destroyed, while our earth is poisoned; we can sit in our safe corners mute as bottles, and we will still be no less afraid.

In my house this year we are celebrating the feast of Kwanza, the African-American festival of harvest which begins the day after Christmas and lasts for seven days. There are seven principles of Kwanza, one for each day. The first principle is Umoja, which means unity, the decision to strive for and maintain unity in self and community. The principle for yesterday, the second day, was Kujichagulia—self-determination—the decision to define ourselves, name ourselves, and speak for ourselves, instead of being defined and spoken for by others. Today is the third day of Kwanza, and the principle for today is Ujima—collective work and responsibility—the decision to build and maintain ourselves and our communities together and to recognize and solve our problems together.

Each of us is here now because in one way or another we share a commitment to language and to the power of language, and to the reclaiming of that language which has been made to work against us. In the transformation of silence into language and action, it is vitally necessary for each one of us to establish or examine her function in that transformation and to recognize her role as vital within that transformation.

For those of us who write, it is necessary to scrutinize not only the truth of what we speak, but the truth of that language by which we speak it. For others, it is to share and spread also those words that are meaningful to us. But primarily for us all, it is necessary to teach by living and speaking those truths which we believe and know beyond understanding. Because in this way alone we can survive, by taking part in a process of life that is creative and continuing, that is growth.

And it is never without fear—of visibility, of the harsh light of scrutiny and perhaps judgment, of pain, of death. But we have lived through all of those already, in silence, except death. And I remind myself all the time now that if I were to have been born mute, or had maintained an oath of silence my whole life long for safety, I would still have suffered, and I would still die. It is very good for establishing perspective.

And where the words of women are crying to be heard, we must each of us recognize our responsibility to seek those words out, to read them and share them and examine them in their pertinence to our lives. That we not hide behind the mockeries of separations that have been imposed upon us and which so often we accept as our own. For instance, "I can't possibly teach Black women's writing—their experience is so different from mine." Yet how many years have you spent teaching Plato and Shakespeare and Proust? Or another, "She's a white woman and what could she possibly have to say to me?" Or, "She's a lesbian, what would my husband say, or my chairman?" Or again, "This woman writes of her sons and I have no children." And all the other endless ways in which we rob ourselves of ourselves and each other.

We can learn to work and speak when we are afraid in the same way we have learned to work and speak when we are tired. For we have been socialized to respect fear more than our own needs for language and definition, and while we wait in silence for that final luxury of fearlessness, the weight of that silence will choke us.

The fact that we are here and that I speak these words is an attempt to break that silence and bridge some of those differences between us, for it is not difference which immobilizes us, but silence. And there are so many silences to be broken.

UROLOGIC AND CUTANEOUS REVIEW
Classifications of Homosexuality (1916)

In the early twentieth century, medical practitioners and researchers became interested in questions of sex and gender and began classifying the varieties of sexual orientation and gender. Some researchers, like Magnus Hirschfeld in Germany, used scientific research to argue that human beings had naturally occurring variances in sexuality, and called for the decriminalization of homosexuality. Others used it in order to search for "cures" for biological ailments. The medical journal Urologic and Cutaneous Review, *which appeared throughout the first half of the twentieth century, published the latest research in sex, sexuality, and other medical issues dealing with male and female genitalia.*

Discussing seriously a paper by L. Pierce Clark,[1] Havelock Ellis[2] points out that Clark divides homosexuals into two types: the homosexual subject and the homosexual object. The former is what is called the true invert. He feels as a man and is attracted by virile men. The other is attracted by boys and feminine men. He is a neurotic and is under a compulsive neurosis. Ellis shows that the true invert is, at the least, as often a victim of neurosis. This classification is neither new nor newly put, nor does it include all types of homosexuality. Some thirty-two years ago it was pointed out that homosexuality and other perversions were dependent on many states, such as: Those which originate in imperative conceptions. Those due to congenital defect. Those which are incident to insanity, periods of involution, or to neurotic states. Those which result from vice. These last arise from the fact that nerves too frequently irritated by a given stimulus require a new stimulus to rouse them. Those in a neuropathic diathesis where sexual functions are not normally performed.[3]

Dr. Tarnowsky divides sexual perverts into acquired and congenital tendency types. In the last the child develops normally and only at puberty do abnormalities appear. The first sex manifestation of these beings is not toward females, but toward males. The boy is more ashamed to undress himself before strange men than before females. He later seeks the society and caresses of men. He feels a strong affection to a well-developed man, and follows him everywhere. At puberty strong sexual desires with emissions occur, with sexual dreams in which he plays a woman's part. Later the sexual passion finds vent in mutual onanism with the loved object; less frequently, in active and passive paederasty.[4]

Sexual perversion may occur in consequence of an insane delusion. In this connection, he cites the cue of Raggi,[5] in which an insane patient, in consequence of largely developed breasts, constructed the delusion that he was a woman.

In the group of acquired paederasty are placed cases in which paederasty has resulted from friendship with a congenital sexual pervert; the cases in which flagellation played a sexual part, etc. These are in many cases vices rather than abnormalities. Dr. Tarnowsky is of opinion that in the East paederasty has not the same moral and medical significance as in Europe.

Paederasty, according to Tarnowsky, may also be a product of senile and of paretic dementia. Krafft-Ebing's[6] classification includes general sexual abnormalities.

This classification under sexual perversion proper includes the bisexuals just now so much discussed; the pronounced types but not the instabilities who are far more common. These last are represented by a class of cases of which the following is a type:

A girl, fearing pregnancy, forbids normal but permits anal coitus, and from this her lover becomes a paederast. One young Bohemian hebephreniac girl had a funnel-shaped anus, but a virginal vagina and hymen.[7]

Her lover admitted to the alienist that she was very lascivious but refused to permit vaginal coitus. She desired anal coitus and enjoyed it intensely both in bowel and vagina, evidently through excitation of the anogenital centre. The lover while still attracted by females only, became incapable of normal coitus but intensely enjoyed paedicatio. The Clark distinctions were better drawn clinically between uranism and paederasty by Stefanowsky albeit he ignores the atypic forms just as do works on practice on differential diagnosis.

The famous Hanoverian assessor, Karl Ulrichs, has expressed the essence of uranism in the phrase "female soul in a male body."

"The persons afflicted with uranism are called urnings. They are rarely addicted to passive paederasty and almost never to active, as in many instances impotence has been produced by excessive masturbation. According to their manifestations of inversion they are divisible into two types. The platonics or erotomaniacs who are contented with an ideal, respectful love accompanied with erotic rumination (Binet). The second type, the fellators, replace the vaginal cavity to them wanting by the buccal. According to Laurent the title of these last in the prisons of Paris is "butter-merchant." Luys has described several types, above all the case of a young Jew whose picture is taken from the life. In the daily satisfaction of his shameful passion, his lips were hyperaesthetic and the pleasure, whose extinguishment among his victims he aided, and the intensity of the orgasm provoked, far surpassed the intoxication of normal sensuality. He envied in his sensual desires the low prostitutes, who in blind alleys and retired places throw themselves at the feet of debauches for the same purpose. These women he supplicated, gold in hand, to allow him to replace them in their revolting function.

"Active paederasts, the only true paederasts, are attracted by immature youths (gitons) of female feminine aspect. These paederasts comport themselves as males; their volupty remains always virile, since relations with females are frequent with them. Such relations are impossible to "urnings," as they experience toward women an intense "trade rivalry," which often attains the extreme degree of the "woman hater." Preference of paederasts for anal coitus is easily explained by pathological association, established between the idea of such a joy and volupty, such as occurs in many cases of erotic fetishism (or sexual symbolism), as in the adoration of table-cloths, chemises, drawers, night-caps, etc. A similar association conceived during childhood, re-enforced by masturbation and erotic rumination, may with time become indissoluble and indestructible.[8]

NOTES

1. *N.Y. Hospital Bulletin,* Vol. VIII.
2. *Jour. Mental Science,* January, 1916.
3. Kiernan, *Detroit Lancet,* 1884.
4. Aberrant Sexual Appetite, *Neurologic Review,* 1886.
5. *La Salute,* 1882.
6. Psychopathic Sexualis. Chaddock's Translation. 1892.
7. *Medical Standard,* November, 1888.
8. *Alienist and Neurologist,* 1894.

∾

ALFRED C. KINSEY, WARDELL B. POMEROY, AND CLYDE E. MARTIN

Sexual Behavior in the Human Male (1948)

The name Alfred Kinsey is synonymous with sexual research and the human sexuality scale, which places people with sexual attraction only for the opposite sex at a one, and only for the same sex at six. Kinsey argues that the vast majority of Americans lie in between these two poles. Kinsey and his research team compiled the largest study of human sexual behavior and published Sexual Behavior in the Human Male, *which reached the top of the* New York Times *bestseller list and opened up the public's eyes to the varieties of human sexual experience.*

HISTORICAL INTRODUCTION

The present volume is a progress report from a case history study on human sex behavior. The study has been under way during the past nine years. Throughout these years, it has had the sponsorship and support of Indiana University, and during the past six years the support of the National Research Council's Committee for Research on Problems of Sex, with funds granted by the Medical Division of The Rockefeller

Foundation. It is a fact-finding survey in which an attempt is being made to discover what people do sexually, and what factors account for differences in sexual behavior among individuals, and among various segments of the population.

For some time now there has been an increasing awareness among many people of the desirability of obtaining data about sex which would represent an accumulation of scientific fact completely divorced from questions of moral value and social custom. Practicing physicians find thousands of their patients in need of such objective data. Psychiatrists and analysts find that a majority of their patients need help in resolving sexual conflicts that have arisen in their lives. An increasing number of persons would like to bring an educated intelligence into the consideration of such matters as sexual adjustments in marriage, the sexual guidance of children, the pre-marital sexual adjustments of youth, sex education, sexual activities which are in conflict with the mores, and problems confronting persons who are interested in the social control of behavior through religion, custom, and the forces of the law. Before it is possible to think scientifically on any of these matters, more needs to be known about the actual behavior of people, and about the inter-relationships of that behavior with the biologic and social aspects of their histories.

Hitherto, there have not been sufficient answers to these questions, for human sexual behavior represents one of the least explored segments of biology, psychology, and sociology. Scientifically more has been known about the sexual behavior of some of the farm and laboratory animals. In our Western European-American culture, sexual responses, more than any other physiologic activities, have been subject to religious evaluation, social taboo, and formal legislation. It is obvious that the failure to learn more about human sexual activity is the outcome of the influence which the custom and the law have had upon scientists as individuals, and of the not immaterial restrictions which have been imposed upon scientific investigations in this field.

There are cultures which more freely accept sexual activities as matters of everyday physiology (e.g., Malinowski 1929), while maintaining extensive rituals and establishing taboos around feeding activities. One may wonder what scientific knowledge we would have of digestive functions if the primary taboos in our own society concerned food and feeding. Sexual responses, however, involve emotional changes which are more intense than those associated with any other sort of physiologic activity. For that reason it is difficult to comprehend how any society could become as concerned about respiratory functioning, about digestive functioning, about excretory functioning, or about any of the other physiologic processes. It is probable that the close association of sex, religious values, rituals, and custom in most of the civilizations of the world, has been primarily consequent on the emotional content of sexual behavior.

Sexual activities may affect persons other than those who are directly involved, or do damage to the social organization as a whole. Defenders of the custom frequently contend that this is the sufficient explanation of society's interest in the individual's sexual behavior; but this is probably a post factum rationalization that fails to take into account the historic data on the origin of the custom (May

1931, Westermarck 1936). It is ordinarily said that criminal law is designed to protect property and to protect persons, and if society's only interest in controlling sex behavior were to protect persons, then the criminal codes concerned with assault and battery should provide adequate protection. The fact that there is a body of sex laws which are apart from the laws protecting persons is evidence of their distinct function, namely that of protecting custom. Just because they have this function, sex customs and the sex laws seem more significant and are defended with more emotion than the laws that concern property or person. The failure of the scientist to go further than he has in studies of sex is undoubtedly a reflection of society's attitudes in this field.

Scientists have been uncertain whether any large portion of the population was willing that a thoroughly objective, fact-finding investigation of sex should be made. It is quite probable that an investigation of the sort undertaken here would have been more difficult some years ago; but we have found that there is now an abundant and widespread interest in possibilities of such a study. Thousands of persons have helped by contributing records of their own sexual activities, by interesting others in the research, and by providing the sort of constant support and encouragement without which the pursuit of this study would have been much more difficult, if not impossible. Even the scientist seems to have underestimated the faith of the man of the street in the scientific method, his respect for the results of scientific research, and his confidence that his own life and the whole of the social organization will ultimately benefit from the accumulation of scientifically established data.

OBJECTIVES IN THE PRESENT STUDY

The present study, then, represents an attempt to accumulate an objectively determined body of fact about sex which strictly avoids social or moral interpretations of the fact. Each person who reads this report will want to make interpretations in accordance with his understanding of moral values and social significances; but that is not part of the scientific method and, indeed, scientists have no special capacities for making such evaluations.

The data in this study are being secured through first-hand interviews. These, so far, have been limited to persons resident in the United States. Histories have come from every state in the Union, but more particularly from the northeastern quarter of the country, in the area bounded by Massachusetts, Michigan, Tennessee, and Kansas. It is intended that the ultimate sample shall represent a cross-section of the entire population, from all parts of the United States. The study has already included persons who belong to the following groups:

> Males, females
> Whites, Negroes, other races
> Single, married, previously married

Ages three to ninety

Adolescent at different ages

Various educational levels

Various occupational classes

Various social levels

Urban, rural, mixed backgrounds

Various religious groups

Various degrees of adherence to religious groups, or with no religion

Various geographic origins . . .

HOMOSEXUAL PLAY

On the whole, the homosexual child play is found in more histories, occurs more frequently, and becomes more specific than the pre-adolescent heterosexual play. This depends, as so much of the adult homosexual activity depends, on the greater accessibility of the boy's own sex. In the younger boy, it is also fostered by his socially encouraged disdain for girls' ways, by his admiration for masculine prowess, and by his desire to emulate older boys. The anatomy and functional capacities of male genitalia interest the younger boy to a degree that is not appreciated by older males who have become heterosexually conditioned and who are continuously on the defensive against reactions which might be interpreted as homosexual.

About half of the older males (48%), and nearer two-thirds (60%) of the boys who were pre-adolescent at the time they contributed their histories, recall homosexual activity in their pre-adolescent years. The mean age of the first homosexual contact is about nine years, two and half months (9.21 years).

The order of appearance of the several homosexual techniques is: exhibition of genitalia, manual manipulation of genitalia, anal or oral contacts with genitalia, and urethral insertions. Exhibition is much the most common form of homosexual play (in 99.8 per cent of all the histories which have any activity). It appears in the sex play of the youngest children, where much of it is incidental, definitely casual, and quite fruitless as far as erotic arousal is concerned. The most extreme development of exhibitionism occurs among the older pre-adolescents and younger adolescent males who have discovered the significance of self masturbation and may have acquired proficiency in effecting orgasm. By that time there is a social value in establishing one's ability, and many a boy exhibits his masturbatory techniques to lone companions or to whole groups of boys. In the latter case, there may be simultaneous exhibition as a group activity. The boy's emotional reaction in such a performance is undoubtedly enhanced by the presence of the other boys. There are teen-age boys who continue this exhibitionistic activity throughout their high school years, some of them even entering into compacts with their closest friends to refrain from self masturbation except when in the presence of each other. In confining such social performances to self masturbation, these boys avoid conflicts over the homosexual. By this time, however, the psychic reactions may be homosexual enough, although it may be difficult to persuade these individuals to admit it. . . .

HOMOSEXUAL ACTIVITY AND AGE

Homosexual activity in the human male is much more frequent than is ordinarily realized. In the youngest unmarried group, more than a quarter (27.3%) of the males have some homosexual activity to the point of orgasm. The incidence among these single males rises in successive age groups until it reaches a maximum of 38.7 per cent between 36 and 40 years of age.

High frequencies do not occur as often in the homosexual as they do in some other kinds of sexual activity. Populations are more homogeneous in regard to this outlet. This may reflect the difficulties involved in having frequent and regular relations in a socially taboo activity. Nevertheless, there are a few of the younger adolescent males who have homosexual frequencies of 7 or more per week, and between 26 and 30 the maximum frequencies run to 15 per week. By 50 years of age the most active individual is averaging only 5.0 per week.

For single, active populations, the mean frequencies of homosexual contacts rise more or less steadily from near once per week (0.8 per week) for the younger adolescent boys to nearly twice as often (1.7 per week) for males between the ages of 31 and 35. They stand above once a week through age 50.

In the population as a whole, among boys in their teens, about 8 per cent of the total sexual outlet is derived from the homosexual. Calculating only for the single males who are actually participating, the average active male in his teens gets about 18 per cent of his outlet from that source, and the figure is increasingly higher until, at 50 years of age, the average male who is still single and actively involved gets 54 per cent of his outlet from the homosexual. This, and pre-marital intercourse with prostitutes, are the only sources of outlet which become an increasing part of the sexual activity of single males. For most other kinds of outlet, as we have shown, the figures drop with advancing age. Since there is a steady decline in frequency of total sexual outlet for the average male, and since there is an increase both in frequencies and in percentage of total outlet derived from the homosexual, it is obvious that this outlet acquires a definitely greater significance, and a very real significance, in the lives of most unmarried males who have anything at all to do with it. There is considerable conflict among younger males over participation in such socially taboo activity, and there is evidence that a much higher percentage of younger males is attracted and aroused than ever engages in overt homosexual activities to the point of orgasm. Gradually, over a period of years, many males who are aroused by homosexual situations become more frank in their acceptance and more direct in their pursuit of complete relations, although some of them are still much restrained by fear of blackmail.

Homosexual contact as an extra-marital activity is recorded by about 10 per cent of the teen-age and young 20-year old married males. By 50 years of age, it is admitted by only 1 per cent of the still married males, but this latter figure is undoubtedly below the fact. Average frequencies fluctuate between once a week and once in two or three weeks for the married males who have any such contacts; and there is no distinct age trend. From 4 to 9 per cent of the total outlet of these married males is drawn from the homosexual source, but again there is no apparent age trend.

≈

GEORGE CHAUNCEY
Gay New York (1994)

George Chauncey, professor of history at the University of Chicago, is one of the foremost scholars of gay U.S. history. His groundbreaking work, Gay New York, *helped bring to light the vast and diverse gay world that flourished in New York in the first half of the century, before the formation of visibly gay organizations like the 1950s groups the Mattachine Society and the Daughters of Bilitis, and long before the Stonewall rebellion in 1969. Chauncey also emphasizes that class and racial identities are central to understanding distinct queer and other sexual identities.*

INTRODUCTION

I

In the half-century between 1890 and the beginning of the Second World War, a highly visible, remarkably complex, and continually changing gay male world took shape in New York City. That world included several gay neighborhood enclaves, widely publicized dances and other social events, and a host of commercial establishments where gay men gathered, ranging from saloons, speakeasies, and bars to cheap cafeterias and elegant restaurants. The men who participated in that world forged a distinctive culture with its own language and customs, its own traditions and folk histories, its own heroes and heroines. They organized male beauty contests at Coney Island and drag balls in Harlem; they performed at gay clubs in the Village and at tourist traps in Times Square. Gay writers and performers produced a flurry of gay literature and theater in the 1920s and early 1930s; gay impresarios organized cultural events that sustained and enhanced gay men's communal ties and group identity. Some gay men were involved in long-term monogamous relationships they called marriages; others participated in an extensive sexual underground that by the beginning of the century included well-known cruising areas in the city's parks and streets, gay bathhouses, and saloons with back rooms where men met for sex.

The gay world that flourished before World War II has been almost entirely forgotten in popular memory and overlooked by professional historians; it is not supposed to have existed. This book seeks to restore that world to history, to chart its geography, and to recapture its culture and politics. In doing so, it challenges three widespread myths about the history of gay life before the rise of the gay movement, which I call the myths of isolation, invisibility, and internalization.

The myth of isolation holds that anti-gay hostility prevented the development of an extensive gay subculture and forced gay men to lead solitary lives in the decades before the rise of the gay liberation movement. As one exceptionally well informed writer and critic recently put it, the 1969 Stonewall rebellion not only marked the beginning of the militant gay movement but was

> the critical . . . event that unleashed a vast reconstitution of gay society: gay bars, baths, bookstores, and restaurants opened, gay softball teams, newspapers, political organizations, and choruses proliferated. Gay groups of all sorts popped up while gay neighborhoods emerged in our larger, and many of our smaller cities. This was and is a vast social revolution . . . a new community came into being in an astonishingly short period of time.

This has become the common wisdom for understandable reasons, for the policing of the gay world before Stonewall was even more extensive and draconian than is generally realized. A battery of laws criminalized not only gay men's narrowly "sexual" behavior, but also their association with one another, their cultural styles, and their efforts to organize and speak on their own behalf. Their social marginalization gave the police and popular vigilantes even broader informal authority to harass them; anyone discovered to be homosexual was threatened with loss of livelihood and loss of social respect. Hundreds of men were arrested each year in New York City alone for violating such laws.

But the laws were enforced only irregularly, and indifference or curiosity—rather than hostility or fear—characterized many New Yorkers' response to the gay world for much of the half-century before the war. Gay men had to take precautions, but, like other marginalized peoples, they were able to construct spheres of relative cultural autonomy in the interstices of a city governed by hostile powers. They forged an immense gay world of overlapping social networks in the city's streets, private apartments, bathhouses, cafeterias, and saloons, and they celebrated that world's existence at regularly held communal events such as the massive drag (or transvestite) balls that attracted thousands of participants and spectators in the 1920s. By the 1890s, gay men had made the Bowery a center of gay life, and by the 1920s they had created three distinct gay neighborhood enclaves in Greenwich Village, Harlem, and Times Square, each with a different class and ethnic character, gay cultural style, and public reputation.

Some men rejected the dominant culture of the gay world and others passed through it only fleetingly, but it played a central role in the lives of many others. Along with sexual camaraderie, it offered them practical support in negotiating the demands of urban life, for many people used their gay social circles to find jobs, apartments, romance, and their closest friendships. Their regular association and ties of mutual dependence fostered their allegiance to one another, but gay culture was even more important to them for the emotional support it provided as they developed values and identities significantly different from those prescribed by the dominant culture. Indeed, two New Yorkers who conducted research on imprisoned working-class homosexuals in the 1930s expressed concern about the effects of gay men's participation in homosexual society precisely because it made it possible for them to reject the prescriptions of the dominant culture and to forge an alternative culture of their own. "The homosexual's withdrawal, enforced or voluntary, into a world of his own tends to remove him from touch with reality," they warned in 1941, almost thirty years before the birth of the gay liberation movement at Stonewall. "It promotes the feeling of homosexual solidarity, and withdraws this group more and more from conventional folkways and confirms them in their feeling that they compose a community within the community, with a special and artificial life of their own." Once men discovered the gay world, they knew they were not alone.

The myth of invisibility holds that, even if a gay world existed, it was kept invisible and thus remained difficult for isolated gay men to find. But gay men were highly visible figures in early-twentieth-century New York, in part because gay life was more integrated into the everyday life of the city in the prewar decades than it would be after World War II—in part because so many gay men boldly announced their presence by wearing red ties, bleached hair, and the era's other insignia of homosexuality. Gay men gathered on the same street corners and in many of the same saloons and dance halls that other working-class men did, they participated in the same salons that other bohemians did, and they rented the same halls for parties, fancy balls, and theatrical events that other youths did. "Our streets and beaches are overrun by . . . fairies," declared one New Yorker in 1918, and nongay people encountered them in speakeasies, shops, and rooming houses as well. They read about them in the newspapers, watched them perform in clubs, and saw them portrayed on almost every vaudeville and burlesque stage as well as in many films. Indeed, many New Yorkers viewed the gay subculture's most dramatic manifestations as part of the spectacle that defined the distinctive character of their city. Tourists visited the Bowery, the Village, and Harlem in part to view gay men's haunts. In the early 1930s, at the height of popular fascination with gay culture, literally thousands of them attended the city's drag balls to gawk at the drag queens on display there, while newspapers filled their pages with sketches of the most sensational gowns.

The drag queens on parade at the balls and the effeminate homosexual men, usually called "fairies," who managed to be flamboyant even in a suit were the most visible representatives of gay life and played a more central role in the gay world in the prewar years than they do now. But while they made parts of the gay world highly visible to outsiders, even more of that world remained invisible to outsiders. Given the risks gay men faced, most of them hid their homosexuality from their straight workmates, relatives, and neighbors as well as the police. But being forced to hide from the dominant culture did not keep them hidden from each other. Gay men developed a highly sophisticated system of subcultural codes—codes of dress, speech, and style—that enabled them to recognize one another on the streets, at work, and at parties and bars, and to carry on intricate conversations whose coded meaning was unintelligible to potentially hostile people around them. The very need for such codes, it is usually (and rightly) argued, is evidence of the degree to which gay men had to hide. But the elaboration of such codes also indicates the extraordinary resilience of the men who lived under such constraints and their success in communicating with each other despite them. Even those parts of the gay world that were invisible to the dominant society were visible to gay men themselves.

The myth of internalization holds that gay men uncritically internalized the dominant culture's view of them as sick, perverted, and immoral, and that their self-hatred led them to accept the policing of their lives rather than resist it. As one of the most perceptive gay social critics has put it, "When we hid our homosexuality in the past, it was not only because of fear of social pressure but even more because of deeply internalized self-hatred . . . [which was] very pervasive. Homosexuals themselves long resisted the idea of being somehow distinct from other people." But many gay men celebrated their difference from the norm, and some of them organized to resist anti-gay policing. From the late nineteenth century on, a handful of gay New Yorkers wrote polemical articles and books, sent letters to hostile newspapers and published their own, and urged jurists and doctors to change their views. In the 1930s, gay bars challenged their prohibition in the courts, and gays and lesbians organized groups to advocate the homosexual cause. A larger number of men dressed and carried themselves in the streets in ways that proclaimed their homosexuality as boldly as any political button would, even though they risked violence and arrest for doing so.

Most gay men did not speak out against anti-gay policing so openly, but to take this as evidence that they had internalized anti-gay attitudes is to ignore the strength of the forces arrayed against them, to misinterpret silence as acquiescence, and to construe resistance in the narrowest of terms—as the organization of formal political groups and petitions. The history of gay resistance must be understood to extend beyond formal political organizing to include the strategies of everyday resistance that men devised in order to claim space for themselves in the midst of a hostile society. Given the effective prohibition of gay sociability and the swift and certain consequences that most men could expect if their homosexuality were revealed, both the willingness of some men to carry themselves openly *and* the ability of other gay men to create and hide an extensive gay social world need to be considered forms of resistance to overwhelming social pressure. The full panoply of tactics gay men devised for communicating, claiming space, and affirming themselves—the kind of resistant social practices that the political theorist James Scott has called the tactics of the weak—proved to be remarkably successful in the generations before a more formal gay political movement developed. Such tactics did not directly challenge anti-gay policing in the way that the movement would, but in the face of that policing they allowed many gay men not just to survive but to flourish—to build happy, self-confident, and loving lives.

One striking sign of the strength of the gay male subculture was its ability to provide its members with the resources necessary to reject the dominant culture's definition of them as sick, criminal, and unworthy. Some gay men internalized the anti-homosexual attitudes pervasive in their society. Many others bitterly resented the dominant culture's insistence that their homosexuality rendered them virtual women and despised the men among them who seemed to embrace an "effeminate" style. But the "unconventional folkways" of gay culture noted by the two 1930s researchers were more successful in helping men counteract the hostile attitudes of their society than we usually imagine. Many gay men resisted the medical judgment that they were mentally ill and needed treatment, despite the fact that medical discourse was one of the most powerful anti-gay forces in American culture (and one to which some recent social theories have attributed almost limitless cultural power). Numerous doctors reported their astonishment at discovering in their clinical interviews with "inverts" that their subjects rejected the efforts of science, religion, popular opinion, and the law to condemn them as moral degenerates. One doctor lamented that the working-class "fags" he interviewed in New York's city jail in the early 1920s actually claimed they were *proud* to be degenerates, [and] do not want nor care to be cured." Indeed, it became the reluctant consensus among doctors that most inverts saw nothing wrong with their homosexuality; it was this attitude, they repeatedly noted, that threatened to make the "problem" of homosexuality so intractable.

All three myths about prewar gay history are represented in the image of the closet, the spatial metaphor people typically use to characterize gay life before the advent of gay liberation as well as their own lives before they "came out." Before Stonewall (let alone before World War II), it is often said, gay people lived in a closet that kept them isolated, invisible, and vulnerable to anti-gay ideology. While it is hard to imagine the closet as anything other than a prison, we often blame people in the past for not having had the courage to break out of it (as if a powerful system were not at work to keep them in), or we condescendingly assume they had internalized the prevalent hatred of homosexuality and thought they deserved to be there. Even at our most charitable, we often imagine that people in the closet kept their gayness hidden not only from hostile straight people but from other gay people as well, and, possibly, even from themselves.

Given the ubiquity of the term today and how central the metaphor of the closet is to the ways we think about gay history before the 1960s, it is bracing—and instructive—to note that it was never used by gay people themselves before then. Nowhere does it appear before the 1960s in the records of the gay movement or in the novels, diaries, or letters of gay men and lesbians. The fact that gay people in the past did not speak of or conceive of themselves as living in a closet does not preclude us from using the term retrospectively as an analytic category, but it does suggest that we need to use it more cautiously and precisely, and to pay attention to the very different terms people used to describe themselves and their social worlds.

Many gay men, for instance, described negotiating their presence in an often hostile world as living a double life, or wearing a mask and taking it off. Each image has a valence different from "closet," for each suggests not gay men's isolation, but their ability—as well as their need—to move between different personas and different lives, one straight, the other gay, to wear their hair up, as another common phrase put it, or let their hair down. Many men kept their gay lives hidden from potentially hostile straight observers (by "putting their hair up"), in other words, but that did not mean they were hidden or isolated from each other—they often, as they said, "dropped hairpins" that only other gay men would notice. Leading a double life in which they often passed as straight (and sometimes married) allowed them to have jobs and status a queer would have been denied while still participating in what they called "homosexual society" or "the life." For some, the personal cost of "passing" was great. But for others it was minimal, and many men positively enjoyed having a "secret life" more complex and extensive than outsiders could imagine. Indeed, the gay life of many men was so full and wide-ranging that by the 1930s they used another—but more expansive—spatial metaphor to describe it: not the gay closet, but the *gay world*.

The expansiveness and communal character of the gay world before World War II can also be discerned in the way people used another familiar term, "coming out." Like much of campy gay terminology, "coming out" was an arch play on the language of women's culture—in this case the expression used to refer to the ritual of a debutante's being formally introduced to, or "coming out" into, the society of her cultural peers. (This is often remembered as exclusively a ritual of WASP high society, but it was also common in the social worlds of African-Americans and other groups.) A gay man's coming out originally referred to his being formally presented to the largest collective manifestation of prewar gay society, the enormous drag balls that were patterned on the debutante and masquerade balls of the dominant culture and were regularly held in New York, Chicago, New Orleans, Baltimore, and other cities. An article published in the *Baltimore Afro-American* in the spring of 1931 under the headline "1931 Debutantes Bow at Local 'Pansy' Ball" drew the parallel explicitly and unselfconsciously: "The coming out of new debutantes into homosexual society," its first sentence announced, "was the outstanding feature of Baltimore's eighth annual frolic of the pansies when the Art Club was host to the neuter gender at the Elks' Hall, Friday night."

Gay people in the prewar years, then, did not speak of *coming out of* what we call the "gay closet" but rather of *coming out into* what they called "homosexual society" or the "gay world," a world neither so small, nor so isolated, nor, often, so hidden as "closet" implies. The Baltimore debutantes, after all, came out in the presence of hundreds of straight as well as gay and lesbian spectators at the public hall of the fraternal order of Elks. Their sisters in New York were likely to be presented to thousands of spectators, many of whom had traveled from other cities, in some of the best-known ballrooms of the city, including the Savoy and Rockland Palace in Harlem and the Astor Hotel and Madison Square Garden in midtown. Although only a small fraction of gay men actually "came out" at such a ball or in the presence of straight onlookers, this kind of initiation into gay society served as a model for the initiation—and integration—into the gay world for other men as well. . . .

III

Although the gay male world of the prewar years was remarkably visible and integrated into the straight world, it was, as the centrality of the drag balls suggests, a world very different from our own. Above all, it was not a world in which men were divided into "homosexuals" and "heterosexuals." This is, on the face of it, a startling claim, since it is almost impossible today to think about sexuality without imagining that it is organized along an axis of homosexuality and heterosexuality; a person is either one or the other, or possibly both—but even the third category of "bisexuality" depends for its meaning on its intermediate position on the axis defined by those two poles. The belief that one's sexuality is centrally defined by one's homosexuality or heterosexuality is hegemonic in contemporary culture: it is so fundamental to the way people think about the world that it is taken for granted, assumed to be natural and timeless, and needs no defense. Whether homosexuality is good or chosen or determined, natural or unnatural, healthy or sick is debated, for such opinions are in the realm of ideology and thus subject to contestation, and we are living at a time when a previously dominant ideological position, that homosexuality is immoral or pathological, faces a powerful and increasingly successful challenge from an alternative ideology, which regards homosexuality as neutral, healthy, or even good. But the underlying premise of that debate—that some people are homosexuals, and that all people are either homosexuals, heterosexuals, or bisexuals—is hardly questioned.

This book argues that in important respects the hetero–homosexual binarism, the sexual regime now hegemonic in American culture, is a stunningly recent creation. Particularly in working-class culture, homosexual behavior per se became the primary basis for the labeling and self-identification of men as "queer" only around the middle of the twentieth century; before then, most men were so labeled only if they displayed a much broader inversion of their ascribed gender status by assuming the sexual and other cultural roles ascribed to women. The abnormality (or "queerness") of the "fairy," that is, was defined as much by his "woman-like" character or "effeminacy" as his solicitation of male sexual partners; the "man" who responded to his solicitations—no matter how often—was not considered abnormal, a "homosexual," so long as he abided by masculine gender conventions. Indeed, the centrality of effeminacy to the representation of the "fairy" allowed many conventionally masculine men, especially unmarried men living in sex-segregated immigrant communities, to engage in extensive sexual activity with other men without risking stigmatization and the loss of their status as "normal men."

Only in the 1930s, 1940s, and 1950s did the now-conventional division of men into "homosexuals" and "heterosexuals," based on the sex of their sexual partners, replace the division of men into "fairies" and "normal men" on the basis of their imaginary gender status as the hegemonic way of understanding sexuality. Moreover, the transition from one sexual regime to the next was an uneven process, marked by significant class and ethnic differences. Multiple systems of sexual classification coexisted throughout the period in New York's divergent neighborhood cultures: men socialized into different class and ethnic systems of gender, family life, and sexual mores tended to understand and organize their homosexual practices in different ways. Most significantly, exclusive heterosexuality became a precondition for a man's identification as "normal" in middle-class culture at least two generations before it did so in much of Euro-American and African-American working-class culture.

One way to introduce the differences between the conceptual schemas by which male sexual relations and identities were organized in the first and second halves of the twentieth century (as well as this book's use of terminology) is to review the changes in the vernacular terms used for homosexually active men, and, in particular, the way in which gay came to mean "homosexual." This does not mean reconstructing a lineage of static meanings—simply noting, for instance, that gay meant "prostitute" before it meant "homosexual." In keeping with the methodology of the study as a whole, it means instead reconstructing how men used the different terms tactically in diverse cultural settings to position themselves and negotiate their relations with other men, gay and straight alike.

Although many individuals at any given time, as one might expect, used the available terms interchangeably and imprecisely, the broad contours of lexical evolution reveal much about the changes in the organization of male sexual practices and identities. For many of the terms used in the early twentieth century were not synonymous with *homosexual* or *heterosexual,* but represent a different conceptual mapping of male sexual practices, predicated on assumptions about the character of men engaging in those practices that are no longer widely shared or credible. *Queer, fairy, trade, gay,* and other terms each had a specific connotation and signified specific subjectivities, and the ascendancy of *gay* as the preeminent term (for gay men among gay men) in the 1940s reflected a major reconceptualization of homosexual behavior and of "homosexuals" and "heterosexuals." Demonstrating that such terms signified distinct social categories not equivalent to "homosexual" and that men used many of them for themselves will also explain why I have employed them throughout this study, even though some of them now have pejorative connotations that may initially cause the reader to recoil.

Gay emerged as a coded homosexual term and as a widely known term for homosexuals in the context of the complex relationship between men known as "fairies" and those known as "queers." According to Gershon Legman, who published a lexicon of homosexual argot in 1941, *fairy* (as a noun) and *queer* (as an adjective) were the terms most commonly used by "queer" and "normal" people alike to refer to "homosexuals" before World War II. Regulatory agents—police, doctors, and private investigators alike—generally used technical terms such as *invert, pervert, degenerate,* or, less commonly, *homosexual* (or *homosexualist,* or simply *homo*), but they also knew and frequently used the vernacular *fairy* as well. In 1917, for instance, an agent of an anti-vice society reported to his supervisor on a "crowd of homosexualists, commonly known as 'fairies.'" Another agent of the society reported ten years later that he had noticed a "colored pervert" in a subway washroom, but added that in identifying the "pervert" to another man in the washroom he had used the more commonplace term: "I said, 'He is a fairy.'"

While most gay men would have understood most of the terms in use for homosexual matters, some terms were more likely to be used in certain social milieus than others. *Fag* was widely used in the 1930s, but almost exclusively by "normals" (the usual word then for those who were not queers); gay men used the word *faggot* instead, but it was used more commonly by blacks than whites. An investigator who visited a "woman's party" at a 137th Street tenement in Harlem in 1928, for instance, reported that one of the women there told him, "Everybody here is either a bull dagger [lesbian] or faggot.'" The investigator, a black man working for an anti-vice society, appears to have believed that the term was less well known than *fairy* to the "normal" white population. When he mentioned in another report that two men at a Harlem restaurant were "said to be 'noted faggots,'" he quickly explained to his white supervisor this meant they were "fairies." While gay white men also used the term *faggot* (although less often than blacks), they rarely referred to themselves as being "in the life," a phrase commonly used by black men and women.

Most of the vernacular terms used by "normal" observers for fairies, such as *she-man, nance,* and *sissy,* as well as *fairy* itself, emphasized the centrality of effeminacy to their character. In the 1920s and 1930s, especially, such men were also often called *pansies,* and the names of other flowers such as daisy and buttercup were applied so commonly to gay men that they were sometimes simply called "horticultural lads." ("Ship me home," said a "nance" to a florist in a joke told in 1932. "I'm a pansy.") The flamboyant style adopted by "flaming faggots" or "fairies," as well as its consistency with outsiders' stereotypes, made them highly visible figures on the streets of New York and the predominant image of *all* queers in the straight mind.

Not all homosexual men in the prewar era thought of themselves as "flaming faggots," though. While the terms *queer, fairy,* and *faggot* were often used interchangeably by outside observers (and sometimes even by the men they observed), each term also had a more precise meaning among gay men that could be invoked to distinguish its object from other homosexually active men. By the 1910s and 1920s, the men who identified themselves as part of a distinct category of men primarily on the basis of their homosexual interest rather than their womanlike gender status usually called themselves *queer.* Essentially synonymous with "homosexual," *queer* presupposed the statistical normalcy—and normative character—of men's sexual interest in women; tellingly, queers referred to their counter-parts as "normal men" (or "straight men") rather than as "heterosexuals." But *queer* did not presume that the men it denoted were effeminate, for many queers were repelled by the style of the fairy and his loss of manly status, and almost all were careful to distinguish themselves from such men. They might use *queer* to refer to any man who was not "normal," but they usually applied terms such as *fairy, faggot,* and *queen* only to those men who dressed or behaved in what they considered to be a flamboyantly effeminate manner. They were so careful to draw such distinctions in part because the dominant culture failed to do so.

Many fairies and queers socialized into the dominant prewar homosexual culture considered the ideal sexual partner to be "trade," a "real man," that is, ideally a sailor, a soldier, or some other embodiment of the aggressive masculine ideal, who was neither homosexually interested nor effeminately gendered himself but who would accept the sexual advances of a queer. While some gay men used the term *trade* to refer only to men who insisted on payment for a sexual encounter, others applied it more broadly to any "normal" man who accepted a queer's sexual advances. The centrality of effeminacy to the definition of the fairy in the dominant culture enabled trade to have sex with both the queers and fairies without risking being labeled queer themselves, so long as they maintained a masculine demeanor and sexual role. Just as significantly, even those queers who had little interest in trade recognized that trade constituted a widely admired ideal type in the subcul-ture and accepted the premise that trade were the "normal men" they claimed to be.

Ultimately men who detested the word *fairy* and the social category it signi-fied were the ones to embrace *gay* as an alternative label for themselves. But they did not initiate its usage in gay culture. The complexity of the emergence of the term's homosexual meanings is illustrated by a story told by a gay hairdresser, Dick Addi-son, about an incident in 1937 when he was a fourteen-year-old "flaming faggot" in a Jewish working-class section of New York:

> A group of us hung out at a park in the Bronx where older boys would come and pick us up. One boy who'd been hanging out with us for a while came back once, crying, saying the boy he'd left with wanted him to suck his thing. "I don't want to do *that!*" he cried. "But why are you hanging out with us if you aren't gay?" we asked him. "Oh, I'm *gay,*" he exclaimed, throwing his hands in the air like an hys-terical queen, "but I don't want to do *that.*" This boy liked the gay life—the clothes, the way people talked and walked and held themselves—but, if you can believe it, he didn't realize there was more to being gay than that!

Gay, as the story indicates, was a code word. Gay men could use it to identify themselves to other gays without revealing their identity to those not in the wise, for not everyone—certainly not the boy in this story (unless he was simply using the word's protean character to joke with the group)—knew that it implied a specif-ically sexual preference. But it did not simply mean "homosexual," either. For all the boys, the "gay life" referred as well to the flamboyance in dress and speech associated with the fairies. Indeed, it was the fairies (the especially flamboyant gay men), such as the ones Addison associated with, who used the word most in the 1920s and 1930s. Will Finch, a social worker who began to identify himself as "queer" while in New York in the early 1930s, recalled in 1951 that the word *gay* "originated with the flaming faggots as a 'camp' word, used to apply to absolutely everything in any way pleasant or desirable (not as 'homosexual'), . . . [and only began] to mean 'homosexual' later on."

The earliest such uses of *gay* are unknown, but the "flaming faggots" Finch remembered doubtless used the word because of the host of apposite connotations it had acquired over the years. Originally referring simply to things pleasurable, by the seventeenth century *gay* had come to refer more specifically to a life of *immoral* pleasures and dissipation (and by the nineteenth century to prostitution, when applied to women), a meaning that the "faggots" could easily have drawn on to refer to the homosexual life. *Gay* also referred to something brightly colored or someone showily dressed—and thus could easily be used to describe the flamboyant costumes adopted by many fairies, as well as things at once brilliant and specious, the epitome of camp. One can hear these meanings echo through the decades in Finch's comment in 1963 that he still "associate[d] the word with the hand waving, limp-wristed faggot, squealing 'Oh, it's *gay!*'" One hears them as well in the dialogue in several novels written in the late 1920s and early 1930s by gay men with a camp sensibility and an intimate knowledge of the homosexual scene. "I say," said Osbert to Harold in *The Young and Evil,* perhaps the campiest novel of all, "you look positively gay in the new clothes. Oh, said Harold, you're lovely *too,* dear, and gave him a big kiss on the forehead, much to Osbert's dismay." A chorus boy gushed to his friend in another, rather more overwritten 1934 novel, "'I'm lush. I'm gay. I'm wicked. I'm everything that flames.'" And Cary Grant's famous line in the 1938 film *Bringing Up Baby* played on several of these meanings: he leapt into the air, flounced his arms, and shrieked "I just went gay all of a sudden," *not* because he had fallen in love with a man, but because he was asked why he had put on a woman's nightgown. The possibility of a more precisely sexual meaning would not have been lost on anyone familiar with fairy stereotypes.

The word's use by the "flaming faggots" (or "fairies"), the most prominent figures in homosexual society, led to its adoption as a code word by "queers" who rejected the effeminacy and overtness of the fairy but nonetheless identified themselves as homosexual. Because the word's use in gay environments had given it homosexual associations that were unknown to people not involved in the gay world, more circumspect gay men could use it to identify themselves secretly to each other in a straight setting. A properly intoned reference or two to a "gay bar" or to "having a gay time" served to alert the listener familiar with homosexual culture. . . .

Younger men rejected *queer* as a pejorative name that others had given them, which highlighted their difference from other men. Even though many "queers" had also rejected the effeminacy of the fairies, younger men were well aware that in the eyes of straight men their "queerness" hinged on their supposed gender deviance. In the 1930s and 1940s, a series of press campaigns claiming that murderous "sex deviates" threatened the nation's women and children gave "queerness" an even more sinister and undesirable set of connotations. In calling themselves *gay,* a new generation of men insisted on the right to name themselves, to claim their status as men, and to reject the "effeminate" styles of the older generation. Some men, especially older ones like Finch, continued to prefer *queer* to *gay,* in part because of *gay's* initial association with the fairies. Younger men found it easier to forget the origins of *gay* in the campy banter of the very queens whom they wished to reject.

Testimony given at hearings held by the State Liquor Authority (SLA) from the 1930s to the 1960s to review the closing of bars accused of serving homosexuals provides striking evidence of the growing use of the word *gay.* At none of the hearings held before the war did an SLA agent or bar patron use the word to refer to the patrons. At a hearing held in 1939, for instance, one of the Authority's undercover investigators testified that the bar in question was patronized by "homosexuals or fairies, fags commonly called." Another investigator also called the bar's patrons "fags," but noted that the "fags" preferred to call themselves "fairies." A few moments later he referred to a group of "normal" people having a good time at a party as "people that were gay," indicating that the term, in his mind, still had no homosexual connotations. Twenty years later, however, SLA agents casually used *gay* to mean homosexual, as did the *gay* men they were investigating. One agent testified in 1960 that he had simply asked a man at a suspected bar whether he was "straight or gay." "I am as gay as the Pope" came the knowing reply. ("Which Pope?" asked the startled investigator. "Any Pope," he was assured.)

Once the word was widely diffused within the gay world, it was introduced to people outside that world by writers who specialized in familiarizing their readers with New York's seamier side. Jack Lait and Lee Mortimer, for instance, confided to the readers of their 1948 *Confidential* guide to the city that "not all New York's queer (or, as they say it, 'gay') people live in Greenwich Village." In 1956, the scandal magazine *Tip-Off* played on the expectation that some of its readers would understand the term—and others would want to—by putting a report on homosexuals' supposed "strangle-hold on the theatre" under the headline, "Why They Call Broadway the 'Gay' White Way." By 1960, liquor authority attorneys prosecuting a gay bar were so certain a bartender in a heavily gay neighborhood such as Greenwich Village could be expected to understand the word that they used one bartender's claim that he was unsure of its meaning as a basis for questioning his candor. "You live only a few blocks from . . . the heart of Greenwich Village," an attorney demanded incredulously, "and you are not familiar with the meaning of the word gay?"[49] The word had become familiar to hip New Yorkers and others fully a decade before the gay liberation movement introduced it to the rest of the nation, and parts of the "respectable" press began using it in the late 1960s and early 1970s.

The ascendancy of *gay* as the primary self-referential term used within the gay world reflected the subtle shifting occurring in the boundaries drawn among male sexual actors in the middle decades of the century. Earlier terms—*fairy, queer,* and *trade* most commonly—had distinguished various types of homosexually active men: effeminate homosexuals, more conventional homosexuals, and masculine heterosexuals who would accept homosexual advances, to use today's nomenclature. *Gay* tended to group all these types together, to deemphasize their differences by emphasizing the *similarity* in character they had presumably demonstrated by their choice of male sexual partners. This reconfiguration of sexual categories occurred in two stages.

First, gay men, like the prewar queers but unlike the fairies, defined themselves as gay primarily on the basis of their homosexual interest rather than effeminacy, and many of them, in a break with older homosexual cultural norms, adopted a new, self-consciously "masculine" style. Nonetheless, they did not regard all men who had sex with men as gay; men could still be trade, but they were defined as trade primarily on the basis of their purported heterosexuality rather than their masculinity (though modified as "rough" trade, the term still emphasized a man's masculine character). A new dichotomous system of classification, based on sexual object choice rather than gender status, had begun to supersede the old.

In the second stage of cultural redefinition, trade virtually disappeared as a sexual identity (if not as a sexual role) within the gay world, as men began to regard *anyone* who participated in a homosexual encounter as "gay," and, conversely, to insist that men could be defined as "straight" only on the basis of a total absence of homosexual interest and behavior. Alfred Gross, publicly a leader in psychological research and social work related to homosexuals in New York from the 1930s through the 1960s and secretly a gay man himself, derided the distinction between homosexuals and trade in a speech he gave in 1947. Fairies, he contended, "are preoccupied with getting and holding their 'man.'" But, he remonstrated, they refuse "to recognize that the male, no matter how roughly he might be attired, how coarse his manners, how brutal or sadistic he may be, if he be willing to submit regularly to homosexual attentions, is every whit as homosexual as the man who plays what is considered the female role in the sex act."

A growing number of gay men subscribed to this more limited view of the behavior allowed men if they were to be labeled "straight"; by the 1970s, most regarded a self-proclaimed "piece of trade" who regularly let homosexuals have sex with him not as heterosexual but as someone unable to recognize, or accept, or admit his "true nature" as a homosexual. . . .

The ascendancy of *gay* reflected, then, a reorganization of sexual categories and the transition from an early-twentieth-century culture divided into "queers" and "men" on the basis of gender status to a late-twentieth-century culture divided into "homosexuals" and "heterosexuals" on the basis of sexual object choice. Each set of terms represented a way of defining, constituting, and containing male "sexuality," by labeling, differentiating, and explaining the character of (homo)sexually active men. Any such taxonomy is necessarily inadequate as a measure of sexual behavior, but its construction is itself a significant social practice. It provides a means of defining the deviant, whose existence serves both to delineate the boundaries of acceptable behavior for all men and to contain the threat of deviance, at once stigmatizing it and suggesting that it is confined to a "deviant" minority.

2

Are We Free to Be You and Me?

QUEER SEXUALITY IN AMERICA, NOW AND THEN

What is gender and why has it been so central to the shaping of sexuality over the last 100 years? Sexuality and gender, two overlapping but distinct categories of social organization and identity, are essential to understanding what it means to be an American queer. It would be impossible to understand one category without the other, as these two categories have been central to the making of modern selves. As the readings from Chapter 1 demonstrate, from the turn of the century, sexologists and many others presumed that biological sex and gender presentation shaped and even determined sexuality, sexual desire, and sexual preference. If you "walked like a woman, talked like a woman, and acted like a woman," but your biological equipment was male, the default and stigmatizing assumption was homosexuality. Similarly, lesbians who have played with gender, known in the early twentieth century as "mannish women" and later as butch dykes, have historically defied conventional expectations of femininity. By wearing pants, smoking in public, or learning to drive, lesbians suffered overt discrimination and moral censure for rejecting the constraints and limitations of femininity. But a complex range of gender presentations existed in queer communities that were also shaped by race and class as much as sexual identity. Some working-class women, for example, found it easier to land a higher-paying industrial job if they presented themselves as men. From the very start of the organization of queer subcultures, the relationships between gender and sexualities have always been far more complicated than those outside the cultures have presumed.

The 1940s and 1950s showed how quickly war and peace could change the social climate in terms of gender and sexuality. With the U.S. entrance into World War II, queer women and men flocked to major cities and found one another, breaking down distinctions between rural and urban, and solidified metropolitan areas' dominance in building vibrant queer communities. Women, queer and not, entered into occupations from which they had been previously excluded but that now demanded their labor as patriotic duty, while so many men were away on the front. No longer did it seem odd or even questionable for millions of women to work in factories, military bases, and offices and to socialize in public without any men around. But wartime also posed risks: the military officially and systematically engaged in psychiatric stigmatization by questioning enlistees about their sexual orientation and discharged "deviants" as security threats.

When the war ended, the scrutiny of sexual orientation and increased policing of gender roles returned with a vengeance. The rise (some would say cult) of heterosexual domesticity emerged as a symbol of postwar prosperity. Instead of rationing meat consumption to support the state, the new Cold War patriotism emulated the wholesome ideals of Ward and June Cleaver. Young adults were exhorted to marry young, bear several polite children, buy a house in the newly constructed suburbs, and partake in the amazing new wonders of home appliances. Although queer subcultures didn't necessarily go completely underground, the increasingly conservative social climate of the postwar United States contributed to a more subdued, controlled landscape of possibilities in terms of gender presentation and sexual identity or orientation.

The 1950s civil rights movement and the social movements of second-wave feminism and gay liberation in the 1960s changed everything, and since then, most scholars would agree that nothing has ever been the same. Middle-class feminists, tired of patriarchal assumptions that relegated their lives to the relative boredom of home and children, vigorously critiqued the stifling and sexist gender expectations of U.S. society. Many second-wave feminists insisted on the right to live freely without the debilitating fears and restrictions shaped by gender inequality, such as rape, domestic violence, and sexual harassment. Feminists also insisted on the right to choose when and whether to procreate and the right to equal work for equal pay. Meanwhile, gay liberationists called into question the need to conform to limiting paradigms of heterosexuality. Gay men created subcultures in major cities that facilitated greater personal experimentation and expression of sexual pleasure. Some second-wave feminists thought that the path to gender equality demanded a separation from men. From this, second-wave feminism and lesbian culture merged into the phenomenon of lesbian separatism. Lesbian feminists—many of whom had only recently identified as heterosexual—combined their critique of gender and sexuality by rejecting participation in the patriarchy (often realized through the creation of women-only collectives). Part of this movement worked to reject butch-femme (i.e., masculine/feminine) gender expressions in lesbian relationships in favor of more androgyny in the streets and between the sheets.

Among African American queers, gender meant something entirely different. As the classic documentary *Paris Is Burning* shows, young, poor African American queer men often used gender play as a way of expressing new forms of identity, often in response to the racism of U.S. society. At the same time, black nationalism and separatism placed new kinds of restrictions on gender expression and sexuality *within* African American communities. As several queer African American scholars and writers have shown, forms of social oppression and conformity should always be examined together; when organizing around one at the exclusion of the other, activists often created new forms of oppression in place of the old.

As a symbol of the changes around gender and sexuality, the enormously popular 1970s record and television show *Free to Be You and Me* marked a watershed in the feminist movement with their advocacy of looser gender expectations for boys and girls. A pet project of outspoken feminist Marlo Thomas, *Free to Be You and Me* used songs, stories, and poems to encourage girls to imagine lives full of possibilities beyond the stereotypical teacher, nurse, and secretary available to prior generations. At the same time, *Free to Be You and Me* also validated boys' feelings and desires that were historically suppressed. Ex–football star Rosie Grier, ostensibly a paragon of tough masculinity, sang "It's Alright to Cry," and Alan Alda explained why "William wants a doll." An entire generation of urban and suburban kids grew up singing these songs that humorously and somewhat subversively planted the ideas of feminism and sexual freedom in little hearts and minds everywhere.

In the past twenty years Americans have witnessed another gender/sexual revolution of sorts with the emergence of transgender politics. Transgenderism, the decision and ability to change from the gender to which one has been assigned at birth to another chosen gender, complicates gay-straight and masculine-feminine binaries in ways that early second-wave feminists and gay liberationists could hardly have imagined. To be transgender has often meant to struggle with a system that punishes people for crossing gender lines in terms of dress, behavior, and identity. Many transgender people, including Kate Bornstein and Loren Cameron in the following sections, talk about their process of transitioning from one gender to another as a move toward integrating how one feels on the inside with what one looks like and how one is treated on the outside. Most transgender activists and theorists initially participated in feminist or queer political movements, and very often, both. Transgender people have pushed the broader lesbian and gay rights movement to take seriously the idea that gender differences and sexual freedom are as important as sexual orientation in the expansion of human rights and civil liberties. In some ways, transgender activists are bringing back political and cultural issues that had been salient in the early twentieth century.

Just as some transgender people blur the boundaries between genders, in many American gay male circles there is an increased fear of gender blurring as more and more gay men define themselves as "straight acting," by which they mean that they conform to some notion of idealized masculinity. Gay men, especially white gay men, have so absorbed ideal masculinity that in the early twenty-first century, they have among the highest rates of body dysmorphia, eating disorders, steroid abuse, and cosmetic surgery, far higher than rates among "straight" men. Ironically, gay men's attempts to "act more straight" and present themselves as masculine as possible come at the same time that their straight male counterparts are learning to be queer. Television shows, male fashion magazines, and even their female partners are encouraging straight men to embrace many of the refined lifestyle markers imagined to unite gay men. Queer women in the early twenty-first century are also reshaping gender expectations. There has been a return to classic butch-femme gender roles that defined lesbian communities in the 1940s, 1950s, and 1960s. It seems that gender and sexuality have never been more intertwined than now.

GEORGE HENRY

Sex Variants (1941)

Besides Alfred Kinsey, psychiatrist George Henry was probably the most well-known sex researcher in the 1930s and 1940s. His team, known as the Committee for the Study of Sex Researchers, put out the first ever large-scale collaborative study of sex research in 1941.

FOREWORD

The Committee for the Study of Sex Variants was founded in the spring of 1935. At its first meeting held in March 1935, the Committee formulated and adopted the following policy in regard to its interests and activities:

1. To correlate the various scientific interests in the field of sex study.
2. To serve as a scientific agency for the furtherance of research on sex variation.
3. To appoint advisory subcommittees for projects sponsored or to be sponsored by the Committee.

The purposes of the Committee were stated in rather broad terms as follows:

> To undertake, support and promote investigations and scientific research touching upon and embracing the clinical, psychological and sociological aspects of variations from normal sex behavior and of subjects related thereto, especially (but not exclusively) through laboratory research and clinical study.

> To disseminate information concerning these subjects of investigation and scientific research and matters connected with or related thereto.

> To do all things incidental to or suitable for the complete accomplishment of these aforesaid purposes.

The Committee has the impression that the interest in research in the field of sex has broadened in the last few years and that the public welfare will be served by publication of the results of this research. Medical, psychological and sociological studies of sex are receiving some mention in the daily press. The public begins to realize that punitive measures alone in dealing with cases of "sex crime" are inadequate and that the sex offender must be studied if progress in the prevention as well as in the treatment of sexual maladjustment is to be achieved.

Eugen Kahn
Chairman of Executive Committee
Committee for the Study of Sex Variants, Inc.

. . .

BISEXUAL CASES

Donald H.

Much sexual irregularity in family. Father a Don Juan, selfish and sensual. Mother a female replica of the father. Both ventured upon outskirts of homosexuality. Mother's first husband bisexual. Divorced by second husband, the father. Donald virtually had no parents. Mother an invalid and father too bored to remain home. Donald embarrassed by speech impediment and poor muscular coordination. Physicians thought play with other children too exciting. Teased in school. Made friends with servants. Instructed in all sorts of sexual activities. Married an aggressive Lesbian. Became impotent. Divorced. Married another Lesbian. Homosexual relations continued.

Bisexual. Mutual. Struggle to be active.

Sydney H.

Nearly half of family unpleasantly aggressive. Sydney exposed to violently aggressive and domineering members. Passivity and tendency to withdraw from harsh realities characteristic of both Sydney and his father. Sydney closely attached to mother. Curious about sex and easily led; couldn't resist advances of others. Rebelled against mother's chaperonage. Feels frustrated. Prefers solitary masturbation and witnessing sexual activities of others. Impractical, artistic recluse with body of a laborer.

Bisexual. Passive, masculine. Schizoid.

HOMOSEXUAL CASES

Thomas B.

Father had violent outbursts of temper; abused family. Mother passive and defenseless. Thomas not robust; timid; afraid of father. Lacked affection. Childhood masturbation. Feared dire consequences. Quiet and bookish. Susceptible to advances of affectionate men. Alliances provide affection and tenderness which he missed in childhood.

Homosexual. Mutual.

Nathan T.

Rigid and severe father dominated home. Nathan a timid, effeminate, spoiled child, protected by sweet and tender mother. Enuresis. Somnambulism. Afraid of rough boys. Considered a sissy. Looked like a girl. Sister dressed him up as a girl. No curiosity about girls. Wicked to have extramarital relations with a girl. Experimentation with a Lesbian. Disliked odor of women. Fear of impotence. Disillusioned. Affairs with men. Enjoyed visual and olfactory stimuli. Sex with dogs and with strangers, i.e., with men picked up on street. Gonorrhea.

Homosexual. Mutual.

NARCISSISTIC CASES

Rafael G.

Men in family handsome; Don Juan type. Youngest and favorite child. Slept with mother. Attached to her. Played with girls. Autoerotism and sex play in boarding school for boys. Active relations with younger boys. After sex with girls not satisfied until he masturbates. Goes with girls to conceal homosexuality. Fears growing old and becoming a degenerate old man. Decided he will not commit suicide until after his mother dies.

Homosexual. Heterosexual relations. Masturbation. Narcissistic.

Reginald M.

Father dominated and thwarted by wealthy wife; became hypochondriacal. Men on either side of family not especially virile. Reginald unable to cope with younger brother. Mother's favorite. Health delicate. Played with dolls and girls. Homosexual and exhibitionistic activities. Failure in business; couldn't face mother; alcoholism.

Active, aggressive homosexual. Sensual. Narcissistic.

. . .

BISEXUAL CASES

. . .

Pearl M.

Family characterized by sexual promiscuity and illegitimacy. Pearl called a half-white bastard. Taken to visit grandfather in prison; children knew he was a murderer. Mother's conduct justified her bad reputation. Pearl's first husband alcoholic, tubercular, irresponsible; died. Second husband indifferent, unfaithful. Pearl affectionate and had many admirers. After two failures in marriage yielded to advances of other women. Still passive, submissive and self-sacrificing. Disappointed in not having children.

Bisexual. Passive feminine. Homosexuality imposed through inadequacies of husbands.

Mae C.

Grandparents on both sides divorced. Parents have common bond of having suffered from family discord. Poorly adjusted to each other. Mae only child. Father encourages her to be boyish. Mother teaches her to be ladylike. Mother becomes partial invalid. Mae assumes responsibility. Father makes advances to Mae. Deserted by father. Accepts help of father's friend, a married man. Repays in sex and with a son. Neglected. Courted by Lesbian. Hopes for marriage with father of her son. Disillusioned. Loses son. Alcoholism. Death.

Bisexual. Preferred to be heterosexual.

HOMOSEXUAL CASES

Irene K.

Stubbornness and rigidity of paternal grandparents caused partially successful rebellion of father and his generation, and emancipation of Irene. Rebellion was consistent reaction. Father aggressive, hypocritical. Mother a sweet little lamb who reacted to stress with neurotic invalidism. Irene determined she would never be treated by a man as father treated her mother. All experiences with men disastrous. Marriage a fiasco. Alcoholism. Contemptuous of men. Resentful of feminine helplessness. Delights in doing a man's job better than he can. Marvelous to be a woman and have a man's brain. Finally succumbs to aggressive boyish girl.

Passive, masculine homosexual.

Virginia K.

Men in family inadequate and irresponsible. Maternal grandmother tyrannical, puritanical. Father worshipped his mother; spoiled by her. Mother headstrong, stubborn, sadistic, brutal, head of family. Frequent open quarrels between parents. Virginia felt sorry for father; resented mother. Physical illnesses brought attention of nurses. Envious of beautiful sister. Frightened by menstruation. Initiated to sex by girl at summer camp. Conflict with mother over homosexuality. Virginia won.

Homosexual. Active and passive.

. . .

NARCISSISTIC CASES

. . .

Rose S.

High proportion of psychotic, psychopathic and sexually maladjusted in family. On maternal side women consistently dominant. Parents hated each other. Rose in constant fear that father would desert family or quarrel with mother and beat children. Grew up in hostile environment. Attempted suicide. Resented being a girl. Married divorced man old enough to be her father. Child born. Fell madly in love with married woman. Deserted husband and child. Passionate affairs with both men and women.

Bisexual. Inclined to be active, sensual homosexual. Somewhat narcissistic.

Regina C.

Conflict between masculinity and femininity increases with succeeding generations. Always wanted to be a boy. Parents emphasized her masculine characteristics. Mother dominant and pampered. Regina rebellious. Affectionate with girls; competitive with boys. Thought of pregnancy revolting. Marries effeminate man against advice. Heterosexual experimentation a failure. Has lost desire for women. Helps adolescent girls with their abortions.

Bisexual. Heterosexual and homosexual experimentation. Rebellious. Narcissistic.

THE GYNECOLOGY OF HOMOSEXUALITY

The *genital findings* in the 31 sex variant women for whom full notation is found may be summarized as follows:

In general:

1. The vulva is large in its dimensions.
2. The labia minora are long, front to back.
3. The labia minora protrude between the labia majora, and are wrinkled, thickened or brawny.
4. The prepuce is large and wrinkled or in folds.
5. The clitoris is notably erectile in two-thirds, with the glans distinctly larger than the average in the antero-posterior diameter.
6. Erotism is clearly in evidence on examination, as shown by dusky flush of the parts, with free flow of clear, glairy mucus, and with definite clitoris erection.
7. The hymen is elastic and insensitive, worn or nicked.
8. The vagina is distensible.
9. The uterus tends to be small, menstruation normal, with cervix catarrh or inflammation absent, save in two cases.
10. The nipple is erectile in two-thirds.

All these findings *can* be the result of strong sex urge, plus

(a) Vulvar and vulvovaginal self-friction; or
(b) Homosexual digital or oral play; or
(c) Heterosexual manual or coital techniques, singly, or in any combination.

∾

AMERICAN PSYCHIATRIC ASSOCIATION
Sexual Deviations (1968, 1980)

The Diagnostic and Statistical Manual of Mental Disorders *(DSM) has been a staple for psychiatrists since its first publication in 1952. The issue of whether homosexuality is a psychiatric disease has been one of the more controversial matters that has faced the framers of the various DSMs over the last few decades. The very first edition, DSM-I, classified homosexuality as a sexual deviation, as did DSM-II in 1968. However, in December 1973, DSM-II was modified by the board of trustees of the American Psychiatric Association (APA), who replaced it with "sexual orientation disturbance."*

SEXUAL DEVIATIONS (DSM II, 1968)

This category is for individuals whose sexual interests are directed primarily toward objects other than people of the opposite sex, toward sexual acts not usually associated with coitus, or toward coitus performed under bizarre circumstances as in necrophilia, pedophilia, sexual sadism, and fetishism. Even though many find their practices distasteful, they remain unable to substitute normal sexual behavior for them. This diagnosis is not appropriate for individuals who perform deviant sexual acts because normal sexual objects are not available to them.

302.0 Homosexuality

302.1 Fetishism

302.2 Pedophilia

302.3 Transvestitism

302.4 Exhibitionism

302.5 Voyeurism

302.6 Sadism

302.7 Masochism

302.8 Other sexual deviation

[302.9 Unspecified sexual deviation]

GENDER IDENTITY DISORDERS (DSM III, 1980)

The essential feature of the disorders included in this subclass is an incongruence between anatomic sex and gender identity. Gender identity is the sense of knowing to which sex one belongs, that is, the awareness that "I am a male," or "I am a female." Gender identity is the private experience of gender role, and gender role is the public expression of gender identity. Gender role can be defined as everything that one says and does, including sexual arousal, to indicate to others or to the self the degree to which one is male or female.

Disturbance in gender identity is rare, and should not be confused with the far more common phenomena of feelings of inadequacy in fulfilling the expectations associated with one's gender role. An example would be an individual who perceives himself or herself as being sexually unattractive yet experiences himself or herself unambiguously as a man or woman in accordance with his or her anatomic sex.

302.5x Transsexualism

The essential features of this heterogeneous disorder are a persistent sense of discomfort and inappropriateness about one's anatomic sex and a persistent wish to be rid of one's genitals and to live as a member of the other sex. The diagnosis is made only if the disturbance has been continuous (not limited to periods of stress) for at least two years, is not due to another mental disorder, such as Schizophrenia, and is not associated with physical intersex or genetic abnormality.

Individuals with this disorder usually complain that they are uncomfortable wearing the clothes of their own anatomic sex; frequently this discomfort leads to cross-dressing (dressing in clothes of the other sex). Often they choose to engage in activities that in our culture tend to be associated with the other sex. These individuals often find their genitals repugnant, which may lead to persistent requests for sex reassignment by surgical or hormonal means.

To varying degrees, the behavior, dress, and mannerisms are those of the other sex. With cross-dressing, hormonal treatment, and electrolysis, a few males with the disorder will appear relatively indistinguishable from members of the other sex. However, the anatomic sex of most males and females with the disorder is quite apparent to the alert observer.

Associated features. Generally there is moderate to severe coexisting personality disturbance. Frequently there is considerable anxiety and depression, which the individual may attribute to inability to live in the role of the desired sex. . . .

Age at onset. Individuals who develop Transsexualism often evidenced gender identity problems as children. However, some assert that although they were secretly aware of their gender problem, it was not evident to their family and friends. The age at which the full syndrome appears for those with the "asexual" or "homosexual" course is most often in late adolescence or early adult life. In individuals with the "heterosexual" course, the disorder may have a later onset.

Impairment and complications. Frequently social and occupational functioning are markedly impaired, partly because of associated psychopathology and partly because of problems encountered in attempting to live in the desired gender role.

Depression is common, and can lead to suicide attempts. In rare instances males may mutilate their genitals.

Predisposing factors. Extensive, pervasive, childhood femininity in a boy or childhood masculinity in a girl increases the likelihood of Transsexualism. Transsexualism seems always to develop in the context of a disturbed parent-child relationship. Some cases of Transvestism evolve into Transsexualism. . . .

Diagnostic criteria for Transsexualism

A. Sense of discomfort and inappropriateness about one's anatomic sex.
B. Wish to be rid of one's own genitals and to live as a member of the other sex.
C. The disturbance has been continuous (not limited to periods of stress) for at least two years.
D. Absence of physical intersex or genetic abnormality.
E. Not due to another mental disorder, such as Schizophrenia. . . .

302.60 Gender Identity Disorder of Childhood

The essential features are a persistent feeling of discomfort and inappropriateness in a child about his or her anatomic sex and the desire to be, or insistence that he or she is, of the other sex. In addition, there is a persistent repudiation of the individual's own anatomic attributes. This is not merely the rejection of stereotypical sex role behavior as, for example, in "tomboyishness" in girls or "sissyish" behavior in boys, but rather a profound disturbance of the normal sense of maleness or femaleness.

Girls with this disorder regularly have male peer groups, an avid interest in sports and rough-and-tumble play, and a lack of interest in playing with dolls or playing "house" (unless playing the father or another male role). More rarely, a girl with this disorder claims that she will grow up to become a man (not merely in role), that she is biologically unable to become pregnant, that she will not develop breasts, or that she has, or will grow, a penis.

Boys with this disorder invariably are preoccupied with female stereotypical activities. They may have a preference for dressing in girls' or women's clothes, or may improvise such items from available material when genuine articles are unavailable. (The cross-dressing never causes sexual excitement.) They often have a compelling desire to participate in the games and pastimes of girls. Dolls are often the favorite toy, and girls are regularly the preferred playmates. When playing "house," the role of a female is typically adopted. Rough-and-tumble play or sports are regularly avoided. Gestures and actions are often judged against a standard of cultural stereotype to be feminine, and the boy is invariably subjected to male peer group teasing and rejection, which rarely occurs among girls until adolescence. In rare cases a boy with this disorder claims that his penis or testes are disgusting or will disappear, or that it would be better not to have a penis or testes.

Some children refuse to attend school because of teasing or pressure to dress in attire stereotypical of their sex. Most children with this disorder deny being disturbed by it except as it brings them into conflict with the expectations of their family or peers.

❦

LOREN CAMERON

Introduction to *Body Alchemy: Transsexual Portraits* (1996)

One of the most well-known transgender authors and photographers, Loren Cameron (1959–) was born a girl in Pasadena, California. She began transitioning from female to male in 1987 and in 1996 published Body Alchemy: Transsexual Portraits, *one of the first photography books that empathetically documents and explores transgender men's lives and bodies. The book won two prestigious Lambda Literary Awards, and Cameron's photography of transgender people has been exhibited in several solo shows. He recently published an e-book entitled* Man Tool: The Nuts and Bolts of Female to Male Surgery.

INTRODUCTION

My affinity for photography began as early as I can remember. My parents had lots of photo books with pictures of The War and pre–World War Two America. There, I first saw images by Walker Evans and Dorothea Lange, who greatly influenced my artistic and aesthetic sensibilities. My father had stories of his own about what it was like to grow up in Iowa near the end of the Great Depression: he and his siblings would scour the railroad tracks to find bits of coal that had fallen from the trains' coal cars, and he quit school at thirteen so he could work to feed his family. Through Lange's photographs, I gained a visual understanding of my father's stories about working-class survival. Her images touched me deeply and helped me understand his tough attitude about living and his generation's no-nonsense work ethic, as well as the universality of the human condition of pain, strife and the will to persevere.

I've looked to these images from the past to learn something of compassion and a sense of the heroic. In my own life, along with my father's words, they have taught me to honor labor and to keep putting one foot in front of the other. Being drawn to photography as a medium of expression seems only natural for me, given the emotional impact it has had on my life. It has been the most powerful teaching tool for me to date, and I feel the message in my work isn't very different from Lange's or Evans': it is a vision about strength and will and everyday people.

A tomboy as a child, I shunned dresses and rolling down my socks. I loved playing Army games, and my favorite doll was a G.I. Joe. When my mother died in 1968, I moved from Pasadena, California to rural Arkansas to live with my father, his wife and her two teenage children. I didn't see my three sisters again until I was nearly twenty.

My father's farm was just outside a small rural town of thirteen hundred people at the foot of the Ozark Mountains. He raised horses for the love of them and was employed at the nearby nuclear plant. A lot of my adolescence and early teens were spent working with my father, building fences and feeding the horses. In my spare time after school, I explored the lush and wild countryside with my small pack of canine companions. Many afternoons were lazed-away on the bank of a pond while I fished for perch and daydreamed.

At the onset of puberty, that slightly insane time in all our lives, I grew very restless and became a regular fixture down at the local greasy spoon in town. I dressed in overalls and workboots and learned to swear like a trucker and smoke cigarettes and marijuana. I loved anything daring and adventurous. My friends and I rafted swollen rivers, drag-raced, rode crazy horses and ran from cops.

During my teens and even before then, I had begun to feel terrifically uncomfortable as a female-bodied person. When I was twelve years old, I heard of people changing sex, and I even wrote away for information. But how could I tell? Who would understand what even I could barely verbalize? I could only wear baggy clothing to hide my ever-developing breasts and somehow learn to cope with the inconvenience of menstruation. At about seventeen, I had barely begun to experiment sexually with boys when one of my older female friends returned home on leave from the Army. As we took a pleasant drive down a dirt road, she very carefully inquired about whether I had ever considered being a lesbian. The thought hadn't even occurred to me. I was elated at the suggestion! Why not? If I couldn't be a boy, then I could be a dyke! Come to think of it, women were very attractive!

Unfortunately, my excitement wasn't shared by my heterosexual friends. Like greased lightning, the news of my new-found identity got around town. It took even less time for all of my friends to turn their backs on me. I was in my junior year of high school where I had been unexpectedly elected class president and student council president. All of a sudden, I was outcast.

Finding no support or solace, I quit school and ran away from home. I spent the next couple of years struggling to survive and taking long bus rides across the States, trying to see the world beyond that small place. Working labor jobs—fruit picking and construction clean-up—I barely got by. I returned to Arkansas, not having found the place to call home, and worked until I felt the urge to buy the next bus ticket. I ran a truckstop fuel station for a while, then I got a job on a youth conservation-corps crew. One day, while I was mixing cement for a rock wall we were building, these two very lesbian-looking women approached from a nearby campground. They were from San Francisco. Within a few hours of friendly conversation, these seemingly sophisticated dykes convinced me that my fame and fortune were to be found in a city by the ocean. Weeks later, I purchased my last bus ticket, grabbed my duffel bag and went out West.

I had lived in the San Francisco lesbian scene for nine years, when at twenty-six, I finally began to address my discomfort about my gender. I can only speculate about the timing. Maybe it was because I was finally living by myself and didn't have to contend with any negative peer pressure, or maybe I was finally old enough to deal with it. Other things had changed too. I had quit smoking pot and tobacco, which I suspect had, until then, suppressed my feelings. In addition, I was recovering from the failure of a very passionate relationship that had left me devastated. For the first time in my life, I wasn't numb.

The need to change became all-consuming: I started the step-by-step process of therapy, doctors and surgeons. Taking testosterone as hormone therapy and developing a body-building regimen, I ever so slowly and painfully began to reinvent myself. I photographed myself and sent amateur snapshots to friends and family in order to show them how happy I was; I wanted them to get used to the idea of my body being different. If they could see my new beard and chest sans breasts, perhaps it would be easier for them to accept my new identity. You know, so they would stop calling me "she." I was excited, too, much like when I had discovered my sexuality as a teenager. Only this time, I refused to feel any shame. I was creating a beautiful new body image, and I was proud of it.

What was initially a crude documentation of my own personal journey gradually evolved into an impassioned mission. Impulsively, I began to photograph other transsexuals that I knew, feeling compelled to make images of their emotional and physical triumphs. I was fueled by my need to be validated and wanted, in turn, to validate them. I wanted the world to see us, I mean, really see us.

Since I'd had no formal training, I took a basic photography class and learned to print my images. My first work was done with a simple Pentax K1000. Within a year, I managed to have my first show, which earned critical attention. After several more exhibitions, I graduated from thirty-five millimeter to medium format. Still preferring the simplicity of a manually operated camera, I bought a used Pentax six-by-seven body and a new one thirty-five macro lens. Finding the rectangular negative more appealing than the shape of a two-and-one-quarter inch square, I decided to continue using a field camera. Besides, this Pentax was as durable as a tank: I could drop it and still be in the running. Transitioning to a larger negative helped me regard myself more seriously as a professional photographer, and the crisp, beautiful quality of the photographs inspired new images.

Despite the financial challenge, The Work has taken on a life of its own, and I am pressed to keep producing. I use a shutter-release bulb in my self-portraits because I usually work alone; my camera doesn't have a shutter timer, so I have to press the shutter button myself. I actually prefer this method to ensure that the work is entirely of my own vision. People have asked me, however, why I don't try to conceal the bulb in the photographs. At times, given the composition of a photograph, concealing the bulb may not be possible. I also feel a certain pride in making a decent image without seeing through the lens, so I don't really mind that the bulb is visible. Its presence serves as a metaphor: I am creating my own image alone, an act that reflects the transsexual experience as well.

For the longest time, transsexuals and especially transsexual men (female-to-males) have been virtually invisible to the dominant culture. Marginalized even within the gay and lesbian subculture, transsexuals have occupied no real space of our own. In the last decade or so, more and more transsexual people have been speaking out about our experiences. We are beginning to represent ourselves for the first time and to develop our own voice. *Body Alchemy* is the first photo documentation of transsexual men from within our community.

As I have observed another movement paralleling that of transsexuals, it is my intention to embrace and include in this work those people who may identify more comfortably as "transgender," or "gender transgressive." A growing number of people are and have been questioning the more usual representations of gender. Some have had chemical and surgical enhancement, and many have not. Inhabiting a less static gender identification than that of typical transsexuals, they are exploring and experiencing a fluid range of gender embodiment. My own intimate partner, Kayt, is one such individual. Ironically, it has been through knowing and loving her that I have gained an even deeper understanding of the mutable soul. Her flexible consciousness has encouraged me to be generous in my thinking and less rigid about the way others self-define, or in fact, when they choose not to.

In an effort to address these issues, I have produced a very personal project with Kayt. Along with my photo essay and its symbolic representations of the two of us, I have invited Kayt to write about her experience of being transgendered and about our sometimes conventional, sometimes unconventional relationship. It is my hope that this inclusion will offer yet another perspective on what it means to be transgendered.

HEROES

The first time transsexual men marched in the San Francisco Gay Pride Parade in 1994, I had an incredible day. Holding one end of a banner that read *FTM TRANS PRIDE,* I walked bare-chested with my head held high. It was a frightening experience: just a handful of us braved the hordes with literally hundreds of thousands of people scrutinizing us. We were all nervous, and I remember whispering repeatedly to my banner mate to slow his pace because I wanted to absorb it all and fix the moment in my mind forever. I wanted to watch people's reactions to us, and more than anything, I wanted to walk with dignity.

As we passed, a silence fell over the crowd until we heard a timid offering of applause, occasionally punctuated with an outbreak of cheers. I glanced at my comrades to see their broad smiles when we heard hoorahs. Every now and then, I glimpsed in the crowd a face full of contempt for us or saw an acquaintance who pretended not to see me wave. I felt a disturbing jumble of sadness and angry defiance; I forced myself to look into their eyes until they turned away.

Whether she or he has marched in a parade or not, I think every transsexual understands what we felt that day. Each one of us has had to take a stand about our identity. When I photograph transsexuals, men or women, I ask about their histories. I know they have labored to arrive at the place where I've found them. They tell me about losing jobs and friends while going through transition, and how they fought to keep them. They talk about the people who love them and how difficult it is to make them understand. I see the strain in their faces as they speak to me, and I know they've been through so much. But more than anything, I hear the relief in their voices. Satisfied with their changed bodies, they each tell me how much better they feel, and that they would do it all again if they had to. I marvel at their strength: like tempered steel, it is the kind that propels armies and liberationists, a single-minded conviction. When I look through my lens at them, I recognize the power of such willfulness. I want the world to know the force of their beauty.

~

KATE BORNSTEIN
My Gender Workbook (1998)

As a performance artist, political activist, and author, Kate Bornstein has a gender identity and life history that defy categorization and classification. Biologically born and raised a boy outside of Fargo, North Dakota, Kate transitioned into a different gender as an adult. She began exploring the cultural meanings of gender in her highly acclaimed performance art and books such as My Gender Workbook *and* Gender Outlaw: Men, Women, and the Rest of Us. *Kate's performance art and writing about gender are known for their humor and scathing wit, and she has broadly influenced artists and writers concerned with gender politics, both in and outside the academy.*

SO . . . ARE YOU A REAL MAN? A REAL WOMAN?

At first glance that seems to be a simple pair of questions. Most people when asked those questions would smile and say, "Of course I'm a real man," or "Of course I'm a real woman." It's not something most of us question. The difficult part comes when we're asked to remember the times we've been made to feel we're not quite as manly or as womanly as we could be or should be. Maybe it was the day we found ourselves deeply afraid or weeping uncontrollably, and we (or someone else) questioned how much of a man we really are. Maybe we've not been able to get pregnant, or maybe we haven't wanted to, and we (or someone else) questioned how much of a woman we really are. There are so many qualifications for those categories, aren't there? We make jokes like "Real men don't eat quiche," or admonitions like "A real woman would be married by now." Not that anyone has ever written all these qualifications down, mind you. People have tried, but there's been too much disagreement about what constitutes a "real man," and what constitutes a "real woman" for there to be one acceptable document containing the absolute definitions of either of those categories of identity. So by trial and error we learn the reality of our real manhood and real womanhood. We build our own definitions for these, and we're very pleased to know people who agree with our definitions. When enough people agree with us, we begin to assume it's natural.

Well, here's a question: If gender is so natural, then why hasn't it been written down and codified? Most everything else that's considered "natural" has been codified. Why isn't there some agreed-upon manual we could hand our children and say, "Here, honey. This is what a real man is. Learn this well." Why do we mystify these categories to such a degree that we assume "everyone knows" what real men and real women are?

Let's keep looking at your Gender Aptitude when it comes to the subject of these categories called "real men" and "real women."

YOUR GENDER APTITUDE, SECTION II: PERCEPTIONS

1. Do you stand up to pee?
   A. Yup, most of the time.
   B. No, never.
   C. Well, I've tried it a few times.
   D. It all depends on the effect I want to create.

2. Have you ever worn the clothes of "the opposite sex"?
   A. Hey, give me a break. No way!
   B. Yes, but when I wear them, they're for the *right* sex.
   C. What sex in the world would be opposite of me?
   D. Several of the above.

3. Do you shave?
   A. Yup. Except when I'm growing my beard or mustache.
   B. Depends. I go back and forth on the hairy armpit thing.
   C. Where?
   D. Yes, but not myself.

4. When you go into a department store to buy yourself clothing, do you shop mostly in a department labeled for your assigned gender?
   A. Well, duh! Where else?

    B. No, because sometimes the other departments have stuff that fits me better.

    C. Yes, because it's very important to me to do that.

    D. I will shop in *any* department for *anything* that's fabulous.

5. *Are there things you* can *do in the world because of your gender that others can't do because of theirs?*

    A. Yes, but that's just the way the world is.

    B. Yeah, but *they* get paid well for doing what *they* can do.

    C. I used to think so.

    D. Honey, I've never let a little thing like gender get in my way.

6. *Are there things you* can't *do in the world because of your gender that others can?*

    A. No. Well, maybe I can't have a baby, but who wants to? Ha ha ha!

    B. Well, duh. Of course!

    C. I used to think it was because of my gender, yeah.

    D. Maybe a long time ago, back before I met the Scarecrow, the Tin Man, and the Lion.

7. *When the store clerk asks, "How can I help you, sir," you*

    A. Smile.

    B. Wince.

    C. Curse.

    D. Curtsy.

8. *When the store clerk looks up at you inquiringly and says, "Yes, ma'am?" you*

    A. Wish you'd grown that mustache after all.

    B. Smile.

    C. Purr.

    D. Brightly exclaim, "Gee I'm sorry . . . would you like to try for Door Number Three?"

9. *Basic black looks best . . .*

    A. On my new BMW.

    B. With pearls.

    C. With anything.

    D. Well, dip me in honey and throw me to the Goth chicks.

10. *Have you read the book* Gender Outlaw *by Kate Bornstein?*

    A. Nope. Is it a Western?

    B. I'd say what I really think about that book, but I'm nervous about how that might affect my aptitude score.

C. Yes, and I loved it!

D. I could've written it better.

Give yourself 5 points if you checked A, 3 points if you checked B, 1 point for C, and no points for D.

Write your score for this section here. _____

THE ELUSIVE "REAL ME"

I'm thinking we live in the latter days of what might as well be called the "Age of Identity." The part of ourselves we show to others might be called an identity. Ideally, our identities are an accurate reflection of who we feel we are. Some people give this identity a name; they call it "The Real Me."

There are books, television shows, college-level courses, tapes, videos, focus groups, cults, all promising that we can learn to be an identity called "the real me." Why, I'm wondering, would we need to learn to be that, unless there was so much pressure coming from the rest of the world, making us not be "the real me." There are obviously enough people in the world who think they're not being "the real me" to keep all these other people in business trying to teach them. People who recover from alcoholism become "the real me." Lesbians, gays, and bisexual people coming out of the closet and embracing their desires become "the real me." Men who learn to cry discover another kind of "real me." People born-again into anything from fundamentalism to feminism claim to have discovered "the real me." More to the point, some transsexual people believe when they've gone from one gender to another that they've arrived at "the real me." Well, what is that identity? And what's "the real me" got to do with being a "real man" or a "real woman"? And most importantly, does your gender (identity) match up with who you feel yourself to be? Do you think your gender is an accurate reflection of everything you are? Everything you could possibly be? Does your gender match up with the real you? . . .

AND JUST WHO DO YOU THINK YOU ARE, ANYWAY?

You're *not* the same person you were ten minutes ago.

None of us is.

Each of us makes dozens if not hundreds of minor decisions in the space of ten minutes. And unless we're truly hermits, each of us is subject to influences by and connections with the world around us that change the course of our lives. No, they're not dramatic changes, but they are changes nonetheless.

Maybe someone smiled at you on the street this morning and made you feel good. Maybe you heard something on the news just now that made you wonder how much say you have in our government. Perhaps it was a phone call from a long-lost friend. It could have been a bit of email, or some passage or question in this book, or a piece of poetry, or just a bird landing on your windowsill that made you change your mind about the state of your life. Interactions of most every type have a tendency to change us; that's what growth is all about. We're so used to these minichanges that we give them no thought, but the fact is we're not the same people we used to be.

> *I've gone through some pretty dramatic changes. I've changed my gender, several times in fact. But I think the question we should be asking ourselves is: "Why is that so dramatic?" I'm not saying it's not dramatic. I think it is. I'm just asking what is it that the culture taught me to make me think that changing gender is dramatic?*

We change our attitudes, our careers, our relationships. Even our age changes minute by minute. We change our politics, our moods, and our sexual preferences. We change our outlook, we change our minds, we change our sympathies. Yet when someone changes hir gender, we put hir on some television talk show. Well, here's what I think: I think we all of us *do* change our genders. All the time. Maybe it's not as dramatic as some tabloid headline screaming "She Was A He!" But we do, each of us, change our gender. In response to each interaction we have with a new or different person, we subtly shift the *kind* of man or woman, boy or girl, or whatever gender we're being at the moment. We're usually not the same *kind* of man or woman with our lover as we are with our boss or a parent. When we're introduced for the first time to someone we find attractive, we shift into being a different *kind of* man or woman than we are with our childhood friends. We all change our genders. I'm just saying it's time we knew exactly what we are doing and why. So, let's get on with the next section of our Gender Aptitude questionnaire and see just how flexible your gender might be. Hang on, we're going to dig a bit deeper now.

YOUR GENDER APTITUDE, SECTION IV: FLEXIBILITY

1. When the kind of person to whom you are normally attracted begins to flirt heavily with you, you
   A. Envision the great sex you're going to have later tonight.
   B. Try to get to know this person a bit better.
   C. Panic because it's been so long and you wonder if you know how to do it right anymore.
   D. Flirt right back, matching move for move.

2. When the kind of person that normally turns you off begins to flirt heavily with you, you
   A. Hit the person.
   B. Leave.

    C. Tell them, "Honey, you flirt with this hand."

    D. See if there's anything about it you can enjoy as long as it's only flirting.

3. *When was the last time you were aware of something about your gender that was holding you back in the world?*

    A. I can't recall a time like that.

    B. Do you want that in minutes or seconds?

    C. Do you mean the times I did something about it, or the times it overwhelmed me?

    D. It was just before I changed my gender the last time.

4. *How many genders do you really think there are?*

    A. Two.

    B. Well, there are two sexes. Is that what you mean?

    C. I'm going to guess there are lots of genders and two sexes.

    D. When do you want me to stop counting?

5. *Do you feel it's possible for someone to change hir gender?*

    A. No. And what does "hir" mean, Flake-o?

    B. I think people can try, but no. Not really, no.

    C. Yes, with proper supervision, surgery, and hormones. I think so.

    D. How many times?

6. *What do you believe the essential sign of gender to be?*

    A. The presence or absence of a penis.

    B. A combination of genitalia, secondary sex characteristics, hormones, and chromosomes.

    C. It's an energy thing. People have male or female energy.

    D. Whatever.

7. *If someone tells you they're neither a man nor a woman, and you find out they mean it, you think to yourself*

    A. This person is either kidding or is really, really sick.

    B. The poor, brave dear!

    C. Whoa! What a trip!

    D. I found another one at last!

8. *If you meet someone who you think is one gender, but you find out they used to be another gender, you think to yourself*

    A. Is this some costume party?

    B. The poor, brave dear!

    C. Wow, and I didn't even know!

    D. Yeah, yeah. But can you do a good Elvis?

9. *If you see someone on the street whose gender is unclear to you, do you*
   A. Dismiss that person as a freak?
   B. Try to figure out if it's a man or a woman?
   C. Mentally give them a makeover so they can pass better as one or the other?
   D. Notice they're staring at you, trying to figure out what you are?

10. *Is the male/female dichotomy something natural?*
   A. Well, duh. Of course.
   B. It's probably a combination of nature and nurture.
   C. Probably, but there are a lot of exceptions walking around!
   D. There's a male/female dichotomy? On what planet?

Give yourself 5 points for each A answer, 3 points for every B, 1 point for a C, and no points for any D answers.

Write your score for this section here. _____

3
Out and About
QUEER SPACES IN AMERICA,
NOW AND THEN

Every time we teach queer studies classes, students who do not identify as queer inevitably pose the question, "Why are there gay bars and gay neighborhoods? You don't find places labeled 'straight' bars and 'straight neighborhoods.'" As with every excellent question, we always ask the students why they think it might be the case that there are places on the map that, for those in the know, have labels like "gay bar," "gay ghetto," or "gay neighborhood."

The idea of a place being marked by the queerness of its inhabitants, or by the marginality of its residents, is nothing new. In medieval cities, for example, Jews lived in separate parts of towns, and in the sixteenth century, the Venice city council established the first ghetto in history for its Jewish residents. The ghetto served several purposes. Christian Venetians felt protected from Jews, and more importantly, Jews felt protected from Christian Venetians. Jews had power over their ghetto. They could observe Jewish holidays without fear of retribution; they could congregate together without fear of violence. Queer space in the United States is marked by similar power dynamics. To call a place or space "queer" is a way to communicate who has power and who does not, who belongs and who does not, and who feels the need for one's own space and who does not.

The idea that a particular place—whether a neighborhood, bar, or building— is marked by the sexual identity or sexual interests of its inhabitants is a much newer phenomenon than the Jewish ghetto. In the United States, it wasn't until the twentieth century that certain parts of town were known as places where "queers" spent time, socialized, and even had public sex. In an age when people and things moved around by ship, most of those places were near ports, where people were constantly coming and going, and where people could maintain some sense of anonymity. These were places in which nonnormative forms of sexuality thrived. In the early twentieth-century United States, queers socialized in parts of town that were already

53

marked as licentious and naughty. Not surprisingly, these parts of town, streets, and parks were also places that attracted members of the urban working classes, who were seen as the primary consumers and producers of illicit sex, debauchery, and anything that violated middle-class Victorian American standards.

But sexuality was only one way of marking separate spaces on the map. Race, class, and gender have always shaped how certain places have been associated with certain groups of people. In New York, Harlem was the place both of and for African Americans and of and for African American queers. Some have even argued that because Harlem was already marked space, because of its association with black people, it was easier for it to become marked as queer space. Further downtown, Greenwich Village became the lefty, progressive part of town, where "women with short hair" and "men with long hair" socialized, and increasingly, also lived. As the *Alienist and Neurologist* article included here shows, places and spaces across the country were racialized and sexualized throughout the twentieth century. There were some places where social boundaries could be crossed, and other places where such transgressions were socially unacceptable. Dance halls and bars were *not* for the upper classes and in many cases were also not for white folk. But they were places where racial and sexual boundaries could be crossed.

It is not an accident that much of the textual gay material from the early twentieth-century United States focuses on men, and that we did not see a visible, *public* queer culture for women until the 1930s and World War II. For women, it was more difficult to mark public queer space, because it was more difficult for women to be public. Middle-class white women were not permitted to socialize in smoky bars in the Bowery in the same way that working-class women could. For that matter, women who displayed their sexuality in any way, queer or otherwise, were frequently marked as prostitutes, as women violating social norms. For mid- dle- and upper-class white women, same-sex socialization took place in women's colleges, progressive movements, and during the women's suffrage movement spanning the 1910s. Were all of these places marked as queer? Obviously not. But could upper-middle-class white women express same-sex love in these environ- ments? Yes. Working-class women, on the other hand, had an easier time than upper-class women in creating explicitly queer space, precisely because they could be more public than upper-class women. Working-class women were creating queer space all over the country, not just in large urban areas like New York City and San Francisco. For example, New York City had separate *neighborhoods* for white queers and for African American queers. In contrast, the working-class les- bian bars of wartime Buffalo accommodated women of different races who could socialize and even date, something that seems to have been more difficult in cities with larger, and therefore more segmented, queer spaces. Although the focus of Elizabeth Lapovsky Kennedy and Madeline Davis's research is on bars as lesbian space, the subtitle of their book, *The History of a Lesbian Community,* shows that "community," an elusive concept that suggests links among people in particular places and spaces, happened in bars, parks, and for men, in bathhouses and rest- rooms. In times and places when queerness was more marginalized, before the age of community centers, high school gay-straight alliances, and support groups, queers made community in subtle places that were less visible to the "untrained" eye.

During World War II, with hundreds of thousands of young horny Americans leaving home, queer spaces appeared in some unlikely places—on battleships, in training camps, and in cities that had large contingents of recruits on leave looking for a bed at the local YMCA. Historians like Allan Berube have argued that although queer spaces existed before the war, World War II put so many people on the move that queerness came out in the open across the country. For women especially, who historically did not have as much power to move around and live publicly, the war provided unprecedented opportunities for same-sex socialization.

After the war, in an era of Cold War McCarthyite repression, the military, which became marked as queer space during the war, was "cleansed" of its queerness, and gay space moved further underground. Police raids on bars and public cruising parks for gay men meant that queer space became both a site of community building and a place of potential state-sponsored violence. In the 1950s, driven by fear not just of social violence and ostracism but of police violence, gay bars became even more important sites for building queer community.

The 1960s counterculture rebellion, feminism, the civil rights and Black Power movements, and anti–Vietnam War protests broke open the culture of repression and laid the groundwork for the 1969 Stonewall rebellion, which many people mark as the beginning of the gay liberation movement (see Chapter 8). For the first time, queers "came out" visibly and publicly and created new communities, places, and spaces for themselves. In San Francisco, the Castro neighborhood became one of the most visible and politically powerful "gay ghettos" in the world, and eventually elected the first openly gay man, Harvey Milk, to the San Francisco City Council. In New York a thriving gay culture turned places like Greenwich Village and, as author Andrew Holleran shows, Cherry Grove and Fire Island, into queer destinations. Certain places on the map were known by both queers *and* non-queers as queer places. In the 1970s, radical lesbian separatists began forming separate communes that were "men-free." In 1976, the Michigan Womyn's Music Festival created a social space for womyn-centered womyn to socialize and celebrate a week without men, free of patriarchy.

As queerness became more visible and public, and as white upper-middle-class queers gained visibility as consumers and political actors, queers began to form their own neighborhoods in most major U.S. cities. From the Castro and Greenwich Village to Dupont Circle and West Hollywood, queers clustered for many of the same reasons Jews had clustered—to gain political and social power over a place in an environment of homophobia. Queers in Los Angeles took this act of gaining political power to its logical conclusion by turning the gay neighborhood West Hollywood into an incorporated city with a queer city council, queer community centers, and the headquarters of the Metropolitan Community Church, the nationally known queer church.

In the twenty-first century, queers have moved far beyond bars, parks, and neighborhoods in the creation of queer space. Since the 1970s, American queers have created new kinds of spaces that form the basis of a queer community that now has political and economic power. Queers have cruises, resorts, teen homeless shelters, senior homes, medical facilities, cafes, bookstores, restaurants, support groups, floors in college dorms, and even memorials to past oppression. At the same time, because of this unprecedented visibility of queer space, some queers have also left queer space and integrated into unmarked space. There are queers living in middle-class suburbs, flirting in sports bars, and sharing rooms in mainstream hotels. Some see this as the decline of queer space. They fear that when queers assimilate into bourgeois social values and when U.S. society begins to embrace "socially acceptable queers," there will be no more need for queer space. If it is socially acceptable for queers to flirt in a sports bar (which is in fact questionable), then is there still a need for separate queer space? Perhaps in an age when one's sexual identity is no longer a marker of difference, then queer space will also no longer be marked as different. But as long as queers still feel uncomfortable flirting in straight bars, aging queers are still afraid to share a room in retirement communities with their same-sex lovers, and students are still afraid to talk to their friends about their same-sex love, queer space will remain a part of the U.S. social landscape.

But even queer space is marked by power. To claim queer space is a statement about perceived power over a particular space, and it is also about regulating access to that space. Although many queers celebrate the integration and visibility of queer space, others lament the new forms of exclusion that operate in these spaces. Neighborhoods like the Castro, West Hollywood, Chelsea in New York, and Dupont Circle in Washington, D.C., are the reserve of upper-middle-class gay white men. Many lesbians and queer people of color have left these newly gentrified neighborhoods for affordable housing and less commercialized queer space in places like Oakland, Echo Park, Harlem, and the U Street corridor in D.C. There is a sense among some that the successes in taking power over place and space have come at a cost—the cost of the radicalism and marginality that results when one's space is defined in response to oppression and marginalization. Even the Michigan Womyn's Music Festival, the bastion of progressive, noncommercial, politically engaged queer community, is now the object of criticism for its exclusion of transgender people from its womyn-born-womyn celebration.

The new battles over space and the fact that these are battles *among* queers as much as they are *between* queers and heterosexuals suggests that the map of America has indeed fundamentally changed and that queer space has become a visible integral part of the United States.

ALIENIST AND NEUROLOGIST

Homosexual Complexion Perverts in St. Louis: Note on a Feature of Psychopathy (1907)

The journal Alienist and Neurologist, *which appeared from 1880 to 1920, was one of few U.S. journals, including the* Urologic and Cutaneous Review *and* Lancet, *of the era that published news and research about sexuality from eminent sex researchers.* Alienist *was a late nineteenth-century term for psychiatrist. This article shows the ways social commentators fused race and sexuality and how black men were frequently feminized by the white press. In this case, racism also manifested itself as anti-queer state-sponsored violence.*

Male negroes masquerading in woman's garb and carousing and dancing with white men is the latest St. Louis record of neurotic and psychopathic sexual perversion. Some of them drove to the levee dive and dance hall at which they were arrested in their masters' auto cars. All were gowned as women at the miscegenation dance and the negroes called each other feminine names. They were all arrested, taken before Judge Tracy and gave bond to appear for trial, at three hundred dollars each, signed by a white man.

The detectives say that the levee resort at which these black perverts were arrested, is a rendezvous for scores of West End butlers, cooks and chauffeurs. Apartments in the house are handsomely furnished and white men are met there. The names of these negro perverts, their feminine aliases and addresses appear in the press notices of their arrest, but the names of the white degenerates consorting with them are not given.

Social reverse complexion homosexual affinities are rarer than non reverse color affinities, yet even white women sometimes prefer colored men to white men and *vice versa.* Homosexuality may be found among blacks, though this phase of sexual perversion is not so common or at least has not been so recorded, as between white males or white females. I have recorded but one male instance in my own personal observation, viz: that of gentleman George, for a time a valet and later a cook who loved to masquerade in woman's attire including bonnet and shoes and could never be induced to wear any shoe but a woman's soft gaiter and who had pierced ears for rings and wore the latter at times when not laughed at too much and when they were not in pawn, for he was impecunious and easily victimized by peddlers from whom he would buy chromo pictures, mantel clocks, rings and women's combs and ornamental trinkets at fabulous unfair prices.

George's peculiar predilection was for white men. He would say he "had no use for niggers" though he made his home for awhile with an aged and kindly colored woman acquaintance who trusted him for board when out of funds.

George had many foolish ways and dress propensities for a man, such as preferring a chemise for a night shirt. He had a right inguinal scrotal hernia requiring the constant wearing of a truss though he was exceedingly careless about this and suffered frequent pain because thereof, requiring my assistance. He had normal appearing masculine genitalia and could have raised a slight beard and mustache though he kept himself closely shaven, he wore his hair long though its growth was rather scant.

A Moll, Krafft-Ebing, Havelock Ellis or Kiernan might find material in St. Louis for further contributions to their studies of reverse sexual instinct. The contraire sexual empfingdung has had other illustrations here. St. Louis has duplicated the woman stabber of Berlin since she set her mark at a million inhabitants. These perverted creatures appear to be features of million peopled cities and they come into the light, if the police are vigilant. The reverse erotopath abounds among the nerve center degraded as well as the insistent and persistent erotopath of cliteromania or satyriac imperative propulsion.

Note: These St. Louis negro perverts gave feminine names that might belong to English or American ladies of any city. The curious may find them and the names the blacks assumed at the record office of the police courts.

❧

ELIZABETH LAPOVSKY KENNEDY AND MADELINE DAVIS

"I Could Hardly Wait to Get Back to That Bar": Lesbian Bar Culture in the 1930s and 1940s (1993)

Elizabeth Lapovsky Kennedy and Madeline Davis took hundreds of oral histories to produce this masterful re-creation of lesbian life in Buffalo, New York, in the 1930s through the 1960s. The book, Boots of Leather, Slippers of Gold, *opened up new research into gay and lesbian life in working-class cities and brought many of the techniques of women's history—collecting oral histories from those who did not leave written record—to the study of sexuality.*

"To me there was nothing greater than a gay bar years ago."

—Vic

"Sure we had good times, but they were making the best of a bad situation."
—Little Gerry

In the 1930s, 1940s, and 1950s, lesbians socialized in bars for relaxation and fun, just like many other Americans. But at the same time, bars (or, during prohibition, speakeasies) and public house parties were central to twentieth-century lesbian resistance. By finding ways to socialize together, individuals ended the crushing isolation of lesbian oppression and created the possibility for group consciousness and activity. In addition, by forming community in a public setting outside of the protected and restricted boundaries of their own living rooms, lesbians also began the struggle for public recognition and acceptance. The time lesbians and gays spent relaxing in bars was perhaps sweeter than for other Americans, because they were truly the only places that lesbians had to socialize; but it was also more dangerous, bringing lesbians into conflict with a hostile society—the law, family, and work. Thus, bar communities were not only the center of sociability and relaxation in the gay world, they were also a crucible for politics.

A small, though significant, body of writing exists on the complex nature of lesbian and gay bar life, but little, if any, considers changing forms of lesbian resistance. Due to the popularity of Radclyffe Hall's *The Well of Loneliness,* its depressing image of bars as seedy places where lesbians went to find solace for their individual afflictions has become embedded in the Western imagination. Lesbian pulp novels, as well as journalistic fiction of the 1950s and 1960s, were the first to convey the centrality of bars to lesbian life, portraying both their allure and their depressing limitations. In the 1960s, pioneering research in the social sciences established that bars were the central institution for creating lesbian and gay culture, and for teaching gays about their identity. Nancy Achilles shows that bars provide a place of socialization, a means of maintaining social cohesion, a context for each individual to confirm gay identity, and a setting for the formation of alliances against the police. Ethel Sawyer documents how Black lesbian behavior is shaped by the norms and values of the bar subculture. Although this research has been invaluable for subsequent scholarship, it is limited by an aura of timelessness and the lack of a framework for understanding resistance.

The new social history of lesbians and gays, despite its emphasis on changing forms of gay politics, has tended to extend these earlier approaches and treat bar communities as an unchanging part of the gay landscape. When we began researching how the bar culture of the mid-twentieth century contributed to the formation of gay liberation, we also held a static model of bar culture. Our discoveries led us to tell a significantly different story: In the context of the changing social conditions of the twentieth century, lesbians acted to shape the possibilities for their future. . . .

For lesbians to establish a public social life was a challenge; each opportunity had to be created and persistently pursued. Bars were the only possible place for working-class lesbians to congregate outside of private homes. They were generally unwelcome in most social settings. Open spaces like parks or beaches, commonly used by gay men, were too exposed for women to express interest in other women without constant male surveillance and harassment. This was a time when it was still dangerous for unescorted women to be out on the street. In addition, many working-class lesbians could not even use their own homes for gatherings. If they were young they often lived with their parents, and once mature and living alone, most could not afford large apartments. Those who had apartments of an adequate size ran the risk of harassment from neighbors and/or the law should they entertain a large gathering.

Even the use of bars by lesbians was dubious. Bars have been profoundly men's dominion throughout U.S. history, to the extent that the active social life of single working-class girls at the turn of the century did not include bars. The temperance movement, the most significant women's campaign in relation to bars, fought not to allow women in, but to get men out. In New York City before the First World War, working women increasingly entered saloons particularly to avail themselves of the reasonably priced good food available to men, but their presence was still controversial. Often saloon owners would not allow women, single or escorted, at the bar, but would serve them in a room in the back. The fragile relation of women to bars continued through World War II, when several cities, including Chicago, passed laws prohibiting women's entrance into bars, in an attempt to limit the spread of venereal disease. (Buffalo seriously considered such a move but did not undertake it.) In this situation, most bars which catered to lesbians were usually located in areas known for moral permissiveness, and the availability of women for male pleasure. Such areas were therefore extremely dangerous for unescorted women.

That lesbians were able to come together and build community in bars is a testimony to their tenacity, their drive to find others like themselves, and their desire for erotic relations with other women. In the 1930s gay and lesbian bars were already well established in New York City—in Harlem and Greenwich Village—but not throughout the country in smaller cities. John D'Emilio and Allan Berube identify the 1940s as the turning point, when gay and lesbian social life became firmly established in bars in most cities of the U.S. In part this change has to do with the general trend in U.S. capitalism toward the increasing commercialization and sexualization of leisure culture and the concomitant increased acceptance of sexual expression. But the immediate catalyst for these 1940s changes was World War II. By uprooting an entire generation, the war helped to channel urban gay life into a particular path of growth—away from stable private networks and toward public commercial establishments serving the needs of a displaced, transient, and young clientele.

John D'Emilio and Allan Berube argue that the bringing together of sixteen million men in the armed forces radically transformed gay-male social life in the U.S. Even though the armed services excluded homosexuals, most gays and lesbians who applied were already expert at hiding their gayness, and were not detected. The discussion of the military's exclusionary policy in newspapers, books, and pamphlets and the routine questions about homosexual interest in the physical examination combined with an intensely same sex environment to heighten young men's awareness of their homosexual potential. Soldiers explored these new interests on leave in major cities, where the fervor of the war made many people anxious to support and help servicemen, and their numbers were too large to be controlled by the Military Police. As a result male gay life became firmly lodged in commercial establishments. This same analysis cannot apply directly to women since they did not join the armed forces in significant numbers—in 1943 the number of women in the armed services was less than 300,000—and therefore enlisted women never had a powerful presence in civilian life.

The story of the impact of the war on lesbian social life still needs to be told and is the subject of this chapter. Moving from the fragmented lesbian culture of the 1930s to the well established bar culture of white lesbians in the 1940s, we explore the kinds of culture and consciousness that lesbians created in bar communities, paying particular attention to the strategies they developed when their new culture increased the risk of public visibility. We reflect on the reasons for the changes in lesbian social life, delineating the role of lesbians in shaping their own history.

SEARCHING FOR LESBIANS IN THE 1930s

Narrators identify the 1930s as qualitatively more difficult than any period to follow. They consider World War II the turning point in lesbian life and judge it impossible for anyone who did not live through the 1930s to imagine what they were like. Arden and Leslie, two white butches who are well-known from their many years in the bars, console themselves about the difficulty of having had to live through such hard times by reflecting on how much harder it must have been for those who came out before them.

> "Can you imagine what it was like in the 1900s when all the women had to wear those long skirts. How could you show it? How could women live together? I guess only a few could do it, who had an independent income. But even so how could they leave their families? It was hard to leave when I was young."

At this point in the interview, we share a bit of women's history and describe the intense friendships between married women in the nineteenth century. But this does not strike the narrators as part of their lesbian heritage. They are unquestionably modern lesbians, who identify themselves as different from other women because they desire to build a specifically sexual life with women outside of marriage. Leslie responds, "There must have been some who didn't marry." Arden then worries, "Those who didn't marry would be stuck at home." But her faith in the indomitable spirit of the modern lesbian wins out: "Some must have run away. But if they ran away who could work? . . . There must have been a lot of masturbation and repression in those days."

Despite the severe oppression, narrators took for granted their ability to create independent lives as lesbians during the 1930s based on opportunities for work and housing. For them, the painful difficulty of the 1930s was the intense isolation. "When I finished high school, I knew who I was and that I was attracted to girls, but I didn't know another person on earth like myself. That would not happen today." (Leslie) Arden had two gay friends, a man and a woman, while growing up in her neighborhood, but this did not significantly lessen her feelings of being alone. Lesbians knew that society did not approve of or accept who they were, and that they should hide it. "I can't imagine how we knew it, but we certainly knew it," Leslie states emphatically, and gives the following example:

> "I was very rough on my shoes and they had to be replaced every two weeks. My father worked at the railroad, and was tired of buying me shoes so frequently. So he took me to where he bought his shoes, and told the man, 'Put a pair of shoes on her that she can't wear out in two weeks.' The man felt sorry for me and would bring out the daintiest shoes and my father said 'no.' He thought he was punishing me. I couldn't let my father know that I liked them. Inside I was elated, absolutely elated. But I knew I couldn't let my father know, because he thought he was punishing me. I lived in those shoes. My mother did not like them. She would say, 'Why the hell do you always have them on?'"

Debra, a respected Black butch who grew up in the South, expresses her intuition of the need for secrecy about the sexual affair she had begun in school at the age of thirteen in 1934 in Virginia, with a woman who was three years older.

> "I [was] thirteen. And I [was] going to school, and it was a very beautiful young lady in school, but she was about three years older than me. And I used to ask her to let me take her books home, carry her books for her. And I was very much interested in that girl. So finally when I was fourteen we went out. And after we went out I knew then that was what I wanted. I really wanted her. And finally I got her and we stayed together for about three years. We weren't living together now, we were seeing each other, and it was kept from my family and also kept from hers. Because at that time, well we felt that . . . we actually felt ourselves that it wasn't a natural thing to do. . . . We had heard it somewhere, as kids, you know how you hear people talking. And we felt that it was something wrong with us."

When asked if she and her girlfriend were scared, she replies, "No I don't think so. But I often think what would have happened if they had caught us. Because she was white and I was Black. And at that time, Boy! It would have been very bad." Some narrators were less fortunate and were caught for expressing their sexual feelings as adolescents during the 1930s and were chastised and punished. Leslie recalls:

> "My mother and I had a room in a rooming house. I was doing my homework with the girl downstairs, and people in the neighborhood had clued this girl's

mother in to the fact that I was 'kind of funny' and they were watching me. I leaned over and kissed the girl, and the mother was looking in the window. She came in and made a fuss. My mother came and kept calling me 'a dirty rotten thing,' and whacked me around, and told me to get upstairs. That kind of thing cooled me down."

The isolation, punishment, and ignorance did not deter narrators from acknowledging in their teens their preference for women. Arden remembers how people talked about her in her neighborhood, but it didn't change her. "I did not conform and had no intention of it." Debra took a little more time to fully accept who she was: "And I guess I was about eighteen before I found out it wasn't anything wrong with me. It was my preference. If I wanted a girl that was my business. And I carried it like that throughout life. I didn't go around broadcasting it, but I didn't try to hide it either."

The process of knowing oneself, admitting one's difference, generated the desire to find others like oneself. This was difficult because Buffalo's few gay bars were both hidden and short-lived. Also, cultural references to lesbianism were extremely limited. The only literary source on lesbianism known to narrators was Radclyffe Hall's *The Well of Loneliness,* which was published in the U.S. in 1929 and read by several narrators during adolescence in the 1930s. Therefore, the search for other lesbians required initiative and persistence, not to mention courage. For white narrators, this meant primarily finding gay and lesbian bars; for Black narrators, it meant finding a community that socialized together at parties. . . .

Leslie, who came out in Buffalo in the 1930s, had no gay acquaintances while growing up and took longer to find a lesbian bar. After years of isolation, she was introduced in the late 1930s to the Hillside, a bar on Seneca Street, far from the center of town, beyond the streetcar line. A woman who "got around" told her about this bar, which was a farmhouse. After a few unsuccessful tries, the two of them finally bought gas for the car and kept going until they found it.

> "When we went in, there was a straight couple dancing and we didn't really see anything else. We bought some drinks and then the straight couple left and some boys went up to the juke box and started dancing. Two men together dancing. I had never seen this before. I couldn't stop looking. My friend had to tell me to close my mouth, I was standing there with my mouth wide open, like a hick, I was so excited. I met several women there."

The Hillside lasted about a year, and Leslie did not become part of a stable social group there. But, by the late 1930s, other gay bars began to open, all of which lasted well into the 1940s. It was in one of these that she established friendships that would continue for years. . . .

Black lesbian life in the 1930s seems to have been somewhat different. Debra, who came to Buffalo in 1938, met her first lesbian friends through her church group, which was racially mixed. They socialized at parties:

"We didn't go to bars, we usually went to someone's house, if we wanted to do any drinking at all. She [her first partner in Buffalo] knew quite a few gay people, but at the time, they didn't go out and broadcast it. There would be quite a few of them like maybe [on] a Friday night or a Saturday night like that."

The parties were fairly large with usually more than 20 people. "It was almost the same as the bar life, but . . . going out to the bars, they couldn't do the things that they wanted to do like dance and stuff like that, so they would meet at someone's house where they could let their hair down." White lesbians also socialized at parties during the 1930s, particularly during the middle of the decade, when for several years there were no gay bars in Buffalo. . . .

Narrators remember that the bars—and we imagine the same would be true of parties—made a tremendous difference in their social lives. Before locating the bars, they ran around with one special friend and went back and forth to each other's houses, because they didn't know other people. Once they went out to the bars, Leslie and Arden reminisce that they met other people and "things started to happen. . . . There was quite a bit of exchange. The bars were important for meeting people. How could you approach someone in a straight bar? You couldn't."

Debra concurs on the difficulty of meeting people at this time.

"Well yes, it's different from now, because now you go out there and you meet one of them, and you like her and you figure that she likes you, you're going to let her know that. Well at that time you wouldn't because you didn't know exactly how she felt. You didn't know whether she was the type that was going to broadcast it and other people would find out. Do you understand what I mean? So you would be a little leery. At that time it was always best to let them hit on you first, then you know where you stood. . . . But it was plenty of gay people at that time, but as I said, they kept it in the closet and they were more careful about exposing [themselves]."

Going to the bars also made a difference in lesbian consciousness. Butches who regularly frequented the bars understood the value of proclaiming themselves and had definite opinions about those who did not. Arden captures this distinction in her reminiscing about women she knew in her bowling leagues during the 1950s. "I never saw such a bunch of gay girls who would not admit it."

Lesbians of the period were highly motivated to go out. They were pushing beyond the limitations of socializing in their own houses with close friends. In addition to frequenting parties and gay bars, when they were available, they went to the entertainment bars—the Little Harlem, the Club Moonglo, the Vendome, Pearl's, and the Lucky Clover—in the Black section of Buffalo. They were all located close to one another on or near "the Avenue," as Michigan from Broadway south was called. Many famous Black entertainers of the time, such as Billy Eckstine and Lena Horne, performed at these bars. Since it was expensive to get into the back room, lesbians would sit in the front and try to hear the music. These were not gay bars, but they were hospitable to lesbians. They had a mixed Black and white clientele that included gamblers, call girls, and lesbians, as well as people who went primarily to enjoy the show. Arden, who frequented these bars in the 1930s, explains why lesbians were welcome: "Because it was free and open and there was no pretense. Remember, there was not too much money around. They were only too glad to have you buy drinks." The easy acceptance of lesbians suggests that the cosmopolitan culture of the Harlem Renaissance had extended to the Entertainment Clubs in Buffalo's Black section.

This neighborhood and these bars remained important for lesbians' good times, at least through the 1940s. Debra, who used to do most of her socializing in these bars during the 1940s, characterizes them in much the same way as Arden. She remembers that they had a mixed Black and white clientele and were popular with gays. "I knew it wasn't [a gay bar] but you did meet a lot of gay people there. Remember, entertainers and stuff coming in at all times. . . . Naturally if you didn't know anything about gay people you wouldn't know if they were gay or not. . . . That's how I met a lot of gay people."

Lesbians have warm memories of "the Avenue," and unquestionably felt at home there. In the 1940s, Arden used to go up and down "the Avenue" at night, and on weekends she would even go in the daytime. She remembers the owner of the Little Harlem, Ann Montgomery, tossing mail out the window, and asking her to take it to the post box. Ann Montgomery would then say, "Go into the bar and ask George [the bartender] to give you what you want." Arden, a gallant butch, who was more than willing to please a distinguished lady, would always say "it wasn't necessary." Ann Montgomery was a dynamic woman with a colorful reputation. One night she even referred publicly to Arden as a lesbian, indicating that she was fully aware of who patronized her bar. Arden still remembers this event vividly with pride and embarrassment forty-five years later.

> "There was a whole slew of people at the bar and Ann came in and told the bartender to give everyone a drink. They were all Black at the bar. I was the only white. The bartender hesitated when he got to me and Ann said, 'Yes, give that lesbian a drink too.' I nearly died. There I was with all those Black racketeers. They never bothered you though."

The special place of the Little Harlem and the other entertainment bars in lesbian life in the 1930s and 1940s can be seen in the way narrators distinguished these bars from straight bars. When asked if a bar we had seen advertised in a 1940s newspaper was gay, Arden and Leslie concur: "It was not gay. It was mostly men, straight men, and not a place for us, not for homos. You'd be better off in the Little Harlem" (Leslie). Although the entertainment bars were not gay space in the sense that gays and lesbians could not be open about who they were, they did provide a space where lesbians were comfortable and could have a good time, without having to fear being ridiculed or harassed.

WAYNE MYSLIK

Renegotiating the Social/Sexual Identities of Places: Gay Communities as Safe Havens or Sites of Resistance? (1994)

Wayne Myslik's article examining the meaning of safe space shows that safety is not simply physical. In fact, Myslik shows that despite a sense of safety in gay neighborhoods, gay neighborhoods are magnets for antigay violence precisely because they are known as gay places. Myslik also documents the depressing yet pervasive sense among gay white men in Washington, D.C., of the Clinton years that despite newfound political and social freedom, most gay men expected to be victims of violence.

INTRODUCTION

> *It was late at night. I was walking to my car. At first they followed me in their car for a couple of blocks. I tried to lose them. Then they cut me off and got out of the car and chased me down. They kept screaming "rich faggot." I think there were four of them. They were wearing high school football jackets. They beat me up pretty bad.*
>
> —Don, 27

> *I was walking down Connecticut Ave [near Dupont Circle] with another man . . . people driving down the street hanging out of the car screamed "faggot" and threw a bottle . . . young high-school kids. A friend was physically beaten up outside the DC Eagle twice by groups of people who knocked him down. I know about a stabbing and drive-by shootings at Tracks.*
>
> —David, 37

Most major American cities have neighborhoods that are popular with gay men or that are predominantly gay. Exhibiting varying degrees of gay commercial and residential concentration, these areas offer opportunities for socialization with other gay men and provide access to specialized services ranging from bookstores to bars to clinics. In this chapter, I am particularly concerned with what I will call "queer spaces." These are areas that, being more than just concentrations of gay men, have come to be identified in and outside the gay community as gay spaces. By exhibiting a degree of social control by the gay community, queer spaces create the perception of being "safe spaces."

The concept of a "safe space" is an important one for gay men, who are at risk of prejudice, discrimination and physical and verbal violence throughout their daily lives. Queer spaces are generally perceived as safe havens from this discrimination and violence, but they often serve as destinations of choice for "gay bashers." The experiences of Don [and] David . . . above refer to events in such queer spaces, near gay establishments, or near the homes of gay people. They portray the reality that incidents of heterosexist violence are common in these "safe havens." Why do gay men continue to identify queer spaces as safe spaces? To answer this question, we must consider the concepts of fear and safety and focus on the social contexts in which heterosexist violence, and reactions to such violence, take place. To do this, I will explore the following themes: (1) heterosexism as a cultural system and its enforcement, (2) violence against gay men, (3) issues of crime, safety, fear and vulnerability, (4) gay men's perceptions of straight places and queer places, and (5) power, politics, and territory as expressed in the landscape.

In approaching this issue from a geographical perspective, I intend to provide some insight into the role queer spaces play in helping gay men cope with the realities of heterosexism, and the violence that often accompanies it. This study discusses the experiences and perceptions of the white gay men who in many ways dominate the cultural landscape of the Dupont Circle neighborhood of Washington, DC. Although many of these observations are not generalizable to other groups, they do raise important questions about how all of us perceive our places in the cities in which we live. . . .

HETEROSEXISM

It's so oppressively straight there [Georgetown].[1] I feel out of my element. They don't even conceive of it . . . that gay people might exist. I'm scared, I guess.
—Geoffrey, 27

I cease anything that may be construed as gay behavior. You have to act asexual.
—Ron, 23

I'm supposed to act a certain way. I'm only tolerated within certain parameters.
—Frank, 37

I always feel like when I walk through a het crowd, maybe someone can tell something is different. I can't relax for fear that I will get a verbal attack, a strange or awkward look.
—David, 37

The System
Feminist theorists have demonstrated the degree to which gender relations are reflected in and constitutive of the patriarchal organization of space in Western culture (see, for example, England 1991; McDowell 1983). Intersecting this gender-ordered construction of society is the sexual ordering of space and place under what

Valentine has called "heteropatriarchy, that is, a process of sociosexual power relations which reflects and reproduces male dominance" (1993: 396).

Western society is based on the notion that the natural purpose of sexuality is for reproduction and that sexual identity is linked inextricably to the individual's role in the reproductive family. Organized around the construction of heterosexuality as the dominant and "normal" form of sexual identity, this view of sexuality is directly dependent upon a binary system of masculine and feminine gender identities that are believed to coincide directly with male- and female-sexed bodies. Gay men thus become outlaws, alien to this heteropatriarchal system.

The current use of the term "family values" by the religious right in attacks against gay civil rights is a cogent example of the extent to which a heteropatriarchal society sees gay men as alien to the familial system. Sexual relations between gay lovers are illegal in many areas, gay marriages are not recognized and the courts frequently deny the rights of gay men to be parents by taking their children from them. With vicious irony, the religious right then labels gays as "anti-family."

Providing abundant evidence of the gendering of urban public space, feminist geographers have been very successful in breaking down the traditional distinction between public and private space that sees sexuality as limited to the private domain (see Peake 1993; Valentine 1993). They have shown that all space has a gender identity and that most spaces, public and private, are masculine dominated. Just as spaces may be identified as masculine or male-dominated, though, urban spaces also have asexual identity. Virtually all such space is heterosexually dominated. As Davis has pointed out, however, "heterosexism and homophobia are social constructions with spatial impacts that are not always clearly visible in the physical landscape" (1994: 2). Indeed, as Geoffrey notes when he says "they don't even conceive of it . . . that gay people might exist," most people are blissfully ignorant of the degree to which sexuality, and in particular, heterosexuality, permeates space. Illustrative of this ignorance is the often heard statement that gays would be tolerated if they didn't "flaunt" their homosexuality. Inherent in this statement is the assumption that heterosexuality is itself not flaunted or expressed outside the home. However, engagement announcements, bridal showers, wedding ceremonies and rings, joint tax returns, booking a double bed at a hotel, shopping together for a new mattress, casual references in conversation to a husband or wife, a brief peck on the cheek when greeting or leaving a spouse, photos of spouses on desks at work, holding hands at the beach, and even divorces are all public announcements and affirmations of one's heterosexuality. The "normality" of heterosexuality is so deeply ingrained in Western culture that it is not even seen. Gay men, though, are keenly aware of this "heterosexual assumption," its visibility, and its impact on their lives. As Ron and Frank have noticed, gay men are tolerated only so long as their gay identity, their homosexuality, remains hidden. When it becomes visible, one is at risk of attack. A t-shirt popular among many gay men states, "I don't mind straight people, as long as they act gay in public."

In nearly all public spaces, then, there is no tolerance for departure from a heterosexual gender-identity and its attendant patterns of behavior. Gay men learn that in the workplace, in bars, in shopping malls, on the street, in virtually every physical or social space in which they travel, sexual orientation must never be visible. For most gay men, adapting behavior between gay and straight spaces to hide their sexual identity becomes natural and nearly unconscious. They do it as automatically as other men change their behavior when they take off a sweatshirt and put on a business suit.

The Enforcement

According to Gary Comstock's extensive survey of male victims of anti-gay violence, perpetrators are typically white (67 percent) males (99 percent) under 21 years old (50 percent) and outnumber their victims. This observation is supported by the survey I conducted of gay men in Washington. Of those who were victimized and knew the race and age of the perpetrator, nearly all identified their attackers as white, male, teenaged or early twenties. All were outnumbered by their attackers. It is perhaps most significant that perpetrators of anti-gay violence do not typically exhibit expected criminal attitudes and behaviors. They rarely have the histories of criminal activity or psychological disorders typical of other violent criminals. It is commonly observed, by victims as well as defense attorneys, that perpetrators of anti-gay violence are "average boys exhibiting typical behavior" (Comstock 1991: 93).

The explanation of how such violent behavior can be deemed "typical" must be found in the socialization of men in American society. Men are socialized to be dominant and aggressive, to conform strongly to established sex roles and to ridicule or punish those who deviate from those roles. Most American men continue to identify gay men and women according to stereotypes of the effeminate "sissy" or the masculine "bull dyke." This association of homosexuality with deviation from accepted gender roles and violation of mandatory heterosexuality interacts with the gender-role socialization of men. Gay men thus become identified as a group requiring ridicule, policing and/or punishment.

Furthermore, the role of adolescence in modern Western society interacts with male socialization to produce a group of people with a greater social incentive to target gay men. Since the nineteenth century, adolescence has become a "kind of temporal warehouse or greenhouse in which young people are parked until needed" (Comstock 1991: 103). Here they are forced to wait for social maturity, before they are told that they may fully participate in society in the roles of wife, husband, parent or worker. Although at their sexual prime, adolescents are told that they are not ready to take on the responsibilities of family. Furthermore, they are forced to compete for boring, part-time and temporary work in the service sector. "Ready to develop primary and independent affective relationships and to take on occupational challenges, they remain their parents' children, dependents with minimal earning power" (Comstock 1991: 103).

Placed in this frustrating position, denied any sense of power or control over their lives, but encouraged to anticipate such control and responsibility in the future, it is hardly surprising that adolescents should resort to activities and behaviors that strengthen and affirm their social status. The socially constructed powerlessness of adolescents, then, is a partial cause of problem behavior, which can be understood as identity-building and power-seeking at the expense of others who also lack power in the social order. Such adolescents can affirm their power only over others with similar or lower status in society. Their targets, therefore, are members of groups shunned and denigrated by adults. Their violent actions are perversions and exaggerations of that adult behavior.

Gay men thus serve as a fixed low-status standard away from which adolescents move up in social standing. Those with the highest social expectations, white males who are held back from high-status positions they are told they deserve by virtue of gender and race, are most likely to express frustration and demonstrate power over lower-status groups. It is not surprising, then, that middle-class adolescents, with the highest expectations for the future, are disproportionately represented among the perpetrators of heterosexist violence. It would be particularly interesting to see what percentage of these adolescent males also commit hate-based crimes against groups such as blacks and Jews, or develop histories of violence against women.

These behaviors are often ignored or even condoned by parents and reinforced by the institutions of society. Churches preach that homosexuality is a sin, schools fail to protect gay youths from harassment, police inadequately respond to assaults, and the courts give perpetrators light sentences. Victims are often blamed for their attacks, and often suffer secondary victimization at the hands of police, medical and judicial officials (Anderson 1982: 146). It is well known that the majority of incidents of heterosexual violence go unreported, the victims often fearing further abuse from the justice system (Herek and Berrill 1992: 289). Most of the men who spoke to me in Washington expressed a cautious optimism about relations between the police and the gay community. Several believed the situation has improved in the past few years. However, even the most optimistic men who spoke to me are reluctant to give the police the benefit of the doubt. Incidents of discrimination or ill treatment by the police are quickly reported throughout the community and are not forgotten for years. Although the police are seen as potentially helpful, it would be unsafe to trust or rely upon them.

We can thus see most incidents of anti-gay violence as the acts of young men attempting to affirm their individual status within their peer group and their group status in society. They accomplish this by demonstrating their adherence to gender roles and asserting social and sexual dominance over a lower-status group whose marginalization by society identifies them as acceptable targets. Attacks on such groups are inadequately proscribed by society and may even be rewarded. These acts of violence are not personal expressions of intolerance of homosexuality, but of societal intolerance, or cultural heterosexism, which grants permission for their actions and mitigates their responsibility for the consequences. Heterosexist violence, therefore, like violence against women, must be understood in the broader context of social dominance based within the structures of privilege derived from race, gender and sexuality.

The Violence

Since the Second World War, gay men have made significant progress in increasing their visibility in American society and in creating organizations that are fighting for their civil rights. Since the Stonewall Riots of 1969, gay social, cultural and political organizations have appeared in nearly every major city, moving out of rented halls and private homes into permanent office spaces and purchased buildings.[2] This creation of visible queer spaces has been met with a drastic increase in violence against gay men and their property. In their comparison of thirteen major surveys of anti-gay violence, Herek and Berrill found that 80 percent of gay men and women surveyed had been verbally harassed, 44 percent were threatened with violence, 33 percent had been chased or followed, 25 percent were pelted with objects and 19 percent were physically assaulted (Berrill 1992: 26). Another study found that gay men are at least four times as likely as the general population to be violently attacked (Comstock 1991: 55).

A report put out by the National Gay and Lesbian Task Force in early 1994 reports that incidents of violence against gay men increased by 127 percent between 1988 and 1993. This study has suggested that, for the first time since such surveys have been conducted, reports of certain types of anti-gay incidents have decreased (NGLTF 1994). Although the NGLTF has been wary of drawing conclusions from this study, it would appear that a pattern of hotspots is developing. Reports of minor harassment have declined, while reports of physical violence are increasing in certain local communities, particularly in those where gay rights issues are being confronted. In Washington, DC, the organization Gays and Lesbians Opposing Violence has issued a report in response to the NGLTF survey which indicates that violence in the District of Columbia continues to increase.

Queer spaces, those areas in which gay men are known to congregate and have been designated as safe spaces, are, ironically, the most frequent settings for this violence, exceeding by 28 percent straight public areas. As an area becomes more generally recognized as a gay neighborhood or queer space, the violence increases and perpetrators travel in search of their targets. The Castro District in San Francisco illustrates this point well. Statistics gathered by the grassroots organization Communities United Against Violence showed that in the 1970s 93 percent of reported assailants were youths from the neighboring Mission and Filmore districts. By 1981, when the Castro had a well-established reputation as a gay neighborhood, the percentage of perpetrators who were traveling from more distant areas had more than doubled (Comstock 1991: 61). It is clear that as the reputation spreads in the media that an area is a gay neighborhood or queer space, the violence increases. Queer spaces become hunting grounds.

CRIME AND SAFETY

I fully expect to be harassed sometime.

—Robert, 32

I expect that as long as I live there will be homophobes trying to outmaneuver me.

　　　　　　　　　　　　　　　　　　　　　　　　　　—Scott, 42

I don't think this problem is going to get any better. . . . There are going to be more and more gangs and gay bashing.

　　　　　　　　　　　　　　　　　　　　　　　　　　—Rod, 28

I always have the feeling that if I were recognized as gay, chances are it would happen.

　　　　　　　　　　　　　　　　　　　　　　　　　　—Bob, 44

I'm afraid whenever I walk down an unfamiliar street and I don't see any other gay people.

　　　　　　　　　　　　　　　　　　　　　　　　　　—Frank, 37

Gay men are not unaware of their risk of victimization. In a national survey conducted in 1984, 83 percent of gay men said they believe they might become the victim of heterosexist violence in the future (Comstock 1991). In my survey of gay men in the Dupont Circle neighborhood of Washington, DC, nearly 85 percent said they expect to be victimized in the future. The perception of vulnerability expressed in the quotations above can affect an individual in many different ways. It can be related to fear, anxiety and stress which can affect the personal and professional life. It can lead to editing behavior, forgoing activities and severely limiting the quality of life. Along with the effect on an individual's quality of life, limiting behavior in response to such crime serves to perpetuate the invisibility of gay men, strengthening the heterosexist and homophobic system that gives rise to the violence in the first place.

Fear, Vulnerability and Behavior

Since the early 1970s, several disciplines including criminology, sociology, psychology and geography have recognized that fear of crime is an important social problem and that numerous social, spatial and psychological factors contribute to the phenomenon. Understanding in particular that fear of crime is only loosely linked to the real presence of crime in an area, most studies since the late 1970s have focused on the independence of fear from victimization. The empirical research has typically examined communities experiencing socioeconomic decline, characterized by a low rate of crime but a very high fear of crime.

Few studies, however, have examined the inverse of this relationship, in communities where there is a high crime rate or high expectation of crime but low level of fear. It is not difficult to imagine how a community with a low crime rate can nonetheless come to experience fear. However, it seems counterintuitive that a community with a high crime rate, in which individuals expect to be victimized, could be characterized by the absence of any fear or anxiety and the presence of a strong sense of safety. I found just such a counter-intuitive relationship in the gay community of Dupont Circle.

Most early studies of fear of crime relied on national or city-wide crime surveys, did little to distinguish between fear of different types of crime and were generally concerned with determining the predictive value of certain demographic characteristics, such as age, sex or income. These studies provide little explanatory insight. Studies by social psychologists are more useful in explaining the relationship between perceptions of crime, fear and precautionary behavior (see, for example, van der Wurff 1989). However, such studies rarely have looked beyond individual cognitive processes to place fear of crime in a broader societal context.

Geographers and their spatially minded colleagues have understood for some time that the physical and social environments interact to produce certain perceptions of crime or safety. This view, referred to as the disorder model, is described succinctly by Bursik and Grasmick, "Fear is a response to the perception that the area is becoming characterized by a growing number of signs of disorder and incivility . . . that indicate that the social order of the neighborhood is eroding" (1991: 101). Residents cannot be assured that others will adhere to a shared set of expectations about behavior. At least three broad aspects of the social environment can be identified as contributing to fear of crime relatively independently of the experience of victimization. The first is environmental incivility, in the form of abandoned buildings, vandalism and graffiti; the second is a lack of community spirit or community satisfaction; and the third is racial tension, most often the result of changes in the racial composition of the area (Smith 1986).

More recently, feminist researchers have created a significant literature on women's fear of crime which analyzes the position of women in society and its significance for fear of crime (see, for example, Pain 1991; Riger 1991; Valentine 1989). These studies recognize that women are subject to a form of violent crime, rape, which is rarely a concern for men. Women express strong feelings of vulnerability to rape because of the likelihood of serious injury in addition to the rape, the perception that they could not physically defend themselves and the lack of protection they receive from society.

Few of these studies, however, have been able to separate perception of crime, feelings of vulnerability, fear and behavior changes from each other. Although difficult to discern from a study of a group that experiences high levels of vulnerability, fear and behavior modification, this distinction is significant. Not all groups are socialized to experience or express emotions such as fear in the same way. For example, many men will recognize that crime is a hazard in their neighborhood and take steps to prevent their victimization, but they will be loath to admit that they experience fear, much less that it is a significant motivation for their behavior. Women, however, are more likely to identify fear as a motivating factor. Furthermore, many men are not even consciously aware of the behavior changes they do make. When these changes are observed, many men will attribute them to "common sense" rather than a reaction to fear or concern for crime. It is misleading, therefore, to rely on the term "fear" in discussion of crime perception. It is more accurate to discuss the breakdown of feelings of safety or security. Their absence from a neighborhood can be expected to reflect the presence of a general sense of safety in the community. . . .

Territory

> *This is our territory, an area we've claimed.*
>
> —Stuart, 26

When asked what it means to be "safe" as a gay man, nearly half of the men who spoke to me defined safety not in physical terms or in terms of violence and crime, but as "living openly as a gay person," "being comfortable in my sexuality." Many gay men explain that they feel safe in queer spaces because of a sense of safety in numbers. Interestingly, though, these men do not believe that other gay men are more likely than straights to come to the assistance of a bashing victim. In fact, several suggested that gay men, out of fear for their own safety, might be less likely to intervene in an attack or bashing. The safety they feel, therefore, is clearly an emotional and psychological safety that comes from being in an area in which one has some sense of belonging or social control, even in the absence of physical control.

Dupont Circle is territory that has been claimed by the gay men of Washington. Although there are violent exceptions, the residents of Dupont Circle have come to expect others to adhere to certain behavioral patterns, the most significant of which is a tolerance of open expressions of homosexuality and the open association of gay men. When Stuart states, "This is our territory," he is not only attesting to his claim on the Dupont Circle neighborhood, but reaffirming that claim. For gay individuals, alienated and with no sense of power, control or order in any other part of the city, this sense of claimed territory takes on an enormous emotional significance.

CONCLUSION

Queer spaces are not, in fact, safe havens from the threat of violence that follows gay men throughout their lives. Ironically, the congregation of people which provides an emotional and psychological safety itself undermines physical safety by advertising the existence and location of a target group. "Safe" spaces in turn become hunting grounds.

However, despite the evidence that gay men are especially targeted in these areas, queer spaces in many respects alter the traditional power relationship between heterosexuals and homosexuals. In most areas of the city, gay men feel uncomfortable or vulnerable and, consciously or unconsciously, alter their behavior to hide their sexual identity. As sites of resistance to the oppressions of a heterosexist and homophobic society, however, queer spaces create the strong sense of empowerment that allows men to look past the dangers of being gay in the city and to feel safe and at home. Overwhelmingly, they consider the psychological and social benefits of open association worth the physical risk taken in queer spaces. For gay men, coping with the presence of violence is an act of negotiating power in society.

NOTES

1. Georgetown is a wealthy neighborhood near Dupont Circle which is home to Georgetown University and a strip of shops and bars crowded with presumably straight college students. Owing to its palpably heterosexual atmosphere and the numbers of drunken young men, many gay men list Georgetown as the neighborhood they feel least safe.

2. On 26 June 1969 a police raid on the Stonewall Inn, a gay bar in New York City, set off a riot that is considered by many as the symbolic beginning of the modern gay rights movement.

REFERENCES

Anderson, Craig L. 1982. "Males as Sexual Assault Victims: Multiple Levels of Trauma." *Journal of Homosexuality* 7: 145–62.

Berrill, Kevin T. 1992. "Anti-gay Violence and Victimization in the United States: An Overview." Pp. 19–26 in Gregory M. Herek and Kevin T. Berrill, eds., *Hate Crimes: Confronting Violence against Lesbians and Gay Men.* Newbury Park, CA: Sage.

Bursik, Robert J., Jr., and Harold G. Grasmick. 1991. *Neighborhoods and Crime: The Dimensions of Effective Community Control.* New York: Lexington Books.

Comstock, Gary David. 1991. *Violence against Lesbians and Gay Men.* New York: Columbia University Press.

Davis, T. 1994. "Gay Territories, Queer Spaces: Reinforcing and Destroying the Power of the 'Gay Ghetto.'" Paper presented at Syracuse University Symposia, Syracuse, NY, 11 February.

England, Kim. 1991. "Gender Relations and the Spatial Structure of the City." *Geoforum* 22 (2): 135–47.

Herek, Gregory M., and Kevin T. Berrill. 1992. "Primary and Secondary Victimization in Anti-gay Hate Crimes: Official Response and Public Policy." Pp. 289–305 in Gregory M. Herek and Kevin T. Berrill, eds., *Hate Crimes: Confronting Violence against Lesbians and Gay Men.* Newbury Park, CA: Sage.

McDowell, L. 1983. "Towards an Understanding of the Gender Division of Urban Space." *Environment and Planning D: Society and Space* 1: 59–72.

National Gay and Lesbian Task Force. 1994. *Anti-Gay/Lesbian Violence, Victimization, and Defamation in 1993.* Washington, DC: NGLTF Policy Institute.

Pain, R. 1991. "Space, Sexual Violence, and Social Control: Integrating Geographical and Feminist Analyses of Women's Fear of Crime." *Progress in Human Geography* 15: 415–32.

Peake, L. 1993. "'Race' and Sexuality: Challenging the Patriarchal Structuring of Urban Social Space." *Environment and Planning D: Society and Space* 11: 415–32.

Riger, Stephanie. 1991. "On Women." In Dan A. Lewis, ed. *Reactions to Crime.* Newbury Park, CA: Sage.

Smith, S. 1986. *Crime, Space, and Society.* Cambridge, UK: Cambridge University Press.

Valentine, G. 1989. "The Geography of Women's Fear." *Area* 21: 385–90.

———. 1993. "(Hetero)sexing Space: Lesbian Perceptions and Experiences of Everyday Spaces." *Environment and Planning D: Society and Space* 11: 395–413.

van der Wurff, Adri, Leendert van Staalduinen, and Peter Stringer. 1989. "Fear of Crime in Residential Environments: Testing a Social Psychological Model." *Journal of Social Psychology* 129 (2): 141–60.

≈

BONNIE J. MORRIS
At the Michigan Womyn's Music Festival (2003)

For the past thirty years, one of the largest women-only musical gatherings in the world takes place in a rural forest in Michigan. The festival attracts thousands of diverse lesbians who camp, perform music, and attend workshops that focus on personal and political transformation. The festival, as chronicled by Bonnie Morris, has become the site of many political struggles in lesbian communities, from the controversy over sado-masochism in the 1980s to recent debates over transgender identity.

> *"For one week in August every year, women only populate the largest town in Oceana County."*
>
> —Deborah Lewis, "The Original Womyn's Woodstock,"
> in *The Woman-Centered Economy*,
> edited by Midge Stocker, 1995

It's only June, but I've already started to pack, and all over North America thousands of women are feeling the same hypnotic urge to assemble their tent stakes and bug spray, flashlights and plaid flannel. This August we'll all be heading to Michigan again, some of us for the 28th year; and though the uninitiated remain skeptical—waiting in line for over-spiced tofu? attending confrontational anti-racism workshops amid wet hay bales? encountering one's rabbi naked in a sweat lodge?—loyal workers like me can't wait to pick up a hammer and plunge in again. Get the stages ready, scatter the wood chips to make trails, nail down the rugs for the campers in wheelchairs, fire up the simmering kettles of corn, and prepare for hours of political processing. Bring it on, set it up, for they're coming to "the land," and when the gates swing open on the first day of that August week somewhere north of Grand Rapids, the magic of Brigadoon—or "Wombstock"—is here again.

At 28, outlasting most women's bookstores and many relationships, the Michigan Womyn's Music Festival is still going strong, and its sliding-scale work-exchange prices for a week of camping, concerts, and hot vegetarian meals remain the best deal in the world for lesbians who want a joyful immersion in dynamic music, crafts, and culture. Just beyond the three excellent stages, sprinkled by the ever-present threat of rain, are all the elements that keep Michigan both revered and vilified in the gay and lesbian press. Yes, there's still nude mud wrestling, worker stress, Goddess worship, the Perseid meteor showers, kissing workshops, and an understanding that the front rows are deaf seating, with interpreters onstage. This is not the corporate Lilith Fair, the industry-underwritten Lollapalooza, however rad those rockfests claimed to be. Here, you have to do a work shift to get in. Whether you condemned the entire genre of women's music before investigating it or were the first in the mosh-pit when June Millington played with Bitch and Animal last summer, whether you now harangue the festival to welcome transfolks officially or still revel in its longtime radical woman-born-only admission policy, you can't write about American lesbian history without bowing before the house that Lisa Vogel built.

Festival culture, which began in the early 1970s as a venue for radical feminist musicians operating outside of the mainstream recording industry, offered a rural alternative to the bars, coffeehouses and protest marches that were more readily available to East and West Coast urbanites. If we trust that Dorothy was right, Oz truly did turn out to be no farther than her own backyard. The Midwest, with its wide-open spaces and muscular farm women, spawned homegrown lesbian landscapes that have endured against all odds. The slightly older National Women's Music Festival, which began in 1974, rests on its laurels as the first and longest continually meeting festival. But National has always met on university campuses. Its audiences have been guests of public educational institutions and thus have had to remain clothed. Its public settings have also meant that men were permitted in the audience (though generally not onstage as performers), and men were often visible in the campus dorms or as union techies in the concert theaters. The Michigan festival, which began in 1976, was by 1982 thriving on 650 acres of privately owned land, where the separatist ideal of uninhibited women-only space took root. Making the pilgrimage to the fern forest where one could party without a shirt became *the* rite of passage for political dykes of my generation.

Aside from popularizing the work of countless lesbian performers—whose loyal fan base led to greater mainstream recognition and bookings—the festival is also a workers' community and a working-class success story. Nurtured by the vision of its then-19-year-old founder, Lisa Vogel, the festival was initially run as a collective, then a cooperative, then a company, and now as a private corporation. Staffed entirely by volunteer labor in its first years, the festival now distributes small salaries or honoraria to long-time coordinators (experienced workers helping to run such various crews as security, garbage, childcare, kitchen, and the performance stage and to its reliable, outstanding onstage production techies and sign language interpreters. Over the years, what evolved as uniquely "Michigan" has become standard practice at other women's festivals and at many mainstream conferences: childcare, a sober support area, private and respected meeting space for women of color, interpreting services, accessible facilities for women with a range of disabilities, health care that includes homeopathic remedies, chemical and smoke-free areas, an expectation that racial stereotypes will be avoided and that the necessary hierarchy of work crews and staff will be diverse in age, race, class, ethnicity, ability, nationality—and style. The festival also has to accommodate the burgeoning needs of campers who, returning every year since 1976, are well over fifty and often bringing along their children.

The scale of preparation is immense. As a festival worker since 1990, I'm notorious for writing in my journal throughout the long work-crew community meetings. Now, looking back through those rain-splotched pages, I find this record of our labors: "We used 37,200 feet of twine." "We used 1,250 pounds of ice in the worker kitchen alone." "We ordered 4,416 rolls of toilet paper." "Childcare had 60 girl toddlers under age four; our youngest camper was three months old." "The main kitchen produced a total of 100,000 meals." "We helped unload 150 craftswomen, including one who's eight months pregnant." "130 gallons of water were used for the Dance Brigade performances." "The interpreters worked with 45 Deaf women from five countries." "The massage crew gave over 890 massages . . ."

Few of the thousands of "festiegoers," as they're affectionately known, are aware of the intense workloads, romantic flings, and political standoffs that characterize the smoothly running worker village backstage. The shows begin on time, the rain crew expertly pounces to cover each stage when a single drop falls from the heavens, and healthy meals dished out by cute babes in aprons are just one part of the six-day ticket package. The division that could arise between the producers of lesbian culture (the workers and artists) and the consumers is mitigated by a mandatory four-hour work shift that's required of all those attending. In this way the endless burden of cooking and cleaning is spread among the many. Lonely or bewildered first-timers plunge right into a bawdy work crew, stirring the pot of beans or the barrow full of wood chips, mingling with a roster of new pals from any number of states or foreign lands. The crafts bazaar area offers as many as 150 booths of woman-made products—art, pottery, books, haircuts, djembe drums, sexy toys, and hot new CDs autographed by the smiling musicians themselves.

The festival's collective vibe remains harmonious, with nude bodies of all colors and shapes nestled together under the meteor-flecked night skies. In August 2002 well over 4,000 women and girls flocked to hear artists as diverse as Bitch and Animal, slam poet Alix Olson, mosh-pit faves Le Tigre and the Butchies, folksinger Cheryl Wheeler, pianist Mary Watkins, the Dance Brigade, the drum orchestra of Ubaka Hill, and the late, great Kay Gardner on flute. Economically speaking, however, those 4,000 tickets are about half of what the festival used to sell during the peak (and very crowded) years in the 1980s, and 6,000 remains a target goal. Concerns about breaking even and attracting more paying festiegoers regularly surface during the worker community meetings of recent years. These discussions look closely at both festival finances and lesbian community values. One heartache is the growing number of thoughtless fans and trans-activist protesters who sneak in each year, chowing down on carefully budgeted food and entertainment without giving anything back. For Michigan to stay out of the red and continue bringing top production values to its three stages, music supporters will need to increase their ticket donations on the sliding scale, returning festies will have to bring along more first-time, full-paying pals—and educate the folks back home about the twin evils of Michigan-bashing and fence-hopping.

Regrettably, threats to Michigan's survival now come from some radical LGBT activists as well as from right-wing religious groups. State family-values groups continue to probe the festival and its bulletin-board Internet communications for any proof of "child welfare endangerment" (casual public sex or illegal drug use on the land), so today's festiegoers are warned not to create conditions under which conservative infiltrators—who do exist!—could move in swiftly and shut things down forever. This concern has placed limits on some of the more provocative workshops on sexuality, but it has also re-opened serious dialogue about what public behaviors are appropriate when so many children and adolescents are present with their moms.

Since 1994, when "Camp Trans" activists set up a presence at the festival's front gates to challenge the woman-born-only policy, it has become fashionable for younger LGBT activists to bash Michigan in the name of progressive trans-friendliness. In recent years, activists have been observed fashioning fake admission wristbands in order to come in and disrupt "the system." Other women, including well-known performers and craftswomen, have helped their friends sneak in, despite the festival's existing options of financial assistance and work exchange for genuinely needy fans interested in attending. The big topic in Workerville 2002, as the festival began running out of food, was clear: what's the deal with lesbians who rip off lesbians? How did scamming Michigan become the new radicalism?

Long hours of discussion yielded few conclusions on this trend. Perhaps it comes from the more destructive wing of the anti-globalism street anarchist movement, or the sheer ease with which anyone can knock down an existing institution's ideals and glass windows. Perhaps time has granted the festival sufficient status and notoriety to make it seem an established Goliath against which restless, younger dyke Davids consider taking aim. Yet such sport fails to take into account Michigan's ongoing revolutionary aims: the collective work ethic; the extraordinary dedication to unlearning racism; the same space for toddlers and adolescent girls; the opening ceremonies honoring Native land; the entirely ASL-interpreted stage program and the wheelchair-accessible forest; plus the 24-hour sober support, full medical care for workers and festiegoers, recycling, and vegan meals. No other institution in the *world* offers this range of services on such a large scale for a primarily (but not exclusively) lesbian consumer base. The festival is certainly not some well-financed behemoth like the IMF or Wal-Mart. Whatever one's view on the transgender issue, Michigan ain't "the Establishment." The performers are risk-taking, mostly lesbian artists whose stands on race, sex, and class limit their ability to get mainstream bookings and to have financial security.

Then there are the longtime workers like me, usually over 600 of us, who hammer and nail and schlep and mediate and clean up after campers and performers, just because we dig being part of the story. We're not paid much, and we're not complaining; we donate our time and labor and the best of our skills in order to see our "field of dreams" continue. But when nonpaying campers rip off the dwindling supply of granola and bagels, there will be that much less for the workers in next year's budget. Wherever Michigan's meaning is being debated—in Ph.D. dissertations, in music zines, at trans venues, poetry slams, and LGBT centers—the message needs to be passed along that ripping off the festival's music, melons, and massage care doesn't equal "fighting the power" in corporate America. As one worker wailed succinctly, "We're women! We're dykes! We don't have money!"

Cultural movements and revolutions have always had the challenging task of transmitting their radical values to the next generation—only to find that their ideals have fallen into the generation gap and vanished. For some of my own college students, the over-forty separatists representing festival culture appear as women of their mothers' generation, the very demographic that they naturally resist. And the ageism cuts both ways, as women like me, who began attending Michigan at twenty, now enter our forties and snarl, "In *my* day we *respected* the established performers like Holly Near!"

An interview with festival producer Lisa Vogel that appeared in *The Woman-Centered Economy* (published in 1995 by Third Side Press) included observations that are now a decade old yet ring true for today's situation. It seemed that, as Lisa comments,

> Utopia lost its glow. The community had come to expect more—more polish, more access, more festival. . . . [O]ther festivals had sprung up all over the country, so boycotters could boycott and still get their music, while others simply went to festivals closer to home. . . . [W]ith dialog and trial-and-error, the Michigan Womyn's Music Festival has stabilized . . . about 20 percent each year are "festivirgins"—women attending the festival for the first time.

Even as the festival's long tenure makes it "retro," an easy mark for those who might condescend to dismiss it, it remains the lesbian haj for an ever-delighted pool of first-timers—including, this year, my own girlfriend, who has never before camped in her life. This ritual of accompanying a new partner to buy a sleeping bag, lantern, and waterproof tampon kit for "her first Michigan" has no Hallmark-card equivalent, yet it is a recognizable rite of passage for many lesbian couples in America. As I suggested in my books, *Eden Built By Eves* and *The Question of Sabotage,* outdoor festivals can and do intimidate the noncamper at first—which is why built-in support systems like Michigan's camping areas for older and disabled fans are so important. But when everything comes together perfectly at that opening-night celebration—the dancers onstage, the ritual fire-eaters, the lush tree foliage waving, the Northern lights or shooting stars overhead, the lover nestled in your lap, the giant bag of M&Ms being passed through a crowd of 4,000, the body-painted and punky-leather dykes dancing with new babies on their hips, and white-haired long-timers barking orders into walkie-talkies in thick Festivalese—it's still Oz and Brigadoon. It is undeniably among the truly unique lesbian cultural contributions to American society.

WILLIAM G. HAWKESWOOD
AND ALEX W. COSTLEY

One of the Children:
Gay Black Men in Harlem (1996)

Despite much work on contemporary gay white male communities, there have been few studies of African American gay men. Most people know of the Harlem Renaissance and gayness "then," but few people have studied black gay men "now." One of the Children: Gay Black Men in Harlem is one of the first studies to ask African American gay men in Harlem about their lives.

Many black Americans manage multiple identities. In white-dominated corporate America, for example, black executives may find it expeditious to play down their black identity. In the cultural context of American society, gay black men often are adept at identifying as American, black, or gay, as the occasion demands, and negotiate between one identity and another depending on context.

In Harlem, where a wide range of types of people are accepted, being gay is not necessarily regarded as being deviant. (Compare this with being gay in mainstream white America, where white gay men are trying to overcome the deviant label by pursuing the status of gay as "ethnic" in order to rationalize and justify the equality of their existence alongside other Americans.) Being gay in Harlem means being different, but in a community characterized by diversity.

Whatever the psychological dimensions of a gay identity, it too, like black identity, comprises social and cultural dimensions. These social and cultural elements of gay life and their importance to the construction and maintenance of gay identity are the subject of this chapter.

BEING GAY

Francis: Gay is lovin' men, honey. All kinds o' men. Lovin' men. Now, that's bein' gay.

In Harlem, gay men primarily regard being gay as synonymous with being homosexual. Same-sex sexual behavior was invariably raised as the single practice that distinguished gay men from other types of men ("bisexual" and "straight") in Harlem.

ROLAND: [A gay man] has sex with the same sex. With other men. He prefers to have sex with other men.

GILBERT: [A gay man is] a man who is interested in another man, sexually. He can be feminine or masculine. It doesn't matter. Some men like different things in sex. But they're all gay.

LESLIE: [A gay man is] a man who has sex with another man. It usually involves emotional commitment. A lover relationship.

The most important aspect of gay identity for these gay black men is sexual behavior. It is the one common attribute they share as gay men. All of my respondents indicated that in order to be gay, that is, to be distinguishable from non-gay people, one had to engage in homosexual intercourse with another man.

For some men, however, having a gay identity meant more than just having sex with other men. Being gay also included participation in a gay social life.

BYRON: [A gay man] is homosexual. He has gay friends. He goes to gay places. Does gay things.

LUTHER: Gay means homosexual, you know. A man who likes to have sex with other men, and who lives a gay lifestyle. He has gay friends and does gay things. Like goes to discos and parties.

GILBERT: A gay man has sex with other men. Hangs out in the scene. Has friends. He's out to his family.

ORVILLE: [A gay man is] a homosexual. But it really refers to younger men.

NATE: Most of them are sissies. Real women. I mean, most gay men act and carry on like women. Now you have the hos [whores] and the church women, the wife type and the nymphomaniac. That's what gay men are like.

SHERMAN: Sometimes [a gay man is] a flamboyant male. A man who dresses well. Has great compassion. He lives a gay lifestyle. In gay bars, and parties. He can also be conservative, though. You know, a quiet man. It depends on his personality. And his role in the community. They're all different types of men actually.

LOUIS: To me, personally, it means that you live a separate lifestyle. It's more than just the sex. Gay sex is important. An important part of it. But it's not all. Because being gay means that you do other gay things too. Like having other gay friends. Going to gay places. I mean you really could see that in the seventies. You know, 'cause all the discos were really gay. That was a gay thing. And gay liberation. That told us so much about being gay. So you could see things that were gay. Just gay. Different to the rest of New York. So being gay is all that too. It's history now, too. We have a history.

Many gay black men in Harlem agree that engaging in homosexual behavior was the starting point of their homosexual identity formation. Such homosexual experiences are followed by a variety of social experiences that lead the individual into the gay world. It is in this "cultural scene," composed of both private and public contexts, that the individual learns how to be gay.

The life history of Louis that I give below is an attempt to show how a gay social and political identity emerged in a man raised in a prosperous and stable black family, the kind rarely mentioned in the literature on black society.

Louis was born in 1950, the third of five children and the elder son of May and Charlie Williams. Charlie was a prosperous realtor, born and raised in Harlem. He had completed high school and worked all his life in his uncle's business, which he was eventually to inherit. He hoped one of his sons would take it over, but one was interested in the arts and the other in basketball. May had come north from Georgia, following in the footsteps of two older sisters. One of them had been a successful jazz singer in the after-hours world of wartime Harlem but had succumbed to alcohol "and stuff" in 1946. That was about the time that her other sister had started taking her to Convent Baptist Church, "with all those monied folks." That's where she met the handsome Charlie. "You seen Louis. You ain't seen nothing," she once remarked. "You think Louis is pretty. Child, you shoulda seen his Daddy!"

Charlie's parents weren't too sure about a southern girl as a wife for their city son, but she regularly went to church, so that helped. They contributed to the couple's first home, in a tenement just north of 110th Street. Four children in four years meant that the family quickly outgrew their first apartment, but by then Charlie was doing quite well with "Uncle's help," so the family moved to 140th Street. This is the home that figures earliest in Louis's childhood memories.

The apartment was huge. It had a long entranceway, off which one could enter the three bedrooms or the two bathrooms. In the "rear" were a large living room with an alcove where the television was located, a dining room, and a large kitchen, which housed a breakfast table. Louis shared a bedroom with his younger brother. His two sisters at that time shared a bedroom also. (Louis's third sister was born some fourteen years after him.) He recalls that he got along well with his brother. Both of the boys were out and about a lot. His brother played ball in the park most evenings and weekends, and Louis was able to have his friends over to play in the bedroom. Mostly they played cards or read, and sometimes his best friends would stay the night.

Louis's parents entertained a lot. He suspects that was because of his father's contacts in the business world. His mother was a wonderful cook. He remembers her peach cobbler with special affection. And he insists, "An' nobody, just nobody, cooks ribs like Ma!" On Sundays, Louis's aunt and her church friends would come to eat. That was always a great time to be home, because his aunt would bring over gifts for the children. Mostly they would be small toys or candy, but once she gave the children a bicycle, and Louis was put in charge.

Louis remembers his older sisters were always in school. Naomi and Rona had many friends who were always coming around. He didn't like them too much because they were always making noise and teasing him. His sisters were always allowed to stay up later and watch television. When Naomi was in eighth grade she had a boyfriend, Willie. He was a basketball player whom Louis admired very much. He was tall and dark and very handsome. He favored Isaac, Louis's younger brother, because Isaac was so good at playing ball. Louis also liked to play, but he was heavier and couldn't match Willie or Isaac on the court. But he persisted because he liked Willie so much. Willie and Naomi eventually married after they finished high school, and Willie became a successful professional ball player.

Ruth also married and has four children as well. She and her family live in New Rochelle, near Louis's mother. His brother lives in D.C. and works on and off as an electrician's assistant. "God knows how many nieces and nephews I got in D.C. Isaac has a different woman he's livin' with every time I see him. His trouble is that he's so fine and all these girls chase after him!"

Louis remembers the summers as a child especially. He would be allowed to play in the playground on the corner. It had swings and "things to climb all over." Trees shaded the mothers, grandmothers, and older sisters who took care of the children "in the park." His favorite part of the playground was where the fountain sprayed over the children. Sometimes if he and his sisters were really lucky his mother would take them to Riverside Park or Central Park. One summer he remembers going to the Bronx Zoo. But it was hot and smelly. He remembers riding the elephant and watching the monkeys, but overall it "wasn't all that."

Louis had two very close friends during his early years at 140th Street. His best friend, Billy, lived in the same building, downstairs. Billy was a quiet child. He always liked to read, and sometimes he'd watch television with Louis. In fact, anything that Louis did Billy liked to do as well. Louis liked his friend. He was very good-looking and always supportive of Louis and his wild dreams. Early in life Louis had decided that he would become a famous singer or film star. He used to dress up and pretend to act parts, sometimes in front of the mirror, but most often in front of Billy. Billy would always cheer and clap, and sometimes tell Louis how he could do something better. Louis and Billy attended the same elementary school, a few blocks away from where they lived. They used to walk to and from school every day. One of Louis's older sisters would escort them. Another friend, Johnny, whom Louis had met at school, would join them on the way. Johnny was a year older than Louis and Billy, physically much bigger and more rugged in appearance. Even at elementary school, the girls followed Johnny around. He played basketball and football at school and always drew a large crowd to watch him perform. This was how Louis had heard of him and eventually got to know him. Louis also liked to play basketball, and he and Johnny became a very popular pair both on and off the court.

Louis notes that around about sixth grade he realized that his feelings for his two closest friends were different from the feelings he had toward a lot of his other friends and acquaintances at school and in the immediate neighborhood. He didn't understand them at the time, but at some point, in a bathroom at school, Johnny approached him and touched him. Louis recalls, "I always remember how good that felt. I mean I felt sick inside, you know. I suddenly felt I was in love or something. I just know I felt wonderful."

At some point over the next few months, as their sexual involvement increased, Louis told Johnny that he was in love with him and that he wanted to marry him. Louis had just simply decided that this was the person with whom he wanted to spend the rest of his life. He compared the simplicity of his love at that time to the love of Fabian and Annette, or Bobby and Debbie, in the movies. But he says that it did consume him and made him intensely jealous of all the girls who hung around Johnny at school. He used to get mad at Johnny for even talking with the girls. And Johnny used to get mad at him, eventually saying that Louis was worse than a girl. It was this statement of Johnny's that caused Louis to think that he really was different. Up to this point, Louis's upbringing typifies that of many of my informants who grew up in the 1950s and 1960s. His introduction to same-sex behavior at the hands of a schoolmate is also typical. That experience was the turning point for him and others, an "awakening" as Willis called it, because the realization hit home that they were "different."

In the early 1960s, the word *gay* wasn't used to describe homosexual men in Harlem. But Louis remembers, when he was in high school, the first time that someone called him "homo."

> LOUIS: I had been hanging around with Johnny so much and really sticking close by, so close I guess it was obvious that the two of us were too close. What pissed me off most was that Johnny heard it too and didn't do nothing. I mean he was my hero and I was hurtin' and I guess I expected him to fight this guy.

Louis stayed home from school the next day, feigning illness. That evening when Johnny came over Louis told him that he didn't want to see him anymore. Johnny told him to "get over it," that he had to understand that he, Louis, really was a "homo." Louis was very distressed. He didn't know what it meant. He knew that he was different, but he was happy the way he was. He knew that something was bad about being a "homo," but he felt he had no one but his good friend Johnny to talk to about it. They never did have sex again, but they remained close friends until Johnny went to high school in the Bronx.

Thereafter, Louis concentrated his efforts on his friendship with Billy. Billy was attractive but not as "manly" as Johnny. But there was something that Louis felt about him too. One day on the way home from school, the boys went to Riverside Park to watch the older guys play basketball. They were there quite late, when Billy told Louis to wait a while. Billy went off down by the river and didn't come back for a long time. Just as Louis was about to go looking for him, Billy emerged from the bushes with a man. Looking back, Louis thinks the guy wasn't all that old, but at that time he thought the guy was too old to be hanging out with Billy. Immediately Louis thought that Billy was up to something. On the way home he asked Billy what was going on. But Billy was evasive. He told Louis that the guy was a friend from the neighborhood. But Louis hadn't seen him before. He persisted until Billy finally told him what they were doing. Louis was shocked and pleased. He couldn't wait to blurt out that he and Johnny were doing the same stuff. Billy said he knew but that he hadn't talked to Louis about it because he wasn't sure whether they could still be friends.

Sometime after that evening, Billy took Louis down to the park and eventually, after seeing the same man again, took Louis into the bushes. Louis enjoyed having sex with Billy but said it wasn't the same as with Johnny. He played a different role. And Billy was too close a friend (and confidant) for them to get into too much. They decided not to do it again but to be special friends. "Girlfriends!" Louis laughed.

This initial sexual encounter typically cements a lifelong commitment between two gay friends. Several informants related similar incidents in their development as gay men. Also, we see here the beginning of a gay social network that was to expand through high school and college years. Typically many of these friendships are maintained in adult life.

Louis and Billy both attended George Washington High School in Harlem. They were in the same class right through school, and both were better than average students. Louis won a scholarship to go to college, but Billy did not even graduate.

> LOUIS: Most of our crowd just studied. We all liked our books. None of us was really sports-oriented. We left that to the boys! We supported them and all, 'cause we liked the sports, and the boys, but we only did that because we wanted them. You know. If we got up to anything those days it would be on the way home from school. 'Cause once I was home I wasn't comin' back out. Not in those days. It was "Do your homework, boy!" But it got me into books, and dreaming. Hours and hours of dreaming. That's why I'm here today. Doin' what I'm doin'. Because of those years.

Occasionally at school Louis would engage in sex, usually with some younger guy. He had two good places to take boys when he wanted to have sex—one in the gymnasium, the other down a tree-filled bank.

> LOUIS: I didn't do much at school, really. Not really. I mean I got caught once and that made me cautious. I was having a good time too. The best I'd ever had. And this kid was screaming. He was screaming so loud that's what attracted them. One of the teachers and some students, I think from the basketball team, came and caught us.

But Louis and Billy discovered (or heard about from friends at the same school) several places they could go and see or participate in sex on the way home from school.

> LOUIS: Our favorite were the parks. You could spend hours there, just watching. And some fine motherfuckers would come on up in there. I even had sex once with the captain of the school basketball team. I fucked him real good. He never spoke to me at school, but I had him. If only all those sissies, and those girls, knew that! . . . I had a teacher. I had some prominent people from around Harlem. I had a TV star.

One particular park seems to have been their favorite. It also features in the life histories of many of the other gay black men I met in Harlem. For some of them it is still an important meeting place for sexual encounters, although the current drug epidemic in Harlem has made the gay area of the park somewhat unsafe. Louis and Billy would go there two or three times a week on the way home from school. They spent hours wandering around the paths and watching older men engage in sex. Louis recalls that it was quite an education. Although he had worked out what to do, actually to see the particular act take place was quite thrilling. Occasionally, the guys would go to the park on the weekends. But Louis thought that it was too crowded, and they might have been recognized: "They was all up in there. Everyone. You never know who you gonna run into. And it was too crowded. I didn't like that. They was comin' at you from every direction." But the park was where Louis first engaged in oral sex—"a scary thing, the first time"—and where he and Billy made many of the friendships with gay people their own age that persist today. Public settings for sex such as this feature prominently in the life histories of many gay men. Apart from the fact that access was free, and no age limit was enforced (as for bars), sexual experience was gained, anonymously, and entry into gay life established.

About this time, 1969–1970, the word *gay* became familiar to Louis and his friends. During the summer before their last year in high school, some gay people had rioted downtown, night after night, and fought for their rights to hang out together, to be gay together, and to have sex and relationships with whom they liked. These, of course, were the Stonewall riots, a memorable event in history for gay people the world over. What this event did for Louis and other young gay men in Harlem was to enlighten them about the fact that a whole section of town was gay. Just as Harlem was for blacks, so Greenwich Village was for gays. Louis used to think that he had been born into the wrong part of town. He should have been born and raised in Greenwich Village.

> LOUIS: I used to dream that I had been born in Greenwich Village to these two fierce gay men. They had a beautiful house and I had a very happy life. I dreamt I went to a gay school and met all these beautiful boys, and I fell in love and got married.

But Louis had never been to Greenwich Village.

In July or August 1969, before entering their senior year at high school, Louis Williams and Billy Pritchard emerged from the Interborough Rapid Transit subway line at Christopher Street for the first time. Louis recalls it as a colorful sight.

> LOUIS: The place was full of hippies. I mean I'd seen them on TV, but here they were live. Hundreds of them holding hands and kissing each other. And a lot of them were men kissing men. I remember us like country boys, standing and staring. All these men. Even black ones. And black and white ones together. I remember that really affecting me. To see black and white men together. That was a trip.

The guys didn't venture too far from the subway. They found the Stonewall Inn, in Sheridan Square, and paid homage along with the many others who were milling around outside the boarded-up bar. They soon returned to the subway, having explored enough for a first visit and because they were a little scared in case they got into trouble. Being raised with a heightened awareness of racial differences, they were not sure how they would be accepted downtown. The fact that black and white men were together questioned basic assumptions that Louis held about life. Although being gay obviously cuts across racial barriers and has instilled in Louis a sense of pride in being gay, he has never had a white friend, let alone a white lover. An important event in the development of being gay for all the informants was a "first visit" to a gay section of town or to a gay bar. All expressed some sense of relief, not just at the security of being away from prying family or suspected homophobic neighbors but at the discovery of others like themselves, doing normal things like dancing, drinking, kissing, holding hands, relaxing, and having a good time.

When school started again, Louis and Billy shared their experiences with their gay friends at school. There was much talk about setting up a gay liberation club at school, but they were not sure how "scandalous" that might be. Harlem wasn't ready for them, yet. Some years later such a club was formed at that high school, and on the club's unofficial "honors list" are the names of Louis and Billy, as Stonewallers.

The last year at high school was difficult. Louis wanted to go to college and was aiming at a private school in upstate New York, a liberal arts college that would provide him with the education he would need to become a star. But gay life was developing all over the city. More parks and bars, and even the bathhouse, in Harlem, beckoned to him. Louis remembers it all "bursting forth."

> LOUIS: It was really me bursting forth on all of it. I mean suddenly I found all these things to do. I started drinking a lot, and going to the bars down on 125th Street. There were a whole lot of them. And all the noise and bright lights of the gay scene at that time. And all the men. I could have sex anywhere, anytime, with anyone I wanted. People begged me to go home with them. But I never did. I mean I had sex with them all right, but I wouldn't go to their homes. I was frightened they wouldn't let me go. And I didn't know who'd be at home with them. But I had a ball.

Louis didn't fall in love at this time—fortunately, he says—so he was able to strike a balance between going out, mainly at night and on the weekends, when it was all happening, and staying in when schoolwork demanded it. However, his friend Billy did fall in love.

> LOUIS: Billy met a guy who was working at Macy's. He was handsome, and he had lots of money. At least we thought so. Anyway, I've forgotten his name, but he used to take us out. We'd go to parties all over town, even to his friends' in Brooklyn. Sometimes we'd stay out all night. But that was mainly when we went to the discos. We were trying all sorts of drugs and drinking. But I said only on

the weekends. That was where Billy went wrong. He was going out with these guys all through the week. He didn't come to school. Until he got into real trouble. And his parents found out. And he got a beating. So, he moved out and lived with that guy in Brooklyn. I used to see him sometimes, but I haven't seen him in years now. I don't even know if he's alive.

It was at this time that the education, career plans, and other dreams of many of the gay men I interviewed were derailed. The 1970s, and all that those years meant for gay men in New York City, undoubtedly played a part. Gay liberation, emerging gay social and political organizations, and the establishment of a large gay scene of bars, clubs, and discos provided these men with places to be gay. Suddenly many men found that they could live "gay" lives, even openly, in the company of many like souls. Most of this new lifestyle, however, was conducted late at night because of the marginalization of gay culture by mainstream New York society (and because many gay men wished to remain discreet). This after-hours lifestyle often interfered with other aspects of gay men's lives. Many did not realize that it would cost them money, time, and sometimes their jobs or schooling.

According to Louis's mother, Billy's expulsion from school and his running away from home was the moment when she realized that Louis too was possibly gay. However, after that incident, Louis settled down, stayed home more often, and studied hard. This reduced her concerns about his gayness. She noted that he was young, and it might be a stage that he was going through or a matter of his hanging out with a wild crowd. She never discussed the issue with him and soon forgot about it.

Louis says that Billy's moving away meant that he did not go out as much and that staying at home probably did help his schoolwork. He was delighted in the spring of 1970 to hear that he was going to college. He was so excited about his good fortune that he had trouble settling down to the last weeks of school.

The next four years were a mixture of pleasure and pain. College days provided Louis with an opportunity to shine academically, especially with his acting, directing, and writing. He also enjoyed an active sports life, but his interest was mainly in the other players. Louis described many of the sexual encounters he enjoyed at college. The dormitory situation provided the growing network of gay friends with many opportunities to engage in sexual encounters. Some of these men went on to marry and have families, but many of them, with whom Louis keeps in touch, remained gay. In his junior year, Louis met Terrence, a "tall, handsome, light-skinned boy" who was a superb basketball player and a gentle, understanding friend. They became buddies on and off the court. Eventually they became lovers. Through the following summer, which Louis spent in Washington, D.C., where Terrence came from, the two developed the basis of what was to become a ten-year affair.

After college, Louis moved to D.C. for six years and lived with Terrence. They were a popular couple in the gay community and well known in the discos and bars. They both worked office jobs for different government departments. Louis recalls this as the happiest time of his life. He had the security of a relationship and of a well-paying, full-time job. Unlike many of their friends in D.C. who were struggling to break free from family constraints and improve their socioeconomic status, Louis and Terrence had it made. However, after six years, during which Louis freely admits to a very promiscuous sex life outside of the relationship, the yearning to return to the arts became too great. Not foreseeing the opportunities he desired in D.C., Louis set his sights on New York. Fortunately, Terrence was a willing partner, and the couple moved to New York City in 1981. Louis's constant unemployment, the cost of living in the city, and continued promiscuity, especially on Louis's part, tore the couple apart. Terrence returned to D.C. Although they remain the best of friends and visit each other frequently, Louis is sometimes remorseful. Both men have moved on to other relationships, but Louis remembers that one with Terrence as being exemplary.

4
The Birds and the . . . Birds
QUEER LOVE, SEX, AND ROMANCE
IN AMERICA, NOW AND THEN

When is an orgasm just an orgasm? (We thought that might get your attention.) For American queers (and for Bill Clinton in the 1990s), the answer is, hardly ever. Throughout the twentieth and early twenty-first centuries, the very idea of queer sex has stirred controversy and debate, reflecting general discomfort with discussions of sexuality in general. If anything, queers have prompted all Americans to have more honest and open conversations about sex and sexuality. However, only in the past thirty years have the information, images, and texts by and about queers and sex become widely available. Prior to the feminist and gay liberation movements of the late 1960s, knowledge about queer sex was hard to come by.

In the late nineteenth and early twentieth centuries, Victorian ideas of women as not naturally sexual influenced U.S. culture. For some, this taboo against frank sexual expression translated into "romantic friendships," in which women openly professed deep emotional, but not necessarily sexual, love for one another. Were some of these friendships sexual as well as emotional? Probably. The erotic element of these friendships has been subject to much debate, especially considering the fact that few women involved in such relationships would have ever used the label "lesbian" to describe themselves. However, some women wrote letters to one another that unmistakably described erotic encounters and feelings, including a series of particularly juicy exchanges between anarchist Emma Goldman and former prostitute Almeda Sperry. Nonetheless, until the end of World War I, women had far more latitude to express romantic sentiment in friendships, or, as some came to be known, Boston marriages, than they had to create recognizably sexual female-female relationships. After the Great War, sexologists' ideas about lesbian deviance filtered into popular culture. Women writers discreetly began to document the world of lesbian sex in autobiographies and fiction, such as the descriptions embedded in Radclyffe Hall's 1928 novel, *The Well of Loneliness.*

91

Men who slept with men had an easier time in terms of finding potential partners in public spaces such as parks and bars and in writing about their sexual relationships. Because these men could use and move through public space in such different ways than could women, their sexual subcultures developed much more quickly and extensively for gay men than for lesbians. In the poetic excerpt by Richard Bruce Nugent, entitled "Smoke, Lilies, and Jade," the author obliquely explores the sensual experience of bisexuality with lyrical and metaphoric language. Describing both the delights of the body and the pleasures of 1920s New York, Nugent captures the uncertainty and excitement of the sexual and cultural possibilities that characterized the Harlem Renaissance scene. Queer men's sex lives most often flourished in bathhouses, parks, and public restrooms, especially in major urban areas where one could have anonymous sexual encounters in one part of town and return to "straight" domestic life in another, if they so chose.

In the 1930s, with the words "lesbian" and "homosexual" firmly associated with sexual acts, some queers wrote openly about their sexuality and lovers. Mary Casal, in her 1930 autobiography *The Stone Wall*, describes how sex contributed to good health when she and her partner were always "more fit for good work after having been thus relieved." These early queer writers helped other lesbians and gay men to form subcultures and communities during the difficult times of the Great Depression, when economic struggle and the looming specter of war in Europe prevented or superseded frank and open discussions of sexuality. One can only imagine the kinds of queer sex that took place and the queer relationships that developed during World War II in barracks, on ships, and in ports of call, when men and women, queer and not, were out of their common social networks, trapped in tight quarters away from home for long periods of time. Whether such sex took place because of same-sex desire or because these men and women were living sex-segregated lives, what they did between the sheets was deemed queer.

Before, during, and after World War II, queers met potential lovers surreptitiously in working-class bars, which were frequently subjected to police raids and arrests. Gay men and lesbians sometimes married each other as a respectable "front" to avoid the suspicions and scrutiny of fearful families and coworkers. Some of the only available descriptions of queer sex were found in relatively chaste, breathless, and suggestive lesbian pulp fiction (the queer equivalent of heterosexual romance bodice-rippers). These pulp novels almost always contained moralizing plots about despairing girls gone astray, reflecting social anxiety about queer love and sex at the time. Queer men relied on early bodybuilding magazines that had social license to reveal and revel in the male form, always with genitalia covered.

The 1960s feminist and gay liberation movements threw off the shackles of repression that characterized the 1950s, giving rise to a veritable cornucopia of choices, images, and information about queer sex and sexuality. In the late 1960s, members of the feminist health movement and lesbian activists began self-publishing pamphlets about lesbian sex. A 193-page booklet entitled *Women and Their Bodies*, the precursor to the ground-breaking *Our Bodies, Ourselves*, was first published in 1970. Gay liberationists (mostly men) boldly and proudly embraced pleasure and sexual expression as part of the movement's goal of liberation from oppression and heterosexism.

In the 1970s, the sexual subcultures of gay men and lesbians moved further apart. Gay men created communities around pleasure in all its forms by gathering in neighborhood bars, bathhouses, gay clubs, and summer resorts. Meanwhile, lesbians debated how to smash the patriarchy and created women's music festivals and women-only cultural communities. Unlike gay men, who made sexual freedom a centerpiece of their liberation, lesbians saw sex as a distraction from more important political issues about the status of women more generally. A few women bucked the trend of self-imposed sexual repression and argued that sex was an integral part of lesbian liberation. In 1975, Tee Corinne published the *Cunt Coloring Book*, one of the first depictions of lesbian erotica, and around the same time Barbara Hammer began to create short, experimental lesbian erotic films that featured women's bodies superimposed upon images of nature, such as the famous *Multiple Orgasm* (1977).

By the 1980s, the landscape of queer sex and sexuality changed profoundly. The lesbian "sex wars," as they became known, first exploded on the lesbian scene with the publication of *Coming to Power: Writing and Graphics on Lesbian S/M*, by the San Francisco–based SAMOIS collective. *Coming to Power* sent shock waves through lesbian communities with its graphic depictions of lesbian sexual power exchange and its trenchant critique of "vanilla" sex. Some lesbians began reclaiming the word "dyke," originally used as a mid-century epithet, as a source of power. As the sex wars unfolded, a few lesbians decided to address the dearth of explicit sexual lesbian imagery, and two pioneers in the fledgling lesbian porn industry founded *On Our Backs*, the first dyke-owned and dyke-specific pornography magazine in history, as well as a lesbian porn video company. But although some lesbians were exploring the boundaries of consensual erotic power play and visual images, other lesbians decried this trend in the community and joined forces with many straight feminists who advocated an end to pornography, even lesbian pornography, as a form of violence against women.

For gay men, the 1980s marked a turning point in thinking and talking about sex. The tremendous number of deaths from HIV/AIDS, combined with the indignity caused by the Reagan administration's refusal to acknowledge such suffering, shifted gay men's focus around sex and sexuality from pleasure to danger, from free expression to self-regulation, internal critique, and fear. No longer was an orgasm just an orgasm, if it ever was to begin with, but now a casual orgasm was fraught with uncertainty and potential risk. In addition, the U.S. Supreme Court affirmed states' rights to make queer sex a criminal offense in its 1986 *Bowers v. Hardwick* decision. At this historical juncture, lesbians and gay men worked together to create care networks and organizations that provided essential services for people with HIV/AIDS in the face of so much tragedy.

After years of caring for dying gay men and agitating fruitlessly for government funding and research, queers took to the streets, got in people's faces, and changed the American conversation about sex by "coming out" in droves. In the late

1980s and early 1990s, radical queers founded activist organizations, and academics began to seriously study queer sex and sexuality, creating the body of knowledge now known as queer theory. The emergence of the Internet provided a new and lucrative venue to create and display queer (predominantly gay male) porn, facilitate online communities and chat rooms, and host websites for casual hookups. Lesbians continued to develop a small but thriving culture of sexual texts and images, but as sociological research has shown, in the twenty-first century queer women have less sex and more monogamy than their queer male counterparts.

Queers have debated the merits of monogamy versus nonmonogamy for years. Dossie Easton and Catherine Liszt's excerpt from *The Ethical Slut: A Guide to Infinite Sexual Possibilities* outlines new ways of thinking about queer (and nonqueer) sex and sexual pleasure in the age of AIDS by imagining loving sexual relationships outside the constraints of monogamy. Some early twenty-first-century cable television shows now depict queer sexual nonmonogamy, especially gay male nonmonogamy, and in some ways celebrate queer relationships for successfully integrated nonmonogamy with loving commitment.

So back to our original question: when is an orgasm just an orgasm? In the infancy of the twenty-first century, new challenges and developments regarding queer sex, love, and relationships have emerged: the rise of the radical religious right; the legalization of gay marriage in Massachusetts; the 2003 *Lawrence v. Texas* decision, which told the states that it was unconstitutional to criminalize gay sex; and politicians' threats to amend the U.S. Constitution to ban gay marriage. If queer sex used to be relegated to public toilets, private rooms at women's colleges, and bathhouses, it is now on prime-time television, in the Supreme Court, on right-wing radio, and on occasion in high school sex ed curricula. If queer relationships used to be romantic friendships or double lives in the twentieth century, queer relationships are now being tracked by the U.S. Census. Queer sex, romance, and relationships are everywhere, showing that an orgasm is most definitely not now, nor has it ever been, just an orgasm.

RICHARD BRUCE NUGENT

Smoke, Lilies, and Jade (1926)

Born in Washington, D.C., to a family of high social position in the black community, Richard Bruce Nugent (1906–1987) was one of the premier authors of the Harlem Renaissance. "Shadows," Nugent's first published poem, was rescued from the trash by Nugent's best friend, Langston Hughes, and was eventually sent to Opportunity *magazine. In 1926 Nugent was part of a group of black artists who envisioned a literary periodical called* Fire!!, *which broke with the black literary establishment. His creative involvement included two brush-and-ink drawings and "Smoke, Lilies, and Jade."*

Alex sat up . . . pulled on his shoes and went out . . . it was a beautiful night . . . and so large . . . the dusky blue hung like a curtain in an immense arched doorway . . . fastened with silver tacks . . . to wander in the night was wonderful . . . myriads of inquisitive lights . . . curiously prying into the dark . . . and fading unsatisfied . . . he passed a woman . . . she was not beautiful . . . and he was sad because she did not weep that she would never be beautiful . . . was it Wilde who had said . . . a cigarette is the most perfect pleasure because it leaves one unsatisfied . . . the breeze gave to him a perfume stolen from some wandering lady of the evening . . . it pleased him . . . why was it that men wouldn't use perfumes . . . they should . . . each and every one of them liked perfumes . . . the man who denied that was a liar . . . or a coward . . . but if ever he were to voice that thought . . . express it . . . he would be misunderstood . . . a fine feeling that . . . to be misunderstood . . . it made him feel tragic and great . . . but maybe it would be nicer to be understood . . . but no . . . no great artist is . . . then again neither were fools . . . they were strangely akin these two . . . Alex thought of a sketch he would make . . . a personality sketch of Fania . . . straight classic features tinted proud purple . . . sensuous fine lips . . . gilded for truth . . . eyes . . . half opened and lids colored mysterious green . . . hair black and straight . . . drawn sternly mocking back from the false puritanical forehead . . . maybe he would make Edith too . . . skin a blue . . . infinite like night . . . and eyes . . . slant and gray . . . very complacent like a cat's . . . Mona Lisa lips . . . red and seductive as . . . as pomegranate juice . . . in truth it was fine to be young and hungry and an artist . . . to blow blue smoke from an ivory holder . . . here was the cafeteria . . . it was almost as though it had journeyed to meet him . . . the night was so blue . . . how does blue feel . . . or red or gold or any other color . . . if colors could be heard he could paint most wondrous tunes . . . symphonious . . . think . . . the dulcet clear tone of a blue like night . . . of a red like pomegranate juice . . . like Edith's lips . . . of the fairy tones to be heard in a sunset . . . like rubies shaken in a crystal cup . . . of the symphony of Fania . . . and silver . . . and gold . . . he had heard the sound of gold . . .

but they weren't the sounds he wanted to catch . . . no . . . they must be liquid . . . not so staccato but flowing variations of the same caliber . . . there was no one in the cafe as yet . . . he sat and waited . . . that was a clever idea he had had about color music . . . but after all he was a monstrous clever fellow . . . Jurgen had said that . . . funny how characters in books said the things one wanted to say . . . he would like to know Jurgen . . . how does one go about getting an introduction to a fiction character . . . go up to the brown cover of the book and knock gently . . . and say hello . . . then timidly . . . is Duke Jurgen there . . . or . . . no because if one entered the book in the beginning Jurgen would only be a pawnbroker . . . and one didn't enter a book in the center . . . but what foolishness . . . Alex lit a cigarette . . . but Cabell was a master to have written Jurgen . . . and an artist . . . and a poet . . . Alex blew a cloud of smoke . . . a few lines of one of Langston's poems came to describe Jurgen. . . .

> Somewhat like Ariel
> Somewhat like Puck
> Somewhat like a gutter boy
> Who loves to play in muck.
> Somewhat like Bacchus
> Somewhat like Pan
> And a way with women
> Like a sailor man . . .

Langston must have known Jurgen . . . suppose Jurgen had met Tonio Kroeger . . . what a vagrant thought . . . Kroeger . . . Kroeger . . . Kroeger . . . why here was Rene . . . Alex had almost gone to sleep . . . Alex blew a cone of smoke as he took Rene's hand . . . it was nice to have friends like Rene . . . so comfortable . . . Rene was speaking . . . Borgia joined them . . . and de Diego Padro . . . their talk veered to . . . James Branch Cabell . . . beautiful . . . marvelous . . . Rene had an enchanting accent . . . said sank for thank and souse for south . . . but they couldn't know Cabell's greatness . . . Alex searched the smoke for expression . . . he . . . he . . . well he has created a fantasy mire . . . that's it . . . from clear rich imagery . . . life and silver sands . . . that's nice . . . and silver sands . . . imagine lilies growing in such a mire . . . when they close at night their gilded underside would protect . . . but that's not it at all . . . his thoughts just carried and mingled like . . . like odors . . . suggested but never definite . . . Rene was leaving . . . they all were leaving . . . Alex sauntered slowly back . . . the houses all looked sleepy . . . funny . . . made him feel like writing poetry . . . and about death too . . . an elevated crashed by overhead scattering all his thoughts with its noise . . . making them spread . . . in circles . . . then larger circles . . . just like a splash in a calm pool . . . what had he been thinking . . . of . . . a poem about death . . . but he no longer felt that urge . . . just walk and think and wonder . . . think and remember and smoke . . . blow smoke that mixed with his thoughts and the night . . . he would like to live in a large white palace . . . to wear a long black cape . . . very full and lined with vermilion . . . to have many cushions and to lie there among them . . . talking to his friends . . . lie there in a yellow silk shirt and black velvet trousers . . . like music-review artists talking and pouring strange liquors from curiously beautiful bottles . . . bottles with long slender necks . . . he climbed the noisy stair of the odorous tenement . . . smelled of fish . . . of stale fried fish and dirty milk bottles . . . he rather liked it . . . he liked the acrid smell of horse manure too . . . strong . . . thoughts . . . yes to lie back among strangely fashioned cushions and sip eastern wines and talk . . . Alex threw himself on the bed . . . removed his shoes . . . stretched and relaxed . . . yes and have music waft softly into the darkened and incensed room . . . he blew a cloud of smoke . . . oh the joy of being an artist and of blowing blue smoke through an ivory holder inlaid with red jade and green

$\sim$

the street was so long and narrow . . . so long and narrow . . . and blue . . . in the distance it reached the stars . . . and if he walked long enough . . . far enough . . . he could reach the stars too . . . the narrow blue was so empty . . . quiet . . . Alex walked music . . . it was nice to walk in the blue after a party . . . Zora had shone again . . . her stories . . . she always shone . . . and Monty was glad . . . everyone was glad when Zora shone . . . he was glad he had gone to Monty's party . . . Monty had a nice place in the village . . . nice lights . . . and friends and wine . . . mother would be scandalized that he could think of going to a party . . . without a copper to his name . . . but then mother had never been to Monty's . . . and mother had never seen the street seem long and narrow and blue . . . Alex walked music . . . the click of his heels kept time with a tune in his mind . . . he glanced into a lighted cafe window . . . inside were people sipping coffee . . . men . . . why did they sit there in the loud light . . . didn't they know that outside the street . . . the narrow blue street met the stars . . . that if they walked long enough . . . far enough . . . Alex walked and the click of his heels sounded . . . and had an echo . . . sound being tossed back and forth . . . back and forth . . . someone was approaching . . . and their echoes mingled . . . and gave the sound of castanets . . . Alex liked the sound of the approaching man's footsteps . . . he walked music also . . . he knew the beauty of the narrow blue . . . Alex knew that by the way their echoes mingled . . . he wished he would speak . . . but strangers don't speak at four o'clock in the morning . . . at least if they did he couldn't imagine what would be said . . . maybe pardon me but are you walking toward the stars . . . yes, sir, and if you walk long enough . . . then may I walk with you . . . I want to reach the stars too . . . *perdone me señor tiene usted fósforo* . . . Alex was glad he had been addressed in Spanish . . . to have been asked for a match in English . . . or to have been addressed in English at all . . . would have been blasphemy just then . . . Alex handed him a match . . . he glanced at his companion apprehensively in the match glow . . . he was afraid that his appearance would shatter the blue thoughts . . . and stars . . . ah . . . his face was a perfect complement to his voice . . . and the echo of their steps mingled . . . they walked in silence . . . the castanets of their heels clicking accompaniment . . . the stranger inhaled deeply and with a nod of content and a smile . . . blew a cloud of smoke . . . Alex felt like singing . . . the stranger knew the magic of blue smoke also

. . . they continued in silence . . . the castanets of their heels clicking rhythmically . . . Alex turned in his doorway . . . up the stairs and the stranger waited for him to light the room . . . no need for words . . . they had always known each other . . . as they undressed by the blue dawn . . . Alex knew he had never seen a more perfect being . . . his body was all symmetry and music . . . and Alex called him Beauty . . . long they lay . . . blowing smoke and exchanging thoughts . . . and Alex swallowed with difficulty . . . he felt a glow of tremor . . . and they talked and . . . slept . . . Alex wondered more and more why he liked Adrian so . . . he liked many people . . . Wallie . . . Zora . . . Clement . . . Gloria . . . Langston . . . John . . . Gwenny . . . oh many people . . . and they were friends . . . but Beauty . . . it was different . . . once Alex had admired Beauty's strength . . . and Beauty's eyes had grown soft and he had said . . . I like you more than anyone Dulce . . . Adrian always called him Dulce . . . and Alex had become confused . . . was it that he was so susceptible to beauty that Alex liked Adrian so much . . . but no . . . he knew other people who were beautiful . . . Fania and Gloria . . . Monty and Bunny . . . but he was never confused before them . . . while Beauty . . . Beauty could make him believe in Buddha . . . or imps . . . and no one else could do that . . . that is no one but Melva . . . but then he was in love with Melva . . . and that explained that . . . he would like Beauty to know Melva . . . they were both so perfect . . . such compliments . . . yes he would like Beauty to know Melva because he loved them both . . . there . . . he had thought it . . . actually dared to think it . . . but Beauty must never know . . . Beauty couldn't understand . . . indeed Alex couldn't understand . . . and it pained him . . . almost physically . . . and tired his mind . . . Beauty . . . Beauty was in the air . . . the smoke . . . Beauty . . . Melva . . . Beauty . . . Melva . . . Alex slept . . . and dreamed . . . he was in a field . . . a field of blue smoke and black poppies and red calla lilies . . . he was searching . . . on his hands and knees . . . searching . . . among black poppies and red calla lilies . . . he was searching and pushed aside poppy stems . . . and saw two strong white legs . . . dancer's legs . . . the contours pleased him . . . his eyes wandered . . . on past the muscular hocks to the firm white thighs . . . the rounded buttocks . . . then the lithe narrow waist . . . strong torso and broad deep chest . . . the heavy shoulders . . . the graceful muscled neck . . . squared chin and quizzical lips . . . Grecian nose with its temperamental nostrils . . . the brown eyes looking at him . . . like . . . Monty looked at Zora . . . his hair curly and black and all tousled . . . and it was Beauty . . . and Beauty smiled and looked at him and smiled . . . said . . . I'll wait Alex . . . and Alex became confused and continued his search . . . on his hands and knees . . . pushing aside poppy stems and lily stems . . . a poppy . . . a black poppy . . . a lily . . . a red lily . . . and when he looked back he could no longer see Beauty . . . Alex continued his search . . . through poppies . . . lilies . . . poppies and red calla lilies . . . and suddenly he saw . . . two small feet olive-ivory . . . two well-turned legs curving gracefully from slender ankles . . . and the contours soothed him . . . he followed them . . . past the narrow rounded hips to the tiny waist . . . the fragile firm breasts . . . the graceful slender throat . . . the soft rounded chin . . . slightly parting lips and straight little nose with its slightly flaring nostrils . . . the black eyes with lights in them . . . looking at him . . . the forehead and straight cut black hair . . . and it was Melva . . . and she looked at him and smiled and said . . . I'll wait Alex . . . and Alex became confused and kissed her . . . became confused and continued his search . . . on his hands and knees . . . pushed aside a poppy stem . . . a black-poppy stem . . . pushed aside a lily stem . . . a red-lily stem . . . a poppy . . . a poppy . . . a lily . . . and suddenly he stood erect . . . exultant . . . and in his hand he held . . . an ivory holder . . . inlaid with red jade . . . and green . . . and Alex awoke . . . Beauty's hair tickled his nose . . . Beauty was smiling in his sleep . . . half his face stained flush color by the sun . . . the other half in shadow . . . blue shadow . . . his eyelashes casting cobwebby blue shadows on his cheek . . . his lips were so beautiful . . . quizzical . . . Alex wondered why he always thought of that passage from Wilde's *Salome* . . . when he looked at Beauty's lips . . . I would kiss your lips . . . he *would* like to kiss Beauty's lips . . . Alex flushed warm . . . with shame . . . or was it shame . . . he reached across Beauty for a cigarette . . . Beauty's cheek felt cool to his arm . . . his hair felt soft . . . Alex lay smoking . . . such a dream . . . red calla lilies . . . red calla lilies . . . and . . . what could it all mean . . . did dreams have meanings . . . Fania said . . . and black poppies . . . thousands . . . millions . . . Beauty stirred . . . Alex put out his cigarette . . . closed his eyes . . . he mustn't see Beauty yet . . . speak to him . . . his lips were too hot . . . dry . . . the palms of his hands too cool and moist . . . through his half-closed eyes he could see Beauty . . . propped . . . cheek in hand . . . on one elbow . . . looking at him . . . lips smiling quizzically . . . he wished Beauty wouldn't look so hard . . . Alex was finding it difficult to breathe . . . breathe normally . . . why *must* Beauty look so long . . . and smile *that* way . . . his face seemed nearer . . . it was . . . Alex could feel Beauty's hair on his forehead . . . breathe normally . . . breathe normally . . . could feel Beauty's breath on his nostrils and lips . . . and it was clean and faintly colored with tobacco . . . breathe normally Alex . . . Beauty's lips were nearer . . . Alex closed his eyes . . . how did one act . . . his pulse was hammering . . . from wrist to fingertip . . . wrist to fingertip . . . Beauty's lips touched his . . . his temples throbbed . . . throbbed . . . his pulse hammered from wrist to fingertip . . . Beauty's breath came short now . . . softly staccato . . . breathe normally Alex . . . you are asleep . . . Beauty's lips touched his . . . breathe normally . . . and pressed . . . pressed hard . . . cool . . . his body trembled . . . breathe normally Alex . . . Beauty's lips pressed cool . . . cool and hard . . . how much pressure does it take to waken one . . . Alex sighed . . . moved softly . . . how does one act . . . Beauty's hair barely touched him now . . . his breath was faint on . . . Alex's nostrils and lips . . . Alex stretched and opened his eyes . . . Beauty was looking at him . . . propped on one elbow . . . cheek in his palm . . . Beauty spoke . . . scratch my head please Dulce . . . Alex was breathing normally now . . . propped against the bed head . . . Beauty's head in his lap . . . Beauty spoke . . . I wonder why I like to look at some things Dulce . . . things like smoke and cats . . . and you . . . Alex's pulse no longer hammered from . . . wrist to finger tip . . . wrist to finger tip . . . the rose dusk had become blue night . . . and soon . . . soon they would go out into the blue the little church was crowded . . . warm . . . the rows of benches were brown and sticky . . . Harold was there . . . and Constance and Langston and Bruce and John . . . there was Mr. Robeson . . . how are you Paul . . . a young man was singing . . . Caver . . . Caver was a very self-assured young man . . . such a dream . . . poppies . . . black poppies . . . they were applauding . . . Constance and John were exchanging notes . . . the benches were sticky . . . a young lady was playing the piano . . . fair . . . and red calla lilies . . . who had ever heard of red calla lilies . . . they were applauding . . . a young man was playing the viola . . . what could it all mean . . . so many poppies . . . and Beauty looking at him like . . . like Monty looked at Zora . . . another young man was playing a violin . . . he was the first real artist to perform . . . he had a touch of soul . . . or was it only feeling . . . they were hard to differentiate on the violin . . . and Melva standing in the poppies and lilies . . . Mr. Phillips was singing . . . Mr. Phillips was billed as a basso . . . and he had kissed her . . . they were applauding . . . the first young man was singing again . . . Langston's spiritual . . . Fy-ah-fy-ah Lawd . . . fy-ah's gonna burn ma soul . . . Beauty's hair was so black and curly . . . they were applauding . . . encore . . . Fy-ah Lawd had been a success . . . Langston bowed . . . Langston had written the words . . . Hall bowed . . . Hall had written the music . . . the young man was singing it again . . . Beauty's lips had pressed hard . . . cool . . . cool . . . fy-ah Lawd . . . his breath had trembled . . . fy-ah's gonna burn ma soul . . . they were all leaving . . . first to the roof dance . . . fy-ah Lawd . . . there was Catherine . . . she was beautiful tonight . . . she always was at night . . . Beauty's lips . . . fy-ah Lawd . . . hello Dot . . . why don't you take a boat that sails . . . when are you leaving again . . . and there's Estelle . . . everyone was there . . . fy-ah Lawd . . . Beauty's body had pressed close . . . close . . . fy-ah's gonna burn my soul . . . let's leave . . . have to meet some people at the New World . . . then to Augusta's party . . . Harold . . . John . . . Bruce . . . Connie . . . Langston . . . ready . . . down one hundred thirty-fifth street . . . fy-ah . . . meet these people and leave . . . fy-ah Lawd . . . now to Augusta's party . . . fy-ah's gonna burn ma soul . . . they were at Augusta's . . . Alex half lay . . . half sat on the floor . . . sipping a cocktail . . . such a dream . . . red calla lilies . . . Alex left . . . down the narrow streets . . . fy-ah . . . up the long noisy stairs . . . fy-ahs gonna burn ma soul . . . his head felt swollen . . . expanding . . . contracting . . . expanding . . . contracting . . . he had never been like this before . . . expanding . . . contracting . . . it was that . . . fy-ah . . . fy-ah Lawd . . . and the cocktails . . . and Beauty . . . he felt two cool strong hands on his shoulders . . . it was Beauty . . . lie down Dulce . . . Alex lay down . . . Beauty . . . Alex stopped . . . no no . . . don't say it . . . Beauty mustn't know . . . Beauty couldn't understand . . . are you going to lie down too Beauty . . . the light went out expanding . . . contracting . . . he felt the bed sink as Beauty lay beside him . . . his lips were dry . . . hot . . . the palms of his hands so moist and cool . . . Alex partly closed his eyes . . . from beneath his lashes he could see Beauty's face over his . . . nearer . . . nearer . . . Beauty's hair touched his forehead now . . . he could feel his breath on his nostrils and lips . . . Beauty's breath came short . . . breathe normally Beauty . . . breathe normally . . . Beauty's lips touched his . . . pressed hard . . . cool . . . opened slightly . . . Alex opened his eyes . . . into Beauty's

. . . parted his lips . . . Dulce . . . Beauty's breath was hot and short . . . Alex ran his hand through Beauty's hair . . . Beauty's lips pressed hard against his teeth . . . Alex trembled . . . could feel Beauty's body . . . close against his . . . hot . . . tense . . . white . . . and soft . . . soft . . . soft . . . .

~

they were at Forno's . . . everyone came to Forno's once . . . maybe only once . . . but they came . . . see that big fat woman Beauty . . . Alex pointed to an overly stout and bejeweled lady making her way through the maze of chairs . . . that's Maria Guerrero . . . Beauty looked to see a lady guiding almost the whole opera company to an immense table . . . really Dulce . . . for one who appreciates beauty you do use the most abominable English . . . Alex lit a cigarette . . . and that florid man with white hair . . . that's Carl . . . Beauty smiled . . . The Blind Bow Boy . . . he asked . . . Alex wondered . . . everything seemed so . . . so just the same . . . here they were laughing and joking about people . . . there's Rene . . . Rene this is my friend Adrian . . . after that night . . . and he felt so unembarrassed . . . Rene and Adrian were talking . . . there was Lucrecia Bori . . . she was bowing at their table . . . oh her cousin was with them and Peggy Joyce . . . everyone came to Forno's . . . Alex looked toward the door . . . there was Melva . . . Alex beckoned . . . Melva this is Adrian . . . Beauty held her hand . . . they talked . . . smoked . . . Alex loved Melva . . . in Forno's . . . everyone came there sooner or later . . . maybe only once . . . but . . . .
. . . .
      but . . . up . . . up . . . slow . . . jerk up . . . up . . . not fast . . . not glorious . . . but slow up . . . up into the sun . . . slow . . . sure like fate . . . poised on the brim . . . the brim of life . . . two shining rails straight down . . . Melva's head was on his shoulder . . . his arm was around her . . . poised . . . down . . . gasping straight down . . . straight like sin . . . down . . . the curving shiny rail rushed up to meet them . . . hit the bottom then . . . shoot up . . . fast . . . glorious . . . up into the sun . . . Melva gasped . . . Alex's arm tightened . . . all goes up . . . then down . . . straight like hell . . . all breath squeezed out of them . . . Melva's head on his shoulder . . . up . . . up . . . Alex kissed her . . . down . . . they stepped out of the car . . . walking music . . . now over to the Ferris Wheel . . . out and up . . . Melva's hand was soft in his . . . out and up . . . over mortals . . . mortals drinking nectar . . . five cents a glass . . . her cheek was soft on his . . . up . . . up . . . till the world seemed small . . . tiny . . . the ocean seemed tiny and blue . . . up . . . up and out . . . over the sun . . . the tiny red sun . . . Alex kissed her . . . up . . . up . . . their tongues touched . . . up . . . seventh heaven . . . the sea had swallowed the sun . . . up and out . . . her breath was perfumed . . . Alex kissed her . . . drift down . . . soft . . . soft . . . the sun had left the sky flushed . . . drift down . . . soft down . . . back to earth . . . visit the mortals sipping nectar at five cents a glass . . . Melva's lips brushed his . . . then out among the mortals . . . and the sun had left a flush on Melva's cheeks . . . they walked hand in hand . . . and the moon came out . . . they walked in silence on the silver strip . . . and the sea sang for them . . . they walked toward the moon . . . we'll hang our hats on the crook of the moon Melva . . . softly on the silver strip . . . his hands molded her features and her cheeks were soft and warm to his touch

. . . where is Adrian . . . Alex . . . Melva trod silver . . . Alex trod sand . . . Alex trod sand . . . the sea *sang* for her . . . Beauty . . . her hand felt cold in his . . . Beauty . . . the sea *dinned* . . . Beauty . . . he led the way to the train . . . and the train dinned . . . Beauty . . . dinned . . . dinned . . . her cheek *had* been soft . . . Beauty . . . Beauty . . . her breath *had* been perfumed . . . Beauty . . . Beauty . . . the sands *had* been silver . . . Beauty . . . Beauty . . . they left the train . . . Melva walked music . . . Melva said . . . don't make me blush again . . . and kissed him . . . Alex stood on the steps after she left him . . . and the night was black . . . down long streets to . . . Alex lit a cigarette . . . and his heels clicked . . . Beauty . . . Melva . . . Beauty . . . Melva . . . and the smoke made the night blue . . . Melva had said . . . don't make me blush again . . . and kissed him . . . and the street had been blue . . . one *can* love two at the same time . . . Melva had kissed him . . . one *can* . . . and the street had been blue . . . one *can* . . . and the room was clouded with blue smoke . . . drifting vapors of smoke and thoughts . . . Beauty's hair was so black . . . and soft . . . blue smoke from an ivory holder . . . was that why he loved Beauty . . . one *can* . . . or because his body was beautiful . . . and white and warm . . . or because his eyes . . . one *can* love

~

CHRISTI CASSIDY
Opening Pandora's Box (2004)

First published in 1984, On Our Backs *is the only nationally distributed pornographic magazine designed by and for lesbians. Debi Sundahl and Nan Kinney, the initial publishers, were frustrated by the pervasive antipornography stances of most lesbian and feminist organizations at the time and wanted a magazine to address the dearth of lesbian erotica.* On Our Backs *has consistently published underrepresented images of lesbian sex and sexuality. This article is the twentieth-anniversary editorial.*

It was 30 degrees below zero with nasty winds blowing and four-foot drifts of snow around the cabin where Nan Kinney and Debi Sundahl were living in the winter of 1982. They had a wood stove for heat. Lovers of three years, they had come to the icy climes of northern Minnesota to explore their spirituality, and ended up discovering their sexuality—and aspects of it much deeper and more obscure than just their desire for women. What they learned, and what happened next, would (in Deb's words) "turn the lesbian nation on its ear."

In the midst of the virulent anti-sex, anti-porn atmosphere of the lesbian community at the time, Nan and Debi were desperate for images of women together. Real lesbians. Having real sex. And where were images of the butch-femme couples who echoed their own relationship? They had experimented with SM but found no pictures of women engaged in power play, either.

So they hatched a plan. They would move to San Francisco, where Samois (a lesbian SM group) was located. "The only books we could find in Minneapolis were *Coming to Power* by the Samois Collective and *Sapphistry* by [Samois member] Pat Califia," Deb recalls. Clearly, a pilgrimage to Babylon by the Bay was their destiny.

San Francisco was and still is one of the most tolerant cities in the U.S., so they packed their bags and drove west in a drive-away Park Avenue Buick stuffed to the gills with suitcases they hauled onto the train after dropping the car off in tiny Walnut Creek.

"Everybody went to the Samois meetings, everybody who was at all interested in sex. The butch-femme couples too, not just leather," Nan says. They immediately became friends with Pat Califia and Gayle Rubin and started helping with the Samois newsletter.

"There was no defining moment," Deb says. "*On Our Backs* was evolutionary, grown organically. We were working for Samois and knew we wanted to have our own business. We wanted to build something."

"We were mad that the politically correct dykes were controlling the lesbian media," Nan says.

"It was flannel shirts and jeans, all very asexual," Deb puts in. "Butch-femme had a history—we had read Joan Nestle's article about the history of 1950s butch-femme—and we wanted to show that. We were lesbians and we liked sex. It was a lesbian sex magazine. We put the word *lesbian* right on the cover of the first issue."

"But we knew from Samois it was a political statement to make a magazine," Nan says. "We were in the right time and place, and we were the right age to just do it."

After Samois went defunct, Nan and Deb set up shop in a flat in the Mission District with Myrna Elana, a friend from Samois who would edit the first issue of what became *On Our Backs,* "entertainment for the adventurous lesbian."

It was a struggle. Tireless networking and working to save money for the first issue led them to stage two lesbian-only strip shows at a club called the Baybrick Inn to finance the first issue. The Tuesday night strip shows, called "BurLEZK," continued for three years. Meanwhile, Debi continued working as a stripper first at the Lusty Lady, and then at the Mitchell Brothers, where she met Nina Hartley ("long before she was a famous porn star!" Deb laughs). Nan ploughed a jackhammer day after day on the streets of San Francisco for PG&E.

But by June 1984 their dream had become a reality. With a print run of 2,000 they sold the first issue of *On Our Backs* at the Gay Pride fair and made enough money to pay the printer. "And without the Mac and desktop publishing, we never would have been able to put out another issue of the magazine," Nan adds.

Susie Bright, *On Our Backs'* well-known and canny editor from 1984 until 1991, contributed to that groundbreaking first issue, and became editor beginning with the second issue. At the time the only employee of Good Vibrations, Bright wrote the personal advice column "Toys for Us," which morphed into her popular Q&A and became the basis for *Susie Sexpert's Lesbian Sex World.*

"'Lesbian sex! Right here,'" says Deborah. "We were calling it out from the booth at Gay Pride twenty years ago."

Nan and Deb sold 500 copies at Gay Pride. They lugged 1,500 copies back to the flat and wondered how they were going to sell them. "We inherited the Samois list, and we got a list of all the feminist bookstores," says Deb. But they soon ran into anti-pornography policies among the booksellers. "Only five percent took it. Oscar Wilde in New York, the gay men's leather stores took it, but Amazon in Minneapolis? No, they were one of the last holdouts." It wasn't until the magazine started selling back issues over the next years that they sold the remaining 1,000 copies of that first issue. By 1989, a full 95 percent of all the feminist and gay bookstores carried the magazine.

Just this year, a "very good" copy of that first issue of *On Our Backs* sold on eBay for $80.00.

At the time, reactions were intense and polarized. "A magazine for adventurous lesbians is just what we need. I enjoyed the stories so much it prompted me to take hand to clit and relieve the tension," wrote one reader from Philadelphia. But a Washington, D.C., reader disagreed: "For years we as lesbian-feminists have been fighting male pornography. . . . It shocks and abhors me to find that women have stooped to the same methods of selling." Overall, though, the response was positive, as in this response from a reader in Pacific Grove, CA: "Just what I've been waiting for! Thought I was the only dyke in the whole world who loves erotica!"

The writer Jewelle Gomez says now, "*On Our Backs* was just what lesbian feminism needed and at just the right time. Lesbian feminists still need sex to keep us from being too self-righteous and too dry—figuratively and literally!"

Blatantly flaunting its sense of humor, a trait sorely lacking in many feminist publications of the time, *On Our Backs'* name itself, coined by Gayle Rubin, was a lampoon of the fiercely anti-porn feminist newspaper *off our backs*. As Maria Elena Buszek wrote in *Of Varga Girls and Riot Grrls: The Varga Girl and WWII in the Pin-up's Feminist History,* "With contributing writers such as Susie Bright and Joan Nestle, and photographers like Tee Corinne and Honey Lee Cottrell, *On Our Backs* hilariously subverted *Playboy's* concept of a 'pleasure primer for masculine tastes' to live up to its slogan, 'Entertainment for the adventurous lesbian.'" Also contributing to the first few issues were Gomez, Bright, Jill Posner, Califia, Morgan Gwenwald, Dorothy Allison, Lee Lynch, Phyllis Christopher, and Linda Smukler. To any student of lesbian culture, these names still resonate.

In addition, *On Our Backs* paid its contributors, which even the more open literary magazines could not always do. "Nobody else paid, but we always did," says Deborah, who now runs Isis Media, which produces erotic and educational material on female ejaculation. "We might have been late sometimes, but lesbians' work was valuable, and we wanted to acknowledge that."

Eventually they were able to pay a full staff, including health insurance, and support themselves, with help from the lucrative videos they were making under the name Fatale Video, the magazine, and a mail-order business they'd set up to sell dildos, sex toys, and other goodies that would appeal to their readers. (Full disclosure: I work with Nan on Fatale Media, and Nan is my lover.)

There were rocky times, but ultimately, Nan says, "We really had the staying power because of the people behind it," including Bright, Posner, Christopher, editors Shar Rednour and Marcy Sheiner, and art director Robin Simmons.

"At meetings we'd ask ourselves, how's it look, is it still forward-reaching enough, creative enough? Are we still pushing the envelope, are we using all our creative juices enough to make something cool?" Deb adds after a moment, "It was classy, not sleazy."

"I feel happy, blessed really, to have met all the people I met through *On Our Backs*. This whole crowd of wild, radical lesbians, this whole group of daring women willing to put themselves out there," Nan says without hesitation. "If I hadn't done *On Our Backs*, I wouldn't have had this level of comfort in my own sexuality."

"Your butch identity was totally validated," Deb interjects. "Nan was the first woman in San Francisco to wear a suit—a real suit and tie—every week to the strip club. Femmes, it'd make 'em wet. Butches got with the program when they saw how excited their femmes were!"

"That's what I mean. I thought, 'Oh, phew, there are other women like me.' The whole panorama of how women can be sexual . . . I didn't realize what a huge Pandora's box we were opening."

MICHAEL CALLEN

Mike Goes to the Baths (1984)

This piece chronicles gay male bathhouse sex in the early years of the AIDS epidemic. In the early and mid-1980s, while Ronald Reagan was president, public health officials frequently clashed with gay men over the role bathhouses should or should not play in queer sexual life. To public health administrators and some gay men like Mike, they spread disease and destroyed gay community. To others, gay bathhouses were the only space where gay men could be free of the watchful eye of heterosexual society. These early "sex wars," about whether gay men should maintain sexual freedom, albeit in the new confines of safer sex rules, or should start to establish more monogamous, coupled sexual relations, dovetailed with lesbian sex war debates about sadomasochism and pornography as violence against women.

I cannot actually remember the last time I went to the baths in New York City before I was officially diagnosed with AIDS in the summer of 1982. I am certain, however, that the last bathhouse I attended was the St. Marks Baths; but what I did and how I felt about it and what diseases I gave or got, I can't recall. My last visit to this institution, which played such a significant role in my life, must have occurred sometime between December 1981 (when I was first diagnosed as being severely immunosuppressed) and say, March 1982.

Impressions:

Club Baths located next to Ortiz Funeral Home: how convenient. Like Sweeney Todd's recycling center.

Entered. $17.50 ($10 to renew membership; $7.50 for a locker). Monday nite, 7:30 to 9:30. Twenty people. About eight blacks, five Hispanics, two Asians, and five whites.

There is a bulletin board. No risk reduction information. Glass display case: aspirin, vitamins (HIM . . . for the sexually active male . . .); Ramses; petroleum-based lubricant (to dissolve condoms?); poppers; cock rings, etc. Suggestion box.

In fairness, except for man in sling being momentarily fisted, I saw no unsafe sex. But everyone who was in a room was lying on his stomach; I saw no takers. [No] sex going on. Masturbation in porno room.

I toured the place hoping to find some info. None. I showered; I sat in jacuzzi; checked out steam room. Labyrinthine. I spoke to a black man in a room on the third floor—in the room where I first got fucked, by a man named Caleb, on a trip to NYC from Boston. Historic. Weird feelings that this was where it had all begun for me—getting fucked, that is.

The black man I spoke with was nice. Seemed about 40–45. He asked if I wanted to smoke a joint. I said no. I asked him if he lived in Manhattan. He said he lived by Geo. Washington Bridge. I said, is that 59th street? He chuckled. 168th Street. He works for Columbia Presbyterian Hospital.

I sighed real deep. He asked what was the matter. I said, "I feel weird. I hadn't been to the baths in two and a half years." It was weird to be back. I blurted out: "Aren't you worried about AIDS?" He said, "no." I asked him, "why not?" He said he could tell who was dangerous and who wasn't. How? He said he could just tell: they looked tired, like they'd been into weird shit, fisting, drugs. He said he was selective. I asked him if he was limiting what he would do. He said, no, he still did all the things he always had. He said he hadn't been to the baths in a long time either, but he just somehow felt safe; he said he could tell who was sick and he was selective. I felt weird about the irony. I wanted to blurt out: Can you tell about me? Do I look like someone with AIDS? I didn't for a couple of reasons: I wanted to find out more . . . what he knew of AIDS and where he'd heard about it. I asked him if he read a lot about AIDS. He groaned and said, yeah, too much. But he's stopped reading. It was too much. I asked him if he attended any GMHC forums. He said, no, but he'd attended one at Columbia Presbyterian which was "pretty comprehensive." There was silence.

I told him I was gonna go and to take care. He got up to leave also and said that it was o.k. He told me to relax; he said I really wanted to be here or I wouldn't be here and that all I needed to do was relax. He said I could come back to see him later if I wanted to. He was very nice.

I made more rounds.

[Another man] cruised me. Finally, I spoke to him in his room. I sighed. He said "what's the matter?" I said, "aren't you worried about AIDS?" He got frightened and pulled back. He said, "My English not so good. You got AIDS or something?" I said no (I made a quick decision; I thought if I said yes, he would totally freak out; he seemed very nervous). I said that I knew there were people with AIDS who were going to the baths and that some of them only had safe sex but others probably had unsafe sex. I'm not sure he understood much of what I was saying. I asked him where he was from. He said Israel. I asked him if they had bathhouses like this in Israel. He relaxed and laughed and said "No." We talked about Israel and the [gay] movie from Israel I had seen (he hadn't seen it or heard of it—I couldn't remember the name). Finally, after silence, I said "Take care; see you around."

I was totally demoralized. I thought of my conversations with Dennis Altman. It really is a race/class issue. It is no accident that most of the people here were blacks and Hispanics.

I thought about the importance of having the pamphlets and poster translated into Spanish.

I made one last round and discovered that in the orgy room, it was very dark and a fat man was in the stirrups being briefly fisted. Others started to come in to watch. The man fisting stopped. Others milled and malingered. One man dropped to his knees to suck another, but was pushed away. I left.

As I was checking out, I decided to ask the cashier if they had GMHC's new safe sex pamphlet. He looked at me funny and said "Why?" I said I was just interested, that's all. He sighed and started pulling out drawers, moving boxes, looking for the brochures. Finally, he found one and handed it to me, took my key and towel and I left.

I felt really weird about going. In the first place, I hated giving the $17.50 to these death factories. I thought, Jack Campbell was on the board of NGLTF! Some political consciousness. I thought, the Club is where most out of towners—those who most need the information—are likely to come because CBC advertises so heavily. I thought, even if they don't have the Safer Sex Committee Poster, GMHC has been saying that they've had the Physicians for Human Rights poster up in bathhouses for several months. Bullshit.

I thought finally about Roger Enlow's refusal to require bathhouse owners to display the posters and brochures. He's wrong, that's all. What to do? Do I go to the straight press and blow the lid off? What is my goal?

Review: I have spoken wherever possible about the dangers of promiscuity in NYC. I took my own income tax return and published *How to Have Sex in an Epidemic*. GMHC refused to distribute it. The state of New York refused to distribute it. I attended the first secret bathhouse meeting over a year ago. I am on the Interagency Task Force and have emphasized the need for appropriate education. I am on the Bathhouse Subcommittee of the Institute's advisory panel: should I ask for reimbursement of the $17.50?

The question is not whether or not to close; the question is how they'll be closed!

Wednesday: The East Side Sauna

I had never been to the East Side Sauna, largely, I suppose, because of its name. I had a West Villager's chauvinistic disdain for anything even vaguely upper "east side." I had lived for close to a year on 3rd Avenue and 77th and had been quite miserable. Looking back I can now see that I was unhappy during that period because I was constantly sick and desperately lonely, but at the time, it was easier to blame my malaise on geography.

Taking the E train up to 53rd street, I tried to distract myself from the pressing question of motivation by reading Gore Vidal's *Lincoln*. Still, I wondered uncomfortably, why are you going to the baths? I can only speculate and try to draw the confusion which prompted me to tour the ruins of my health and youth. First, let me confess that there was indeed an erotic component. Although I was as positive as any weak-willed human can be that I was not going to engage in any sexual activity that involved the exchange of bodily fluids (how clinical!), I was on the one hand eager to have at least some sexual response; it has been so long since I've felt anything approximating genital sexual desire. But on the other hand, I have been publicly asking those who still go to the baths a question I now asked myself: how is it possible to have any healthy sexual response in a setting in which you know—or reasonably believe—others around you are engaging in acts that are killing them? In his inimitable style, Richard B. compared a gay man going to the baths for unsafe sex in New York in 1984 to a Jew who returned to Auschwitz to masturbate. In my apocalyptic railings against bathhouses in recent months I had been equally reductive: bathhouses are little more than death houses; to enter a bathhouse in 1984 is suicidal and arguably homicidal. So, I wanted to have some sexual response but I was, at the same time, horrified that I might. What would it all mean? [. . .]

We announced in "We Know Who We Are" that "The party that was the '70s is over." Walking the halls of this bathhouse, I was more than ever convinced that this is true. The point missed by many formulating "safer sex" guidelines—and I include myself in this criticism—is that what a subset of us eroticized in the '70s was spontaneity and abandon. In addition to the 1,000 or so gay men who've made the ultimate sacrifice as soldiers in the sexual revolution, we have lost a way of life. The equation has changed, but we have not—the settings have not. A demoralization and anguish of untold proportions hung in the silence of the halls at the East Side Sauna. The image that struck me was one of little boys lost—each wandering around aimlessly, looking for mommy or daddy, holding on to his penis for what small comfort might be left in this hostile, frightening world. Each seemed utterly selfish in his despair: two men approaching one another in a hallway would, in an instant, search the face of the other for some sign that contact, comfort was possible and not finding it, would pass without a word on to the next candidate. The eyes seem to beg: is it you? Are you the one who will love me?

Perhaps I project. But perhaps not. The expressions haunted me. I had seen them—or expressions quite like them—somewhere before. It was only later that I remembered where: in the endless *Life* magazine photos of children of war. The look is one of innocence incongruously overlaid with a profoundly adult sense of loss—the loss of a culture, a way of life. [. . .]

The East Side Sauna is '70s high tech—which means grey industrial carpet covering platforms and walls, tasteful indirect (is indirection the hallmark of gay style?) lighting and the artful use of mirrors. All bathhouses are labyrinthine and the image of experimental rats running a maze for some imagined reward only to receive an electric shock for a wrong turn would not be inappropriate.

Since there was no price difference between a locker and a room purchased for 4 hours (as opposed to 8), I purchased a room. Or rather a cubicle. 6 x 5, plywood walls (painted grey, of course), and the ubiquitous dimmer. I went from 7:30 to 9:30 and the place was packed. At certain bathhouses, you can get some sense of how crowded it is by counting the number of key holders that have keys hanging from them (representing empty rooms) versus the number that have signature cards with check-out time noted on them (representing rented rooms). I counted fifteen across times six rows, with some miscellaneous key holders, for a total of approximately 100 available rooms (this excluded lockers). Of this, I would estimate that 60–65 were occupied. In short, the place was packed. After undressing, I headed for the "wet area"—which, compared to the facilities at other bathhouses, is a pathetic shower area approximately 8 x 8', a steam room (without much steam, of course) and a dry sauna (without much heat) and a toilet where water drips on you from the ceiling. (A towel on the floor is supposed to soak up the dripping water, but instead is squishy and gross with urine.)

I showered (two of the six showers didn't work—tradition must, after all, be upheld). I entered the steam room and chatted with a man who must have been 50. He seemed like a businessman. He was wearing his glasses in the shower. I told him that I had never been here before. I asked if this was unusually crowded. He said, no, that actually I had missed the peak crowd. The best time to come, he instructed me, was between 4:30 and 7:30 when the businessmen come in before going home.

I asked him if he was afraid of AIDS. He said, "yeah, everyone is." I asked him if he had changed at all as a result. He said, he makes his partners wear condoms. They don't always like it but he insists. He also said he has cut down on the number. He was very friendly.

When I left the shower, this Asian man (drunk?) came up and started fondling my penis. I pushed his hand away and said "No thank you." He persisted. I was more forceful: I said, "no thank you." He persisted. I pushed his hand away again and said "I said, stop!" He looked at me and smiled and then said "your dick was too small anyway." And turned and left. I thought, here is the paradox: One second, you are trying to have intimate relations with a stranger and the next second you are insulting him. How gross! Women, of course, endure this kind of shit all the time when they tell men who are whistling and clucking and making suggestive remarks to fuck off. The men immediately say: "Dyke. You were too ugly anyway. I wouldn't fuck you if you were the last goddamn . . ."

I recalled from the secret bathhouse meeting that the managers of the East Side Sauna had seemed particularly eager for any risk reduction information. They had asked for a copy of "How to Have Sex in an Epidemic." And so I was surprised not to find any AIDS materials. In the TV room there was a Greater Gotham Business Council brochure and the hepatitis B brochure. On a bulletin board just outside this room there were various community announcements (an ad for tickets to an Alvin Ailey concert, the gay Front Runners, etc.) but nothing about AIDS. I found out subsequently that the East Side Sauna had not been given the materials but still, they could have/should have had the GMHC NYPHR posters, which GMHC has been claiming have been available for three months.

The only "unsafe" sex I saw was one man fucking another without condoms in a room with the door open. I heard grunts coming from behind the doors to two other rooms and I saw two men embracing in the hallway and then disappear into a room, but on the whole, I would have to acknowledge that there has been a significant change in behavior, judging from what I remembered about bathhouses from the past.

~

DOSSIE EASTON AND CATHERINE A. LISZT
Paradigms Old and New (1998)

Well-known Bay Area sex radicals Dossie Easton and Catherine Liszt advocate sexual practices and perspectives that contrast with the mainstream gay community's emphasis on monogamy and marriage rights. In this excerpt from The Ethical Slut: A Guide to Infinite Sexual Possibilities, *Easton and Liszt explain their philosophy of sexuality, counter some well-worn myths about sluthood, and provide a comprehensive overview and guide to polyamory, which is also known as consensual nonmonogamy.*

We're sure you don't need us to tell you that the world does not, for the most part, honor sluthood, or think well of those who are sexually explorative. In this chapter we'll discuss some of the ideas and assumptions that have helped make so many sluts feel bad about themselves. While you read them, you might like to think about what all these judgments about sluts tell us about our culture.

"PROMISCUOUS"

This means we enjoy too many sexual partners. This word alone has possibly created more unhappy sluts than any other. (We've also been called "indiscriminate" in our sexuality, which we resent: we can always tell our lovers apart.)

We do not believe that there is such a thing as too much sex, except perhaps on certain happy occasions when our options exceed our abilities, nor do we believe that the ethics we are talking about here have anything to do with moderation or abstinence. Kinsey once defined a "nymphomaniac" as "someone who has more sex than you."

Is having less sex somehow more virtuous than having more? We think not. We measure the ethics of a good slut not by the number of his partners, but by the respect and care with which he treats them.

"AMORAL"

Our culture also tells us that sluts are evil, uncaring, amoral and destructive—Jezebel, Casanova, Don Juan. Watch out! The mythological evil slut is grasping and manipulative, seeking to steal something—virtue, money, self-esteem—from his partners. In some ways, this archetype is based on the idea that sex is a commodity, a coin you trade for something else—stability, children, a wedding ring—and that any other transaction constitutes being cheated and betrayed. (Once when Dossie was recovering from a botched abortion a friendly nurse tried to comfort her by saying, "I know, honey, they all promise to marry you." Dossie managed to keep a straight face—the nurse was friendly and supportive, and it seemed cruel to inform her that she wouldn't have dreamed of marrying the unethical slut who by this time was conspicuous only by his cowardly absence.)

We have rarely observed any Jezebels or Casanovas in our community, but perhaps it is not very satisfying for a thief to steal what is freely given. We do not worry about being robbed of our sexual value by the people we share pleasure with.

"SINFUL"

Some people base their sense of ethics on what God, or their church, or their parents, or their culture, considers okay or not okay. They believe that being good consists of obedience to laws set down by a power greater than themselves. Dossie remembers explaining to some family friends that she had left the church she was raised in because she didn't believe a just God would punish her aunt for getting a (much justified) divorce. The family friends were pretty conservative people, and of an older generation. One of them asked, "Well, if you don't believe God will punish you, why don't you just go around murdering people?" Dossie explained that she doesn't murder people because her internal sense of ethics, her empathy with others, and her desire to feel good about herself all tell her that to harm another person would be a terrible thing for her to do.

To believe that God doesn't like sex is like believing that God doesn't like you: we all wind up carrying a secret shame for our own perfectly natural sexual desires and fulfillments. We prefer the beliefs of a woman we met who is a devoted churchgoer. She told us that when she was about five years old, she discovered the joys of masturbation in the back seat of the family car, tucked under a warm blanket on a long trip. It felt so wonderful that she concluded that the existence of her clitoris was proof positive that God loved her. . . .

"ADDICTED"

More recently we hear about sex addicts and avoidance of intimacy. Sex addiction is usually defined as the substitution of sex for nourishment of other needs, like to allay anxiety or bolster sagging self-esteem. Such people may have compulsive needs to "score," to succeed sexually with a large number of partners, or to get validation for their sexual attractiveness over and over, as if they need constant reassurance because at the core they do not see themselves as attractive and lovable.

Sex can be misused as a substitute for connection, emotional relationship or a solid sense of internal security based on knowing your own worth. Some sexual abuse survivors become what is called "sexualized" in a childhood where the closest approximation to adult attention, validation and affection they had was molestation. Such survivors may need to expand their options and learn other ways to get their needs met. On the other hand, "sex addict" seems to be the latest incarnation of cultural judgment about sluts: a good friend of Catherine's once told her, quite seriously, that the reason Catherine was so contented was that she was a sex addict who had managed to find a way to make a lifestyle out of her addiction.

If you are working on any of these issues, we suggest that you put some thought into how you would like your sexuality to be different in the future. Some twelve-step groups and therapists may try to tell you that anything but the most conservative of sexual behaviors is wrong, or unhealthy, or "into your addiction"; we encourage you to trust your own beliefs and find yourself a more supportive environment. If your goal is monogamy, that's fine, and if your goal is to stop seeking sex in the place of friendship, or any other behavior pattern that you wish to re-sculpt, that's fine too. We do not believe that successfully recovering sex addicts have to be monogamous unless they want to be.

"EASY"

Is there, we wonder, some virtue in being difficult?

MYTHS ABOUT SLUTS

One of the challenges facing the ethical slut is our culture's insistence that, simply because "everybody knows" something, it must inevitably be true. A lot of these cultural paradigms have become almost invisible; people take them as much for granted as the air they breathe or the ground they walk on. Questioning what "everybody knows" is sometimes difficult and disorienting, but we have found it to be rewarding—questioning is the first step toward creating a new paradigm, one that may fit you better.

We urge you to regard with great skepticism any sentence that begins "Everybody knows that . . ." or "Common sense tells us that . . ." or "It's common knowledge that . . ." Often, these phrases are signposts for cultural belief systems which may be antisexual, monogamy-centrist and/or codependent.

Cultural belief systems can be very deeply rooted in literature, law and archetype, which means that shaking them from your own personal ethos can be difficult. But the first step in exploring them is, of course, recognizing them.

Here, then, are some of the pervasive myths that we have heard all our lives, and have come to understand are most often untrue and destructive to our relationships and our lives.

Myth 1: Long-term monogamous relationships are the only real *relationships.*
Lifetime monogamy as an ideal is a relatively new concept in human history, and makes us unique among primates. There is nothing that can be achieved within a long-term monogamous relationship that cannot be achieved without one—business partnership, deep romantic attachment, stable parenting, personal growth, and care and companionship during the aging process are all well within the abilities of the slut.

People who believe this myth may feel that something is wrong with them if they aren't in a committed twosome—if they prefer to remain "free agents," if they discover themselves loving more than one person at a time, if they have tried one or more traditional relationships that didn't work out. Instead of questioning the myth, they question themselves. Such people often have a very romantic view of couplehood—that Mr. or Ms. Right will automatically solve all their problems, fill all the gaps, make their lives complete.

One friend of ours points out that if something goes wrong in a monogamous marriage, nobody takes that as evidence against the practicality of monogamy—but if something goes awry in an open relationship, many folks instantly take that as proof that nonmonogamy doesn't work.

A subset of this myth is the belief that if you're really in love, you will automatically lose all interest in others, and thus, if you're having sexual or romantic feelings toward anyone but your partner, you're not really in love. This myth has cost many people a great deal of happiness through the centuries, yet is untrue to the point of absurdity; a ring around the finger does not cause a nerve block to the genitals. Even happily monogamous couples recognize the realities of outside sexual and romantic desire: if Jimmy Carter could lust in his heart, so can you.

Myth 2: Sexual desire is a destructive force.
This one goes all the way back to the Garden of Eden, and leads to a lot of crazy-making double standards. In this worldview, men are hopelessly sexually voracious and predatory, and women are supposed to control and civilize them by being pure, asexual and withholding. Thus the openly sexual woman destroys civilization.

Many people also believe that unashamed sexual desire, particularly desire for many people, destroys the family—yet we suspect that far more families have been destroyed by bitter divorces over adultery than have ever been disturbed by ethical consensual nonmonogamy.

Myth 3: Loving someone makes it OK to control his behavior.
This kind of territorial reasoning is designed, we guess, to make people feel secure—but we don't believe that anybody has the right, much less the obligation, to control the behavior of another functioning adult. Being treated according to this myth doesn't make us feel secure, it makes us feel furious. The old "awww, she's jealous—she must really care about me" reasoning, or the scene in which the girl falls in love with the boy when he punches out a rival suitor, is symptomatic of a very disturbed set of personal boundaries which can lead to a great deal of unhappiness.

This myth also leads to the belief, so often promulgated in Hollywood films and popular literature, that fucking someone else is something you do to your partner, not for yourself—and is, moreover, the very worst thing you can do to someone. (For many years, adultery was the only legally acceptable grounds for divorce, leaving those who had unfortunately married batterers or drunks in a very difficult position.) People who believe this often believe that nonmonogamy must be nonconsensual, in order to protect the sensibilities of the "betrayed" partner.

Myth 4: Jealousy is inevitable and impossible to overcome.
Jealousy is, without a doubt, a very common experience in our culture—so much so that a person who doesn't experience jealousy is looked at as a bit odd, or in denial. But the fact is that a situation which would cause intense jealousy for one person can be no big deal for another. Some people get jealous when their honey takes a sip out of someone else's Coke, others happily watch their beloved wave bye-bye for a month of amorous sporting with a friend at the far end of the country. Jealousy is common, but far from inevitable.

Some people also believe that jealousy is such a shattering emotion that they have no choice but to succumb to it. On the contrary, we have found that jealousy is an emotion like any other: it feels bad (sometimes very bad), but it is not intolerable; sometimes the best thing to do with jealousy is simply to allow yourself to feel it. We have also found that many of the thinking patterns which lead to jealousy can be unlearned, and that unlearning them is often a useful process. Later in this book, we will discuss jealousy in much greater detail.

Myth 5: Outside involvements reduce intimacy in the primary relationship and impede problem-solving.

Most marriage counselors are taught that when a member of an otherwise happily married couple has an "affair," this must be a symptom of unresolved conflict or unfulfilled needs that should be dealt with in the primary relationship. Sometimes this is true, and equally often it is not. The problem is that this myth leaves no room for the possibility of growthful and constructive open sexual lifestyles. It is cruel and insensitive to interpret an affair as a symptom of sickness in the relationship, as it leaves the "cheated-on" partner—who may already be feeling insecure—to wonder what is wrong with him. Meanwhile, the "cheating" partner gets told that she is only "acting out" to get back at her primary partner, and she really doesn't want, need or even like her lover.

Many people have sex outside their primary relationships for reasons that have nothing to do with any inadequacy in their partner or in the relationship. Perhaps this outside relationship allows a particular kind of intimacy that the primary partner doesn't even want, such as fetish behavior or particular sexual activities, and thus constitutes a resolution of an otherwise insoluble conflict. Or perhaps it meets other needs—such as a need for uncomplicated physical sex without the trappings of relationship, or for sex with someone of a gender other than one's partner's, or for sex at a time when it is otherwise not available (during travel or a partner's illness, for example). Or it may simply be a natural extension of an emotional and/or physical attraction to someone besides the primary partner.

An outside involvement does not in any way have to subtract from the intimacy you share with your partner unless you let it. And we sincerely hope you won't.

Myth 6: "Swept away by love."

Hollywood tells us that "love means never having to say you're sorry," and we, fools that we are, believe it. This myth has it that if you're really in love with someone, you never have to argue, disagree, communicate, negotiate or do any other kind of work. It also tells us that love means we automatically get turned on by our beloved, and that we never have to do anything to deliberately kindle passion. Those who believe this myth may find themselves feeling that their love has failed every time they need to schedule a discussion or to have a courteous (or not-so-courteous) disagreement. They may also believe that any sexual behavior that doesn't fit their criteria for "normal" sex—from fantasies to vibrators—is "artificial," and indicates that something is lacking in the quality of their love.

WHAT WE BELIEVE

So we just spent a whole section telling you about all the concepts and mythologies the world may believe about sluts. Now, we'll tell you our side of the story—the way we look at our lives and the lives of the people we know.

You Are Already Whole

Jane Austen wrote, "It is a truth universally acknowledged that a single man in possession of a good fortune must be in want of a wife." While we think Jane probably had her tongue firmly planted in her cheek, a great many people do believe that to be single is to be somehow incomplete, and that they need to find their "other half." A lot of the myths we mentioned in the previous section are based in that belief.

We believe, on the other hand, that the fundamental sexual unit is one person; adding more people to that unit may be intimate, fun and companionable but does not complete anybody. The only thing in this world that you can control is yourself—your own reactions, desires and behaviors. Thus, a fundamental step in ethical sluthood is to bring your locus of control into yourself—to recognize the difference between your "stuff" and other people's. When you do this, you become able to complete yourself. That's why we call this "integrity."

You may notice that the parts of this book are based in that idea: in Part I, we talk about the ideas and concepts you need to grasp within yourself; in Part II, we talk about interactions with other sluts; and in Part III, we discuss interactions with the world. (In Part IV, we cover the fun stuff that didn't fit in anywhere else.) Similarly, throughout the book, every time we introduce a new idea or concept, we will start by discussing how it works for the individual—you need to understand these concepts, and how they apply to you, before you can begin communicating your needs and ideas to the other people in your life. When you have built a satisfying relationship with yourself, then you have something of great worth to share with others.

Starvation Economies

Many people believe, explicitly or implicitly, that romantic love, intimacy and connection are finite capabilities of which there is never enough to go around, and that if you give some to one person, you must be taking some away from another.

We call this belief a "starvation economy"; we'll talk much more about it in Part II. Many of us learn to think this way in childhood, from parents who have little intimacy or attention for us, so we learn that there is only a limited amount of love in the world and we have to fight for whatever we get—often in cutthroat competition with our brothers and sisters.

People who operate from starvation economies can become very possessive about the people, things and ideas that matter to them. They are working from a paradigm that anything they get comes from a small pool of not-enough, and must thus be taken from someone else—and, similarly, that anything anyone else gets must be taken from them.

It is important to distinguish between starvation economies and real-world limits. Time, for example, is a real-world limit; even the most dedicated slut has only twenty-four hours every day. Love is not a real-world limit: the mother of nine children can love each of them as much as the mother of an only child.

Our belief is that the human capacity for sex and love and intimacy is far greater than most people think—possibly infinite—and that having a lot of satisfying connections simply makes it possible for you to have a lot more. Imagine what it would feel like to live in an abundance of sex and love, to feel that you had all of both that you could possibly want, free of any feelings of deprivation or neediness. Imagine how strong you would feel if you got to exercise your "love muscles" that much, and how much love you would have to give!

Openness Can Be the Solution, Not the Problem

Is sexual adventurousness simply a way to avoid intimacy? Not usually, in our experience.

While it is certainly possible to use your outside relationships in order to avoid problems or intimacy in your primary relationship, we do not agree that this pattern is inevitable or even common. Many people, in fact, find that their outside relationships can *increase* their intimacy with their primary partner by reducing the pressures on that relationship, and by giving them a safe place to express issues that may have them feeling "stuck" in the primary relationship.

These are our beliefs. You get to have beliefs of your own. What matters to us is not that you agree with us, but that you question the prevailing paradigm and decide for yourself what you believe. Thousands and thousands of ethical sluts are proving every day that the old "everybody knows" myths don't have to be true.

We encourage you to explore your own realities and create your own ethos— one that spurs you onward in your evolution, that supports you as you grow, and that reflects your pride and happiness in your newfound relationships.

∽

DWIGHT A. MCBRIDE
It's a White Man's World (2005)

Dwight McBride has written numerous books on race, culture, and literature. His book Black Like Us *was the first anthology to bring together the voices of queer African American writers in a single volume, thereby creating a canon for queer African American literature. The editors also dealt with both the exclusion of questions of race from queer literary studies and the heteronormativity of African American literary studies and culture. This chapter from his most autobiographical work again explores the intersections of race and sexuality. He coins the term "the gay marketplace of desire" to show that gay male desire is embedded in a racist marketplace that shapes U.S. culture.*

[A] cultural site that has fascinated me in my investigation of the gay marketplace of desire is that of gay male personal ads. Since the late 1980s to the present day, they made the incredible transition from phone-based ads and print ads to the electronic, online format. That transition was itself important in at least two sig-nal ways: the advent and use of photos in ads and the simplifying and privatizing of the placing of ads. That is, ad placing became less cumbersome and even more anonymous, which opened up the possibility of doing so to an entire group of men who might not have otherwise considered the prospect (including, among others, men on the so called "down low" or the DL, and men who identify as "bi-curi-ous"). With print ads, one had to commit far enough to the idea of placing an ad to at least complete the necessary paper work and post it to the newspaper or mag-azine where it was being placed, or call it in over the telephone (not a very appeal-ing prospect for the nervous anonymity seeker). With the advent of online ads, this not only further privatized the act of placing an ad, but also made the mechanics of it so simple that even those who may not be entirely committed to the idea of ad placing could experiment with the possibility without much difficulty. This both broadened the base of potential ad placers and increased the revenue flow in that industry, resulting in what is now a proliferation of Web sites where gay men can place and read such ads for a nominal fee.

Some Web sites have evolved to include the more sophisticated technology of chat rooms, where men can talk to potential dates, mates, hook-ups, or sex part-ners in real time. AOL (America Online) is the most likely household name in this regard among gay men. Daniel Mendelsohn provides an elaborate and somewhat illuminating discussion of AOL in this regard in his book *The Elusive Embrace: Desire and the Riddle of Identity.* Most sites these days also include pictures along with your self-styled profile that may be viewed by other users on the system. One of the sites with which I experimented, M4M4SEX (http://m4m4sex.com), not only breaks down its database so that you can search men by city, but also allows its users to place public and private pictures on the web. The public picture is the one that appears with your ad/profile and may be viewed by anyone who visits the site (the thumbnail public image is all you can see unless you are a member, in which case you can click onto the larger picture). The private image may only be viewed when a user on the system sends e-mail (filtered through the site so that no actual e-mail addresses have to be exchanged) to another user. At that point, the user may grant the person to whom he sends a message the right to view his pri-vate picture.

What should not go unremarked upon here are the complex levels of privacy that are clearly at work. Indeed, these sites are often constructed to maximally pro-tect the privacy of users' personal information: real names are rarely used as your user name, messages are exchanged through the system so no actual e-mail addresses have to be exchanged, and private images are usually able to be viewed only after being granted access to them. Each of these progressive privacy levels are easily exploitable by users, as one might well imagine, to protect their anonymity, to stave off those in whom they may not be interested, and to encourage those in whom they wish to express further interest. This extra sense of privacy, along with the fact that one is dealing only in virtual bodies and does not (except by choice and mutual agreement) have to face real bodies or real embodied persons, makes it far more possible than in a gay bar, for example, to get in touch with exactly what it is we want. And, under cover of anonymity, it becomes possible to be far clearer, more honest, and unapologetically (even if at times brutally) discriminating about what it is we want. Indeed, even the desires that most of us know enough about "political correctness" and gay propriety to realize we should have some shame around can be expressed with abandon online. The Internet freed us even from the PC shackles of the gay bar, a place where we no longer even need to patronize some and pretend to others about the often exclusive and predictably hegemonic nature of our desires on the one hand, or about the problematic fetishistic nature of them on the other. For some this might be liberating, a form of ultimate sexual liberation, perhaps. But is that equally so for all of us? . . .

Having said that, it remains to review a sampling of ads I collected just under two years ago from the M4M4SEX Web site. These ads are all from Chicago-based customers. No names are used, as is the case on the Web site. Each of the ads appeared on the site below a matching thumbnail photograph, which we of course cannot reproduce here. Just beneath each photograph (before the ad appears) is a coded user name. Each ad begins with a headline followed by the ad itself. I have added in brackets a brief description of the photos, the writing of which poses its own difficulties of visual assessment, which I do not address here. Let me state up front that I do not here take on the obvious references to bare backing and HIV brought up by these ads. Though related, I might argue, such a full discussion lies beyond the scope of this current project. There are many abbreviations used which are unique to this genre of gay online commerce. Where relevant, I translate them:

Chrischicago [close-cropped shot of a brown penis only]
Looking for hot oral and more . . .
Hey guys, I'm 30, mixed black & Scottish, 5'9, 175 lbs, masc., 7" cut. I'm in Chicago regularly, and looking to have some fun with hot white guys while I'm here. I love oral, body contact, nipple sucking, being rimmed, and fucking.

Edgewsxyguy [torso shot of a toned white body with perfect abs, cropped just above the lips and just below where trimmed pubic hairs begin]
Hot Euroguy looking . . .
29/5'11"/160/ slim—defined / abs / great shape / gdlkng and masculine, uncut: -) Looking for a hottie for safe play, possible LTR. Caucasians only, be D/D free and in shape, no fems pls . . .

Hotlover4you [handsome face (framed by short cropped hair) and toned pectorals of a smiling, square-jawed, handsome white man]
Hot stud for hot latinos
5'9, 165pnds,brn/brn,musc,tan,smooth. Looking for hot latin guys who love to fuck! very oral and mostly bottom. must be clean and safe.

> Looking to meet masculine gbm NOW. 36, 5-10" 160lbs, hot tight body, 8"
> mushroomhead dick, versatile sex pig with few limits, love trying new things, toys, ice
> cubes, ropes, etc. . . .

Taken together, these ads tell us a great deal about the gay marketplace of desire, what constitutes value in that marketplace, and who has access to making the "rational choice" of sex or love object in that same marketplace. These mores, clearly racialized as they are, also speak to the depth of American racism. There is no part of our lives, thinking, and experience that it does not reach.

In this world of personals where privacy and anonymity reign, black men pander to white fantasies about what white men want them to be (even to talking in black dialect); white men freely acknowledge without being condemned as hubristic that they are "very good-looking" ("VGL") since it is only an admission of the obvious logic of the marketplace of desire at work; white men apologize for not liking black guys ("sorry bois . . . not interested in black men") without the least thought of how offensive or racist such a gesture might be; indeed, it would seem that whiteness is the all-around salient variable that increases one's value in the gay marketplace of desire. A white man (in some cases, a "light-skinned latin man" may suffice—that is, if he is "clean and safe"), who is "very good-looking," with "a large penis," a "hot tight body," and a masculine affect ("no fems" allowed after all), represents the ideal type, the sexy and desirable man that we should all want in the personals world.

It should not surprise us, however, that this same type abounds in the world of corporate banking and finance as well. Though I cannot be certain about the question of penis size, I have always marveled at how white, "good-looking," tight-bodied, and testosterone-laden the men are who populate the business schools at UCLA where I was a graduate student and at Northwestern where I currently teach. And it did not surprise me when I recently recalled a line from the 1997 film *Boiler Room* (a latter-day remake of the older *Wall Street*—which is referenced in the film), when the recruiter for the firm, J. T. Marlin (played by Ben Affleck), says to his young recruits: "You will be a millionaire. . . . You are the future big swinging dicks of this firm. Now, you all look money-hungry and that's good. Anybody that tells you money is the root of all evil, doesn't fucking have any. They say money can't buy happiness; look at the fucking smile on my face: ear to ear, baby." Perhaps the thing that ties these two worlds together—these worlds in which power and value of one sort or another is amassed, sold, and consumed in a thoroughly well-ordered marketplace that unfairly advantages those who have capital of one sort or another over those who do not—is the parallel between the gift of capital and the gift of whiteness. Both define the rules of the marketplace in which we all must at some level circulate. Much like capital, whiteness is seldom something one earns, but is more often a matter of birth. As such, whiteness is a valuable commodity in a fundamentally racist culture. Its value is so compelling, so complete, that it reaches even to the most intimate parts of our lives as sexual, desiring, and loving subjects. So much is this the case that Funguylkvw (i.e., fun guy in Lakeview)—a "good-looking" white guy himself—provides in his ad a not so very implied critique of the market-place of desire recognizing its corruption. His ability to do so, however, to be able to stand above the system and critique it in the way that he does and to still full-well expect to have the "hot sex" to which he alludes in his ad, comes from his position as a good-looking white guy in the marketplace as well. The people in a position to make the "rational choice" according to the dominant racial logic fueling the gay marketplace of desire are also people who in their disavowal still benefit from it. In this way, the knowledge that makes it possible for Funguylkvw to disavow the working of the marketplace, as he does here, is the same logic that makes other white men in the marketplace apologize ("Sorry, built white guys only"), and still others congratulate black men . . . for being their first sexual encounter with blackness. These men make these gestures from privileged positions in the marketplace of desire. Indeed, the declaration of a black man in exercising his exclusive desire for other black men does not resonate with equal systemic weight in the gay marketplace of desire. How could it in a marketplace where the reign of the value of whiteness is so thoroughly established?

5

Where Are Our White Picket Fences?

QUEER RELATIONSHIPS AND FAMILIES IN AMERICA, NOW AND THEN

On September 1, 2002, the *New York Times*, the arbiter of moderate liberal U.S. politics and values, published the following announcement: "Daniel Andrew Gross and Steven Goldstein will affirm their partnership today in a civil union ceremony at the Shoe Acres Inn and Restaurant in North Hero, Vermont." Such mundane words launched a mini-revolution. It was the first time in the venerable newspaper's 150-year history that a same-sex couple had its social *and* sexual relationship publicly recognized and honored.

Was the public celebration of a same-sex relationship something new? Yes and no. Since the nineteenth century, upper-middle-class white women living together had their relationships recognized in the form of "Boston marriages." Historian Lilian Faderman has documented many very visible upper-middle-class female partnerships in the nineteenth- and early twentieth-century United States. But the sexual nature of such relationships was rarely acknowledged and most of these women remained officially "single" until they died. In a heterosexual world, if there was no man present, there was no formal relationship. From Boston marriages to *New York Times* same-sex commitment ceremony announcements, queer relationships have come a long way.

As for families with children, queers have always had children, since most queers lived in socially sanctioned marriages until the second half of the twentieth century. Until this time, queers had to lead double lives, by which we mean that queers performed "straight" roles in heterosexual relationships, marriages, and families while simultaneously participating in a second "queer world." For this reason, it would be odd for queers *not* to have had children, since they were indeed participating in heterosexual society. Some of the queers who visited public cruising

123

grounds in 1920s New York or who founded early gay rights organizations in the 1950s had children while married.

But since the 1970s and, for the first time in U.S. history, queers have not had to lead double lives and they are now able to bring their relationships and their queerness together to form new kinds of families. Judith Stacey, one of the foremost scholars of American families, argues that the queer family, as opposed to queers having children in a heterosexual family, is one of the most radical reconfigurations of the family in modern history. For the first time in history, queers now have their same-sex relationships and their radically reconfigured families recognized *socially* and *legally*.

The modern queer family was made possible by the advent of the civil rights movement, the sexual revolution, and transformations in all family forms, which made divorced, two-house, interracial, and single-parent families common. The 1960s saw both the invention of the birth control pill, which gave women more control over planning their families, and the end of antimiscegenation laws, which had prohibited interracial marriage in dozens of states around the country. The breakdown of the male-driven, upper-middle-class bourgeois family created space for new kinds of family to emerge. The children's documentary *That's a Family* suggests that the modern queer family is one of many new forms of family that has developed as a result of women working and divorcing, of grandparents gaining custody over children, of interracial families becoming legally acceptable, and of heterosexual couples choosing *not* to have children.

Queers can now build the kinds of families they want, in part due to the development of new reproductive technologies. For example, a single queer woman can go to a reproductive clinic, request sperm, inseminate herself, and have a child without the assistance of a man. Two women can do the same. In light of this reproductive revolution, it is no wonder that the 1980s were characterized by a "lesbian baby boom," a time when women in same-sex relationships could build families without the presence of a man.

Gay men wanting to parent were having different conversations than lesbians. Regardless of the technological revolution, reproductive technologies did not prove quite as liberating for queer men, who still lacked a womb. The baby boom and the possibility of gay fatherhood came to gay men much later, once adoption became a more realistic possibility and queers themselves began to see the family as something other than two parents and two kids. Some pursued coparenting, when more than two parents of both sexes and any sexual orientation intentionally come together to procreate and parent children. Others have chosen to adopt children, although adoption also takes myriad forms, such as sperm donation, when a man helps a lesbian couple have kids, or open adoption, when biological mothers maintain some connection to their biological children and adoptive parents. Still others adopt children from other countries or from U.S. foster care or private agencies. All of these new mechanisms have changed the meanings of family and allowed queers to envision their own families with children in new and revolutionary ways.

Dan Savage describes the making of his queer male family using the adoption system, which by definition requires gay men to engage with state politics and the law to build family. Other queer men have developed relationships with women in order to build new kinds of families with more than two parents. Now that queers can get legally married in some parts of the country and therefore gain the legal privileges of marriage, building queer families seems all that much easier.

So why the sudden desire for queers to have children? Is it merely the legal and biological possibility of having kids or is there something social and cultural going on in the United States that has made queer families not only possible but also desirable? In an age when queers can choose not to lead double lives, some queers can also choose to lead lives that resemble those of hetero-Americans. The opposite is also the case. Hetero-Americans can choose to cohabitate, lead single lives, or not have children. With the breakdown of the rules governing relationships and family making, families have become more a matter of choice than social obligation.

Some queers choose to have their own white picket fences, but the presence of children in queer communities has forced queers to reexamine what it means to be queer. With increasing queer visibility on the streets and on television, "queer" no longer seems to be as taboo as it once might have been. Queers now have the possibility to integrate into nonqueer space for the first time. Queers can build families for themselves, although doing so successfully often requires that they don't look too different from the families of their nonqueer counterparts.

Queers and their children have forced queer communities to respond to the needs of openly queer parents. The Michigan Womyn's Music Festival has reexamined its policies about public sex, since there are an increasing number of young children present at the festival. Some gay men with children no longer go to gay pride parades that celebrate (often quite publicly) queer sex and sexuality, and some queer institutions have changed their funding and programming priorities.

Some critics, like Suzanna Danuta Walters, decry the rise of marriage and family as a decline in the queerness of queers. For Walters and many others, the rise of the modern queer family simultaneously signals the decline of radical queer culture and, in some ways, of everything that marked queers as different. Others criticize the new emphasis on queer relationships and family because these are seen as social privileges for those who can assimilate into white upper-middle-class society. For working-class queers, queers of color, and transgender queers, the suburban two-child picket fence household is not a realistic possibility. In many quarters, queers are still afraid of being fired from their jobs, of being cut off from their families of birth, and of not being able to pay their bills on time or stay in their homes as the cost of living continues to rise. Some ask the question, "Is the rise of the modern queer family a white, middle-class phenomenon?" It is not a coincidence that our authors in this section are overwhelmingly white and upper-middle-class.

For others, the ability for queer families to participate openly in public schools, soccer leagues, and summer camps is a sign of increased power and demonstrates the way these institutions have been forced to change in response to the presence and demands of queer families. Whether it is assimilation and the loss of radical queerness or transformative integration and the rise of the new family, no one disagrees that in some social strata, queer relationships and queer families and their straight counterparts are starting to look more and more alike.

DAN SAVAGE

Younger Brother Dynamics (2000)

Dan Savage (1964–), humorist and writer, published his acclaimed book The Kid *about two gay men adopting a kid. Savage's irreverent humor and frank talk about complex social issues, which have been so widely popularized in his column, "Savage Love," come to the adoption process in this book.*

My boyfriend likes to listen to dance music when he drives. He likes to listen to dance music when he cooks, cleans, wakes, sleeps, reads, picks his nose, and screws. There isn't much he doesn't enjoy doing listening to dance music. I'll listen to dance music when I'm under recreational general anesthesia (that is, if I'm really high), or if I'm in a dance club somewhere, dancing. Since I don't get high or go to clubs often, I don't listen to dance music much. As for listening to dance music out of context—no drugs, no dance club, no *dancing*—well, frankly, I don't see the point.

But Terry was techno before techno was cool, and his attachment to dance music has been a rich source of conflict in our relationship. We've both made sacrifices on the bloody altar of coupledom: I no longer listen to the radio while I go to sleep, to give one piddling example, as he can't sleep with the radio on; he no longer goes clubbing all night long (if I couldn't have a radio in the bedroom, then, by God, his ass had better be in my bed to justify the sacrifice). But he's been having a hard time completely letting go of dance music because much of his pre-me social life revolved around it. After monogamy, dance music has been our single biggest "issue." Monogamy was a quickie fight, over and done with: he didn't want me sleeping around, and I didn't want to fight. Should a day come when I do put someone else's dick in my mouth, he won't dump me because: (a) I'd do all I could to make certain he never found out; and (b) if he did find out, well, he's promised to work through it.

We'd been together two years, so our fights had become highly ritualized ceremonies, and the dance-music-in-the-car fight was one we had down pat. We were in a car, driving to Portland, Oregon, and he was subjecting me to Iceland's pixie lunatic, Björk. 1 didn't think this was fair, as I don't like dance music, and when we were doing ninety on I-5, I couldn't escape.

The fight didn't begin at the start of the trip. They never do. I'm a conflict-avoidance champ, and if we fought at the beginning of every road trip I would, like a dog that associates a ride in the car with a trip to the vet, refuse to get in the car. Had I anticipated this fight, I would have insisted that we fly, or take the train, or ship ourselves UPS, or get to Portland on some form of transport that puts nice, reasonable people in charge of the music. But Terry was tricky, taking advantage of my memory problems. Before we got in the car, and for about the first forty-five minutes of any trip, Terry was on his best behavior. He lulled me into the car with false promises of books on tape, or conversation. Then, when we were too far from home to turn back, and going too fast for me to jump, he put on a CD he knew I'd object to—*chunk-ka tcha, chunk-ka tcha, chunk-ka tcha*—and with fleeing not an option, I had no choice but to turn and fight.

"You know I can't stand dance music, especially in a car, so why do you do this?" I said, typically. "While I'll happily put up with Björk at home, because I can leave, or blow my brains out, or beat you to death with a hammer, I think it is unfair of you to subject me to Björk when I'm trapped in a car."

And we were off! I didn't have a driver's license, Terry pointed out, which forced him to do all the driving. Therefore, he should get to pick the music. Yes, but while he might have a license, he didn't own a car, and I happened to be paying for this rental. Therefore, as the automobile's temporary legal guardian, I should have some say in the music I was subjected to. I was being unreasonable, he said. He was being selfish, I responded. Yi, yi, grrr, icha-yiy, Björk sings.

Thinking it was a compromise, the boyfriend turned the music down. All we could hear now was the beat: boom-boom-boom. Which, as it happens, was the thing about dance music that drove me out of my mind. I was not satisfied. I sulked. He drove. He said something bitchy. I said something bitchy. We fought on for about twenty-five more miles, and finally, unable to enjoy Björk for my bitching and sulking, the boyfriend snapped off the CD player, and we sat in silence.

An hour and fifteen minutes of silence later, we were in Portland.

We'd driven down to Portland from Seattle on a wet spring day because, in our wisdom and maturity, my boyfriend and I had decided to become parents. We were in Portland to get pregnant.

This was my first visit to Portland. During the seven years I'd lived in Seattle, just three hours away, it had never before occurred to me to visit Portland. Seattle's a hilly, damp place with a lot of water and trees. Portland's a hilly, damp place with a lot of water and trees. Portland and Seattle both have Pioneer Squares, Hamburger Marys, homeless street punks, and huge bookstores. Why would anyone who lives in Seattle vacation in Portland?

My boyfriend Terry, however, was very familiar with Portland. His father spent a couple of years dying here in the mid-nineties. Daryl, Terry's father, had non-alcohol-related cirrhosis of the liver. Daryl went to Portland's Oregon Health State University hospital for a liver transplant, but when they opened him up, they found cancer. They cut out the cancer, put in the new liver, and sewed Daryl up. But the cancer returned, and promptly attacked Daryl's new liver. When they opened him up a second time, the doctors decided he was too far gone to "waste" another liver on, his own bad luck for not being Mickey Mantle. It was in Portland that Terry, his mother, and his brother were informed that their husband and father had less than a year to live.

Three months later Daryl Miller was dead.

For Terry, Portland was the city of bad news. The hospital where Terry's father got his liver and a little while later the bad news squatted on a hill overlooking the Willamette River. It looked like a cross between L.A.'s Getty Center and a clump of East German apartment blocks, and there was no escaping the sight of OHSU as you drove into Portland. As we crossed the Steel Bridge over the Willamette on our way to the Mallory Hotel, the hospital where Daryl died came into view. Looking grim, Terry pointed it out to me.

"I hate this place," Terry said. "I hate fucking Portland." The bridge dipped down and we drove into Portland's old downtown as OHSU slipped out of sight.

The adoption agency we were pinning our hopes on was based in Portland. It had offices in Seattle, and with the exception of a required two-day seminar in Portland, all the preparation—the paperwork, the intake interviews, the jumping through hoops—could be accomplished in Seattle. Once the two-day seminar was over, Terry insisted, we were never coming back to Portland. Ever.

Our agency did "open" as opposed to "closed" adoptions. In an open adoption, the pregnant woman, called the birth mother in agency-speak, selects a family for her child, and has a mutually agreeable amount of ongoing contact with her child, usually two or three visits a year, with photos and letters exchanged at set times. In an open adoption, there are no secrets: the kid grows up knowing he was adopted, and knowing who his bio-parents are. Our agency was the first and still is one of the few in the country to do truly open adoptions. Since a lot of people were unfamiliar with the concept, and since some were spooked by it, the agency's managers felt they needed at least two days to explain how it all worked.

It also gave the agency a chance to weed out couples who didn't get it. Since the agency placed more children than any other in the Pacific Northwest, couples who weren't into openness sometimes attempted to adopt a kid through the agency. These couples might come to resent or fear the birth mom after they got their baby, and attempt to interfere with her right to visit, or make her feel unwelcome when she did. The agency felt it was in the best interest of all concerned that the children they placed wound up with couples truly committed to the concept.

So here we were in Portland, checked into the Mallory, this fussy ol' lady of a hotel, ready to demonstrate our commitment. But if we didn't get out of our hotel room in the next fifteen minutes, we weren't going to make it to the seminar on time, which would make a bad impression, which would call into question our commitment. And if we didn't get a kid out of this, the drive and the fight would all have been for nothing.

But we couldn't leave, because my boyfriend had locked himself in the bathroom and wouldn't come out.

Which was my fault. While I'd been right to stand my ground about blasting dance music in the car, I should have dropped it after I'd gotten my way. But I kept right on picking, making snide remarks about Björk when we were getting out of the car and walking into the hotel. Had Terry won, he would've done the same to me. After monogamy and dance music, picking was our biggest issue. We both had older brothers; I was the third of four kids, and he was the second of two. Younger brothers are less powerful than older brothers, so persistence and stamina are our survival/revenge strategies. Older siblings may hit harder, but younger brothers move faster, and we are relentless. And like all younger brothers everywhere, neither of us knew when to stop. We took jokes, wrestling matches, and "playful" fights past the point where they were fun or sexy, right up to the point where someone, usually me, got hurt.

In straight relationships the younger-brother dynamic is sometimes present, but only when a younger brother is present, and most women date only one younger brother at a time. Only in gay relationships can two younger brothers come together. The younger-brother dynamic was why, when the hotel receptionist asked us how our drive down was, I opened my fool mouth and said, "Fine, except for the Icelandic lunatic in the car with us." I'd gone too far and someone—Terry this time—got hurt. But I was not responsible for my actions; my birth order made me do it.

From inside the bathroom, the boyfriend wanted to know why I couldn't let it go. He'd turned Björk off an hour and a half ago. We weren't even in the car anymore. Why couldn't I leave it alone?

"It's stressful enough being in Portland at all," Terry said from behind the green bathroom door. He wasn't locked in the bathroom because he was crying, but because we were fighting, and when we fight we prefer to have a door between us. A closed door. "We have to be the presentable, nonthreatening, happy, happy, happy gay couple in a room full of straight people for two days. Why do you have to pick now to be such a prick?"

"'Cause I'm a brat," I said to the door. "I'm a brat just like you. And what is this locked-in-the-bathroom stuff but your final dig?"

He didn't answer.

"We gotta go be presentable now, Terry."

Silence.

"I'm sorry I called Björk a lunatic. She's a genius."

Nothing.

"Honey, let's go get pregnant. You can name the baby after Björk, teach him Icelandic folk songs, I don't care."

Still nothing. Finally, in desperation, I lied.

"You can listen to whatever music you want in the car all the way back to Seattle."

The door opened. All was forgiven.

∾

SUZANNA DANUTA WALTERS

Take My Domestic Partner, Please: Gays and Marriage in the Era of the Visible (2001)

Suzanna Danuta Walters, an associate professor of sociology and director of the Women's Studies Program at Georgetown University, is a well-known observer of feminist and queer politics. In this piece, Walters discusses changes in the discourse and politics of LGBT movements regarding domesticity, marriage, monogamy, and children.

In the supposedly hip "gay '90s" Americans seem unusually vexed when it comes to gays and families. In poll after poll, even when respondents are in favor of nondiscrimination, the numbers shift radically when it comes to family issues. In a 1993 *U.S. News & World Report* poll ("Straight Talk" 42), 60 percent opposed recognizing legal partnerships for homosexuals, 73 percent opposed same-sex marriages, and 70 percent opposed allowing gays to adopt. In a 1994 *Newsweek* poll (Ingrassia 47), 65 percent of those polled opposed gay adoptions; 62 percent believed gays should not be allowed legally to marry. This is all in the context of polls that show that people overwhelmingly oppose discrimination in housing, employment, health care, and so on. Indeed, in the same *Newsweek* poll, 74 percent favored protecting gays from job discrimination and 81 percent favored equal housing laws. An earlier poll by *Time* magazine, in 1989 (Isaacson et al. 101), showed something quite similar: 69 percent opposed legal recognition of gay couples, 75 percent opposed gays adopting, while 6 percent believed gays should be allowed to inherit each other's property. More recent polls paint a similar picture of increasing support for antidiscrimination legislation while at the same time steady resistance to adoptions by gays, foster parenting by gays, and, of course, gay marriage: an October 1998 Time/CNN poll (Lacayo 32–36) showed that 64 percent opposed gay marriage and 57 percent opposed adoptions by gays.

Yet as much as the right wants to go back to the (fictional, of course) days of June and Ward, Ozzie and Harriet, times do seem to be a-changin'. Domestic partnership laws, gay marriages, donor insemination, adoption—while unthinkable a few years ago—are now part of the larger cultural landscape. Hundreds of universities, cities, towns, and private businesses (including major corporations such as Apple Computers and Disney) have instituted domestic partnership policies, allowing unmarried couples (both homosexual and heterosexual) to share health benefits, housing rights, and other amenities typically accorded only to married heterosexuals. Gays are having children in record numbers, prompting the term "gayby boom" to enter the public lexicon.

Into this changing social field emerges the specter of gay marriages. This is not to say that the subject of gay marriage has never been broached before. Rather, it is to say that "the gay marriage debate" as a public spectacle emerges in the context of a heightened visibility of lesbians and gays. This new visibility affects gays and straights alike, altering gay sensibilities and political strategies and inhabiting straight consciousness as never before. In other words, to understand the gay marriage debate we must have some sense of the strange and confusing moment in which this debate emerges onto the public stage. Gay understandings about marriage, gay desires, gay identities are forged not just through some internal logic but also through the complex negotiations with (heterosexist, hegemonic) popular culture. The huge academic, legal, and journalistic discourse around gay marriage (a discourse I will examine in this chapter) is produced in and around a new public visibility of lesbians and gays. Thus I am interested here in locating this debate within this changing social and cultural field. For surely it must be different to broach gay marriage now than in the context, say, of the 1960s when gay liberationism, the women's movement, and hippie culture explicitly challenged traditional familial models, disavowing marriage and its detritus of commercialized legitimacy. The *historical* question "Why now?" must be merged with the *cultural* examination of how and why marriage gets produced as a "gay desire" and a straight fear.

Gay life and identity, defined so much by the problems of invisibility, subliminal coding, double entendres, and double lives, has now taken on the dubious distinction of public spectacle. But beyond the odes to openness, diversity, and "tolerance," few (except on the right of course!) have questioned the value of this almost obsessive fascination with gay life. At first glance, these stunning changes seem all for the good. But if gays seem like the paragons of trendiness, then they are being simultaneously depicted as the very anti-Christ, the sign of a culture in decay, a society in ruins, the perverse eclipse of rational modernity. As religious fundamentalism grows, becomes mainstream and legitimate, so too does hard-edged homophobia. Hate crimes are on the rise—not just in pure numbers but in the severity and brutality of the acts.[1]

It is assumed that visibility is an unmitigated "good thing," inherently promoting awareness and producing sensitivities. Most people believe that the more lesbians and gays are assimilated into the everyday life of American society, the more readily straight people will "understand" and "accept" them. To some extent, I believe this to be true. As an openly gay person I have ample evidence that seeing gays and lesbians in all walks of life helps to shatter old stereotypes and challenge misinformed judgments. I have seen numerous students and colleagues reevaluate their prejudices when faced with a lesbian professor. Indeed, several years ago, when I announced my pregnancy, a colleague's first words were, "But I never thought you wanted to have a *family!*"—the assumption being, of course, that lesbians and gay men were beyond the realm of family life. While my colleague is not quite on the barricades for gay rights, my everyday presence and that of my daughter have surely made her more aware of the multiple ways of forming family.

Yet, unfortunately, the processes of assimilation and cultural visibility are not solely beneficent. History has shown us—with horrifying detail—the ways in which forms of bigotry sustain themselves and even grow in the face of assimilation. Never have we had so many openly gay elected officials, or so many antigay initiatives. Gay weddings abound on TV as they are being denounced in Congress. Gays are at once the new "Willie Hortons" and the chic flavor of the month. The age of visibility produces both realities: the hopeful moments of rights and inclusion and the fearful moments of victimization and reaction.

As with any minority group, the moment of public visibility marks the beginning of a complex process. The emergence into public view can aid in the process of liberation; surely liberation cannot be won from the space of the crowded closet. Yet the glare of commercial culture can often produce a new kind of invisibility, itself supported by a relentless march toward assimilation. The debates about assimilation are as old as the movement itself. Indeed, every social movement has at some point been faced with similar questions, questions about the benefits of assimilation into the dominant order versus the elaboration of visionary alternatives to that order. But what *is* new today is that these debates are now taking place in full public view, around the watercoolers of corporate America, the hallways of university campuses, the barbecue grills of genteel suburbia, and the streets and malls of both urban and rural areas. No longer restricted to closed-door meetings and internecine battles, these internal debates have been irrevocably externalized. If the enemy was once perceived as invisibility itself, then how is an enemy defined in an era of increased visibility? Is the penetrating gaze of the popular a sign of public acceptance or, rather, the construction of the homosexual as commodity fetish, as sideshow freak?

What profound (and new) alienation must be felt when a gay person looks at a gay wedding cheerfully depicted on TV and then has her/his partner studiously ignored at a family gathering? What does it feel like to be depicted as the cutting edge of chic postmodern style as you are getting fired from your job, rejected by your family, and targeted by right-wing activists? These are new problems, surely, for those coming of age in this new era of visibility. The gap between new expectations and old realities can produce a postmodern funnyhouse of the soul, as gays live out the paradoxes of our times.

NOT ALL IN THE FAMILY: HETEROSEXUAL UNEASE IN THE ERA OF VISIBILITY

Into this strange register of the visible enters the soundbite-ish gay marriage debate, a debate played out in the pages of gay journals but also played out on our TV sets, in glossy mainstream magazines, in prime-time news specials, in our legislative bodies, in legal argumentation, in everyday talk. Gay marriage has wreaked havoc on the public imagination. Indeed, the peculiarly public display that is the marriage ritual emphasizes the centrality of the visible to marriage, in a way that domestic partnerships or even commitment ceremonies can never quite manifest. Weddings are highly commercialized public signs;[2] it is no accident that this imagery has captivated public imagination, pushing aside the more mundane and everyday images of lesbian and gay life by making visible that which we cannot have.

Nowhere is this new gay visibility more pronounced—and more problematic—than on television. Gay weddings have appeared on numerous series, including *Friends* (with Candace Gingrich playing the lesbian minister), the since canceled *Northern Exposure,* and *Roseanne.* For all the obvious newness of this—and its pathbreaking quality—most have forgone the taboo gay kiss and presented gay marriage ceremonies as cuddly, desexualized mirrors of the more familiar heterosexual ritual. Notably absent are the odes to same-sex love and the revisions of traditional vows that most assuredly accompany many gay commitment ceremonies. The *Friends* wedding—while carefully sensitive—went out of its way to portray the gay wedding as an exact replica of its heterosexual counterpart, only with two bridal gowns. The episode focused much more on the heterosexual response to the gay environment than on the gay participants themselves. Indeed, the gay wedding was framed by a secondary plot line concerning the impending divorce of a character's traditional mom, implicitly linking heterosexuality and homosexuality in a liberal scenario of sameness.

It is interesting to note that in three of the major gay weddings handled on TV, it is a heterosexual character who brings the nervous and fighting homosexual couple together when the nuptials are threatened. In *Friends, Northern Exposure,* and even the typically more innovative *Roseanne,* one of the series regulars has a heart-to-heart with one member of the bickering gay couple and helps convince the wavering one to go through with the planned wedding. Often, it is the character who is initially most resistant to the wedding (ex-husband Ross in *Friends* and rich town leader Maurice in *Northern Exposure*). This strange pattern is not, I'm afraid, merely coincidental. Rather, the confidential tête-à-tête between gay outsider and heterosexual insider renders not only homosexuality but *homophobia* benign and palatable. The appalled Maurice, who complains about these "tutti fruttis" ruining the very concept of marriage by engaging in a same-sex version of it, becomes not a bigoted homophobe but, rather, a befuddled and ultimately good-hearted traditionalist. The straight character is reformed and redeemed through his/her expertise in prewedding cold feet, thereby avoiding reckoning with the actual homophobia that surrounds such events. And the gay characters are "redeemed" by participation in a very familiar ritual—the said cold feet.

In this scenario, straight people know more about family life and relationships and are needed to pass that knowledge on to their floundering gay brethren. The implication here is that gays are simply not knowledgeable about the real-life issues of forming families, making commitments, raising kids.[3] Not only does this infantilize the gay characters, it also reintroduces an old canard about homosexuals as childlike, immature, unformed versions of heterosexuals. This backlash scenario argues for the "acceptance" of homosexuals but not as full-fledged people who can handle their own lives.

In addition, there is a certain amount of hubris at the specter of the straight homophobe playing Dear Abby to the jittery gay person. Do these gay people on TV never have *any* gay friends to consult in their various travails? Isolation and assimilation are often the price of tokenism. But at least the *Cosby* family had each other. Gay people on TV appear to have sprung full-blown from the Zeus's head of heterosexuality—the social, political, and cultural context that "births" gay people gives way to the fiction of the fully formed fag, parented by bravely reconstructed heterosexuals. Homophobia is rarely portrayed as just that; rather, it is usually reduced to ignorance, bewilderment, and discomfort. In the television land of gay life, the perpetrators of homophobia (aside from the obvious gaybashers) are not *offenders* but are basically good-hearted souls whose liberal inclinations will win out in the end.

Contrast this delusional neoliberalism with the realities of antigay politics. The same year that witnessed ratings-successful gay weddings on TV also saw the U.S. Congress overwhelmingly support an antigay marriage bill and a putatively progay president sign it. Television abounds with gay weddings while our elected officials rail against marriage (and state after state votes to restrict marriage to heterosexuals)—and polls suggest most Americans agree with the officials and not with the television shows they watch so assiduously. For the religious right, gay marriage is most assuredly the proverbial line in the sand, keeping heterosexuals safe from the invading hordes of gay barbarians eager to say their "I dos" in the Chapel of Love. A full-page ad by the Family Research Council in *The Washington Post* quite explicitly locates marriage as the glue that holds society together—and that keeps out the undesirables. Above a picture of a crumbling wedding cake, the ad encapsulates the "family values" rhetoric and reveals its political heritage: "The institution of marriage was built to last. . . . It was made in heaven . . . Recognized by the state . . . Sanctioned by faith and honored by the community. It has gone hand-in-hand with the rise of civilization. Marriage has survived Marxism. Outlasted Free Love. Outlived Woodstock. Toughed-out the Playboy philosophy. Even endured radical feminism." Opponents of gay marriage are explicitly linking the supposed evils of same-sex love to all the other supposed evils of a secular-humanist society—the ogre of sixties-style sex, drugs, and rock-n-roll meets up with the shibboleth of radical feminism, which encounters the Godzilla of gay marriage. Because the right has used this as a wedge issue in recent elections, gays must, unfortunately, fight the battle on the limited turf that has been set out for us. So mainstream and conservative gays assert the centrality of marriage and pledge their commitment to maintaining its traditions. They respond to right-wing hysteria (e.g., William Bennett's assertion that same-sex marriage "would be the most radical step ever taken in the deconstruction of society's most important institution") by assurances of shared family values and reverence for traditional marriage. It is difficult to hear the more radical gay voices, those that would say to Bennett and his ilk: "Would that it were so! Forward deconstruction! Onward challenge! Hi ho revision!" In this truncated battle, then, the complicated and difficult politics of marriage gets evaporated in a sea of assimilationist paeans to heavenly coupledom.

A PLACE AT THE ALTAR: THE EQUALITY ARGUMENT

If the liberal popular culture depicts gay weddings as cheerfully hetero we-are-the-world assimilation, and straight homophobes depict them as the satanic rituals of secular humanism run amok, then what are gays themselves saying about this contested institution? There are really two debates surrounding the whole issue of gays and marriage. The first is the one we are most familiar with—that between gays arguing for rights to marriage and heterosexuals attempting to limit legally recognized marriage to heterosexual couples. This debate as it stands is fairly simple and one can take a position without much ado. The public gay argument is basically one of equality: how can one justify denying one group of people access to a practice, simply on the basis of their sexual preference? At the most basic level, gays argue that they are being both socially disenfranchised (because marriage brings with it such large and meaningful social approval) and economically discriminated against (marriage confers all sorts of financial rewards, including inheritance, tax filings, health and pension benefits, etc.) by being denied access to such a fundamental social institution. For gays—at least publicly—this is another in a long line of civil rights issues, analogous here to interracial marriages and other forms of systematic exclusion. Prohibiting gays from marriage is one more insult, perpetuating the belief that gays are second-class citizens, unable or unworthy to take up the mantle of full civic membership.

The civil rights/equality arguments for marriage are by now quite familiar and need not be reiterated here. Indeed, I will focus more in this piece on the ideological agendas that underlie—in both explicit and implicit ways—the more impassioned advocates of gay marriage who are not relying solely on an equality argument. That marriage rights would confer benefits—both social and economic—to many lesbians and gays is undeniable. Given the structure of our social and legal system (including our tax structure, inheritance laws, health benefits and responsibilities, childcare and custody and parenting issues—to name just a few), it is certainly understandable that many gay couples would desire access to the same rights and responsibilities, benefits and assumptions that married heterosexuals receive as a matter of course. Numerous writers, including David Chambers, have explicitly spelled out the financial and legal ramifications and strongly argue that gay access to marriage is not only just and fair but would also positively confer tangible benefits that far outweigh additional responsibilities or burdens.

However controversial the phenomenon may be within the gay community, gay wedding ceremonies have become a part of the political landscape. Mass weddings now regularly mark gay pride days and gay rights demonstrations; over five hundred couples participated in such a rite during the 1993 March on Washington and the recent Millennium March began with a similar mass betrothal. In the few polls that have been done, there does seem to be general support within the gay community for legalizing gay marriage. Certainly even those who think the energy misplaced and the institution suspect agree that full civil rights for gays must include the right to marry. In a thoughtful editorial for the *St. Louis Post-Dispatch*,

Amy Adams Squire Strongheart writes with humor and fairness about both sides of the debate within the gay community and concedes the point that the institution of marriage has, at best, a misogynist history. Yet she takes up the mantle of gay marriage, in part because "we lesbians and gays have been told by religion, government and business that we don't matter and that our relationships don't count. But they do count" (1994). She goes on, however, to argue that we must "create a new covenant that is more applicable to the unique nature of our love relationships." Yet for her, I fear, the "unique nature" of our relationships has a decidedly biological bent. Citing the Bible, she argues for a "born with it" thesis, implying that our "differences" are natural and innate (genetic?). So it seems that the difference is not so much about ideology, or history, or vision, but rather that since we are "born different," God surely means for us to have different ceremonies.[4]

However, there is a more complex issue that often gets ignored in the media light of this highly polarized and acrimonious debate, and that is the differences amongst gays *themselves* over marriage. Before I delve into that more complex subject, I must of course note that the basic equality/equal access argument is persuasive and important. Obviously, no thoughtful gay activist should or would take a position that argues for the continual exclusion of lesbians and gays from any institution or practice they choose to join—be it marriage or the military. That said, and my nod to fundamental principles of equality duly noted, the rest of this essay will engage in a much more critical analysis of gay *desire* to join such dubious institutions, and the kinds of ideological positions and cultural assumptions that surround such desire. For desire is, of course, constructed. No one—gay or straight—is born with some inherent desire to throw themselves on the altar, pledging fidelity to one true love and filing joint income taxes. No gene for that. So gay desire to marry must be interrogated, its seeming transparency compromised in order to reveal the complex of cultural and political imaginings that have produced a moment such as this.

There is, of course, a more pragmatic and strategic dimension to this discussion. Like the gays in the military debate, many lesbians and gay men are reluctant to focus so exclusively on this particular issue, believing that the impossibility of victory here will foreclose action on more winnable initiatives. Indeed, the overwhelming support of the Defense of Marriage Act, even among those considered allies and who had previously voted for antidiscrimination legislation, was a sign to many activists that foregrounding marriage was a strategic error of Olympian proportions. In many ways—like the military debate—this issue was forced on gays. While it was never the highest priority among gay organizations and activists, the developments in Hawaii and, later, Vermont, helped push the issue of gay marriages to center stage. It is strangely disconcerting that the two most public issues identified with lesbian and gay rights have been inclusion in marriage and the military, two institutions notorious as sites for the reproduction of some of the most troublesome values and practices around masculinity and violence. But in a dominant culture in which masculinity and violence are such recurrent and persistent tropes, should this be any surprise?

TIES THAT BIND: THE FEMINIST CRITIQUE

For many gay activists and theorists, access to marriage seems as straightforward as access to any social institution. Yet, for many others—lesbians in particular—access to marriage is like asking to have a piece of a very, well, *tasteless* pie. For lesbians— many of whom have been influenced and shaped by feminism—the institution of marriage is irrevocably mired in inequality and male dominance. Feminists from both the second and first waves (I think here particularly of Charlotte Perkins Gilman's eerie documentation of marriage as imprisonment in the feminist classic *The Yellow Wallpaper*) have analyzed marriage as one of the central mechanisms for the subordination of women. In more recent years, of course, feminists have skill- fully revealed the violence at the heart of the marital bond. Wife battery and sexual abuse are now understood not to be simply an unfortunate outcome of idiosyncrat- ically violent men but, rather, deeply embedded in the unequal structure of mar- riage and its sexist ideological underpinnings. Indeed, women are more likely to be violated by spouses than by anyone else. I am always surprised, in fact, when writ- ers supportive of gay marriage blithely speed past this bleak fact, as if to imply that these overwhelming statistics speak nothing of *marriage itself.*

Lesbian feminists (and many feminist gay men) argue that the institution of marriage has a long and rather ugly history that should mitigate against participa- tion by gay people of conscience. Marriage has historically been built on the sup- pression of women and the ownership of women and children by the male "head of household." While ownership no longer literally occurs, heterosexual marriage con- tinues to operate to limit women's options and curtail women's independence. It is only recently that rape in marriage was even conceptualized as a crime, and wife bat- tering continues to be one of the most underreported and underprosecuted offenses. Many gays and feminists argue that marriage is not some neutral institution—or an empty vessel—that can be blissfully transformed by the addition of same-sex partic- ipants. Indeed, marriage was built and organized as a means to institutionalize and enforce very particular and unequal divisions of gender, property, and childcare— divisions that both assumed and attempted to enforce female responsibility for childcare, food production, home maintenance, and male responsibility for mediat- ing the outside world through wage labor and property ownership.

If, as many have argued, gay rights and women's rights are absolutely inter- twined, then any gay argument for marriage that ignores or downplays the relation- ship of the marriage institution to institutionalized male dominance is problematic at best. Indeed, in recent years we have seen a restigmatizing of single women and single mothers—portrayed as either pathetically lonely career gals gone sour (*Ally McBeal*) or as the cancer in the body of domesticity, creating social havoc through reckless child rearing and neglectful daycare. While feminists pushed legislation to make it easier to leave marriages, the push now is to make it more difficult, through challenges to no-fault divorce and a rise in fundamentalist "covenant marriages." If feminists are right—that marriage is one of the cornerstones of the patriarchal fam- ily and a central site for the reproduction of gendered ideologies and behaviors—

then gay inclusion must be seen in that light and therefore examined through that feminist lens. In other words, gay access to marriage must be understood in terms of both sexual exclusion *and* gender domination. Paula Ettelbrick, in particular, has written eloquently of the unavoidable history of marriage as an institution of ownership, property rights, violence, and control that cannot be simply overturned with gay inclusion. In her much-cited debate with Tom Stoddard in the now-defunct gay journal *Out/Look,* Ettelbrick makes a convincing antimarriage argument that hinges on a sophisticated gender-based critique joined with an antiassimilationist gay rights analysis.[5]

Marriage advocates such as William Eskridge, writing in *The Case for Same-Sex Marriage,* grant that marriage has historically been a form of subordination for women but do not believe that it *must* be the case. That seems analogous to the fiction that there can be a "kinder, gentler" capitalism or, in the words of George W. Bush, a "compassionate conservatism."[6] In addition, it ignores the current status of marriage as an institution perpetuating gendered identities and gendered inequalities. Marriage has not only a checkered past; its present is equally troublesome.

TO TAME THE WILD BEAST: GAY MARRIAGE AS ANTIDOTE

If marriage itself reinforces structural inequalities within families, it also privileges state-regulated, long-term pairing over other forms of intimacy and connectedness. Many in the gay movement—like their counterparts in the women's movement—have been critical of marriage not only for its gender inequity and history of violence but also for the ways in which it contributes to a *devaluing* of other ways of being sexual, loving, and nurturing. Many gays believe that families of choice are at least as valid as traditional marriage structures—and certainly as lasting. Anthropologist Kath Weston (1991) and others have written convincingly of the ways in which lesbians and gay men—so often disenfranchised from their families of origin—have created families of choice that serve many of the personal, emotional, and social functions of more traditional familial formations. In creating vast and intricate networks of friends and lovers, gay people have forged intimacies and connections that often seem more lasting and durable than the often tenuous family of origin. Weston argues that these families of choice are not merely replicas of heterosexual families but actually create new forms of mutual responsibility that are outside the more typical—and typically gendered—roles inhabited by women and men in heterosexual families.

This is not just a banal argument for diversity of familial forms; rather, it is about advocating models of love, support, and intimacy that actively dethrone the sexual/familial couple and present instead ever-expanding webs of relationships—ex-lovers, their partners or lovers, old friends, blood kin, and so on. Indeed, one can see this as a gay gift to the bankrupt models of middle-class white heterosexuality that "tend to isolate couples from their larger families and sometimes from friends—especially if they are ex-lovers" (Browning 1997:133).

Yet if gays succeed in sanctifying the couple as the primary social unit (the one that gets financial and legal benefits), does that help to set up a hierarchy of intimacy that replicates the heterosexual one rather than challenging or altering it? Gay marriage might grant visibility and acceptance to gay marrieds, but it will not necessarily challenge homophobia (or the nuclear family) itself; indeed, it might simply demonize nonmarried gays as the "bad gays" (uncivilized, promiscuous, irresponsible) while it reluctantly embraces the "good gays" who settle down and get married. Many gays therefore argue that to participate in this institution is not only to assimilate into the dominant heterosexist way of relating but also to give further credence to an institution that has been built on the backs of both sexism and heterosexism.

While certainly there is no direct correlation between desire to marry and desire to assimilate, testimonies and anecdotal evidence suggest that many gays who desire marriage ceremonies are precisely those gays who are most interested in exhibiting their sameness to straight America. In particular, they are often more religiously identified and more anxious to assert the absolute validity of long-term commitments over other forms of loving. There is no doubt that many gay people—in constructing ceremonies of commitment—try very hard to find ways to render them differently. Because of their very nature, gay ceremonies have a variety and diversity not often witnessed in heterosexual ceremonies. In Ellen Lewin's thoughtful and fascinating tour of lesbian and gay commitment ceremonies, she rightly stresses the often uneasy mixture of the traditional with the "queer" in the formation of these ceremonies, the mixing of genres and ideologies implying a sort of postmodern pastiche of gender-bending imagery.

Nevertheless, the desire to mimic heterosexual pairings is strong (and understandable, given the relative invisibility of alternative forms of loving). Indeed, Lewin betrays just such an assumption when she refers to our "failure to marry." But is it simply a failure, an exclusion, an omission, or can we imagine it as a rejection, a challenge, a bold act of refusal? Lewin identifies gay unease at heterosexual weddings as "excruciating" because of our inability to be "recognized as worthy of such celebration" rather than resulting from our rejection of an institution we find deeply flawed. . . . Is the dream of a seamless inclusion really so foolproof?

Many gays, such as conservative writer and former editor of the *New Republic* Andrew Sullivan, strongly believe that the right to marry is crucial to the "maturity" of the gay movement. Writing early on in 1989, Sullivan argues against domestic partnerships and for legalizing gay marriage. He is wary of the legal ramifications of domestic partnerships (who qualifies?) but is even more concerned that the concept of domestic partnerships undermines the centrality and hegemony of the institution of marriage, arguing that "Society has good reason to extend legal advantages to heterosexuals who choose the formal sanction of marriage over simply living together" (1989:20). His argument, like those of many other conservative gays, is actually a familiar and vaguely Victorian one: marriage tames and civilizes the wild beast that is Man; without it we would be awash in a sea of sexual depravity, flitting madly about from partner to partner, never tending to the business of the day. Like his family values counterparts on the Christian right, Sullivan sees marriage as the "anchor . . . in the chaos of sex and relationships to which we are all prone" (1989:20). Now, many would disagree, arguing instead that the metaphor might not be an anchor but rather an albatross, particularly heavy around the necks of women. Not coincidentally, Sullivan's arguments for marriage are framed within an understanding of the gay movement that interprets the Stonewall generation as washed-out radicals, too blinded by their own perverse desire for liberation to be able to grow up and assimilate. But brave young souls like himself have reckoned with this immaturity and now agree that "a need to rebel has quietly ceded to a desire to belong" (1989:20). More recently, Sullivan has testified before the House judiciary subcommittee hearings on the Defense of Marriage Act, arguing that endorsing same-sex marriage means being in favor of stability, monogamy, and responsibility (U.S. House Hearing 1996); in short, being "profamily" in the worst sort of antifeminist way. His is, as he himself admits, a conservative argument for gay marriage, a claim that same-sex marriage will have two beneficent outcomes: forcing homosexuals into more committed and monogamous relationships and reinforcing the centrality and dominance of marriage as the primary social unit.

Georgetown University law professor William Eskridge recently published a more sophisticated and scholarly version of the Sullivan argument. For Eskridge, there are many reasons to pursue marriage, including the one I find most compelling—the civil equality issue, and Eskridge makes a strong case here. But beyond the obvious (gays should not be excluded from any realm of society), Eskridge echoes Sullivan's argument about the "civilizing" influence of marriage on gay men in particular, men whose wanton promiscuity needs to be tamed by the imposition of marriage. Not only does Eskridge invoke the same ideology of naturally wild men,[7] he also joins Sullivan in framing the argument around a very particular and truncated historical narrative. Eerily like mainstream heterosexual stories of gay life (see particularly Maria Shriver's voice-over in her TV special on the "gay '90s"), Eskridge creates a history of radical gay activists and sexual liberationists giving way to commitment-bound, home-owning, AIDS-fearing "guppies" for whom marriage is the bright light at the end of the tunnel. Not only does this paint a false picture of the demise of gay radicalism (it is still alive and well, thank god) but it also completely ignores the reality of nonwhite, poor, working-class gays—the majority of course. So marriage will civilize nasty promiscuous gay men (and what of lesbians?) and, in so doing, will make them more acceptable (his language) to straights. Like Sullivan, Eskridge too argues for marriage over domestic partnership, because "most lesbians and gay men want something more than domestic partnership; they want to be in a committed relationship at some point in their lifetime" (Eskridge 1996:78). Thus, for these gay men, marriage is the real sign of a committed relationship (thank you Dan Quayle!)—everything else is just silly kid's play. In making his argument for gay marriage as profamily, Eskridge joins in the chorus of single-mother bashing that has characterized the family values debate since Dan Quayle let fly at Murphy Brown by claiming that "some studies have found that children of lesbian couples are better adjusted than children of single heterosexual mothers, presumably because there are two parents in the household. If this finding can be generalized, it yields the ironic point that state prohibitions against same-sex marriages may be antifamily and antichildren" (Eskridge 1996:13). So, in arguing that gay marriage promotes a sound environment for raising children, Eskridge (perhaps unintentionally) falls into the worst sort of conservative assumptions of two-parent stability over just about anything else.[8] In explicitly linking marriage with parenting, Eskridge (and many others, for this has been a consistent point among gay marriage advocates) forgoes a more radical and nuanced critique of the family (and thus ignores the substantive work of feminist scholars) and further conflates partnering (a presumably sexual relationship between consenting adults) and parenting (a relationship of profound structural dependency). This conflation and merger (memorialized in the nursery rhyme "first comes love, then comes marriage, then comes baby in the baby carriage") is the fulcrum of the heterosexist nuclear family, confusing sexual intimacy with family, the desire to parent with sexual desire, interdependency with dependency.[9]

In this conservative argument for gay marriage—and for its civilizing influence on gays in need of civilizing—there is an implicit and often explicit denigration of radical attempts to challenge both marriage and the family. During the early days of both the women's movement and the gay movement, a critique of the family and of marriage was integral to a critique of patriarchy and heterosexism generally. The Gay Liberation Front made a statement in 1969—right after Stonewall—that was crystal clear in its denunciation of marriage: "We expose the institution of marriage as one of the most insidious and basic sustainers of the system."[10] For writers such as Eskridge, Sullivan, and Bruce Bawer (and, one might add, most heterosexuals), this kind of statement is one they would like to forget. For them it is a remnant of an extremist and liberationist past that must be transcended if gays are to fully enter into mainstream society and take their rightful place alongside Mr. and Mrs. Cleaver. But for many of us these are glorious statements of which we are proud. They indicate a thoughtful and thoroughgoing critique of social institutions that have played a serious role in the subjugation of women and the enforcement of heterosexuality. To be liberated from these institutions—and then perhaps to create ones that build not on those shaky foundations but on new and sturdier ones—is seen as a worthy and ethical goal.

Like many others, Eskridge seems to want to have it both ways. He argues that gays have no desire to "shake up" the institution of marriage and familial structures, they only want to be allowed access to them. But these same marriage advocates simultaneously argue that legalizing same-sex marriages will radically alter marriage as we know it and bring substantial change to an historically fraught institution. Typically, the second argument is made by more progressive gay activists and scholars who are painfully aware of the problems in the institution of marriage and are trying to support gay civil rights without promoting a thoughtless assimilationism. But it is not at all clear that adding lesbians and gays to the marriage stew will necessarily alter its flavor, just as it is not at all clear that allowing open gays to serve in the military would alter the structure of the military. Embedded, powerful institutions are funny things. True, no institution is impenetrable or completely inelastic to change. Nevertheless, powerful and hierarchical ones such as the military or marriage are not going to be easily transformed.

BEYOND MARRIAGE: RETHINKING INTIMACY, SEX, COMMUNITY

Yet I do have some sympathy for the internal transformation argument. Indeed, the extraordinary Vermont decision sent unexpected shivers up my spine even as I winced at much of the language used to support it. In that sense, the Christian right is right: the creation of gay and lesbian families *does* pose a fundamental challenge to traditional family values. For if "traditional family values" is just another way of stating the claim that heterosexual, nuclear families (with Dad bringing home the bacon and Mom cooking it up for him and the kids) are the single "correct" form of family, then our families most certainly do stir things up. As much as straights and many gays might want to argue that there is no difference between the way gays create families and the way heterosexuals do, it seems hard to believe that the structure of exclusion and discrimination that surrounds gay life cannot in some way impact gay family life. Because gays parent and partner in a world brimming with hatred, where they have little legal recourse to fight either overt or covert discrimination, gay families can never be simple replicas of heterosexual families.

Yet it is not at all clear that, say, same-sex marriages will present a *fundamental* challenge to the institution of marriage or that gay parents will construct truly new ways of raising children. Is it possible that the creation of gay families through marriage (or commitment ceremonies) and the raising of children is the *least* challenging aspect of gay and lesbian life? Is the formation of gay families the nail in the assimilationist coffin, linking gays irrevocably with mainstream heterosexuality? Or do these moves shake up heterosexual dominance like nothing else, permanently altering the very definitions of family? These are, as we social scientists like to say, empirical questions. But the argument that gay marriage, for example, will *necessarily* alter (sexist, heterosexist) marriage as we know it seems far-fetched. Have the Log Cabinites altered the GOP? If gays marry from within the dominant heterosexual frameworks—invoking dangerous ideologies of familialism, faith, and fidelity—the prospect of internal combustion fizzles out.

In addition, the very place of family is often a fraught one for lesbians and gay men. While the larger social world offers few sites of freedom for gays, the family is all too often the site of the most outrageous rejection and brutality. For so many lesbians and gays, the family is not only the first place where they experienced homophobia but also the place where they felt most betrayed, most alone, most violated. Like battered women beaten by those who pledge their love, the rejection of gay people by their families is one of our ugliest social secrets. Some of the saddest stories gay people tell are the stories of family—remaining in the closet for fear of rejection, being kicked out of the home, being told you are no longer a son/daughter, being kept away from the other kids, being beaten, being told you are sick, telling your mother it is not "her fault," being disinherited, being shunned. It should be no surprise, then, that "family" remains a highly charged arena for lesbians and gay men. It is ironic that one of the coded ways gays have of acknowledging other gays is to ask if they "are family." And in this referencing, we hint at a utopian construction of "families of choice" that is not bound by definitions of blood, of law, of sex, of gender.

My objection to marriage, therefore, rests on any number of arguments. The feminist critique of marriages past and present is, in itself, enough for me. And the gay liberationist argument against assimilation into the dominant heterosexual gestalt—and the way that this assimilation can denude us of our specificity and cultural uniqueness as it claims our allegiance—is a powerful statement against easy adoption of heterosexual mores. But my objection is not simply to marriage as it exists (e.g., with the implication being that if it were less sexist, had a different history, less homophobic, I would embrace it) but, rather, to the valorization of coupledom and familialism that marriage implies.

If granted inclusion in the marriage club, will gays and lesbians be similarly pressured to marry as are their heterosexual counterparts? As many have argued,[11] marriage is hardly a choice. Like its partner in crime, heterosexuality, marriage is largely *compulsory:* if the economic benefits don't get you, the social ones surely will do the trick. As feminists consistently argue, the institution of marriage is inextricably tied to the heterosexual nuclear family, as well as to the merger of parenting and partnering, intimacy and financial interdependency that is so central to our truncated vision of family. Marriage is not simply an isolated institution, nor some innate desire. On the contrary, marriage signifies a whole chain of equivalences and relationships that are therefore naturalized and valorized as the single true model for intimate life: the linking of long-term sexuality with financial interdependence, the merger of partnering with parenting, the assumption of sexual desire chained to emotional intimacy. Lesbians and gays should do all they can to dismantle those conflations and to continue to envision and enact ways of caring and loving that reinvent family, intimacy, parenting. Working to end all marriage as a legal institution (and to instead provide meaningful social and financial supports for relations of dependency and need) would do much more to challenge the noxious politics of family values than getting married ourselves. I'd much rather see a utopian future of unmarried love and lust—for our heterosexual brothers and sisters too—than a dystopian future where marriage and familialism continue to trump values of community and care.

NOTES

1. According to statistics from the Human Rights Campaign (garnered from the FBI), hate crimes against lesbians and gays (or those perceived as lesbian or gay) increased to 14 percent of the total of all reported hate crimes in 1997, up from 11.6 percent in 1996. In

addition, attacks against lesbians and gays are becoming more violent, indicated most dramatically by the brutal murder of Wyoming gay student Matthew Shepard in October 1998.

2. The commercialization of marriage is obviously disturbing as well. What does this say about the supposedly "natural" drive to marry, given its relentless marketing? Gays have gotten in on the act as well. Just the other day I received a catalogue in the mail for "Family Celebrations," billing itself as "America's First Wedding & Special Occasions Catalog for the Gay and Lesbian Community." Yet the emphasis is clearly on weddings or other such ceremonies and firmly embedded in a traditional family motif (even the kid's stuff references two mommies or two daddies). Where is the paraphernalia to celebrate single motherhood? Deep and abiding friendships? Political alliances?

3. The construction of gays as congenitally unable to negotiate the vicissitudes of adulthood (read marriage and kids) is a common theme not only in TV neoliberal discourse but also in gay conservative discourse. (See particularly Bawer 1996; Sullivan 1997.)

4. Sullivan has used the biological argument to different effect in his testimony before the subcommittee on the 1996 Defense of Marriage Act.

5. Paula Ettelbrick (1989) in the much cited debate with Tom Stoddard.

6. This is not to suggest that marriage is identical to capitalism but, rather, to argue *rhetorically* that institutions forged in the fires of structural inequality cannot simply be remade.

7. This ideology is not only Victorian but clearly neoconservative as well: neocon guru George Gilder was making the same argument for the Moral Majority in the '80s.

8. In this chapter I am focusing rather narrowly on gay marriage. For a more extended discussion of gay family life, including issues around child rearing, see my forthcoming book *All the Rage: The Story of Gay Visibility in America.*

9. Feminist legal theorist Martha Fineman has made a controversial and compelling argument that has important implications for rethinking this debate. In her book *The Neutered Mother, the Sexual Family, and Other Twentieth-Century Tragedies* (New York: Routledge, 1995), Fineman argues that in order to create a less gendered social order (and a less unequal one as well) we need to separate parenting and partnering and socially and economically valorize relations of dependency instead of supposed peer relations. The conflation of parenting and partnering (and the assumption that one leads to the other) sets the stage for the conflation of relations of dependency and relations of mutuality. As Fineman argues, most of our social supports go to preserving the marital union, and our supports for dependent children are bound up with our valorization of a two-spousal unit (1995). Indeed, as Chambers reports, spouses cannot be summarily written out of a will, whereas children can. Yet, presumably, the relation of parent to child (or any other relationship of dependency) is not comparable to that of adult sexual partners. Dependencies are in all relationships, to be sure, but to economically and socially support a relationship in which fundamental dependency is not the presumption seems to help create a context for the confusion of intimacy with dependency, social legitimacy with state support. Perhaps gays would do better to support legislation that removes marriage as a legal and economic category, while at the same time creating frameworks to socially, legally, and economically support relations of real dependency: parent to child, caretaker to caretakee, able-bodied to the disabled they care for, etc.

10. "Gay Revolution Comes Out," *The Rat,* August 12–26, 1969, p. 7, cited in Eskridge 1996, p. 53.

11. See especially Polikoff 1996.

REFERENCES

Bawer, Bruce, ed. 1996. *Beyond Queer: Challenging Gay Left Orthodoxy.* New York: Free Press.

Browning, Frank. 1997. "Why Marry?" In Andrew Sullivan, ed., *Same-Sex Marriage: Pro and Con,* p. 133. New York: Vintage (originally in the *New York Times,* April 17, 1996).

Chambers, David. 1996. "What If? The Legal Consequences of Marriage and the Legal Needs of Lesbian and Gay Male Couples." *Michigan Law Review* 95 (2): 447–91.

Eskridge, William N. 1996. *The Case for Same-Sex Marriage: From Sexual Liberty to Civilized Commitment.* New York: Free Press.

Ettelbrick, Paula. 1989. "Since When Is Marriage a Path to Liberation?" *OUT/LOOK National Gay and Lesbian Quarterly* 9: 14–16.

Fineman, Martha Albertson. 1995. *The Neutered Mother, the Sexual Family, and Other Twentieth-century Tragedies.* New York: Routledge.

Ingrassia, Michele. 1994. "The Limits of Tolerance?" *Newsweek,* February 14, p. 47.

Isaacson, Walter, et al. 1989. "Should Gays Have Marriage Rights?" *Time,* November 20, p. 101.

Lacayo, Richard. 1998. "The New Gay Struggle." *Time,* October 26, pp. 32–36.

Polikoff, Nancy. 1996. "Marriage as Choice? Since When?" *Gay Community News* 24, no. 3/4 (Winter/Spring): 26–27.

"Straight Talk About Gays." 1993. *U.S. News & World Report,* July 5, p. 42.

Strongheart, Amy Adams Squire. 1994. "A Foundation for Same-Sex Marriage." *St. Louis Post-Dispatch,* February 10, p. 7B.

Sullivan, Andrew. 1989. "Here Comes the Groom." *The New Republic,* August 28, p. 20.

Sullivan, Andrew, ed. 1997. *Same-Sex Marriage: Pro and Con.* New York: Vintage.

U.S. House Hearing. 1996. *Subcommittee on the Constitution of the Committee on the Judiciary, on H.R. 3396,* Defense of Marriage Act. 104th Cong., 2d sess., May 15.

Weston, Kath. 1991. *Families We Choose: Lesbians, Gays, Kinship.* New York: Columbia University Press.

~

JUDITH STACEY
AND ELIZABETH DAVENPORT
Queer Families Quack Back (2002)

In this article, Judith Stacey, a professor of gender and sexuality at New York University, and Elizabeth Davenport, a professor at the University of Southern California, investigate the issues queer families raise in contemporary law and culture. They question whether queer families represent the vanguard of contemporary family formation or whether the embrace of "family values" discourse reflects a more politically conservative turn toward assimilation.

> *That's what I like. . . . How we as queers get to choose our families. It's like picking the right color scheme for your house. We don't have to accept what the state has given us. We accessorize.*
>
> —"George," in Mann, 1999

> *The buzz around this year's Millennium March on Washington doesn't tout glitter or pageantry. It boasts the addition of a "family area" with activities for the kids; it tells you where to rent a baby stroller.*
>
> —Hank Stuever, 2000

"If it looks like a duck, and it walks like a duck, and it quacks like a duck, then it *is* a duck!" Thus ran the verdict pronounced by opponents of the historic legislation by which Vermont became the first state in the USA to grant lesbian and gay couples the right to form civil unions. Debating the bill's provisions in March 2000, hostile lawmakers complained that a civil union was nothing less than marriage by another name, while a flock of little yellow plastic ducks brooded disconsolately on desks throughout the chamber.

Should gay or lesbian couples be allowed by law to marry? Should some form of domestic partnership be recognized as an alternative to marriage, perhaps for heterosexual couples also? Should lesbians and gay men conceive and rear children? Is there really any single way of being "family" nowadays? Such questions preoccupy citizens and policy-makers alike at the dawn of the new millennium, not only in the United States but in parliaments and public squares around the world. Just a month before the Vermont debate, Canada amended its federal regulations pertaining to spouses to extend to same-sex couples all rights and obligations enjoyed by those of mixed sex. The weekend prior to that, thousands of noisy demonstrators gathered in Paris to protest against the French government's decision to offer unmarried couples, regardless of gender, many benefits and duties that French married couples receive. *"Oui au mariage"* (yes to marriage), they chanted, implying that those who would not, or could not, marry should not be entitled to equality in the eyes of the law.

But if it looks like a duck, and it walks like a duck, is it then a duck . . .? Nowhere in the world as yet can same-sex couples actually marry under exactly the same terms and in exactly the same manner as their heterosexual counterparts. Although the conservative owners of the little yellow ducks in Vermont failed to defeat the civil unions bill, they did successfully reserve the word "marriage" for the union of a man and a woman. Likewise, Canadian law recognizes only married persons as spouses and classifies gay and lesbian partners along with unmarried heterosexual couples of at least twelve months' duration as common law mates. And the French government has never proposed extending *mariage* itself to those whom it now legally acknowledges as registered partners.

But that marriage, and such related issues as the legal relationship of a non-biological parent to his or her children, should have become part of the much-vaunted "homosexual agenda" at all would have appeared ludicrous had anyone prophesied it even a short time ago. Most gay liberationists of the 1960s and 1970s had no interest in imitating or assimilating into heterosexual norms. Those who first broke down the tightly secured door of the closet, deliberately spilling its contents all over the floor, never imagined they might be clearing the way for a new culture of domesticity. The queens of Stonewall so quickly laid to one side by gay and lesbian couples proudly chasing the latest advances in reproductive technology in the quest for their own little princes and princesses—who would have guessed it?

In this chapter we examine the queer political environment in which our putative ducklings—gay and lesbian families in their many plumed varieties—must sink or swim. In the course of what follows, we ask whether lesbian, gay, and other queer genres of kinship represent the brave new families of the twenty-first century, pointing to ways that those in more conventional families might also renegotiate the demands of love and labor. Or conversely, does the gay movement's embrace of family discourse in fact signify capitulation—a retirement from activism to couch potato viewing of *Leave it to Beaver* reruns?

NO PLACE LIKE HOME:
THE POSTMODERN FAMILY CONDITION

Let us begin with a bird's eye view of the context in which queer families of all kinds have hatched. The first thing to notice is how easily these fowl blend into their surrounding terrain. An image of "Beaver" rather than a duck evokes the "fabled family of Western nostalgia," signifying the bygone 1950s era of the modern nuclear family system to which we can no longer return. *Leave it to Beaver*, a popular TV sitcom of that era, idealized a world when proper men were breadwinners and proper women homemakers, when marriage was for life and homosexuality was not a fit topic for family dinner table conversation. However, even before the sitcom could make it into reruns, a global post-industrial world began to supplant the industrial economy that had underwritten the Cleavers' family regime. The "patriarchal bargain" of the modern family order (Kandiyoti, 1988)—in which women subordinated their individual interests to those of husbands and children in exchange for economic support and social respectability—would soon unravel. Rates of maternal employment, developments in contraception and reproductive technology, and no-fault divorce petitions advanced apace, while feminist and gay liberation movements spurred women and men to question received understandings of gender, sexuality, and family life and to pursue what sociologist Anthony Giddens (1992) terms the modern ideal of a "pure relationship" of "confluent love."

In place of the supposedly "normal" American family immortalized by 1950s sitcoms, most people today seek love and intimacy within the denaturalized world of the postmodern family condition. The postmodern family represents no new normal family structure, but instead an irreversible condition of family diversity, choice, flux, and contest. The sequence and packaging of romance, courtship, love, marriage, sex, conception, gestation, parenthood, and death are no longer predictable. Now that there is no consensus on the form a normal family should assume, every kind of family has become an alternative family. Lesbigay or queer families occupy pride of place in this cultural smorgasbord which includes familiar varieties that were historically most prevalent among the poor—such as stepfamilies, unwed motherhood, blended families, bi-national families, divorce-extended kin, cohabiting coupledom, and grandparent-headed families—along with such newer developments as at-home fatherhood, deadbeat dads, and open adoption—as well as innovations made possible by new commerce and technology—surrogacy, sperm banks, ovum exchange, genetic screening, gender selection, frozen embryos, and the no-longer-distant specter of human cloning.

As family innovations proliferate, the mass media energetically broadcast provocative images on a global scale. British journalists gave front-page coverage in late 1999 to the story of a gay male couple who challenged the time-honored passage of citizenship through the mother's line. Returning home to London with infant twins borne by an American surrogate mother, the two men were identified as "parent one" and "parent two" on the babies' birth certificates (Gibb, 1999; BBC, 2000). Singer Melissa Etheridge, her former partner Julie Cypher, and David Crosby, their proud celebrity sperm donor, have graced the glossy pages of entertainment monthlies as symbols of new ways to be family. Hollywood gave its first twenty-first century Oscar for best actress to Hilary Swank for her performance as the transgendered "boyfriend" of Chloe Sevigny in *Boys Don't Cry* (to traditionalists' dismay, the transgendered can truly quack like ducks by legally entering into marriage with a "same-gendered" partner). And in *The Adventures of Priscilla, Queen of the Desert,* the young son of one of the bus travelers is portrayed enthusiastically applauding the drag show that dad and his mates perform in a little Australian outback town where the boy lives with his mother.

Of course, similar topics now grace the pages of academic journals in numerous disciplines (from sociology, psychology and law, to political science, anthropology, cultural studies, religion, history, and medicine). Whereas appropriate motherhood has long been the focus of scholarly debate, now fathers too have become contested subjects—whether as deadbeat or at-home dads, or as cells in turkey basters. Scholars on the conservative end of the spectrum have begun to claim that not only can children experience too little fathering (as in the case of fathers absent through disappearance or divorce, imprisonment or inertia), but also too much (as in the case of gay men co-parenting).

Perhaps it should not surprise us that the sight of such unfamiliar courses of intimacy gives conservative diners indigestion. Confronted by so much novelty, threatened forces train their rifles at the handiest targets, and campaigns for lesbigay family rights have become difficult to miss. Queer families occupy the vanguard of the postmodern family condition, because they make the denaturalized and contingent character of family and kinship impossible to ignore. How irresistible these sitting ducks must appear to backlash troops mustered for target practice; and their frustration can only be magnified as they begin to suspect the futility of their cause.

For by the turn of the millennium, it was already obvious that the historic move toward the legalization of gay marriage had gathered such a head of steam that it was no longer a matter of *if*, but of *when* or *where* it would first secure full legal status. And indeed, in April 2001, the Netherlands led the way and same gendered couples began to be wed. Other nations seem likely to follow suit, including Denmark, Sweden, Canada, and Norway.

Even in the United States, where progress will undoubtedly be slower, popular antigay sentiment is steadily declining. Early in 2000, *Newsweek* conducted a poll which showed 83 percent of all Americans favoring protection from discrimination at work for gay people (up from 56 percent in 1977), with almost 60 percent considering gay partners entitled to shared health benefits, and more than one-third supporting the legalization of gay marriage (Leland, 2000). Those viewing homosexuality as a sin were down to 46 percent (from 54 percent only two years earlier, in 1998). And indeed, in California, a poll taken in the aftermath of a bitterly fought ballot initiative—designed to restrict marriage to the union of a man and a woman—indicated that the "debate" itself raised consciousness in this regard: while 42 percent of Californians said they considered homosexuality morally wrong, no fewer than 54 percent came out against homophobia (Warren, 2000). Another poll found 41 percent of all Americans saying yes to civil unions as a means of extending benefits normally associated with marriage ("Poll Finds Split on Gay Rights and Marriages," 2000). Early French surveys concerning the new civil unions (*pactes civils de solidarité*, or PACS, as the French more colorfully name them) indicated that almost half the population approved of offering them to gay and lesbian couples, and an even greater percentage supported PACS for straight couples. Indeed, startlingly high numbers of heterosexuals have presented themselves to be "PACS-ed" even though for them marriage remains an option ("French Couples Take Plunge That Falls Short of Marriage," 2000).

But although other nations have surged ahead of the United States on the road to making marriage open to all, jurisdictions in the USA lead in providing legal pathways for planned lesbigay parenthood. Here, dramatic legal, popular, and technological gains in the area of lesbian and gay parental rights have preceded the advent of civil unions or marriage. Consistent with this trend, the *Newsweek* poll (Leland, 2000) showed a higher proportion of respondents favoring adoption rights for gay partners (39 percent) than the percentage approving marriage (34 percent).

QUEER FAMILY VALUES: A CASE OF CONFORMITY?

Although gay family rights issues now enjoy immense grassroots support among lesbians and gay men in many corners of the world, not all gay theorists or activists find this trend ducky. The same ideological and strategic differences that characterize other contemporary lesbian, gay, and queer discourses undergird the family quarrels: should the ultimate goal be normalization or subversion? Do the politics of accommodation or resistance promise to pave the royal road to "Home"?

Scholars and activists of diverse ideological leanings continue to debate the consequences of legalizing same-sex marriage. They ask whether it augurs to democratize and degender the institution of marriage, or simply to exacerbate existing inequalities between haves and have-nots, couples and singles, women and men, and among members of different racial and ethnic groups. Would gay marriage increase social acceptance of lesbians and gays, or would it merely promote sexual conservatism and conformist, white picket-fence values? Lesbian and gay studies scholars also cross quills over domestic partnership legislation. Is this best viewed as a desirable and even preferable alternative, a strategic stepping stone, or as a second-class stepsister to full marriage rights? Similarly, what can be said about the current character of gay family relationships? Are they indeed more egalitarian and less violent than their heterosexual counterparts, as enthusiasts frequently claim? Are gay people—gay male people in particular—less inclined to monogamy, and if so, is that cause for regret or applause? Are queer family forms inherently more innovative, more unstable, and/or more considered than mainstream ones?

At the very least it is evident that lesbians and gay men do not share a common set of family values with each other, not to mention with those who occupy less common frequencies on the queer rainbow bandwidth. Indeed, the very notion of "queer family values" is somewhat oxymoronic, signifying a quixotic wish to fuse subversion with normalization. Even so, for just this reason queer family values may serve as a fitting parodic figure to represent the paradigmatic paradoxes of postmodern intimacy! After examining some of the thickets and thorns of these debates, we will argue for the somewhat frustrating claim that the best answer to most of these questions is "all of the above." That is to say, contemporary lesbigay or queer family agendas necessarily house elements of liberation and accommodation, political success and co-option, hand in hand. . . .

HEATHER'S MOMMIES AND OTHER RELATIVES: RESEARCHING QUEER FAMILIES

In a cartoon published not so long ago in the *New Yorker,* a brisk-looking elementary school teacher poses a decidedly postmodern math problem to her young charges. "If Heather has two mommies," she asks, "and each of them has two brothers, and one of those brothers has another man for a 'roommate,' how many uncles does Heather have?"[1] The question artfully exposes the way in which the mapping of a family tree, a project rather more commonly assigned by elementary school teachers, is problematic to a child whose family does not match assumed genealogical norms. Must a household reflect some particular cultural pattern (father, mother, and 2.1 children of assorted gender, for example) in order to be considered a family by others?

The notion of "families we choose" (the discourse-setting title of anthropologist Kath Weston's 1991 study of lesbian and gay families in and around San Francisco) challenges essentialist understandings of kinship. Weston identified the

widespread gay experience of rejection by families of origin and the need to construct alternative support structures (a need dramatically heightened by the first rav-
ages of the AIDS epidemic among gay men) as foundational to the creativity with
which lesbians and gay men began structuring their own families of choice during
the last decades of the twentieth century. Multi-household support networks, the
blending of selected biological and chosen kin, and early lesbian experiments in
planned parenthood via donor insemination were but some of the "chosen" family
forms she investigated.

Families We Choose rightly serves as a portal into the lesbian and gay studies
literature on family formation, for it presciently traced the historic shift—at a time
when that shift was still young and raw—from the anti-family stance of the early
gay liberation movement to the sense of entitlement increasingly voiced by gays and
lesbians in their struggle for family recognition and rights as enjoyed by others.
Such demands, as Weston noted, are not inherently reactionary, reformist, or even
progressive. Whether gay family discourse replicates or resists mainstream family
"values" depends upon the particular social and political context. She read the move
toward establishing families of choice as a sign of a growing sense of political confidence and entitlement among lesbians and gay men. Even Weston might have
been surprised, however, to find that within the decade, gay and lesbian parents and
their children would become the feted subjects of cover stories in *Newsweek* and
other mainstream publications.

AND BABY MAKES THREE (OR TWO, OR FIVE): PARENTING IN QUEER FAMILIES

How many uncles does—or should—Heather acknowledge, indeed? And a few years
later, will students find themselves asking in high school biology how Heather herself was conceived . . . by artificial insemination from one of the uncles to his sister's
female partner, or by sperm donated by an unknown biological "parent" (or even,
nowadays, sperm stored by one of the "moms" in anticipation of a lesbian coupling,
prior to her undergoing male-to-female sex reassignation surgery)? With ovum
exchange or fusion? With a pre-birth custody decree attached? Or one of the many
other variants rapidly gaining in popularity? Two or more gay men sharing with one,
two or more women in the raising of children sharing all their genetic material? And
any other co-mothers out there? A former partner, perhaps, and her own new partner, all equally, or perhaps competitively, devoted to Heather and to her healthy
growth to maturity? Or non-sexual co-parents, defying the modern Western norm
that the family be inherently sexual by definition? Or other kinship relations consciously forged in ways that might be emulated by heterosexual parents also?

The "gayby boom" (or, more accurately, "lesbaby boom") of the past two
decades has been nothing short of spectacular. By the late 1970s, as Weston (1991)
documented, lesbians on the west coast and in other urban centers of the United
States had begun deciding to bear their own biological children (aided by new

assisted reproduction techniques). By the 1990s, gay men were joining the planned parenthood brigade, via adoption, surrogacy, or joint parenting arrangements. Prior to this time, of course, children raised by gay men or lesbians had typically been born in the context of an earlier heterosexual relationship, and few parents who came out of the closet in those days were able to win contests for custody of their children.

Heterosexual procreation and parenthood, after all, represent the ideological lynchpin of Western gender and family conventions. The advent of planned lesbian and gay parenting has spawned a growing mixture of political controversies in the USA and Europe, as well as a new social science industry. Do children need a biological or a social father? A mother? All, or none of the above? Are lesbian and gay parents better, worse, or different from straight parents, and how do their children fare? Queer parenting experiments and the custody rights issues these pose have, interestingly, birthed a natural laboratory for the study of the effects of parental gender and sexual orientation upon child development.

As might be expected, conservative scholars have predicted dire outcomes; and their pejorative views dominated the perspectives of judges and legislators who dealt with the first wave of child custody conflicts and demands. Conservatives claim, for example, that homosexual parents are more sexually promiscuous and more likely to molest their own children; that their children suffer a greater risk of losing a parent to AIDS, substance abuse, or suicide; that the children are more apt to be confused about gender and sexual identities and to become homosexual themselves; that the social stigma and embarrassment of having a homosexual parent unfairly ostracize children and damage their ability to form peer relationships; and that as a consequence of all this, such children suffer higher levels of depression and other emotional difficulties (e.g., Cameron and Cameron, 1996; Cameron et al., 1996; Wardle, 1997). Opponents of homosexual parenthood insist also that children of lesbians suffer the supposed ill effects of "fatherlessness." "It is now undeniable," a Brigham Young professor of family law asserts, "that, just as a mother's influence is crucial to the secure, healthy, and full development of a child, [a] paternal presence in the life of a child is essential to the child emotionally and physically" (Wardle, 1997: 860).

On the contrary, although the research record has limitations, more than two decades of studies have failed to substantiate such claims. The vast majority of studies to date attempt to compare child outcomes among offspring reared by heterosexual and lesbian mothers. However, since most of these children were born within heterosexual marriages which later dissolved, it has proved very difficult to isolate the effects of parental sexual orientation from such factors as divorce, coming out, step-parenting, or declines and other changes in living standards. But a new literature is growing up as fast as the children themselves, to study the children of self-identified lesbians and gay men consciously choosing to become parents through various means.

This research remains fledgling and constrained by methodological challenges, but thus far researchers almost uniformly report no meaningful differences in the measures of child outcomes they have employed; and this emerging social scientific consensus has helped to shift custody policies and decisions in a more progressive direction. Over time, increasing numbers of state courts and legislatures are extending custody, adoption, and foster care rights to lesbian and gay parents. Not surprisingly, this trend has provoked a backlash assault on the reputed ideological purposes of such research and renewed, sporadically successful, efforts to restrict parenting rights explicitly to heterosexuals.[2]

The available research, however, in our view, suffers more from its defensive response to homophobia than from ideological partisanship. For although few reputable social scientists now subscribe to the view that homosexual parents subject their children to serious risks, too many sympathetic researchers have felt compelled to adopt an implicitly heteronormative defense of gay parenting which accepts heterosexual parenting as the gold standard and therefore sets out to investigate whether or not homosexual parents are indeed inferior. Too often scholars seem to believe that this precludes discovering any differences in child outcomes at all. Thus a characteristically defensive review of research on lesbian-mother families concludes: "a rapidly growing and highly consistent body of empirical work has failed to identify significant differences between lesbian mothers and their heterosexual counterparts or the children raised by these groups. Researchers have been unable to establish empirically that detriment results to children from being raised by lesbian mothers" (Falk, 1994: 151).

While it is easy to understand and sympathize with the reasoning behind this defensive stance, the impulse to downplay or deny any finding of difference serves to forfeit a unique opportunity for exploring the effects of parental gender and sexual identity, ideology, and behavior on children. This is particularly unfortunate for the domain of gender and sexual theory. Indeed, foreclosing the most interesting questions, researchers report findings that some might find perverse, defensively claiming that children of gay and lesbian parents turn out to be heterosexual in virtually the same proportion as those raised by heterosexual parents. However, while there is no evidence that parental sexual orientation per se has a notable impact on children's general psychological, intellectual or social development (nor reason that it should, apart from the social stigma involved), it seems as likely as it should be acceptable that gay parents affirmatively expose their children to a greater range of gender and sexual options. Indeed, there are scattered findings in the published studies that support such a view (see Tasker and Golombok, 1997; Stacey and Biblarz, 2001).

Moreover, should the day in fact come when homosexuality is no longer stigmatized, would it matter anyway how many kids did turn out to be gay? It should ᴇem self-evident to all but the most biased observer that more heterosexual parents, as well as the dominant culture, are likely to attempt to influence their children to follow in their heterosexual footsteps than are gay parents to deliberately "bring their kids up gay" (to quote Eve Kosofsky Sedgwick's teasingly titled monograph). As Sedgwick (1993: 76) wryly notes, "advice on how to help your kids turn out gay, not to mention your students, your parishioners, your therapy clients, or your military subordinates, is less ubiquitous than you might think."

The other minor differences reported in the research on lesbian parenting derive from the special demographic characteristics, values, and quality of relationships such parents currently represent. Given the social and economic requisites involved, lesbians (and especially gay men) who choose to become parents tend to be older and better educated than parents in general, and more often reside in urban settings. And as the means of assisted reproduction and independent adoption are more readily available to those in dominant social groups, such parents are more likely to be white and comparatively affluent. Not surprisingly, the majority of studies to date focus on the group easiest to identify, namely, white lesbian mothers in major cities, and their children. Their tantalizing findings prompt a rash of questions in their turn. Lesbian co-mothers studied, for example, seem to have higher parenting skills than heterosexual stepfathers. But is this related to their sexual orientation, their gender, or other factors? Do gay fathers parent any differently than dads in general, and, if so, why? Would the findings be the same if more racially diverse populations of gay parents were included? And, indeed, are the very categories "lesbian mother" and "gay father" ethnocentric, historically transitional and conceptually flawed, as queer theory would imply, since they presume sexual orientation to be fixed and dichotomous rather than fluid, inconsistent, and more multiple? Might we not learn more of interest by studying the gender and number of parents in given families, and their diverse biological and social routes to parenthood, rather than emphasizing effects of their sexual orientation?

Valerie Lehr helpfully summarizes some of the issues researchers might usefully seek to address in this context:

> By highlighting the contradictory roles that queer people create when we enter families, we can perhaps identify some of the challenges that queer families pose for dominant understandings of family: How do we understand lesbian nonbiological mothers who live with a child's biological mother? Are lesbian partners mothers or fathers in those relationships? Can a lesbian be a father? Similarly, how do we understand the roles played by two male parents? Are they fathers, mothers, or some of each? . . . If a child has three or more parents, how do we identify them? (1999: 103)

Or, as Graff (1999) puts it, bemoaning her own lack of legal status as a potential co-parent, "if a dead man, or an uncle, or an absent cuckold, or a holy ghost, or a sperm-bank-supplemented husband can be a sociological 'father,' why can't I?" (ibid.: 105).

LIBERTY, EQUALITY, DIVERSITY?

While some researchers spend their efforts measuring lesbigay families against tacit heteronormative standards, others are more interested in assessing whether queer family relationships are superior—more liberated and liberating—than the *ancien régime* of compulsory heterosexual marriage and gender-divided parenting. Three prominent areas of current concern involve sexual practice and ethics, distributions of labor and power, and racial or ethnic differences in family formation and ideology.

The thorny issue of variance in sexual practice and ethics is not of course one unique to gay people. Values with regard to monogamy, promiscuity, sexual sport, and sex outside of love and relationships are ubiquitous subjects of debate among sexual ethicists and the general public, not to mention the US Congress! Many gay men, however, pursue this dispute with particular energy, passion and creativity. For the gay male "culture of desire"—which queer theorists like Frank Browning (1994) affirm—creates special challenges for those gay men who question the colonization of sexuality in the name of respectability or of redemption or of "safe" sex after the devastating terrors of AIDS, but who nonetheless seek the semblance of intimate family bonds. Navigating some of the choppiest channels in the currents of eros and domesticity, such gay men experimentally invent new genres of the "sexual" family. That is precisely what makes homosexuality so threatening to self-appointed defenders of civilization, Browning claims:

> What is wrong with us homosexual people to straight society is that we are always available (potentially); what threatens them [*sic*] is their anxiety that all men harbor a desire to be penetrated and to surrender to the universal impulse toward wildness, an impulse that if allowed to go unchecked would proliferate into a thousand jungles of desire. (1994: 100)

Although data on sexual practice is difficult to gather and decode, most research supports the view that quite a few gay men do indeed seem to walk on the wild side with greater abandon than most of the rest of the population. *Homosexualities,* A. P. Bell and M. S. Weinberg's (1978) classic study on this matter, reports quite formidable levels of gay male sexual activity. Almost half of the white gay men interviewed and one-third of black gay men claimed to have had at least 500 different sex partners in their lives, and more than 90 percent of the white gay men reported 25 partners or more. Moreover, more than one-quarter of the white gay men reported sexual activity with more than 50 partners during the year of the study, a second quarter indicated between 20 and 50, and more than half of the 29 percent who considered themselves, coupled at the time of their interview depicted their relationships as non-monogamous. Similarly, Gary Dowsett's (1996) *Practicing Desire,* an ethnographic study of gay male sexual practice in Australia, records extensive numbers of sexual partners. The majority of lesbians in the Bell and Weinberg (1978) study, by contrast, claimed to have had fewer than ten partners, with another quarter reporting fewer than five. Almost three-quarters of the women said that they were currently in a stable relationship with another woman which integrated love and sex (despite a culture of jokes about lesbian bed-death), and far more of these than the men believed that sexual infidelity would cause their relationship to fail. And, indeed, despite their greater tolerance for open relationships, Bell and Weinberg record considerable instability in gay male couple relationships.

More recently, voices claim to detect a move away from sexual libertinism, particularly among younger gay men, partly the result of AIDS, and partly a classic historical/political generational shift. Some critics complain that current family discourse represents a conservative retreat from the defense of sexual liberty and pleasure (paralleling feminist sex wars over pornography). "Sex Panic" critics, like Browning (1994), Warner (1993, 1999), Douglas Crimp (1988), and Kobena Mercer (1994), castigate prominent mainstream gay authors, including Sullivan (1995, 1997), Bawer (1993), Michelangelo Signorile (1997), and Gabriel Rotello (1997), for fostering such a retreat. And while lesbians certainly divide along similar ideological lines, it is as striking as it is unsurprising that this is a discourse dominated by men.

But who, if anyone, dominates the household when couples cannot resort to default mode gender scripts? Studies of the division of domestic labor and power have become a major area of sociological research ever since feminists focused attention on the politics of housework. Because same-sex couples offer an exceptional social laboratory for gender theory and practice, research on how gay and lesbian couples and co-parents share household duties and expenses is a thriving enterprise, assessing the great gay hope that their relationships are more egalitarian and just than heterosexual ones. The record thus far provides grounds for both self-congratulation and caution. *American Couples,* the 1983 classic study by Philip Blumstein and Pepper Schwartz, which compared married and cohabiting straight couples with their gay male and lesbian counterparts, did find that gender served as a potent determinant across the spectrum of money, work, and sex. Lesbians were most likely to share domestic tasks equally, they reported, and gay men to divide them by interest, but both were more egalitarian and more economically autonomous than married couples. Later studies of lesbian co-parents report similar results. For example, Raymond Chan, Risa Brooks et al. (1998) found that lesbian co-mothers shared childcare tasks more equally than heterosexual parents and that more egalitarian couples were also more satisfied with their relationships. Likewise, Maureen Sullivan (1996) found that lesbian co-parents tended to perform equal childcare duties and enjoy equal status in the home as long as both remained employed. But if one (and not necessarily the birth mother) became a full-time homemaker, her breadwinner partner seemed to assume more of the kind of decision-making power that male breadwinners have traditionally enjoyed. A recent ethnographic study, however, more skeptically asks if such findings owe more to romantic, self-congratulatory ideological investments than to quotidian practice. After closely observing more than fifty families, Christopher Carrington (1999) claims that domestic tasks were, in fact, far from equally shared, but that investment in egalitarianism led lesbians to credit partners who contribute little with more than they in fact do, while dominant gay male partners worked hard to counter any perceived emasculation of the more domesticated partner by stressing that partner's non-domestic activities.

The fond myth that a same-gendered relationship is inherently shielded from patriarchal patterns of dominance and subordination can even make lesbians and gays particularly vulnerable to more threatening consequences. For it fosters a tendency to deny what divorce lawyers have known all along, namely that attempts to anchor romantic affairs in the turbulent waters of domesticity are beset by all kinds of dangers, including violence in the home. The emergence of disappointing data pointing to the prevalence of partner abuse among gay men and lesbians—which preliminary surveys indicate to be no less rampant than in heterosexual relationships—has led to community-based efforts to provide domestic violence intervention and prevention services, at least in urban centers (National Coalition of Anti-Violence Programs, 1997, 1998, 1999). Service providers emphasize the need for concerted efforts to increase the sensitivity of health care and law enforcement agencies to victims of same-gendered domestic violence. For example, a battered lesbian rightly fears that her partner can gain the same access as she to the network of women's shelters, and a gay man might report an assault by his partner as perpetrated by a stranger. Confronting the tendency within lesbian and gay groups to deny the existence of such violence remains a major challenge. Lesbians, in particular, have been reluctant to acknowledge that loving women does not in itself grant them immunity from domestic abuse. And feminist theory must confront the complex question of whether and why families in all their new varieties might retain as much potential for violence and danger as when gender seemed to explain all.

However long the "families we choose" literature may be on matters of liberty and equality, it falls significantly behind—like much else in lesbian and gay studies—on matters of racial and ethnic diversity. This is a disproportionately white discourse, both among authors and subjects, reflecting the unwitting ethnocentrism of categories like gay, queer, and choice. After all, communities constructed around sexual identity tend to be white-dominated in Western countries, because the identification of "gay" with "white" points to the relatively privileged position of those who can afford to make sexuality the central axis of their identity.[3] As the late Joseph Beam, a black gay poet, observed with some bitterness before he died of AIDS: "We ain't family. Very clearly, gay male means: white, middle-class, youthful, nautilized, and probably butch; there is no room for black gay men within the confines of this gay pentagon" (1986: 14). And, of course, the word "family" itself often signifies differently among communities of color, not to mention among peoples of non-Western nations.

Consequently, the emergent literature on the family formations of lesbigay people of color builds on the premise that most are likely to regard the racial groups to which they belong as a stronger source of solidarity and identity (and marginality) than they do their sexual affinities. Indeed, lesbigay people of color appear to be more apt than whites to remain semi-closeted, embedded within their own racial kin groups and neighborhoods, and to pursue homoerotic interests within racial bonds (see, e.g., Hawkeswood, 1996). Keith Boykin, Executive Director of the National Black Gay and Lesbian Leadership Forum, recounts how he came to such a stance: "The shared racial identity develops a much stronger family bond than any presumed identity based on sexual orientation. I never polled my family members, but ultimately I decided that some would be more disturbed by my dating a white woman, while others would be more upset by my dating a black man" (1996: 23).

Likewise, gay men and lesbians of color are less likely to participate in the planned gayby boom, partly because of economic barriers which disproportionately affect people of color, partly because they are less likely to live within communities which support and foster this choice, and partly because of the relative paucity of non-white sperm donors. As Boykin notes, "Homophobia and heterosexism are frequently seen not as prejudices but as survival skills for the black race or the black individual" (1996: 167). Black gay and lesbian people—where their existence is even acknowledged—are sometimes viewed by their own families, communities, and churches as lacking commitment to the race on a similar scale to heterosexuals who intermarry. Boykin admits that a "black man who dates only men raises the specter of the extinction of the family name, potentially causes embarrassment to the family, and often suggests an irresponsible disregard for the need to create strong, black families" (ibid.: 23). A black gay couple caring for their own children are likely not counted a "strong, black family" in this sense. . . .

Indeed, one can readily argue that the improvisational diversity of family practices which African-Americans and South Africans forged in response to racial subordination and poverty—such as "other-mothering" and multi-household families—foreshadowed many features of the postmodern family condition in the West as a whole. Certainly, the explosive national discourse on black "matriarchy" in the USA provoked by the 1965 *Moynihan Report* foreshadowed preoccupations of the contemporary politics of "family values" more generally, as in the Murphy Brown discourse. That is why, in theory, it seems clear that forging a "rainbow coalition" to support queer family values could benefit both communities of color and gay people of every hue. Translating such theory into practice, however, will require far more awareness and respect than has yet been achieved for the genuine diversity of family definitions, priorities and vulnerabilities that divide racial and ethnic communities here and elsewhere.

SO DUCK OR NO DUCK?

If it looks like a duck, and it walks like a duck, and it quacks like a duck, then is it a duck? We began by asking whether the Vermont experiment in creating civil unions for same-sex couples represents marriage in all but name. So does it? Does the demand of so many lesbian and gay people, in so many parts of the world at once, for equal recognition of their pairings presage an irreversible move toward the embrace of conventional forms of family life? Are lesbigay family forms really just the same as everyone else's, differing only by the gender combination of sexually bonded adults? Does gay marriage really threaten to undo civilization, as conservatives fear? As Frank Browning observes, "Worse even than the sexual perversions they practice, gay people's more damning threat to traditionalists is their claim to family parity, their claim to family life as a right" (1994: 142).

Given our claim that queer family developments signal the frontier of global changes in family structure inherent in the postmodern family condition, we could say that in that sense, families created by lesbians and gay men are truly not distinct from other families. They simply heighten the visibility of the fact of irreversible diversity. They bring us face to face with inescapable contests over legitimate relations of gender, sexuality, and family. The decline of the modem (Western) nuclear family system, as we have noted, has left us with no prevailing culturally mandated family pattern—as any third-grader trying to fill in those blanks on a traditional family tree quickly discovers. All forms of intimacy now contend with instability, contradiction, experimentation. Yet family life itself has by no means been discarded. Instead, many are reinventing it with ingenuity and passion. And here gay men and women (and especially those who defy dichotomization as men or women at all) are leading the pack.

The political meanings of family sentiments, practices, and discourse among gay men and lesbians cannot be defined by checking any one box (progressive, reactionary, and so forth), other than the one marked "all of the above." Most reforms are two-edged, often contradictory, and can be read as progressive and co-optive, subversive and accommodationist all at once, depending upon social, economic, and political contexts. Extending marriage to same-gendered couples, as we saw, could simultaneously redefine the institution by eroding gender meanings and homophobia, but also exacerbate class inequities and couple privilege, further marginalizing the single, dissidents, sexual radicals, and all who lack economic resources. Choosing to bear children might help to combat homophobia as Heather's mommies take their place as soccer moms, at PTA meetings, and in church and temple, and other children come to see two mommies as yet another norm. But it could also foster more puritanical and conformist values, as critics charge, and sap collective energies from other ongoing political and social battles, as well as ignoring the needs of the elderly gay, or of disenfranchised youth.

The way a society treats its gay families has broad implications for all families. Just as we refuse to protect the family bonds of children because their parent(s) are gay, denying them equal access to health care or to inheritance or to appropriate custody arrangements, so too we punish children for other parental infractions, such as being born to a single mother on welfare or belonging to another group subject to social prejudice. Queer family discourse is not likely to disappear until we come to understand that, as one of us has argued elsewhere, "all our families are queer." Gay and lesbian families simply display with added intensity the characteristics of broader family and social realities today, helping to expose the dangerous disjunction between popular "family values" rhetoric and the complex lived realities of contemporary families. Not the same as other families, nor an alternative to "the family," lesbigay families expose the social and historical character of every definition of family. Promoting queer family values within a multi-hued rainbow coalition to support all shapes and colors of families could establish family diversity itself as normal in a democracy.

EPILOGUE

Perhaps we might end by suggesting that newly emerging gay and lesbian family forms might better be compared not to plastic ducks but to the ugly duckling of the children's fairy-tale. Hatched as if in prophetic anticipation of the current technological revolution in methods of reproduction as one of a brood of ducklings, one offspring quickly appears different from his nest-mates. Everyone who sees the ugly duckling considers him disturbingly queer. "Quack, Quack! Get out of town!" they derisively sing. But in time, the queer duckling quacks back, for to his own surprise and theirs he survives their taunts and emerges a magnificent swan, the pride of the pond. Not a duck at all, although the egg from which he came had been laid among their kind. And wouldn't it be dull if the only species our pond could sustain were identical little yellow plastic ducks?

NOTES

1. *The New Yorker,* 8 March, 1999, with reference to Leslea Newman, 1991. *Heather Has Two Mommies.* Boston: Alyson Publications.

2. In Utah, for example, Wardle drafted regulations limiting adoption and foster care placements to households in which all adults were related by blood or marriage (later passed by the state legislature), shortly after publishing his 1997 article impugning the methods, merits, and motives of social science research on lesbian and gay parenting.

3. Note Steven Seidman's assertion that: "Lesbians and gay men of color have contested the notion of a unitary gay subject and the idea that the meaning and experience of being gay are socially uniform. Indeed, they argue that a discourse that abstracts a notion of gay identity from considerations of race and class is oppressive because it invariably implies a white, middle-class standpoint" (1993: 120). Valerie Lehr (1999) suggests that the fact that racial/ethnic identity is more likely to be central to self-definition for people of color in the USA may result in greater sexual freedom because of the consequently lessened need to embrace a fixed sexual identity. She further wonders, conversely, whether bisexuality is undercounted in white communities.

REFERENCES

Bawer, Bruce. 1993. *A Place at the Table: The Gay Individual in American Society.* New York: Poseidon.

Beam, Joseph. 1986. "Leaving the Shadows Behind," in Joseph Beam, ed., *In the Life: A Black Gay Anthology.* Boston: Alyson Publications.

Bell, Alan P., and Martin S. Weinberg. 1978. *Homosexualities: A Study of Diversity among Men and Women.* London: Mitchell Beazley.

Boykin, Keith. 1996. *One More River to Cross: Black and Gay in America.* New York: Anchor.

British Broadcasting Corporation. 2000. "Gay Couple's Babies 'Denied Citizenship.'" *BBC News Online,* 2 January, www.news.bbc.co.uk.

Browning, Frank. 1994. *The Culture of Desire: Paradox and Perversity in Gay Lives Today.* New York: Random House.

Cameron, Paul, and Kirk Cameron. 1996. "Homosexual Parents." *Adolescence* 31: 757–76.

Cameron, Paul, Kirk Cameron, and Thomas Landess. 1996. "Errors by the American Psychiatric Association, the American Psychological Association, and the National Educational Association in Representing Homosexuality in Amicus Briefs about Amendment 2 to the U.S. Supreme Court." *Psychological Reports* 79: 383–404.

Carrington, Christopher. 1999. *No Place Like Home: Relationships and Family Life among Lesbians and Gay Men.* Chicago: University of Chicago Press.

Chan, Raymond W., Risa C. Brooks, et al. 1998. "Division of Labor among Lesbian and Heterosexual Parents: Association with Children's Adjustment." *Journal of Family Psychology* 12 (3): 402–19.

Crimp, Douglas. 1988. AIDS: *Cultural Analysis/Cultural Activism.* Cambridge: MIT Press.

Dowsett, Gary W. 1996. *Practicing Desire: Homosexual Sex in the Era of AIDS.* Stanford, CA: Stanford University Press.

Falk, Patrick J. 1994. "The Gap between Psychosocial Assumptions and Empirical Research in Lesbian-Mother Child Custody Cases." Pp. 131–56 in A. E. Gottfried and A. W. Gottfried, eds., *Redefining Families: Implications for Children's Development.* New York: Plenum.

"French Couples Take Plunge That Falls Short of Marriage." 2000. *New York Times,* 18 April, p. 1.

Gibb, Frances. 1999. "Gay Couple Will Be the Legal Parents of Twins." *Times,* 28 October, p. 5.

Giddens, Anthony. 1992. *The Transformation of Intimacy: Sexuality, Love, and Eroticism in Modern Societies.* Palo Alto, CA: Stanford University Press.

Graff, E. J. 1999. *What Is Marriage For? The Strange Social History of Our Most Intimate Institution.* Boston: Beacon Press.

Hawkeswood, William G. 1996. *One of the Children: Gay Black Men in Harlem.* Berkeley: University of California Press.

Kandiyoti, Deniz. 1988. "Bargaining with Patriarchy." *Gender and Society* 2 (3): 274–90.

Lehr, Valerie. 1999. *Queer Family Values: Debunking the Myth of the Nuclear Family.* Philadelphia: Temple University Press.

Leland, John. 2000. "Shades of Gay." *Newsweek,* 20 March, pp. 46–49.

Mercer, Kobena. 1994. *Welcome to the Jungle: New Positions in Cultural Studies.* New York: Routledge.

National Coalition of Anti-Violence Programs. 1997. *Annual Report on Lesbian, Gay, Bisexual, Transgender Domestic Violence.* Los Angeles: NCAVP.

———. 1998. *Annual Report on Lesbian, Gay, Bisexual, Transgender Domestic Violence.* Los Angeles: NCAVP.

———. 1999. *Annual Report on Lesbian, Gay, Bisexual, Transgender Domestic Violence.* Los Angeles: NCAVP.

"Poll Finds Split on Gay Rights and Marriages." 2000. *Los Angeles Times,* 1 June, p. A31.

Rotello, Gabriel. 1997. *Sexual Ecology: AIDS and the Destiny of Gay Men.* New York: Dutton.

Sedgwick, Eve Kosofsky. 1993. "How to Bring Your Kids Up Gay." Pp. 69–81 in Michael Warner, ed., *Fear of a Queer Planet: Queer Politics and Social Theory.* Minneapolis: University of Minnesota Press.

Seidman, Steven. 1993. "Identity and Politics in a 'Postmodern' Gay Culture: Some Historical and Conceptual Notes." Pp. 105–42 in Michael Warner, ed., *Fear of a Queer Planet: Queer Politics and Social Theory.* Minneapolis: University of Minnesota Press.

Signorile, Michelangelo. 1997. *Life Outside: The Signorile Report on Gay Men—Sex, Drugs, Muscles, and the Passages of Life.* New York: HarperCollins.

Stacey, Judith, and Timothy Biblarz. 2001. "(How) Does the Sexual Orientation of Parents Matter?" *American Sociological Review* 66 (2): 159–83.

Sullivan, Andrew. 1995. *Virtually Normal: An Argument about Homosexuality.* New York: Knopf.

———. 1997. *Same-Sex Marriage: Pro and Con—A Reader.* New York: Vintage.

Sullivan, Maureen. 1996. "Rozzie and Harriet? Gender and Family Patterns of Lesbian Coparents." *Gender and Society* 19 (6): 747–67.

Tasker, Fiona L., and Susan Golombock. 1997. *Growing Up in a Lesbian Family.* New York: Guilford.

Wardle, Lynn D. 1997. "The Potential Impact of Homosexual Parenting on Children." *University of Illinois Law Review,* 833–919.

Warner, Michael. 1993. *Fear of a Queer Planet: Queer Politics and Social Theory.* Minneapolis: University of Minnesota Press.

———. 1999. "Normal and Normaller: Beyond Gay Marriage." *Gay and Lesbian Quarterly* 5 (2): 119–71.

Warren, Jennifer. 2000. "Gays Gaining Acceptance in State, Poll Finds." *Los Angeles Times,* 14 June, pp. A1, A27.

Weston, Kath. 1991. *Families We Choose: Lesbians, Gays, Kinship.* New York: Columbia University Press.

⮑

DANIEL GROSS AND STEVEN GOLDSTEIN

Weddings/Celebrations (2002)

The landmark October 2002 publication of Daniel Gross and Steven Goldstein's wedding announcement opened up a new era in queer visibility in the United States. For the first time a major mainstream publication included same-sex ceremonies alongside traditional weddings. The newspaper even changed the name of the column from "Wedding Announcements" to "Weddings/Commitments," marking not just queer inclusion but also a shift in how Americans understand committed love.

Daniel Andrew Gross and Steven Goldstein will affirm their partnership today in a civil union ceremony at the Shore Acres Inn and Restaurant in North Hero, Vt.

Assistant Judge Barney Bloom of State Superior Court in Montpelier will preside. Last evening, Rabbi David M. Steinberg led an exchange of Jewish vows at the Musée des Beaux-Arts of Montreal.

Mr. Goldstein, 40, is the founder and owner of Attention America, a public affairs consulting firm in Manhattan. He was a co-manager of Jon S. Corzine's campaign in 2000 for the Senate from New Jersey. A summa cum laude graduate of Brandeis, Mr. Goldstein holds a master's degree in public policy from Harvard and a master's in journalism and a law degree from Columbia.

He is a son of Carole and Dennis Goldstein of Bayside, Queens. His mother is a fund-raiser for the Friends of the Lukas Foundation, which she helped found to support the Lukas Community, a village for adults with developmental disabilities in Temple, N.H. His father is the founder and senior partner of the Barrister Reporting Service, a court transcription concern in Manhattan.

Mr. Gross, 32, is a vice president of GE Capital in Stamford, Conn., working on the financing of international projects like power plants and pipelines. He graduated cum laude from Yale, from which he also received an M.B.A. and a master's degree in environmental management. He was a Fulbright scholar in 1994–95 in Thailand, studying and teaching natural resources management at the Asian Institute of Technology near Bangkok.

He is a son of Merle and Barry Gross of Chicago. His mother ran Merle Ltd., a former coat manufacturer in Chicago. His father retired as a partner in Shefsky & Froelich, a Chicago law firm.

The couple met in October 1992 in Washington, where Mr. Goldstein was working as a television news producer and Mr. Gross as a consultant. Mr. Goldstein was one of 35 respondents to a personal ad that Mr. Gross had placed in *Washington City Paper.* It read: "Nice Jewish boy, 5 feet 8 inches, 22, funny, well-read, dilettantish, self-deprecating, Ivy League, the kind of boy Mom fantasized about." They arranged to meet one evening at Kramerbooks & Afterwords, and had their second date the next night.

That Thanksgiving, Mr. Gross went home to visit his parents. "My mom said, 'You seem like everything's great,'" he recalled. "'You seem like you're in love.' I said, 'I am.' They said, 'That's great.' I said, 'His name is Steven.' My mother said, 'Oy,' and was silent for a while."

Both sets of parents now support the relationship.

While Mr. Gross was in Thailand, Mr. Goldstein had a $1,500 telephone bill one month. They were apart again while Mr. Gross was in graduate school. Finally, in 1998, they moved to New York together.

They postponed a commitment ceremony until leaders of Reform Judaism had voted to support rabbis who perform same-sex unions and Vermont had given legal recognition to civil unions, both events in 2000.

"Sept. 11 accelerated the process," Mr. Goldstein said. "We all began to think of our own mortality."

∽

CHIEF JUSTICE MARGARET MARSHALL

Ruling in *Goodridge v. Massachusetts Department of Health* (2003)

This court decision, also sometimes called the same-sex marriage case, made Massachusetts the first state in the United States to allow legal marriage between any two people regardless of sex or gender. The court action prompted some in the state to call for an amendment to the state constitution defining marriage as a union of a man and a woman, but to date, the proposed amendment to the constitution, which would take the issue away from the courts and bring it back to the legislature, has not moved forward. The first legal same-sex marriage took place in Massachusetts on May 17, 2004.

March 4, 2003–November 18, 2003

Present: Marshall, C. J., Greaney, Ireland, Spina, Cowin, Sosman, & Cordy, JJ.

MARSHALL, C. J. Marriage is a vital social institution. The exclusive commitment of two individuals to each other nurtures love and mutual support; it brings stability to our society. For those who choose to marry, and for their children, marriage provides an abundance of legal, financial, and social benefits. In return it imposes weighty legal, financial, and social obligations. The question before us is whether, consistent with the Massachusetts Constitution, the Commonwealth may deny the protections, benefits, and obligations conferred by civil marriage to two individuals of the same sex who wish to marry. We conclude that it may not. The Massachusetts Constitution affirms the dignity and equality of all individuals. It forbids the creation of second-class citizens. In reaching our conclusion we have given full deference to the arguments made by the Commonwealth. But it has failed to identify any constitutionally adequate reason for denying civil marriage to same-sex couples.

We are mindful that our decision marks a change in the history of our marriage law. Many people hold deep-seated religious, moral, and ethical convictions that marriage should be limited to the union of one man and one woman, and that homosexual conduct is immoral. Many hold equally strong religious, moral, and ethical convictions that same-sex couples are entitled to be married, and that homosexual persons should be treated no differently than their heterosexual neighbors. Neither view answers the question before us. Our concern is with the Massachusetts Constitution as a charter of governance for every person properly within its reach. "Our obligation is to define the liberty of all, not to mandate our own moral code." *Lawrence v. Texas*, 123 S.Ct. 2472, 2480 (2003) *(Lawrence)*, quoting *Planned Parenthood of Southeastern Pa. v. Casey*, 505 U.S. 833, 850 (1992).

Whether the Commonwealth may use its formidable regulatory authority to bar same-sex couples from civil marriage is a question not previously addressed by a Massachusetts appellate court. It is a question the United States Supreme Court left open as a matter of Federal law in *Lawrence, supra* at 2484, where it was not an issue. There, the Court affirmed that the core concept of common human dignity protected by the Fourteenth Amendment to the United States Constitution precludes government intrusion into the deeply personal realms of consensual adult expressions of intimacy and one's choice of an intimate partner. The Court also reaffirmed the central role that decisions whether to marry or have children bear in shaping one's identity; *Id.* at 2481. The Massachusetts Constitution is, if anything, more protective of individual liberty and equality than the Federal Constitution; it may demand broader protection for fundamental rights; and it is less tolerant of government intrusion into the protected spheres of private life.

Barred access to the protections, benefits, and obligations of civil marriage, a person who enters into an intimate, exclusive union with another of the same sex is arbitrarily deprived of membership in one of our community's most rewarding and cherished institutions. That exclusion is incompatible with the constitutional principles of respect for individual autonomy and equality under law.

6

To See and Be Seen

QUEERS IN AMERICAN MEDIA AND ENTERTAINMENT, NOW AND THEN

On the 2004 television lineup, it was the rare network that did not have some form of queer character. If one examined cable television, the most popular shows often had queer characters, and in some cases, queer sexuality. How did U.S. media representations of queers go from the 1934 Hays Code, which forbade any expression of sexuality at all, to the borderline soft-porn soap opera *Queer as Folk*, one of the most popular television shows for the Showtime network in the first years of the twenty-first century?

In fact, in the early days of U.S. cinema, queerness was not as unusual as one might presume. In the words of Vito Russo, popular historian of queerness on-screen, "Characters who were less than men or more than women had their first expression in the zany farce of mistaken identity and transvestite humor inherited from our oldest theatrical traditions." The femininity of these male characters was generally connected with inferiority, a trend that continued in the cinema for many years. But as cinema developed, so too did the way films played with gender and sexuality. Marlene Dietrich wore men's clothing, and limp-wristed men unabashedly flirted with other men. The 1920s and early 1930s were a time of general cultural experimentation both in the United States and in Europe, a time when people played with sexuality in life and in representations. Not only were there queer characters in film, but the new field of animation presented opportunities for artists and cartoonists to present queerness through cartoon characters. Many early cartoon characters at one point or another appeared in drag, kissed members of the same sex, and played with gender and sexuality. Even the cartoons that appeared in the New York tabloid *Brevities* freely portrayed the feminine man, but unlike many of the representations on screen, in *Brevities*, the effeminate men were overtly sexual.

But the 1930s rise of conservative politics in the face of economic depression meant a return of conservative cultural politics as well. The Hays Code, which shaped the U.S. media from the 1930s until the 1980s, restricted overt displays of sexuality in the media, and queerness went underground. As Vito Russo shows, queerness did not actually disappear, but became coded. Characters were "musical" or were "like that." Men exchanged knowing glances that could be interpreted through a "queer lens."

Ironically, at the same time that popular media were becoming more fearful of overt discussions of sexuality, queerness began revealing itself in literature. In 1929, Radclyffe Hall's *The Well of Loneliness* told the story of "sexual deviants" in a more honest and open way than had previously been done. Mary Casal's 1930 *The Stone Wall* told the story of nonnormative female sexuality in an autobiographical voice.

In the period during and after World War II, queerness was everywhere and nowhere, in that if one knew how to read coded visual language, one found queerness everywhere, and those who did not read the code saw nothing. In fiction, the 1950s saw a whole string of lesbian pulp fiction, such as the classic *Beebo Brinker*. Like the earlier lesbian fiction of the 1920s and 1930s, these novels portrayed the "difficult life" of women who love women, and a world of oppression. In gay male fiction, writers like James Baldwin and Gore Vidal wrote about queer men's sex and intimacy in sometimes oblique, sometimes explicit ways.

Baldwin's narrator in his 1956 classic *Giovanni's Room* recalls his sexual awakening with a neighbor:

> He looked at me with his mouth open and his dark eyes very big . . . I laughed and grabbed his head as I had done God knows how many times before, when I was playing with him or when he had annoyed me. But this time when I touched him something happened in him and in me which made this touch different from any touch either of us had ever known. And he did not resist, as he usually did, but lay where I had pulled him, against my chest . . . Joey raised his head as I lowered mine and we kissed, as it were, by accident. Then, for the first time in my life, I was really aware of another person's body, of another person's smell.

Queerness came out of the closet with a vengeance in the 1970s when television shows, movies, and other forms of media and entertainment began breaking open the iron closet of the Hays Code. Musicals like *Cabaret* and television shows like *An American Family* began portraying openly gay characters. It's pointless to argue when the first gay character appeared on television, because the definition of queer representation has radically changed over time. In the 1920s, queerness was about gender play; in the 1980s, it was about sexual identity. In the 1970s, television series began portraying male characters who were in love with other men. Lesbians on screen became popular in the 1980s and 1990s when the queer femme fatale (as played by the likes of Sharon Stone) caused a sensation. Many have marked the 1990s as the decade in which queerness in the media moved from the margins to the mainstream. In 1997, Ellen Degeneres's character "came out," making her the first queer lead character in a television series. From 1997 to 2005, dozens of queer characters graced U.S. television screens. As Suzanna Danuta Walters shows, the new visibility of queerness has only occurred since the 1980s, fundamentally moving queers from the margins to the mainstream of American media.

On stage, one of the most important media moments occurred in 1992 when Tony Kushner's two-part, six-hour epic *Angels in America: A Gay Fantasia on America* won the Tony award and became that year's hit play. The long, philosophical play examines the intersections of queerness and religion at the height of the Reaganite 1980s, a time when queerness was perceived to be under attack by AIDS and by a silent government that was doing little to fight the disease. The play explored visibility, conservative politics, and assimilation and identity in the United States. In the words of the queer main character, Prior Walters, "We won't die secret deaths anymore. The world only spins forward. We will be citizens. The time has come." Kushner's lead character emphasizes that visibility and the ending of silence were keys to transforming the world. In the twenty-first-century United States, visibility happens through the media.

One of the primary reasons for the revolution in mainstream media was the development of queer film, plays, music, and literature. As queers began coming out, forming communities, and making culture, many rebelled against the mainstream media that excluded their work and their representations of queerness, and went on to form an alternative media universe. Queer bookstores stocked literature by and about queers; tiny playhouses in major urban areas produced gay-themed plays and musicals; cafes and summer camps, including the famous Michigan Womyn's Music Festival, created a forum for queer artists to perform music reflecting their American experiences. Gay male writers like Andrew Holleran and Edmund White, along with British writers like David Leavitt, Alan Hollinghurst, and Hanif Kureishi, created quality queer fiction that eventually began to push the edges of the mainstream literary establishment. Kureishi's novels became films, and in 2004, Alan Hollinghurst won the Booker Prize, the most prestigious award in British fiction. For women, writers like Dorothy Allison and Alice Walker used the experiences of feminist fiction writers to write the stories of lesbian women, and unlike gay male fiction, which often portrayed the sexualized worlds of gay men in the 1970s, lesbian fiction was often a form of social criticism and took a more politicized stance than gay male fiction. Some queer writers and artists have questioned whether the queer media make invisible those who are different, especially queers of color. From poet/filmmaker Marlon Riggs to scholar Dwight McBride, African American queer artists and writers have criticized queer representations for presuming that the queer experience could be encapsulated in the upper-middle-class, gay white male experience.

Some ask why, in the first decade of the twenty-first century, queerness has become the new marker of hipness. If queer has simply become a way to make a form of media hip, does it still have any of its political import? Queer culture has gone mainstream. For example, when Barnes and Noble established its gay and lesbian section and the last remaining queer bookstores began closing in major cities, it became clear that the meanings of queer culture had changed forever.

RADCLYFFE HALL

Why Did I Write *The Well of Loneliness?* (1934)

Radclyffe Hall's 1928 English novel The Well of Loneliness *opened up discussion about lesbian love and was a huge scandal when it reached its American audience. Its publication made lesbianism a cause célèbre in some parts of the country, especially among the burgeoning bohemian community of Greenwich Village.*

I only decided to write *The Well of Loneliness* after most profound consideration, and deep study of my subject, and, moreover, I waited to write it until I had made a name for myself as an author, this because I felt that it would, at that time, be difficult for an unknown writer to get a novel on congenital sexual inversion published. Also I wished to offer my name and my literary reputation in support of the cause of the inverted. I knew that I was running the risk of injuring my career as a writer by rousing up a storm of antagonism; but I was prepared to face this possibility because, being myself a congenital invert, I understood the subject from the inside as well as from medical and psychological textbooks. I felt therefore that no one was better qualified to write the subject in fiction than an experienced novelist like myself who was actually one of the people about whom she was writing and was thus in a position to understand their spiritual, mental, and physical reactions, their joys and their sorrows, and above all their unceasing battle against a frequently cruel and nearly always thoughtless and ignorant world, a world which seeks to label a fact in Nature as "unnatural" and thus as being a fair target for ridicule or condemnation.

In my book I endeavoured to portray in Stephen Gordon the finest type of the inverted woman, knowing well that such a type does, in fact, exist side by side with the weaker members. My book had a threefold purpose. Firstly, I hoped that it would encourage the inverted in general to declare themselves, to face up to a hostile world in their true colours, and this with dignity and courage. Secondly, 1 hoped that it would give even greater courage than they already possess to the strong and courageous, and strength and hope to the weak and the hopeless among my own kind, spurring all classes of inverts to a mighty effort to make good through hard work, faithful and loyal attachments—if such attachments are contracted—and, above all, to sober and useful living; in a word spurning all classes of inverts to prove that they are capable of being as good and useful citizens as the best of the so-called normal men and women, and this against truly formidable odds. Thirdly, I hoped that normal men and women of good will would be brought through my book to a fuller and more tolerant understanding of the inverted; that those parents who had chanced to breed male or female inverts would cease from tormenting and condemning their offspring, and thus—as is only too often the case—doing irreparable harm to the highly sensitized nervous system that is characteristic of inversion; above all would cease destroying that self-respect which is the most useful and necessary prop to those of all ages in their journey through life, but particularly to the young invert. I hoped also that my book would reach schoolteachers, welfare workers, indeed all those who had the care of the young, and that it might even prove useful to doctors and psychologists who are often hampered in their work and their studies by meeting only those inverts whose plight has rendered them physically or psychically unfit, those inverts who owing to persecution have become the prey of nervous disorders and cannot thus be considered fair examples of the inverted as a whole. Whether or not I have succeeded in my aim time alone will show.

GENERAL REMARKS

In his commentary at the beginning of my book, Havelock Ellis says: "So far as I know, it is the first English novel which presents, in a completely faithful and uncompromising form, one particular aspect of sexual life as it exists among us today." He is correct I think; at all events when I sat down to write *The Well of Loneliness*, I felt that I was about to undertake the task of a pioneer, and that I must therefore be prepared to face the consequences—frequently unpleasant—that accrue from most pioneer work. As an American journalist of my acquaintance wrote to me wittily when the storm broke: "You have torpedoed the ark, and therefore you mustn't be surprised that Mr. and Mrs. Noah have come out to see what's happened!" . . .

What happened in the United States appears in the "Victory Edition" (1929, Covici, Friede). The account of the attempt made by Mr. Sumner to get my book suppressed in America also, and of the lawsuits that followed, is given in great detail by that brilliant lawyer and champion of literary freedom, Morris Ernst, who, incidentally, fought the forces of retrogression on behalf of my American publishers. This account is indeed well worth reading, and it tells the story of the battle of *The Well of Loneliness* in the United States far better than I could hope to tell it. In the end my book was victorious. I have great cause for gratitude towards America; great cause for gratitude also towards all those eminent American men and women who came forward in defence of the book, and great cause for gratitude towards the three American judges who conducted the last case in so seemly and so eminently just a manner.

Have I suffered through the writing of *The Well of Loneliness?* Yes and no. I certainly felt very strained and weary by the time the battles were ended. Of course many strange and unexpected things happened to me after the English suppression. Until the book was publicly attacked, some of those whom I had supposed to be sincere friends taking their cue from a fine and generous press, perhaps appeared to accept the book in the spirit in which it had been written; but after the public attack—taking their cue from the then antagonistic portion of the press—they leapt on me, howling with the wolves. I was down, as they thought, and so they trampled. But then there rose up many in my defence and among these the most unexpected people: simple working people, the humble and the poor as well as a host of distinguished men and women some of whom I had only known by name until they came forward to defend me.

Very moving and unforgettable sympathy was extended to me by all classes of society. For instance, a subscription was started to pay my legal expenses, which, however, I could not very well accept in view of the fact that I possessed certain assets—I was able to sell my London house and thus procure the necessary ammunition. One very rich man, unknown to me personally, generously offered to pay the whole of my expenses himself, begging me to engage the best possible barristers, while quite a number of poor working men wrote to me saying that if a subscription was started they would like to contribute their hard-earned shillings. And so it was that those dark and distressful days held for me their patches of sunshine. Indeed the sympathy of the British working classes was one of my greatest supports at that time and I am never likely to forget it.

A less agreeable side of the picture is the notoriety that the suppression of the book caused to fall upon me—I could not then escape it nor can I even now six years after the book's publication. I do not like notoriety; it embarrasses me and makes me feel shy, but I realise that it is the price I must pay for having intentionally come out into the open, and no price could ever be too great in my eyes. Nothing is so spiritually degrading for an understanding of one's morale as living a lie, as keeping friends only by false pretences. It is this that drags many an invert down, that whittles away his or her self respect and with it his or her usefulness as a citizen. The worthy among the inverted—those fine men and women whom Nature has seen fit to set apart as variants from the more usual type—hate the lies and the conspiracy of silence that a ruthless society sometimes forces on them. Like their more normal brethren they are honest, simple souls who long to live honestly and to live as themselves; they desire to form a part of the social scheme, to conform in all ways to the social code as it exists at present. Because, though they see its imperfections as every intelligent person must, they realise that nothing in this world can be perfect and that, on the whole, this code as it is—save for its injustice towards themselves—is a workable and necessary proposition unless we are to fall into chaos. Such inverts desire to legalise their unions. Preposterous, do you say? And yet it may come, though I may not be here to welcome its coming.

One last word. It has very frequently been said that *The Well of Loneliness* is my own life, that Morton was my home, Raftery my horse, and Sir Philip and Lady Anna my parents; that Angela Crosby really lived and still lives, and that Mary also is a real person. This is not so, the book is pure fiction so far as such details and such people are concerned; I only drew upon my own experience when I came to write certain fundamental emotions that are characteristic of the inverted. Then, I admit, I did draw upon myself, I drew very ruthlessly upon myself, hoping that by telling my readers the truth, *The Well of Loneliness* would carry conviction.

TONY KUSHNER
Angels in America (1992)

It is hard to imagine a more important moment in queer theater history than Tony Kushner's 1992 production of Angels in America. *The six-hour, two-day show tracks the lives of several characters living in New York in the mid-1980s at the height of the AIDS epidemic. It interweaves discussions of sexuality with religion, all within the context of the conservative Reagan era. The play won numerous awards and has been produced all over the world. In 2003, director Mike Nichols made a film version of the play that also won numerous awards.*

PRIOR: *I. WANT.* You to go away. I'm tired to death of being done to, walked out on, *infected,* fucked over and *now* tortured by some mixed-up, reactionary angel, some . . .
(The Angel lands in front of Prior.)
ANGEL: You can't Outrun your Occupation, Jonah. Hiding from Me one place you will find me in another. I I I I stop down the road, waiting for you.
(She touches him, tenderly, and turns him, cradling him with one arm.)
ANGEL: You Know Me Prophet: Your battered heart, Bleeding Life in the Universe of Wounds.
(The Angel presses the volume against his chest. They both experience something unnameable—painful, joyful in equal measure. There is a terrifying sound. The Angel gently, lovingly lowers Prior to the ground.)
ANGEL: Vessel of the BOOK now: Oh Exemplum Paralyticum: On you in you in your blood we write have written: STASIS!
The END.
(In gales of music, holding the Book aloft, the Angel ascends.
The bedroom disappears. Prior stands, puts on his street clothes and resumes his place beside Belize. They are back on the street in front of the funeral home.)
BELIZE: You have been spending too much time alone.
PRIOR: Not by choice. None of this by choice.
BELIZE: This is . . . worse than nuts, it's . . . well, don't migrate, don't mingle, that's . . . malevolent, some of us didn't exactly *choose* to migrate, know what I'm saying . . .
PRIOR *(Overlapping):* I hardly think it's appropriate for you to get *offended,* I didn't invent this shit it was *visited* on me . . .
BELIZE *(Overlapping on "offended"):* But it *is* offensive or at least monumentally confused and it's not . . . *visited,* Prior. By who? It *is* from you, what else is it?
PRIOR: Something else.
BELIZE: That's crazy.
PRIOR: Then I'm crazy.

BELIZE: No, you're . . .

PRIOR: Then it was an angel.

BELIZE: It was *not* an . . .

PRIOR: Then I'm crazy. The whole world is, why not me?

It's 1986 and there's a *plague,* half my friends are dead and I'm only thirty-one, and every goddamn morning I wake up and I think Louis is next to me in the bed and it takes me long minutes to remember . . . that this is *real,* it isn't just an impossible, terrible dream, so maybe yes I'm flipping out.

BELIZE *(Angry):* You better not. You better fucking not flip out.

This is not dementia. And this is not real. This is just you, Prior, afraid of what's coming, afraid of time. But see that's just not how it goes, the world doesn't spin backwards. Listen to the world, to how fast it goes. . . .

HANNAH: You had a vision.

PRIOR: A vision. Thank you, Maria Ouspenskaya.

I'm not so far gone I can be assuaged by pity and lies.

HANNAH: I don't have pity. It's just not something I have.

(Little pause)

One hundred and seventy years ago, which is recent, an angel of God appeared to Joseph Smith in upstate New York, not far from here. People have visions.

PRIOR: But that's preposterous, that's . . .

HANNAH: It's not polite to call other people's beliefs preposterous.

He had great need of understanding. Our Prophet. His desire made prayer. His prayer made an angel. The angel was real. I believe that.

PRIOR: I don't. And I'm sorry but it's repellent to me. So much of what you believe.

HANNAH: What do I believe?

PRIOR: I'm a homosexual. With AIDS. I can just imagine what you . . .

HANNAH: No you can't. Imagine. The things in my head. You don't make assumptions about me, mister; I won't make them about you.

PRIOR *(A beat; he looks at her, then):* Fair enough.

HANNAH: My son is . . . well, like you.

PRIOR: Homosexual.

HANNAH *(A nod, then):* I flew into a rage when he told me, mad as hornets. At first I assumed it was about his . . . *(She shrugs)*

PRIOR: Homosexuality.

HANNAH: But that wasn't it. Homosexuality. It just seems . . . ungainly. Two men together. It isn't an appetizing notion but then, for me, men in *any* configuration . . . well they're so lumpish and stupid. And stupidity gets me cross.

PRIOR: I wish you would be more true to your demographic profile. Life is confusing enough.

(Little pause. They look at each other.)

PRIOR: You know the Bible, you know ...

HANNAH: Reasonably well, I . . .

PRIOR: The prophets in the Bible, do they . . . ever refuse their vision?

HANNAH: There's scriptural precedent, yes.

PRIOR: And what does God do to them? When they do that?

HANNAH: He . . . Well, he feeds them to whales.

(They both laugh. Prior's laugh brings on breathing trouble.)

HANNAH: Just lie still. You'll be all right.

PRIOR: No. I won't be. My lungs are getting tighter. The fever mounts and you get delirious. And then days of delirium and awful pain and drugs; you start slipping and then.

I really . . . fucked up. I'm scared. I can't do it again.

HANNAH: You shouldn't talk that way. You ought to make a better show of yourself.

PRIOR: Look at this . . . horror.

(He lifts his shirt; his torso is spotted with three or four lesions.)

See? That's not human. That's why I run. Wouldn't you? Wouldn't anybody.

HANNAH: It's a cancer. Nothing more. Nothing more human than that.

PRIOR: Oh God, I want to be done.

HANNAH: An angel is just a belief, with wings and arms that can carry you. It's naught to be afraid of. If it lets you down, reject it. Seek for something new. . . .

PRIOR: I'm almost done.

The fountain's not flowing now, they turn it off in the winter, ice in the pipes. But in the summer it's a sight to see. I want to be around to see it. I plan to be. I hope to be. This disease will be the end of many of us, but not nearly all, and the dead will be commemorated and will struggle on with the living, and we are not going away. We won't die secret deaths anymore. The world only spins forward. We will be citizens. The time has come.

Bye now.

You are fabulous creatures, each and every one.

And I bless you: *More Life.*

The Great Work Begins.

~

SUZANNA DANUTA WALTERS

Prologue to *All the Rage: The Story of Gay Visibility in America* (2003)

In the prologue to her lively book about the increasing visibility of American queers, Suzanna Danuta Walters recounts the dearth of images, support, and resources available to young queers a mere thirty years ago when she first came out of the closet. Walters con-

trasts this paucity with the veritable media explosion that accompanied both Ellen Degeneres's coming out on mainstream television and the brutal murder of Matthew Shepard in the late 1990s. Walters argues that these two cultural moments were an important watershed, which not only galvanized the LGBT rights movement, but also showed the ordinary faces and lives of queer people to main street America.

I think I must have been about 12 or 13 when I first thought I might be gay. I'll never forget the moment I *knew* it to be true, when I kissed a girl for the first time under the stairwell in my school. Like all such kisses, it retrospectively becomes a defining event, although at the time it was simply a thrill. I'll also never forget what it meant to come out, a not-so-sweet sixteen, in what now seems like the medieval 1970s. When I came out, I knew not one other gay teen, although I remember a sensitive boy who avoided my loud coming out like the plague. Now, gay youth groups proliferate and many school systems provide training to staff to alert them to issues of sexual identity. When I came out, I lost many of my high school friends and only found solace with a rather secretive college club. Now, gay teens can meet other gay teens—sometimes even in school-based clubs. Indeed, the Gay, Lesbian and Straight Educational Network (GLSEN) estimates that over seven hundred high school "gay/straight alliances" are registered with the organization, and the numbers continue to grow. When I was a gay teen, harassment was simply what one lived through—the idea of reporting it seemed unimaginable. Now, a young teen in Wisconsin sets a precedent when courts find the school liable for failing to stop anti-gay abuse and awards him close to a million dollars. When I came out, I feared my liberal family would disown me, scorn me, turn away in disgust. Now, kids can refer their folks to PFLAG (Parents and Friends of Lesbians and Gays) for supportive gay-positive re-education. When I came out, invisibility was taken for granted. I can remember vividly scouring the TV guide for any television program that might give me some indication that I existed, and have only a vague memory of an artsy British broadcast on public TV, I must have watched that every time it was replayed. Now, we have Ellen (and Will and Jack and Carter and Willow . . .). When I came out, I was rushed to a psychiatrist. No one ever suggested that I was healthy. Now, the movement to cure gays again rears its ugly head, but this time it is after all the medical and psychiatric organizations have discredited "reparative therapy" and disavowed the idea of homosexuality as an illness.

When I came out, there were no out gay politicians, no gay studies programs in universities, no advertisements that featured gays, no gay TV stars, few out gay actors, little anti-discrimination legislation, no glossy gay magazines, no gay cruises and few gay festivals. There was no gay chic, no gayby boom, no gay MasterCard. Now, there is all this and more. When I came out, my mother and I both assumed a future without children. Lesbian mother seemed like an oxymoron. Now, we share the care of my daughter and know many gay parents. Then, gay parents routinely hid or lost their kids and few questioned the rightness of this. Now, when a lesbian mom loses her kid, her story becomes a supportive TV Movie of the Week and front page news. When I came out, gay marriage was a contradiction in terms. Now, Congress is so scared it might happen that it enacts legislation to forbid it, free-thinking Vermont gives it a tentative nod, and commitment ceremonies are becoming commonplace.

When I came out, I remember being chased, taunted, spit at. It never occurred to me that I could report this. Now, gay and lesbian anti-violence groups are in most major cities and the inclusion of gays in hate crimes laws moves ahead. When I came out, I ran to the bars because it was the only place I thought I could touch another woman without fearing for my life. Now, that quite justified fear remains of course, but there are plenty of spaces of safety besides the bars and bathhouses. When I came out, I thought homosexuality was the problem. Now, homophobia has been named and declaimed from the byways of small-town America to the grand halls of government. When I came out, I could not help but feel alone, isolated, marginalized. While I knew there was a gay rights movement, the pervasive silence of the larger public world kept me from finding it easily, mired as I was in my overpowering sense of difference and aloneness in that difference. Now, that awful closet of isolation and invisibility has been replaced by the wide-open door of public recognition.

Two events, one in 1997 and the other in 1998, dramatically illustrate the new visibility. The coming out of Ellen Morgan on the unevenly successful sitcom *Ellen* was an historic event and in a sense deserved the unprecedented media attention that it garnered. Of course, this televisual fictional event was made juicer and more complicated by the prior coming out of the real life Ellen who plays the character of the same name. Rumors had been circulating for years about DeGeneres's sexuality, and the simultaneous revelation of both the real-life and the fictional Ellen was destined for Hollywood history-making. Indeed, she made the cover of the April 14 *Time* magazine, revealing that, "yep, I'm gay." In addition, she was interviewed by Diane Sawyer on *20/20* (replete with tearful reconciliation with her parents) and put in an appearance on *Oprah* (who also played her therapist on the coming-out episode) the day the episode aired.

There were other television events besides the airing of the actual coming-out episode, because increasingly our mass-mediated cultural world appears as one rebounding, interlocking process rather than a set of discrete objects. In the first place, the show had been airing tongue-in-cheek hints for weeks. Episode after episode included the requisite hints (e.g., Ellen looking in a mirror singing "I feel pretty, oh so pretty. I feel pretty and witty and . . ." ending the song before the word is uttered; or when she is looking at new homes to purchase, she responds to her mother's "where are you?" by popping out of the door and exclaiming "in the closet"). On the talk show circuit, she responded to direct questions about her character's sexuality with coy answers: "The character does find out—and this is where the confusion comes in—that she is Lebanese." On *Good Morning America* she claimed that everything "got totally blown out of proportion. . . . We're adding another character—a guy—and his name is Les Bian."

By the time the actual episode aired, even those most willfully in denial had to admit that Ellen was, indeed, gay. But it did not stop there. In other words, this became a huge and far-reaching media event—no newspaper neglected before-and-after coverage, the news magazines weighed in, and the national gay organizations made this priority number one. The Gay and Lesbian Alliance Against Defamation (GLAAD) sponsored more than fifteen hundred "Come Out with Ellen" home viewing parties, and big-city fundraisers were sponsored by Absolut vodka, replete with celebrity memorabilia including signed scripts from the historic episode and *Ellen* trivia games. GLAAD also fielded thousands of media queries, produced a very popular "Come Out with Ellen" Web page, and served as informal consultants on the coming-out episode (and one of its own—Chastity Bono—even had a guest spot on a later episode).

Protestors showed up at ABC headquarters in Washington, Jerry Falwell referred to her as "Ellen degenerate," a Birmingham, Alabama, affiliate refused to air the episode, and a Birmingham auditorium was filled to capacity (more than twenty-five hundred people) to witness a direct satellite feed of the episode. A teacher in Alameda was attacked by a parent for discussing the episode in her fifth-grade class (although she was later cleared by the school board and by a state panel), and the network charged twice the normal advertising rates for the episode, and got it. More viewers watched the episode than any other single episode in the history of television, with the exception of the final episode of *M*A*S*H* and the "who shot J.R.?" revelatory episode of *Dallas*. Local stations followed the airing with reports of parties and protests, ancillary commentary on the status of gay life, reports on gays in Hollywood and gays in government. Vice President Al Gore made a speech in October of 1997 to the Hollywood Radio and Television Society where he argued that "when the character Ellen came out, millions of Americans were forced to look at sexual orientation in a more open light." The media coverage even surpassed the Dan Quayle silliness with Murphy Brown. Not long after the coming-out episode, the series was canceled.

If Ellen's coming out was cause to celebrate, then the following year's "gay event" was surely cause to mourn. The 1998 murder of gay University of Wyoming student Matthew Shepard illustrates with sad clarity the state of affairs in the era of visibility. For, of course, death by gay bashing is nothing new. Indeed, there are few gay people who have escaped some form of violence. What was striking was not just the horribleness of the crime, nor that it occurred in these supposedly more liberal times. What was astounding to so many was the tidal wave of attention this death garnered. Like the coming out of Ellen, the murder of Matthew grabbed public attention and shook it by its proverbial ears. On TV news, in magazines and newspapers, in public statements and countless memorials, the death of Matthew Shepard became a flash point for gay anger and sympathetic straight grief. While surely Shepard's death was especially ugly (beaten and left tied up on a country road) and his persona especially attractive (nonthreatening, All-American kid from the heartland), that does not wholly explain the depth of the media coverage. In these new times, killing gays still goes on, but it is no longer business as usual. As I joined the mourners on the steps of the Capitol I was struck by the huge presence of the media, politicians crowding to join in, public figures and Hollywood stars weeping at the microphone. Congress joined in the chorus of concern and condemnation. Even the

President immediately denounced the incident and named it as a hate crime, using the opportunity to promote stronger legislation in that area. We should never underestimate the significance of an American President speaking out on anti-gay violence. A young gay man's death, which not so very long ago would have been a nonevent, or at best a news story tucked in the back pages, now captivated a nation seeing its sons and daughters with new eyes.

These two events illustrate the confusing and often incomprehensible tenor of the times. We rejoice at breaking down one barrier only to be faced, again, with the ugliness and brutality of another. Ellen comes out, Matthew dies, and the media turns both into iconic events. Ellen gets canceled and Matthew becomes a memory and the parents of both become advocates for equal rights. In the eye of the storm it is sometimes difficult to make out the contours, to see with clarity, to know for sure which way the wind is shifting. Surely, though, we're not in Kansas anymore.

This book is for everyone. It is for the liberal gays, who are now sitting back in wonder at the dawning of a new age, thinking the battles have largely been won. They haven't. Be vigilant. It is for the radical gays, who view with unbridled cynicism these changes, seeing them as solely superficial at best, nefariously co-optive at worst. Relax, there's more to this sea change than homosexuality lite. It is for the conservative gays, who want to slip silently into the night of American society, unnoticed, unseen, unremarked. Forget it guys, keep your suits on but don't ever force our brightly colored tutus back in the closet. It is for the well-meaning heterosexuals, who think an embrace of sameness is the best gays can hope for. It isn't. We cherish our differences. It is for the heterosexuals who didn't even know we existed. Look around you—we are your sons and daughters, husbands and wives, coworkers, bosses, and next-door neighbors. It is for the not so well-meaning straights, who wish fervently that the gay '90s would fade out as a footnote to history. This is history. And the new millennium holds hopes and fears as paradoxical as the last.

7
Sticks and Stones
BULLYING, BATTERING, AND BEATING
AMERICAN QUEERS, NOW AND THEN

Queerness has a lot to do with violating boundaries, challenging norms, and shaking up social expectations. Queers question what it means to be male and female, what sex means, what kinds of relationships are good, what kinds of family structures should exist, and what it means to be American. Queers have challenged the images Americans see on stage and screen and in newspapers and literature. In the past thirty years, queers have tried to stretch the boundaries of what it means to be American and at the same time have questioned whether any kinds of boundaries are useful for social cohesion. Some queers aim for inclusion within bounded groups; others try to explode those boundaries.

When we speak of violence, we speak broadly about the physical and discursive use of power to maintain social, cultural, and physical boundaries that support dominance of one group over another. We find violence when a queer is screamed at from a passing car, when gay bashing occurs, when television and movies portray queers as diseased or despised, and when high school bullies taunt their (perceived-to-be or out) gay classmates, especially when statistics show that queer teens have a much higher rate of suicide than nonqueer teens. We find violence when women are harassed, assaulted, or raped. We find violence, in different forms, at all times and in all places of American queer history. We ourselves have each been the victims of violence because of our queerness, and it is the rare queer person who has not experienced some form of violence.

We conceive of violence as all of those attempts to use one's power to maintain boundaries by inciting fear in those perceived to be transgressing—whether because of their appearance, their relationships, or their positions in society. As Wayne Myslik shows in his study of antigay violence in queer neighborhoods, most white queer men *assume* violence as a social fact, even if most of them have not experienced physical violence directly. In other words, antiqueer violence has

181

proven successful at inciting fear in queers who are ever more visible. At the same time, queers fear that too much visibility, like holding hands in the wrong part of town, could incite violence.

In the early part of the twentieth century, antiqueer violence was widespread but less visible than in the early twenty-first century. We choose to use the word "antiqueer," as opposed to "homophobic," to suggest a broader cultural phenomenon, one that posits violence as a response to difference or a way of keeping people in their place. "Homophobic" suggests an irrational fear of people who sleep with members of the same sex; antiqueer violence maintains both the gender and sexual social order in a society in which roles and identities are changing. Phobias and identities suggest something wrong, not with the social order but with a person's psyche.

Throughout much of U.S. history, antiqueer violence was often state sponsored. Violence is state sponsored when those who hold state authority use that power to maintain social boundaries. When police harassed queers on the street in the 1920s, when they raided queer bars in the 1950s, or when the military ousted queers from the military, the state was—and it continues to be—involved in antiqueer violence. State-sponsored antiqueer violence included enforcement of antisodomy laws on the books in many states until the Supreme Court made such laws unconstitutional in 2003. Legal violence, although perhaps not as visceral as physical violence, is nonetheless a way of using power to patrol social boundaries (not to mention the humiliation of police raids into people's private bedrooms). Legal violence also gives legal and tacit permission to those who do carry out physical violence, condoning their attempts to protect the outmoded social order.

That said, if in the 1950s the state was seen as a primary source of antiqueer violence, by the new millennium, queers often expect the state to defend them *against* antiqueer violence. Police are expected to prosecute antiqueer crimes; legislatures are expected to pass anti–hate crimes legislation, making violence motivated by hostility toward a group a more serious offense than violence directed against an individual; and many activists are calling on the U.S. military to end the persecution of queers. Some argue that because the state is no longer patrolling the sexual and gender boundaries, other social, religious, and cultural groups have become more violent in their attempt to put queers back in their place.

The shift from state-sponsored to socially driven violence happened over four decades, from the Stonewall rebellion in 1969, which marked the beginning of the end of explicit police violence against queers, to the Supreme Court's overturning of antisodomy laws in 2004. Some argue, however, that the lack of access to marriage for people in same-sex couples and the lack of legal protection for transgender people mark the continuation of state-sponsored violence. Over that same period of time, antiqueer violence has seemed to become more visible, more violent, and better documented.

In 1978, the Castro neighborhood in San Francisco elected Harvey Milk to the San Francisco City Council, the first openly queer elected official in the history of the United States. Milk spoke openly about the fact that his visibility and outspoken transgression of social boundaries made him a target of violence. His predictions came true when city councilmember Dan White murdered Milk and then Mayor George Moscone. These murders caused anger and sadness in San Francisco's gay community, but White's virtual acquittal caused outrage. Successfully arguing that he was temporarily insane after ingesting a large quantity of Twinkies, an event now known infamously as the "Twinkie defense," White received a minimum sentence. The "jury of White's peers" reminded San Franciscans that the murder of a queer—or even an ally of the queer community like Moscone—was not all that serious. Milk's murder, and the outrage it spawned, was only the first of several moments in the contemporary American queer history of violence. In 1998, Matthew Shepard, a twenty-year-old student at the University of Wyoming, was brutally beaten and hung on a fence to die by two young men from Laramie. Shepard's death sparked nationwide vigils, protests, and a spate of legislation making sexual orientation a protected class.

Murder is obviously the most visible form of antiqueer violence, but as the report from the Gay, Lesbian, and Straight Educators Network (GLSEN) shows, antiqueer violence begins in American schools with taunting and teasing on playgrounds and physical abuse in locker rooms, and can cause such trauma that queer youth commit suicide at much higher rates than other youth. These issues are compounded by other social problems like poverty and violence in urban American schools. What the study does not reflect is the degree to which such taunting and physical abuse occur not only in schools (another form of semi–state-sponsored antiqueer violence) but also in these youths' homes. Frequently, queers first experience antiqueer violence from parents and family members who want to patrol the family's boundaries and enforce traditional roles. Because of this, queer youth often end up on the streets and drop out of school. Queer youth have a high homeless and high school dropout rate, and often have less support from family members to respond to state and social antiqueer violence. After all, unlike African American youth, whose parents are also members of the same persecuted minority, queer youth of all ethnic backgrounds usually have no familial introduction into their community and culture. The visibility of queer youth has helped drive this violent response against them, and this violence has generated a queer community response in the form of queer homeless shelters, queer proms, and even queer public high schools like the Harvey Milk Institute in New York City that provide a safe space for students who could not succeed in school because of school violence.

Valerie Jenness, a leading sociologist on gay and lesbian antiviolence projects, shows how gays and lesbians have made antiqueer violence into a social *problem*, rather than simply a social *fact*. By marking something as a problem, Jenness shows how queer activism has been a key factor in highlighting the degree of antiqueer violence in the United States and in showing ways to address such violence.

If violence is a means of patrolling boundaries, then antiqueer violence will continue so long as queers are perceived as *not* fitting into certain boundaries. So long as certain Christian leaders continue to demonize queers as "other," so long as the military continues marking queers as a threat to morale, so long as high schools see a same-sex prom couple as "a problem," antiqueer violence will remain a social problem, not just for queers but for everyone.

LESLIE FEINBERG

Stone Butch Blues (1993)

Leslie Feinberg, born a working-class Jewish girl in Buffalo, wrote this autobiographical novel about her changing gender identity while living in Buffalo and New York in the 1950s to the 1970s. Stone Butch Blues *tells the story of Jess Goldberg, who learns to accept and negotiate her attraction to women and her butch identity. Immediately, she is faced with violence. The police raid the lesbian bars, arrest any woman wearing fewer than three articles of women's clothing, and routinely beat, strip, or rape them. Jess and her friends also face the violence of bashers who attack without cause on dark or well-lighted streets. Her story was one of the earliest to narrate the life of a transgender person and one of the best to describe the violent enforcement of gender norms.*

I didn't want to be different. I longed to be everything grownups wanted, so they would love me. I followed all their rules, tried my best to please. But there was something about me that made them knit their eyebrows and frown. No one ever offered a name for what was wrong with me. That's what made me afraid it was really bad. I only came to recognize its melody through this constant refrain: "Is that a boy or a girl?"

I was one more bad card life had dealt my parents. They were already bitterly disappointed people. My father had grown up determined he wasn't going to be stuck in a factory like his old man; my mother had no intention of being trapped in a marriage.

When they met, they dreamed they were going on an exciting adventure together. When they awoke, my father was working in a factory and my mother had become a housewife. When my mother discovered she was pregnant with me, she told my dad she didn't want to be tied down with a kid. My father insisted she'd be happy once she had the baby. Nature would see to that.

My mother had me to prove him wrong.

My parents were enraged that life had cheated them. They were furious that marriage blocked their last opportunity to escape. Then I came along and I was different. Now they were furious with me. I could hear it in the way they retold the story of my birth.

Rain and wind had lashed the desert while my mother was in labor. That's why she gave birth to me at home. The storm was too violent to be forded. My father was at work, and we had no phone. My mother said she wept so loudly in fear when she realized I was on the way that the Dineh grandmother from across the hall knocked on the door to see what was wrong, and then, realizing my birth was imminent, brought three more women to help.

The Dineh women sang as I was born. That's what my mother told me. They washed me, fanned smoke across my tiny body, and offered me to my mother.

"Put the baby over there," she told them, pointing to a bassinet near the sink. *Put the baby over there.* The words chilled the Indian women. My mother could see that. The story was retold many times as I was growing up, as though the frost that bearded those words could be melted by repeating them in a humorous, ironic way.

Days after I was born the grandmother knocked on our door again, this time because my cries alarmed her. She found me in the bassinet, unwashed. My mother admitted she was afraid to touch me, except to pin on a diaper or stick a bottle in my mouth. The next day the grandmother sent over her daughter, who agreed to keep me during the day while her children were at school, if that was alright. It was and it wasn't. My mother was relieved, I'm sure, although at the same time it was an indictment of her. But she let me go.

And so I grew in two worlds, immersed in the music of two languages. One world was Wheaties and Milton Berle. The other was fry bread and sage. One was cold, but it was mine; the other was warm, but it wasn't.

My parents finally stopped letting me travel across the hall when I was four. They came to pick me up before dinner one night. A number of the women had cooked a big meal and brought all the children together for the feast. They asked my parents if I could stay. My father grew alarmed when he heard one of the women say something to me in a language he didn't understand, and I answered her with words he'd never heard before. He said later he couldn't stand by and watch his own flesh and blood be kidnapped by Indians.

I've only heard bits and pieces about that evening, so I don't know everything that went on. I wish I did. But this part I've heard over and over again: one of the women told my parents I was going to walk a difficult path in life. The exact wording changed in the retelling. Sometimes my mother would pretend to be a fortuneteller, close her eyes, cover her forehead with her fingertips, and say, "I see a difficult life for this child." Other times my father would bellow like the Wizard of Oz, "This child will walk a hard road!"

In any case, my parents yanked me out of there. Before they left, though, the grandmother gave my mother a ring and said it would help to protect me in life. The ring frightened my parents, but they figured all that turquoise and silver must be worth something, so they took it.

That night there was another terrible desert storm, my parents told me, terrifying in its power. The thunder crashed and the lightning illuminated everything.

"Jess Goldberg?" the teacher asked.

"Present," I answered.

The teacher narrowed her eyes at me. "What kind of name is that? Is it short for Jessica?"

I shook my head. "No, ma'am."

"Jess," she repeated. "That's not a girl's name." I dropped my head. Kids around me covered their mouths with their hands to stifle their giggles.

Miss Sanders glared at them until they fell silent. "Is that a Jewish name?" she asked. I nodded, hoping that she was finished. She was not.

"Class, Jess is from the Jewish persuasion. Jess, tell the class where you're from."

I squirmed in my seat. "The desert."

"What? Speak up, Jess."

"I'm from the desert." I could see the kids mugging and rolling their eyes at each other.

"What desert? What state?" She pushed her glasses higher up on her nose.

I froze with fear. I didn't know. "The desert," I shrugged.

Miss Sanders grew visibly impatient. "What made your family decide to come to Buffalo?"

How should I know? Did she think parents told six-year-old kids why they made huge decisions that would impact on their lives? "We drove," I said. Miss Sanders shook her head. I hadn't made a very good first impression.

Sirens screamed. It was the Wednesday morning air raid drill. We crouched down under our desks and covered our heads with our arms. We were warned to treat The Bomb like strangers: don't make eye contact. If you can't see The Bomb, it can't see you.

There was no bomb—this was only practice for the real thing. But I was saved by the siren.

I was sorry we'd moved from the warmth of the desert to this cold, cold city. Nothing could have prepared me for getting out of bed on a winter morning in an unheated apartment in Buffalo. Even warming our clothes in the oven before we put them on didn't help much. After all, we still had to take our pajamas off first. Outside the cold was so fierce that the wind carved up my nose and sliced into my brain. Tears froze in my eyes.

My sister Rachel was still a toddler. I just remember a round snowsuit swaddled with scarves and mittens and hat. No kid, just clothes.

Even when I was bundled up in the dead of winter, with only a couple of inches of my face peeking out from my snowsuit hood and scarf, adults would stop me and ask, "Are you a boy or a girl?" I'd drop my eyes in shame, never questioning their right to ask.

During the summer there wasn't much to do in the projects, but there was plenty of time to do it.

The projects, former Army barracks, now housed the military-contracted aircraft workers and their families. All our fathers went to work in the same plant; all our mothers stayed home.

Old Man Martin was retired. He sat in a lawn chair on his porch listening to the McCarthy hearings on his radio. It was turned up so loud you could hear it all the way down the block. "Gotta watch out," he'd tell me as I passed his house, "communists could be anywhere. Anywhere." I'd nod solemnly and run off to play.

But Old Man Martin and I shared something in common. The radio was my best friend, too. "The Jack Benny Show" and "Fibber McGee and Molly" made me laugh, even when I didn't know what was so funny. "The Shadow" and "The Whistler" chilled me.

Perhaps outside these projects working families already had televisions, but not us. The streets of the project weren't even paved—just gravel and giant Lincoln Logs to mark the parking. Very few new things came down our road. Ponies pulled the carts of the ice man and the knife sharpener. On Saturday they brought the ponies without the carts and sold rides for a penny. A penny also bought a chunk from the ice man—chipped off with his ice pick. The ice was dense and slick and sparkled like a cold diamond that might never melt.

When a television set first appeared in the projects, it was in the living room of the McKensies. All the children in the neighborhood begged our parents to let us go watch "Captain Midnight" on the McKensies' new television. But most of us were not allowed in their home. Although it was 1955, the neighborhood still had some invisible war zones from a fierce strike that had been settled in 1949, the year I was born. "Mac" McKensie had been a scab. Just the word itself was enough to make me shy away from their house. You could still see traces of that word on the front of their coal bin, even though it had been painted over in a slightly different shade of green.

Years later, fathers still argued about the strike over kitchen tables and back-yard barbecue grills. I overheard descriptions of such bloody strike battles, I thought WWII had been fought at the plant. At night when we'd drive my father to his shift, I used to crouch down on the back seat of the car and peek past the plant gates out over the now quiet fields of combat.

There were also gangs in the project, and the kids whose parents had scabbed during the strike made up a small but feared pack. "Hey, pansy! Are you a boy or a girl?" There was no way to avoid them in the small planet of the project. Their sing-song taunts stayed with me long after I'd passed by.

The world judged me harshly and so I moved, or was pushed, toward solitude.

The highway sliced between our projects and a huge field. It was against the rules to cross that road. There wasn't much traffic on it. You'd have to stand in the middle of a lane for a long time in order to get hit. But I wasn't supposed to cross that road. I did though, and no one seemed to notice.

I parted the long brown grass that bordered the road. Once I passed through it I was in my own world.

On the way to the pond I stopped to visit the puppies and dogs in the out-side kennels connected to the back of the ASPCA building. The dogs barked and stood on their hind legs as I approached the fence. "Shhh!" I warned them. I knew no one was supposed to be back here.

A spaniel pushed his nose through the chain-link fence. I rubbed his head. I looked around for the terrier I loved. He had only come to the fence once to greet me, sniffing cautiously. Usually, no matter how I coaxed, he'd lay with his head on his paws, looking at me with mournful eyes. I wished I could take him home. I hoped he went to a kid who loved him.

"Are you a boy or a girl?" I asked the mongrel.

"Ruff, ruff!"

I didn't see the ASPCA man until it was too late. "Hey, kid. What you doing there?"

Caught. "Nothing," I said. "I wasn't doing anything bad. I was just talking to the dogs."

He smiled a little. "Don't put your fingers inside the fence, son. Some of 'em bite."

I felt the tips of my ears grow hot. I nodded. "I was looking for that little one with the black ears. Did a nice family take him?"

The man frowned for a moment. "Yes," he said quietly. "He's real happy now."

I hurried out to the pond to catch polywogs in a jar. I leaned on my elbow and looked up close at the little frogs that climbed up on the sun-baked rocks.

"Caw, caw!" A huge black crow circled above me in the air and landed on a rock nearby. We looked at each other in silence.

"Crow, are you a boy or a girl?"

"Caw, caw!"

I laughed and rolled over on my back. The sky was crayon blue. I pretended I was lying on the white cotton clouds. The earth was damp against my back. The sun was hot, the breeze was cool. I felt happy. Nature held me close and seemed to find no fault with me.

On my way back from the field I passed the Scabbie gang. They had found an unlocked truck parked on an incline. One of the older boys disengaged the emergency brake and made two of the younger boys from my side of the projects run under the truck as it rolled.

"Jessy, Jessy!" they taunted as they rushed toward me.

"Brian says you're a girl, but I think you're a sissy boy," one of them said.

I didn't speak.

"Well, what are you?" he mocked me.

I flapped my arms, "Caw, caw!" I laughed.

One of the boys knocked the jar filled with polywogs from my hand and it smashed on the gravel. I kicked and bit them but they held me and tied my hands behind my back with a piece of clothesline.

"Let's see how you tinkle," one of the boys said as he knocked me down and two of the others struggled to pull off my pants and my underpants. I was filled with horror. I couldn't make them stop. The shame of being half-naked before them—the important half—took all the steam out of me.

They pushed and carried me to old Mrs. Jefferson's house and locked me in the coal bin. It was dark in the bin. The coal was sharp and cut like knives. It hurt too much to lie still, but the more I moved the worse I made the wounds. I was afraid I'd never get out.

It took hours before I heard Mrs. Jefferson in the kitchen. I don't know what she thought when she heard all the thumping and kicking in her coal bin. But when she opened the little trap door on the coal bin and I squirmed out onto her kitchen floor, she looked scared enough to fall down dead. There I stood, covered with coal soot and blood, tied up and half-naked in her kitchen. She mumbled curses under her breath as she untied me and sent me home wrapped in a towel. I had to walk a block and knock on my parents' door before I found refuge.

They were really angry when they saw me. I never understood why. My father spanked me over and over again until my mother restrained his arm with a whisper and her hand.

A week later I caught up with one of the boys from the Scabbie gang. He made the mistake of wandering alone too near our house. I made a muscle and told him to feel it. Then I punched him in the nose. He ran away crying; I felt great, for the first time in days.

My mother called me into our house for dinner. "Who was that boy you were playing with?" I shrugged.

"You were showing him your muscle?"

I froze, wondering how much she had seen.

She smiled. "Sometimes it's better to let boys think they're stronger," she told me. I figured she was just plain crazy if she really believed that.

The phone rang. "I'll get it," my father called out. It was the parent of the kid whose nose I bloodied; I could tell by the way my father glowered at me as he listened.

"I was so ashamed," my mother told my father. He glared at me in the rearview mirror. All I could see were his thick black eyebrows. My mother had been informed that I could no longer attend temple unless I wore a dress, something I fought tooth and nail. At the moment I was wearing a Roy Rogers outfit—without my guns. It was hard enough being the only Jewish family in the projects without being in trouble at the temple. We had to drive a long time to go to the nearest synagogue. My father prayed downstairs. My mother and sister and I had to watch from the balcony, like at the movies.

It seemed like there weren't many Jews in the world. There were some on the radio, but none in my school. Jews weren't allowed on the playground. That's what the older kids told me, and they enforced it.

We were nearing home. My mother shook her head. "Why can't she be like Rachel?"

Rachel looked at me sheepishly. I shrugged. Rachel's dream was a felt skirt with an appliqué poodle and rhinestone-studded plastic shoes.

My father pulled our car to a stop in front of our house. "You go straight to your room, young lady. And stay there." I was bad. I was going to be punished. My head ached with fear. I wished I could find a way to be good. Shame suffocated me.

It was almost sundown. I heard my parents call Rachel to join them in their bedroom to light the Shabbas candles. I knew the shades were drawn. A month before, we'd heard laughter and shouting outside the living room windows while my father was lighting the candles. We raced to the windows and peered out into the dusk. Two teenagers pulled down their pants and mooned us. "Kikes!" they shouted. My father didn't chase them away; he closed the drapes. After that, we started praying in their bedroom with the shades pulled down.

Everyone in my family knew about shame.

Soon afterward my Roy Rogers outfit disappeared from the dirty clothes hamper. My father bought me an Annie Oakley outfit instead.

"No!" I shouted, "I don't want to. I don't want to wear it. I'll feel stupid!"

My father yanked me by the arm. "Young lady, I spent $4.90 for this Annie Oakley outfit and you're going to wear it."

I tried to shake off his hand, but it was clamped painfully on my upper arm. Tears dripped down my cheeks. "I want a Davy Crockett hat."

My father tightened his grip. "I said no."

"But why?" I cried. "Everybody has one except me. Why not?"

His answer was inexplicable. "Because you're a girl."

"I'm sick of people asking me if she's a boy or a girl," I overheard my mother complain to my father. "Everywhere I take her, people ask me."

I was ten years old. I was no longer a little kid and I didn't have a sliver of cuteness to hide behind. The world's patience with me was fraying, and it panicked me.

When I was really small I thought I'd do anything to change whatever was wrong with me. Now I didn't want to change, I just wanted people to stop being mad at me all the time.

One day my parents took my sister and me shopping downtown. As we drove down Allen Street I noticed a grownup whose sex I couldn't figure out.

"Mom, is that a he-she?" I asked out loud.

My parents exchanged amused glances and burst out laughing. My father stared at me in the rearview mirror. "Where did you hear that word?"

I shrugged, not sure I'd ever really heard the word before it had escaped from my mouth.

"What's a he-she?" my sister demanded to know. I was interested in the answer too.

"It's a weirdo," my father laughed. "Like a beatnik."

Rachel and I nodded without understanding.

Suddenly a wave of foreboding swept over me. I felt nauseous and dizzy. But whatever it was that triggered the fear, it was too scary to think about. The feeling ebbed as quickly as it had swelled.

I gently pushed open the door to my parents' bedroom and looked around. I knew they were both at work, but entering their bedroom was forbidden. So I peeked around the room first, just to make sure.

I went directly to my father's closet door. His blue suit was there. That meant he must be wearing the grey one today. A blue suit and a grey suit—that's all any man needed, my father always said. His ties hung neatly on a rack.

It took even more nerve to open my father's dresser drawer. His white shirts were folded and starched stiff as a board. Each one was wrapped around with tissue paper and banded like a gift. The moment I tore off the paper band, I knew I was in trouble. I had no hiding places for garbage that my mother wouldn't find right away. And I realized my father probably knew the precise number of shirts he owned. Even though all of them were white, he probably could tell exactly which one was missing.

But it was too late. Too late. I stripped down to my cotton panties and T-shirt and slid on his shirt. It was so starched my eleven-year-old fingers could hardly get the collar buttoned. I pulled down a tie from the rack. For years I had watched my father deftly twist and flop his ties in a complicated series of moves, but I couldn't figure out the puzzle. I tied it in a clumsy knot. I climbed up on a footstool to lift the suit from the hanger. Its weight surprised me. It fell in a heap. I put on the suit coat and looked in the mirror. A sound came from my throat, sort of a gasp. I liked the little girl looking back at me.

Something was still missing: the ring. I opened my mother's jewelry box. The ring was huge. The silver and turquoise formed a dancing figure. I couldn't tell if the figure was a woman or a man. The ring no longer fit across three of my fingers; now it fit snugly on two.

I stared in the big mirror over my mother's dresser, trying to see far in the future when the clothing would fit, to catch a glimpse of the woman I would become.

I didn't look like any of the girls or women I'd seen in the Sears catalog. The catalog arrived as the seasons changed. I'd be the first in the house to go through it, page by page. All the girls and women looked pretty much the same, so did all the boys and men. I couldn't find myself among the girls. I had never seen any adult woman who looked like I thought I would when I grew up. There were no women on television like the small woman reflected in this mirror, none on the streets. I knew. I was always searching.

For a moment in that mirror I saw the woman I was growing up to be staring back at me. She looked scared and sad. I wondered if I was brave enough to grow up and be her.

I never heard the bedroom door open. By the time I saw my parents it was already too late. Each of them thought they were supposed to pick up my sister at the orthodontist. So they all got home unexpectedly early.

My parents' expressions froze. I was so frightened my face felt numb.

Storm clouds were gathering on my horizon.

∽

MOISÉS KAUFMAN

The Laramie Project (2001)

In 1998, Matthew Shepard, a gay University of Wyoming student, was brutally murdered by Aaron McKinney and Russ Henderson, from Laramie, Wyoming. Like the murder of Harvey Milk twenty years earlier, Shepard's murder sparked street marches across the country in expression of mourning and support and also to protest the continuing violence against queers in the United States. Two years later, New York playwright Moisés Kaufman brought his Tectonic Theater Project to Laramie to interview residents about the murder and its effect on the town. He turned these interviews into The Laramie Project, *an award-winning play and film. In the wake of Shepard's murder, his mother, Judy, and father, Dennis, established the Matthew Shepard Foundation, dedicated to supporting diversity programs in education and to helping organizations establish environments where young people can feel safe.*

MOMENT: AARON MCKINNEY

NARRATOR: During the trial of Aaron McKinney, the prosecution played a tape recording of his confession.

ROB DEBREE: My name is Rob DeBree, sergeant for the Sheriff's Office. You have the right to remain silent. Anything you say can and may be used against you in a court of law.

NARRATOR: The following is an excerpt of that confession.

ROB DEBREE: Okay, so you guys, you and Russ go to the Fireside. So you're at the Fireside by yourselves, right?

AARON MCKINNEY: Yeah.

ROB DEBREE: Okay, where do you go after you leave the Fireside?

AARON MCKINNEY: Some kid wanted a ride home.

ROB DEBREE: What's he look like?

AARON MCKINNEY: Mmm, like a queer. Such a queer dude.

ROB DEBREE: He looks like a queer?

AARON MCKINNEY: Yeah, like a fag, you know?

ROB DEBREE: Okay. How did you meet him?

AARON MCKINNEY: He wanted a ride home and I just thought, well, the dude's drunk, let's just take him home.

ROB DEBREE: When did you and Russ talk about jacking him up?

AARON MCKINNEY: We kinda talked about it at the bar.

ROB DEBREE: Okay, what happened next?

AARON MCKINNEY: We drove him out past Wal-Mart. We got over there, and he starts grabbing my leg and grabbing my genitals. I was like, "Look, I'm not a fuckin' faggot. If you touch me again you're gonna get it." I don't know what the hell he was trying to do but I beat him up pretty bad. Think I killed him.

ROB DEBREE: What'd you beat him with?

AARON MCKINNEY: Blacked out. My fist. My pistol. The butt of the gun. Wondering what happened to me. I had a few beers and, I don't know. It's like I could see what was going on, but I don't know, but I don't know, it was like somebody else was doing it.

ROB DEBREE: What was the first thing that he said or that he did in the truck that made you hit him?

AARON MCKINNEY: Well, he put his hand on my leg, slid his hand like as if he was going to grab my balls.

MOMENT: GAY PANIC

ZACKIE SALMON: When that defense team argued that McKinney did what he did because Matthew made a pass at him . . . I just wanted to vomit, because that's like saying that it's okay. It's like the "Twinkie Defense," when the guy killed Harvey Milk and Moscone. It's the same thing.

REBECCA HILLIKER: As much as, uh, part of me didn't want the defense of them saying that it was a gay bashing or that it was gay panic, part of me is really grateful. Because I was really scared that in the trial they were going to try and say that it was a robbery, or it was about drugs. So when they used "gay panic" as their defense, I felt, this is good, if nothing else the truth is going to be told . . . the truth is coming out.

MOMENT: AARON MCKINNEY (CONTINUED)

ROB DEBREE: Did he ever try to defend himself against you or hit you back?

AARON MCKINNEY: Yeah, sort of. He tried his little swings or whatever but he wasn't very effective.

ROB DEBREE: Okay. How many times did you hit him inside the truck before you guys stopped where you left him?

AARON MCKINNEY: I'd say I hit him two or three times, probably three times with my fists and about six times with the pistol.

ROB DEBREE: Did he ask you to stop?

AARON MCKINNEY: Well, yeah. He was getting the shit kicked out of him.

ROB DEBREE: What did he say?

AARON MCKINNEY: After he asked me to stop most all he was doing was screaming.

Rob DeBree: So Russ kinda dragged him over to the fence, I'm assuming, and tied him up?

Aaron McKinney: Something like that. I just remember Russ was laughing at first but then he got pretty scared.

Rob DeBree: Was Matthew conscious when Russ tied him up?

Aaron McKinney: Yeah. I told him to turn around and don't look at my license plate number 'cause I was scared he would tell the police. And then I asked him what my license plate said. He read it and that's why I hit him a few more times.

Rob DeBree: Just to be sure? *(Pause)* So obviously you don't like gay people?

Aaron McKinney: No, I don't.

Rob DeBree: Would you say you hate them?

Aaron McKinney: Uh, I really don't hate them but, you know, when they start coming on to me and stuff like that I get pretty aggravated.

Rob DeBree: Did he threaten you?

Aaron McKinney: This gay dude?

Rob DeBree: Yeah.

Aaron McKinney: Not really.

Rob DeBree: Can you answer me one thing? Why'd you guys take his shoes?

Aaron McKinney: I don't know. *(Pause)* Now I'm never going to see my son again.

Rob DeBree: I don't know. You'll probably go to court sometime today.

Aaron McKinney: Today? So I'm gonna go in there and just plead guilty or not guilty today?

Rob DeBree: No, no, you're just going to be arraigned today.

Aaron McKinney: He is gonna die for sure?

Rob DeBree: There is no doubt that Mr. Shepard is going to die.

Aaron McKinney: So what are they going to give me, twenty-five to life or just the death penalty and get it over with?

Rob DeBree: That's not our job. That's the judge's job and the jury's.

MOMENT: THE VERDICT

Narrator: Has the jury reached a verdict?

Foreperson: We have, Your Honor.

We the jury, impaneled and sworn to try the above entitled case, after having well and truly tried the matter, unanimously find as follows:

As to the charge of kidnapping, we find the defendant, Aaron James McKinney, guilty.

As to the charge of aggravated robbery, we find the defendant, Aaron James McKinney, guilty.

As to the charge of first-degree felony murder (kidnapping), we find the defendant, Aaron James McKinney, guilty. *(Verdict goes sotto voce. Narration begins.)*

As to the charge of first-degree felony murder (robbery), we find the defendant, Aaron James McKinney, guilty.

As to the charge of premeditated first-degree murder, we find the defendant, Aaron James McKinney, not guilty.

As to the lesser-included offense of second-degree murder, we find the defendant, Aaron James McKinney, guilty.

MOMENT: DENNIS SHEPARD'S STATEMENT

NARRATOR: Aaron McKinney was found guilty of felony murder, which meant the jury could give him the death penalty. That evening, Judy and Dennis Shepard were approached by McKinney's defense team, who pled for their client's life. The following morning, Dennis Shepard made a statement to the Court. Here is some of what he said.

DENNIS SHEPARD: My son Matthew did not look like a winner. He was rather uncoordinated and wore braces from the age of thirteen until the day he died. However, in his all too brief life he proved that he was a winner. On October 6, 1998, my son tried to show the world that he could win again. On October 12, 1998, my firstborn son and my hero lost. On October 12, 1998, my firstborn son and my hero died, fifty days before his twenty-second birthday.

I keep wondering the same thing that I did when I first saw him in the hospital. What would he have become? How could he have changed his piece of the world to make it better?

Matt officially died in a hospital in Fort Collins, Colorado. He actually died on the outskirts of Laramie, tied to a fence. You, Mr. McKinney, with your friend Mr. Henderson left him out there by himself, but he wasn't alone. There were his lifelong friends with him, friends that he had grown up with. You're probably wondering who these friends were. First he had the beautiful night sky and the same stars and moon that we used to see through a telescope. Then he had the daylight and the sun to shine on him. And through it all he was breathing in the scent of pine trees from the snowy range. He heard the wind, the ever-present Wyoming wind, for the last time. He had one more friend with him, he had God. And I feel better knowing he wasn't alone.

Matt's beating, hospitalization, and funeral focused worldwide attention on hate. Good is coming out of evil. People have said enough is enough. I miss my son, but I am proud to be able to say that he is my son.

Judy has been quoted as being against the death penalty. It has been stated that Matt was against the death penalty. Both of these statements are wrong. Matt believed that there were crimes and incidents that justified the death penalty. I too believe in the death penalty. I would like nothing better than to see you die, Mr. McKinney. However, this is the time to begin the healing process. To show mercy to someone who refused to show any mercy. Mr. McKinney, I am going to grant you life, as hard as it is for me to do so, because of Matthew. Every time you celebrate

Christmas, a birthday, the Fourth of July, remember that Matt isn't. Every time you wake up in your prison cell, remember that you had the opportunity and the ability to stop your actions that night. You robbed me of something very precious, and I will never forgive you for that. Mr. McKinney, I give you life in the memory of one who no longer lives. May you have a long life, and may you thank Matthew every day for it.

MOMENT: AFTERMATH

REGGIE FLUTY: Me and DeBree hugged and cried. . . . And, you know, everybody had tears in their eyes, and you're just so thankful, you know, and Mr. Shepard was cryin', and then that got me bawlin' and everybody just—

ROB DEBREE: This is all we've lived and breathed for a year. Daily. This has been my case daily. And now it's over.

REGGIE FLUTY: Maybe now we can go on and we can quit being stuck, you know?

AARON KREIFELS: It just hit me today, the minute that I got out of the courthouse. That the reason that God wanted me to find him is, for he didn't have to die out there alone, you know. And if I wouldn't of came along, they wouldn't of found him for a couple of weeks at least. So it makes me feel really good that he didn't have to die out there alone.

MATT GALLOWAY: I'm just glad it's over. I really am. Testifying in that trial was one of the hardest things I've ever done. And don't get me wrong, I love the stage, I really do, I love it. But it's tricky, because basically what you have is lawyers questioning you from this angle but the answers need to be funneling this way, to the jury. So what you have to do is establish a funneling system. And that's hard for me because I'm a natural conversationalist, so it's just natural instinct that when someone asks you a question, you look at that person to make eye contact. But it's kind of tough when you literally have to scoot over—change your position, in effect, funnel over to where the jury is. But I was able to do that several times over the course of my testimony.

(Everyone is amused and baffled by this last text.)

REGGIE FLUTY: It's time to move on. And I think for even the citizens are having the town painted red so to speak. They're gonna just be glad to maybe get moved on.

∾

VALERIE JENNESS

Social Movement Growth, Domain Expansion, and Framing Processes: The Gay/Lesbian Movement and Violence against Gays and Lesbians as a Social Problem (1995)

Valerie Jenness, chair of the Department of Criminology, Law, and Society and a professor in the Department of Sociology at the University of California, Irvine, is one of the foremost scholars in the areas of social control, public policy, and hate crime legislation. She is the author of numerous books about hate crimes and social problems and regularly testifies before state and federal legislatures as an expert about hate crime bills.

ANTI-GAY AND LESBIAN VIOLENCE AS AN EMERGENT SOCIAL PROBLEM

> *In a 1988 case involving the beating death of an Asian-American gay man, a Broward County [Florida] circuit judge jokingly asked the prosecuting attorney, "That's a crime now, to beat up a homosexual?" The prosecutor answered, "Yes sir. And it's also a crime to kill them." The judge replied, "Times have really changed."*
> —Hentoff, 1990

Hate-motivated conduct in general and hate crimes, in particular recently have emerged to constitute a recognizable social problem in the United States. Although there are no accurate data on the number of hate-motivated crimes committed each year, most reports suggest that violence against individuals based on their race, religion, ethnicity, or sexual orientation is increasing exponentially in this country (Berk, Boyd, and Hamner 1992; Center for Democratic Renewal 1992; Fenn and McNeil 1987; Fernandez 1991; Hernandez 1990; Lee and Fernandez 1990). However, some reports challenge the validity of accounts that indicate an increase in hate-motivated conduct in the United States. For example, in the introduction to *Bias Crime: American Law Enforcement and Legal Responses,* the editor cites New York City data to suggest that "bias incidents were down some 1.4 percent in 1991" (Kelly 1993:6). Regardless of whether they are increasing or decreasing in the United States, acts of hate-motivated violence continue to garner national and international attention (Kelly 1993; Levin and McDevitt 1993; U.S. Department of Justice 1987).

Although there is no agreed upon definition of the term hate crime (Berk, Boyd, and Hamner 1992; Fernandez 1991; Jenness and Grattet 1993; Lee and Fernandez 1990), violence against gays and lesbians increasingly is recognizable as one type of hate crime that is reported to be widespread. By many accounts, violence motivated by homophobia and heterosexism represents the most frequent, visible, violent, and culturally legitimated type of bias-motivated conduct (Berrill 1992; Comstock 1989, 1991; Dean, Wu, and Martin 1992; Herek 1989; National Gay and Lesbian Task Force 1987, 1991; U.S. Department of Justice 1987). In addition, violence against gays and lesbians is reported to constitute one of the most rapidly growing forms of hate crime in the United States (Berrill 1992; Dean, Wu, and Martin 1992; Fenn and McNeil 1987; National Gay and Lesbian Task Force 1987, 1991). Anti-gay and lesbian attacks are reported to include everything from verbal harassment to fatal assaults. As such, they are reported to be undertaken by a range of perpetrators, from members of organized hate groups to members of police departments (Berrill 1992; Center for Democratic Renewal 1992; Collins 1992; Dean, Wu, and Martin 1992; Herek 1989; Herek and Berrill 1990, 1992; Hunter 1992; von Schulthess 1992).

A growing visible concern with violence against gays and lesbians contributes to and reflects its standing as a recognizable social problem. Consistent with the quote at the beginning of this section, one could say that "times have changed" such that a new social problem has been recognized in the United States; indeed, Comstock has declared that anti-gay and lesbian violence is "taking its place among such societal concerns as violence against women, children and ethnic and racial groups" (Comstock 1991:1). The conduct and activities that are commonly referred to as "hate-crimes against gays and lesbians" certainly are not new (Adam 1978; Bensinger 1992; Comstock 1991; Fout 1992; Herek 1989; Katz 1976). However, the increased visibility and subsequent criminalization of these activities over the last two decades are notable (Center for Democratic Renewal 1992; Jenness and Grattet 1993; National Gay and Lesbian Task Force 1987, 1991). Hate-motivated violence against gays and lesbians has attracted considerable attention from a variety of constituencies and numerous forums, including editorials in many prestigious newspapers, official hearings before both houses of Congress, and sustained educational efforts on many university campuses. Such attention has ensured that violence against gays and lesbians remains a source of highly politicized public debate, as well as an impetus for reform in public policy.

On April 23, 1990, President Bush signed into law the Hate Crimes Statistics Act. This Act requires the U.S. Department of Justice to collect data on hate-motivated violence against select groups (Fernandez 1991; U.S. Congress 1992). At the signing of the Act, Bush announced the opening of a national toll-free hotline to report hate-motivated violence, which continues to be operated by the Community Relations Service of the Department of Justice.[1] Although contested by numerous conservative senators on the grounds that gays and lesbians are members of an "affinity group" rather than a minority group (U.S. Congress 1988), the inclusion of a "sexual orientation" provision in the Act constitutes the federal government's only official legislative response to anti-gay and lesbian violence. From the point of view of the National Gay and Lesbian Task Force (1987:20), the federal government's response to anti-gay and lesbian violence "is similar to its initial reaction to the AIDS epidemic, which was viewed as a gay problem of little significance rather than a problem of general concern."

In the last decade, many federal, state, county, and city officials have sponsored new legislation in an effort to control hate crimes, including those directed at gays and lesbians (Bensinger 1992; Hernandez 1990; Jenness and Grattet 1993; Lee and Fernandez 1990; Morasch 1992; Padgett 1984). At least seventeen states have adopted hate crimes statutes that specifically address hate-motivated violence against people because of their sexual preference or sexual orientation (Jenness and Grattet 1993; National Institute Against Prejudice and Violence 1993). Many of the states that do not have hate crimes laws are increasingly relying upon statutes already on the books (e.g., laws against vandalism, trespass, assault, etc.) to seek increased penalties if prosecutors can prove that violence against gays and lesbians, or people presumed to be gay or lesbian, was motivated by homophobia or heterosexism.

Anti-gay and lesbian violence also is being greeted with a range of extra-legal community responses that run the gamut from public education campaigns to enhanced surveillance efforts (Bensinger 1992; Kelly 1993; Lee and Hernandez 1990; Levin and McDevitt 1993). The proliferation of watchdog organizations at the local, state, and federal level has taken place across the United States. Watchdog organizations such as the Center for Democratic Renewal, the Klanwatch Project, and the National Institute Against Prejudice and Violence continue to sponsor efforts designed to track and curb hate violence, including violence against gays and lesbians (Center for Democratic Renewal 1992; National Gay and Lesbian Task Force 1987, 1991; National Institute Against Prejudice and Violence 1993). Similarly, many civil rights organizations, including those funded by the federal government and state governments, have taken up the cause of violence against gays and lesbians as part of larger ongoing efforts to protect civil rights more generally (Kelly 1993).

Public officials' and civil rights groups' responses to hate-motivated violence against gays and lesbians have been inspired and accompanied by similar and contrasting responses emanating from gay and lesbian communities across the United States. According to the National Gay and Lesbian Task Force (1991:22), by 1990, "within lesbian and gay communities across the United States there was an unprecedented level of organizing against violence." Along with hundreds of gay and lesbian resource and community centers, many gay and lesbian organizations have responded to the perceived and experienced threats of violence by establishing and sustaining anti-violence projects. This newfound activism has been consequential for the construction of violence against gays and lesbians as a social problem in the United States. . . .

THE ESTABLISHMENT OF ANTI-VIOLENCE PROJECTS

Anti-violence projects have emerged from within gay and lesbian communities for two general, albeit interrelated, reasons. First, seven of the organizations in this study were founded in response to a specific hate-motivated incident that was subsequently construed as indicative of other, often larger, threats to members of the gay and lesbian community. For example, San Francisco's Community United Against Violence was "born in the wake of one of the worst incidents of anti-lesbian/gay violence,"[2] while New York City's Anti-Violence Project developed "after one particularly nasty incident on 29 March." Similarly, the Connecticut Lesbian and Gay Anti-Violence Project "was formed in the summer of 1988 as a response to the gay-bashing murder of Richard Reihl in Wethersfield, Connecticut." . . .

In contrast to organizations founded in response to a specific incident, 24[3] of the organizations in this study were founded in response to a more generalized awareness of the epidemiology and consequences of violence against gays and lesbians. As Q-Patrol's[4] training manual explains, "Welcome to Q Street Patrol, a community anti-violence project . . . QSP was formed because of the ever increasing hate crimes directed at our community." Similarly, the Lesbian and Gay Men's Community Center in San Diego developed an anti-violence project "in reaction to the rise of incidents and crimes of hate directed at lesbians, gay men, and bisexuals." Many of the organizations emerged in response to the growing realization that hate-motivated violence is intimately connected to other concerns relevant to the status of gays and lesbians, as well as the health of gay and lesbian communities.

. . . Gay and lesbian sponsored anti-violence projects are emerging and being institutionalized as integral to larger efforts to enhance the status of gays and lesbians in the United States. From the point of view of these organizations, anti-gay and lesbian projects are critical insofar as violence against gays and lesbians reflects and contributes to institutionalized heterosexism and attendant homophobia. As Herek (1989:949) has surmised, "antigay hate crimes must be understood, in part, as a logical outgrowth of this pervasive norm of intolerance." With this in mind, it is not surprising that gay and lesbian sponsored anti-violence projects have undertaken sustained efforts to engage in coalition-building. This has, in turn, provided a newfound forum for discussions of race and religion to gain a foothold in the gay and lesbian movement in the United States.

EXTENDING THE POLITICAL TERRAIN

The history of the gay and lesbian movement in this country reveals that it has been, by and large, a white person's movement. As other analysts have documented (Adam 1987; Marcus 1992; Shaw 1988), the more visible and institutionalized SMOs [social movement organizations] sustaining the gay and lesbian movement in the United States have, for the most part, remained color blind in terms of their activities and agendas. Consistent with the historical development of the gay and lesbian movement, discussions of race and racism, as well as religion and anti-Semitism, are visibly absent from the activities sponsored by the SMOs included in this study. For example, none of the anti-violence projects identify as an organization of and/or for gays and lesbians of color. Moreover, while addressing the problem of hate-motivated violence against gays and lesbians, only rarely do these organizations speak to the issues of racism and anti-Semitism and how they provide an institutional and cultural context for the victimization of gays and lesbians of color, as well as gays and lesbians who identify as Jewish. Although some of the organizations sponsor select activities for people of color and acknowledge a political concern for people of color, very few *enact* corresponding activism or tailor their message to gays and lesbians of color. For example, San Francisco's Community United Against Violence and New York City's Anti-Violence Project are the only organizations in this study that print their messages in English and Spanish.

However, *some* gay and lesbian sponsored anti-violence projects devote attention to violence directed at people of color and Jews through their coalition-building efforts and jointly sponsored enterprises. Columbus's Stonewall Union Anti-Violence Project, Portland's Lesbian Community Project, and Cambridge's Campaign to End Homophobia have adopted multicultural perspectives in order to work with other "minority groups" and "progressive allies" to address hate-violence in general and anti-gay and lesbian violence in particular. At different points in their histories, many of the organizations have sponsored activities that focus on broad issues of discrimination. For example, one of the most active organizations in the United States, Portland's Coalition for Human Dignity, has held numerous rallies and marches (the "We Are Not Afraid" rally, the "Rock Against Racism" rally, and the "Dignity and Diversity" march and rally) to demonstrate their opposition to all forms of discrimination and violence directed at minorities. Similarly, the Gays United to Attack Repression and Discrimination in Fort Lauderdale, the Anti-Violence Project of New York, the MaryAnn Finnegan Project of Cleveland, and the Rhode Island Alliance for Lesbian and Gay Civil Rights of Providence have organized direct action efforts that focus on multiple manifestations of hate-motivated violence. The Spokane Gay and Lesbian Community for Dignity and Human Rights, which was founded to "address, combat, and eradicate crimes of violence and harassment toward the gay, lesbian and bisexual community of Spokane," summarizes the logic fueling a focus on multiple forms of oppression in a statement of purpose:

> As we organizers networked with groups targeted for oppression, challenges arose among us—to identify and acknowledge the *hidden barriers* to ending oppression in our own community. We recognized that racism, sexism, and homophobia were common factors shared among a diversity of people and that they helped to create a narrowed vision for equity, protection, safety, and dignity. We stretched ourselves enough to recognize that oppression touches us *all.* Oppression is *inclusive;* thereby, creating solutions to end oppression meant utilizing *inclusive* tactics to end crimes of hate, bias and oppression. The Spokane Gay and Lesbian Com-

munity for Dignity and Human Rights has a vision that a climate for the intolerance of violence and oppression in the Spokane community can be shaped by our united effort to stand together in the spirit of equity. We are committed to taking the leadership in this task of building a common alliance.[5]

On occasion some of these organizations speak to the issue of racism and anti-Semitism and the victimization of people of color and Jews. As part of Chicago's Horizons Community Services' Anti-Violence Project, the 1992 Campaign to Count and Counter Hate Crimes reported the following:

> One example of the intersection of various hatred is the case of a man who was attacked and called a "faggot Jew." Not only was he attacked because he was perceived to be gay, but because he was perceived to be Jewish. A Latina lesbian may be attacked because of her race or her sexual orientation or because she is a woman, or any combination of the three. A black, gay man may also be attacked because of the color of his skin, because he is gay or because of his culture. Horizons recognizes that hatred can be acted out for many reasons and, although we serve gay men, lesbians, and bisexual people, we work with other groups who are working to stop the rising tide of hate crime in this country.

Although acknowledgements such as these are few, they demonstrate that gay and lesbian sponsored anti-violence projects have provided a forum for issues of race and racism, as well as religion and anti-Semitism.[6]

The mere existence of these anti-violence projects opens newfound political terrain for the gay and lesbian movement in this country. The projects and their attendant programs bring newfound visibility to the issue of violence against gays and lesbians and provide a forum for race and religion to be discussed within the gay and lesbian movement. While this extends the territory of the gay and lesbian movement in the United States, select forms of activism sustained by the anti-violence projects serve to "expand the domain" (Best 1990) of the "condition-category" (Ibarra and Kitsuse 1993) such that it is increasingly recognizable as a social problem. . . .

PUBLICIZING REPORTS OF VIOLENCE

Efforts to document anti-gay and lesbian violence generally are undertaken by gay and lesbian sponsored anti-violence projects in order to challenge law enforcement agencies and legislative reports. To mount this challenge, information generated by gay and lesbian sponsored anti-violence projects is distributed to law enforcement agencies, government officials, members of the gay and lesbian community, and the general population. This information highlights the underreporting of both official crime and undetected hate-motivated violence against gays and lesbians. As an example, Detroit's Triangle Foundation reported the following in a recent newsletter:

> In the past year in Michigan, our community experienced numerous incidents of hate crimes and harassments, but the outstanding one was the double murders of Christine Puckett and Sue Pittmann. Our statistics will be reported to the U.S. Department of Justice according to the Hate Crimes Statistics Act. *Michigan police issued NO reports of hate crimes!*

Gay and lesbian community organizations release statistical information to the public, as well as law enforcement and legislative agencies, in three general ways. First, organizations publicize statistics through independently produced and released press kits. Ft. Lauderdale's Gays United to Attack Repression and Discrimination annually releases the "Report of the GUARD Anti-Discrimination Project" to the local community. Second, a number of organizations publish flyers, pamphlets, and/or books containing statistical information on anti-gay and lesbian violence. For example, The Louisiana Gay and Lesbian Political Caucus published a booklet, *Exposing Hatred,* which was based on a 1989 survey of violence and harassment experienced by members of the local gay and lesbian community. As another example, in 1990 the North Carolina Coalition for Gay and Lesbian Equality published *Violence, Discrimination, Threats and Harassment Against Gay Men, Lesbians and AIDS-Affected People.* This report declares that "North Carolina leads the nation in reports of violence, vandalism, and harassment against gay men and lesbians." Third, and finally, many organizations participate in publicizing anti-gay and lesbian violence statistics by forwarding local data to the National Gay and Lesbian Task Force. Much like the Federal Bureau of Investigation's (FBI) Uniform Crime Report (UCR), the National Gay and Lesbian Task Force's Anti-Violence Project compiles statistics gathered from different communities across the United States to produce a national report. This report, *Anti-Gay Violence, Victimization and Defamation* (National Gay and Lesbian Task Force 1987, 1991), is then distributed to libraries, governmental agencies, and political organizations. As the Community Coalition of Alameda explained, "there is a national effort by the National Gay and Lesbian Task Force, the Community United Against Violence, and others to release statistics about violence all at the same time to make more of an impact."

The statistical reports generated by these organizations often include descriptive accounts of particular incidents. The North Carolina Coalition for Gay and Lesbian Equality released a report titled "Homophobia & Human Rights in North Carolina" that contains statistics on anti-gay and lesbian violence, especially murder, assault, and vandalism. Along with statistics, this report published descriptive accounts of numerous homophobic-motivated acts of violence. For example:

> June, Charlotte: A man leaving Scorpio, a gay bar, was hit with a night stick, punched in the stomach and threatened ("If you make a move, I'll kill you"). Then he was robbed from the parking lot. When police arrived, they asked if he had propositioned the assailant. When the victim complained, police Internal Affairs said that the police officer was within his rights to ask this question.

July 10, Morgantown: Three assailants struck on the head and drowned eighteen-year-old Daimon Ray Canipe when the young man defended another man fishing at the same pond from homophobic comments. Canipe's friend James Lewis Williams was also thrown into the lake, but he survived the attack. The assailants were charged with manslaughter *(Morgantown News Herald)*.

July, Chapel Hill: A white male, 26, walking along Franklin Street was attacked. He was hit, thrown against a car, thrown to the ground, and kicked in his ribs by an assailant shouting anti-gay epithets.

Similarly, Community United Against Violence reported the following in a newsletter:

Just recently, in November 1990, a group of women were confronted outside Club Q by a man who hit their car and then shouted "what the fuck are you looking at, you dyke bitches, there's no damage, get back in your car." In the ensuing encounter, at least seven women were physically attacked and two of them injured seriously.

Examples of "real live" cases such as these not only illustrate corresponding statistical information, but act as "horror stories" (Johnson 1989) and "atrocity tales" (Best 1990) as well. Quite frequently, "worst case" examples are put forth to exemplify the problem.[7] This usually is accomplished by detailing the gruesome facts of the injury, the consequences of the victimization, and/or the circumstances surrounding the official handling of the case. In the process, they elicit negative emotion by playing on the common fear that "this could happen to anyone" (Best 1990; Johnson 1989).

In the end, the documentation efforts sustained and publicized by gay and lesbian sponsored anti-violence projects across the United States expand the domain of violence against gays and lesbians in at least three primary ways. First, they encourage victims of anti-gay and lesbian violence to "go public" as a necessary first step toward uncovering and documenting the prevalence and incident rate of "official crime" being perpetrated against gays and lesbians. These organizations provide confidential and supportive avenues for gays and lesbians to report various types of victimization that would otherwise go unnoticed, and thus not included in reports by law enforcement officials and mental health authorities. Second, and related, gay and lesbian anti-violence projects render visible acts of criminal as well as noncriminal violence that generally are not recognized as instances of anti-gay and lesbian violence. In the process, they ensure that more and more conduct is recognized as an instance of anti-gay and lesbian hate-motivated conduct, thus more and more categories of violence against gays and lesbians are revealed. Third, and finally, the proliferation of documentation networks brings visibility to the phenomena now labeled "violence against gays and lesbians." The result is a well-publicized documented rise in anti-gay and lesbian violence in this country, which is, at least in part, attributable to revised documentation methods and greater reporting by the victims (Herek 1989; Herek and Berrill 1990, 1992).

The discovery and documentation of newly recognized forms of violence, coupled with reports of a rise in all or select forms of violence, have provided the condition-category of violence against gays and lesbians with newfound visibility and "empirical credibility." With regard to the former, and as others have already pointed out, visibility is a central resource for social movements and a central component for the successful construction of a social problem (Collins 1989; Gamson, Hoynes, and Sasson 1992; Holstein and Miller 1990; Jones, McFalls, and Gallagaher 1989; Miller 1993). With regard to the latter, claims are empirically credible "to the extent that there are events and occurrences that can be pointed to as documentary evidence" (Snow and Benford 1992:140).[8] In this case, visibility and empirical credibility are evidenced by the emergence and proliferation of crisis intervention and victim assistance programs, educational campaigns, and street patrols. Combined, these forms of activism are an outgrowth of and further contributor to successful domain expansion. Moreover, they constitute the primary vehicle through which the "framing work" (Snow and Benford 1992:136) of these anti-violence projects is accomplished. As Gerhards and Rucht (1992:572) recently concluded:

> No matter how strong, broad, interlinked, and professional the organizational structure for mesomobilization is, it only provides structural basis for mobilization processes. A second crucial task for mobilization is an adequate framing of the issue. . . . To activate the existing structure for concrete support and to attract many micromobilization groups from the mobilization potential, this "hardware" structure has to apply a kind of "software." . . .

CONCLUSION AND DISCUSSION

While gays and lesbians historically have existed in victimizing social environments (Adam 1978, 1987; Herek 1990; Katz 1976; Marcus 1992), over the last decade gay and lesbian communities throughout the United States increasingly have been responsive to anti-gay and lesbian violence (Comstock 1991; Duggan 1992; Galst 1991; Gamson 1989; Hentoff 1990; National Gay and Lesbian Task Force 1987, 1991). In particular, gay and lesbian communities have emerged to bring newfound attention to violence against gays and lesbians, protect gays and lesbians from victimization, and change the conditions that lead to such violence. Descriptively speaking, the anti-violence projects in this study continue to respond to anti-gay and lesbian violence by documenting the incidents and prevalence of anti-gay and lesbian violence, establishing crisis intervention and victim assistance programs, sponsoring education programs, and forming street patrols.

The institutionalization of these SMOs and their attendant activism have ensured that the problem of "hate-" or "bias-" motivated violence includes violence against gays and lesbians. . . . [T]he activism sustaining anti-violence projects in the United States has gone through an evolution whereby an expansion of the reach of the gay and lesbian movement in this country has allowed it to expand the domain of what is now being referred to as "hate crimes" in general and "violence against gays and lesbians" in particular. This, in turn, has set the stage for framing the nature of the phenomenon in a way that has allowed it to be competitive in the social problems marketplace (Best 1990; Hilgartner and Bosk 1988). This research suggests that just as the establishment of gay and lesbian sponsored anti-violence projects has extended the terrain and the "reach" of the gay and lesbian movement in this country, sustained documentation efforts continue to expand the domain of the condition-category now commonly referred to as "violence against gays and lesbians" by rendering it visible and empirically credible.

NOTES

1. The national toll-free hotline initially refused to document calls from victims of anti-gay and lesbian violence.

2. This incident occurred after the "White Night" riots following Dan White's manslaughter conviction for the killings of Supervisor Harvey Milk and Mayor Moscone.

3. The Lesbian and Gay Anti-Violence Project of Santa Rosa. California, did not provide information on its founding. Given the data I relied upon in this work, it is not surprising that often comparable information on each organization was not available. Thus, when reported numbers do not add up it should be assumed that the remaining data are missing.

4. The "Q" in "Q-Patrol" is used to initialize "Queer."

5. Emphasis in the original.

6. Notably, the fact that gays and lesbians embody gender and are firmly situated in a patriarchal culture is (comparatively) ignored by the activism sustaining the gay and lesbian sponsored anti-violence projects in this study (Jenness and Broad 1994).

7. Best (1990:28) notes that "atrocity tales," which are usually selected for their extreme nature, often come to typify the problem and thus become the referent for discussions of the problem.

8. Gamson (1992:69) has noted that the term *credibility* "contains a subtle hedge." It is not that the claims have been proven true, but that they have the appearance of truth.

REFERENCES

Adam, Barry. 1978. *The Survival of Domination.* New York: Elsevier/Greenwood.

——. 1987. *The Rise of a Gay and Lesbian Movement.* Boston, Mass.: Twayne Publishers.

Bensinger, Gad. 1992. "Hate crimes: A new/old problem." *International Journal of Comparative and Applied Criminal Justice* 16:115–123.

Berk, Richard, Elizabeth A. Boyd, and Karl M. Hamner. 1992. "Thinking more clearly about hate-motivated crimes." In *Hate Crimes: Confronting Violence Against Lesbians and Gay Men,* eds. Gregory Herek and Kevin Berrill, 123–143. Newbury Park, Calif.: Sage Publications.

Berrill, Kevin T. 1992. "Anti-gay violence and victimization in the United States: An overview." In *Hate Crimes: Confronting Violence Against Lesbians and Gay Men,* eds. Gregory Herek and Kevin Berrill, 19–45. Newbury Park, Calif.: Sage Publications.

Best, Joel. 1990. *Threatened Children: Rhetoric and Concern About Child Victims.* Chicago, Ill.: University of Chicago Press.

Center for Democratic Renewal. 1992. *When Hate Groups Come to Town.* Montgomery. Ala.: Black Belt Press.

Collins, Michael. 1992. "The gay bashers." In *Hate Crimes: Confronting Violence Against Lesbians and Gay Men*, eds. Gregory Herek and Kevin Berrill, 191–200. Newbury Park, Calif.: Sage Publications.

Collins, Patricia Hill. 1989. "The social construction of invisibility: Black women's poverty in social problems discourse." In *Perspectives on Social Problems*, eds. James A. Holstein and Gale Miller, 77–93. Greenwich, Conn.: JAI Press.

Comstock, Gary. 1989. "Victims of anti-gay and lesbian violence." *Journal of Interpersonal Violence* 4:101–106.

———. 1991. *Violence Against Lesbians and Gay Men.* New York: Columbia University Press.

Dean, Laura, Shanyu Wu, and John L. Martin. 1992. "Trends in violence and discrimination against gay men in New York City: 1984 to 1990." In *Hate Crimes: Confronting Violence Against Lesbians and Gay Men*, eds. Gregory Herek and Kevin Berrill, 46–64. Newbury Park, Calif.: Sage Publications.

Duggan, Lisa. 1992. "Making it perfectly queer." *Socialist Review* 22:11–31.

Fenn, Peter, and Taylor McNeil. 1987. "The response of the criminal justice system to bias crime: An exploratory review." Washington, D.C.: Abt. Associates.

Fernandez, Joseph. 1991. "Bringing hate crimes into focus." *Harvard Civil Rights–Civil Liberties Law Review* 26:261–292.

Fout, John C. 1992. *Forbidden History: The State, Society, and the Regulation of Sexuality in Modern Europe.* Chicago, Ill.: University of Chicago Press.

Galst, Liz. 1991. "Taking it to the streets: Nationwide queer street patrols come out against antilesbian and antigay violence." *Advocate* (August):66–67.

Gamson, Josh. 1989. "Silence, death, and the invisible enemy: AIDS activism and social movement 'newness.'" *Social Problems* 36:351–367.

Gamson, William A. 1992. "The social psychology of collective action." In *Frontiers in Social Movement Theory*, eds. Aldon C. Morris and Carol McClurg Mueller, 53–76. New Haven: Yale University Press.

Gamson, William A., David Croteau, William Hoynes, and Theodore Sasson. 1992. "Media images and the social construction of reality." *Annual Review of Sociology* 18:373–393.

Gerhards, Jurgen, and Dieter Rucht. 1992. "Mesomobilization: Organizing and framing in two protest campaigns in West Germany." *American Journal of Sociology* 98:555–595.

Hentoff, Nat. 1990. "The violently attacked community in America." *Weekly Newspaper of New York,* September 25, n.p.

Herek, Gregory M. 1989. "Hate crimes against lesbians and gay men: Issues for research and policy." *American Psychologist* 44:948–955.

———. 1990. "The social context of hate crimes: Notes on cultural and psychological heterosexism." *Journal of Interpersonal Violence* 5:316–333.

Herek, Gregory M., and Kevin T. Berrill. 1990. "Documenting the victimization of lesbians and gay men: Methodological issues." *Journal of Interpersonal Violence* 5:301–315.

———. 1992. *Hate Crimes: Confronting Violence Against Lesbians and Gay Men.* Newbury Park, Calif.: Sage Publications.

Hernandez, Tanya Katerl. 1990. "Bias crimes: Unconscious racism in the prosecution of racially-motivated violence." *Yale Law Journal* 99:832–864.

Hilgartner, Stephen, and Charles Bosk. 1988. "The rise and fall of social problems: A public arenas model." *American Journal of Sociology* 94:53–78.

Holstein, James A., and Gale Miller. 1990. "Rethinking victimization: An interactional approach to victimology." *Symbolic Interaction* 13:103–122.

Hunter, Joyce. 1992. "Violence against lesbian and gay male youth." In *Hate Crimes: Confronting Violence Against Lesbians and Gay Men*, eds. Gregory Herek and Kevin Berrill, 76–82. Newbury Park, Calif.: Sage Publications.

Ibarra, Peter R., and John I. Kitsuse. 1993. "Vernacular constituents of moral discourse: An interactionist proposal for the study of social problems." In *Constructionist Controversies: Issues in Social Problems Theory*, eds. Gale Miller and James A. Holstein, 21–54. Hawthorne, N.Y.: de Gruyter.

Jenness, Valerie, and Kendal L. Broad. 1994. "Antiviolence activism and the (in)visibility of gender: The expansion of the gay and lesbian movement and the appropriation of the contemporary women's movement." *Gender & Society* 8:402–423.

Jenness, Valerie, and Ryken Grattet. 1993. "The criminalization of hate: The social context of hate crimes in the United States." Paper presented at the annual meeting of the American Sociological Association, Miami, Florida.

Johnson, John M. 1989. "Horror stories and the construction of child abuse." In *Images of Issues: Typifying Contemporary Social Problems*, ed. Joel Best, 5–19. Hawthorne, N.Y.: de Gruyter.

Jones, Brian J., Joseph A. McFalls, Jr., and Bernard J. Gallagher, III. 1989. "Toward a unified model for social problems theory." *Journal for the Theory of Social Behaviour* 19:337–356.

Katz, Jonathan. 1976. *Gay American History.* New York: Crowell.

Kelly, Robert J., ed. 1993. *Bias Crime: American Law Enforcement and Legal Responses.* Chicago, Ill.: Office of International Criminal Justice, University of Illinois.

Lee, Virginia Nia, and Joseph M. Fernandez. 1990. "Legislative responses to hate-motivated violence: The Massachusetts experience and beyond." *Harvard Civil Rights–Civil Liberties Law Review* 25:287–340.

Levin, Jack, and Jack McDevitt. 1993. *Hate Crimes: The Rising Tide of Bloodshed and Bigotry.* New York: Plenum Press.

Marcus, Eric. 1992. *Making History: The Struggle for Gay and Lesbian Equal Rights.* New York: HarperCollins Publishers.

Miller, Leslie. 1993. "Claims-making from the underside: Marginalization and social problems analysis." In *Constructionist Controversies: Issues in Social Problems Theory*, eds. Gale Miller and James A. Holstein, 153–180. Hawthorne, N.Y.: de Gruyter.

Morasch, James. 1992. "The problem of motive in hate crimes: The argument against presumptions of racial motivation." *Journal of Criminal Law and Criminology* 82:659–689.

National Gay and Lesbian Task Force. 1987. *Anti-Gay/Lesbian Violence, Victimization, and Defamation in 1987.* Washington, D.C.: National Gay and Lesbian Task Force Policy Institute.

———. 1991. *Anti-Gay/Lesbian Violence, Victimization, and Defamation in 1990.* Washington, D.C.: National Gay and Lesbian Task Force Policy Institute.

National Institute Against Violence and Prejudice. 1993. *Striking Back at Bigotry: Remedies Under Federal and State Law for Violence Motivated by Racial, Religious, or Ethnic Prejudice.* Baltimore, Md.: Author.

Padgett, Gregory L. 1984. "Racially motivated violence and intimidation: Inadequate state enforcement and federal civil rights remedies." *Journal of Criminal Law and Criminology* 75:103–138.

Shaw, Nancy Stoller. 1988. "Preventing AIDS among women: The role of community organizing." *Socialist Review* 18:76–92.

Snow, David A., and Robert D. Benford. 1992. "Master frames and cycles of protest." In *Frontiers in Social Movement Theory*, eds. Aldon C. Morris and Carol McClurg Mueller, 133–155. New Haven: Yale University Press.

U.S. Congress. 1988. H.R. 575. 100th Congress, 2nd Session.

————. 1992. H.R. 4797. 102nd Congress, 2nd Session.

U.S. Department of Justice. 1987. *Report on Hate Crimes in the United States.* Washington, D.C.: Federal Bureau of Investigation.

von Schulthess, Beatrice. 1992. "Violence in the streets: Anti-lesbian assault and harassment in San Francisco." In *Hate Crimes: Confronting Violence Against Lesbians and Gay Men*, eds. Gregory Herek and Kevin Berrill, 65–75. Newbury Park, Calif.: Sage Publications.

◈

GAY, LESBIAN, AND STRAIGHT EDUCATORS NETWORK (GLSEN)

National School Climate Survey, Key Findings (2003)

The mission of GLSEN is to "assure that each member of every school community is valued and respected regardless of sexual orientation or gender identity/expression." A ten-year-old organization with a staff of thirty, GLSEN helps to found and support gay-straight alliances (GSAs) in schools across the country, organizes yearly conferences, conducts and publishes research, and advocates for safe and welcoming schools everywhere. The national school survey examines how homophobia is institutionalized in schools and outlines steps to create more bias-free school communities.

GLSEN's National School Climate Survey is the only national survey to document the experiences of lesbian, gay, bisexual, and transgender (LGBT) students in America's high schools. Conducted biennially since 1999, the National School Climate Survey fills a crucial void in our collective understanding of the contemporary high school experience.

The results of this survey are intended to inform educators, policymakers, and the public at large, as part of GLSEN's ongoing effort to ensure that all schools are places where students are free to learn, regardless of sexual orientation or gender identity/expression.

The 2003 National School Climate Survey results summarized here continue to track the basic and endemic problem of name-calling, harassment, and violence directed at LGBT students, while offering new information about the impact of these experiences on academic performance and the effect of interventions designed to mend—or at minimum address—the underlying problem. For the first time, the 2003 survey data allowed us to ascertain that school climate is definitely linked to the academic performance and college aspirations of LGBT youth.

Violence, bias, and harassment of LGBT students continue to be the rule—not the exception—in America's schools. And this survey demonstrates that this hostile school climate has a direct and measurable link to LGBT students' ability to learn, their sense of belonging in school, their academic performance, and their educational aspirations.

For complete results of GLSEN's 2003 National School Climate Survey, including complete information about methodology and demographics, please visit www.glsen.org or call GLSEN's Communications Department at (212) 727-0135.

METHODOLOGY

A total of 887 LGBT youth from forty-eight states and the District of Columbia completed the survey. In order to ensure a more representative sample, we had two methods of obtaining participants. In the first, surveys were completed by LGBT youth involved with community-based groups or service organizations. Fifty such groups and organizations were randomly chosen from a master list of over 200 groups nationwide. Of the original fifty groups contacted, thirty-eight returned completed surveys, accounting for a total of 308 surveys of LGBT youth in middle school or high schools. We also made the National School Climate Survey available on the Internet via GLSEN's website. Notices about our on-line survey were posted on LGBT youth-oriented listserves and electronic bulletin boards. Also, notices were emailed to GLSEN chapters and to youth advocacy organizations. Through the on-line version, we obtained completed surveys from an additional 579 LGBT youth. Data was collected from community-based groups from the end of May to the end of August 2003. On-line data collection took place from June to the end of August 2003.

HOMOPHOBIC REMARKS, HARASSMENT, AND SCHOOL SAFETY: HARASSMENT AT SCHOOL IS THE RULE, NOT THE EXCEPTION

As in 1999 and 2001, the overwhelming majority of LGBT students report hearing homophobic remarks. At times, faculty and staff contribute to the problem by either making homophobic comments themselves or failing to intervene when they hear students making them. The survey results further demonstrate that verbal, sexual, and physical harassment are common experiences for LGBT students and that a majority feel unsafe, and many skip school altogether, because they are simply too afraid to go.

Homophobic Remarks/Verbal Harassment

84 percent of LGBT students report being verbally harassed (name calling, threats, etc.) because of their sexual orientation.

91.5 percent of LGBT students report hearing homophobic remarks such as "faggot," "dyke," or the expression "that's so gay" frequently or often.

44.7 percent of LGBT youth of color report being verbally harassed because of both their sexual orientation and race/ethnicity.

82.9 percent of LGBT students report that faculty or staff never intervened or intervened only some of the time when present and homophobic remarks were made.

Physical Harassment/Victimization

39.1 percent of LGBT students report being physically harassed (being shoved, pushed, etc.) because of their sexual orientation.

Within the vulnerable population, transgender students are even more at risk: 55 percent of transgender youth report being physically harassed because of their gender, gender expression, or sexual orientation, as compared with 41 percent of LGBT students who report physical harassment for any one of these reasons, meaning that transgender students are more than 30 percent likelier to suffer physical harassment than LGBT students.

57.9 percent of LGBT students reported having property stolen or deliberately damaged at school, as compared with 35 percent of students in a national sample of all high school students in a 1999 U.S. Department of Justice survey, meaning they were significantly more likely to be victimized by such crimes and attacks.

Sense of Safety at School

64.3 percent of LGBT students report feeling unsafe at their school because of their sexual orientation.

28.6 percent of LGBT students report missing at least one entire day of school in the past month because they felt unsafe. The rate was even higher (35.1 percent) among LGBT youth of color who felt unsafe at school for a variety of reasons (because of their sexual orientation, their race, or both).

BIAS AND ITS IMPACT ON SCHOOL PERFORMANCE AND ASPIRATIONS: HARASSMENT SIGNIFICANTLY RELATED TO DIMINISHED ACHIEVEMENT AND FUTURE EDUCATIONAL ASPIRATIONS

For the first time, we examined how school climate was related to school performance, grade-point average (GPA), and college aspirations for LGBT students. The school performance and college aspirations are significantly diminished for LGBT students who experience harassment.

Students who frequently experienced harassment because of their sexual orientation had GPAs that were more than 10 percent lower than those who did not: average GPA for LGBT students who report frequent verbal harassment: 2.9; average GPA for LGBT students who report only rare or less frequent verbal harassment: 3.3.

Students who experience frequent verbal harassment because of their sexual orientation are less likely than other students to plan to attend college: 13.4 percent of LGBT students who report verbal harassment do not intend to go to college, twice the figure of those LGBT students who report only rare or less frequent verbal harassment (6.7 percent).

LGBT RESOURCES, SCHOOL POLICIES, AND SUPPORT SYSTEMS: POLICIES, PROGRAMS, AND TEACHERS MAKE A DIFFERENCE

Many schools fail to provide resources or support for their LGBT students. However, when supportive faculty or LGBT-related resources are available, LGBT students do better in school and are much more likely to plan to attend college. Furthermore, there is a definitive relationship between schools and communities having policies and laws regarding violence, bias, and harassment against LGBT students and student safety.

37.3 percent of LGBT students do not feel comfortable discussing LGBT issues with their teachers. LGBT students unable to identify supportive teachers or staff were more than twice as likely not to plan to continue their education after secondary school: 24.1 percent of LGBT students with no supportive faculty or staff say they do not intend to go to college. Only 10.1 percent of LGBT students who did report having one or more supportive faculty or staff members say they will not go to college.

LGBT students who can identify supportive faculty or staff do better in school than those who cannot, with grade point averages more than 10 percent higher than their peers: average GPA for LGBT students who cannot identify any supportive faculty or staff: 2.8; average GPA for LGBT students who can identify one or more supportive faculty or staff members: 3.1.

LGBT students in schools with gay-straight alliances (GSAs) were more likely to feel safe in school than students whose schools do not have a GSA: 68.3 percent of LGBT students who report their schools do not have a GSA say they feel unsafe in their schools because of their sexual orientation. Students who said their school has a GSA were less likely to report feeling unsafe at school for the same reason (60.9 percent).

Students who did not have (or did not know of) a policy protecting them from violence and harassment were nearly 40 percent more likely to skip school than those who did: 36.5 percent of LGBT students who said their school did not have a specific harassment policy skipped class in the last month because they felt unsafe, with that number dropping to 26.6 percent among LGBT students who know that there is some sort of harassment policy in place to protect them.

CONCLUSIONS AND RECOMMENDATIONS

GLSEN's 2003 National School Climate Survey presents a striking and troubling picture of the experience of our nation's lesbian, gay, bisexual, and transgender students. For so many, school can be a dangerous and unsafe place.

These findings suggest that schools should consider the following steps to improve school climates and create environments that encourage participation in school activities, improve educational outcomes, and raise future educational aspirations for LGBT students:

- Institute policies that include "sexual orientation and gender identity" as protected classes along with existing categories such as race, religion, and ability, as such policies dramatically reduce absenteeism among LGBT students.
- Provide training for teachers on how to support LGBT students, as building the skills of teachers in supporting LGBT students would not only increase the currently low rate of intervention by teachers in stopping harassment (and thus diminish the negative effects on student achievement) but would also significantly increase the future aspirations of LGBT students in terms of pursuing higher education.
- Create and support programs such as gay-straight student alliances, which can significantly increase students' sense of belonging at school and thereby their likelihood of attending and graduating from high school.

Clearly, more work needs to be done in our nation's schools to create safer climates for all students. Local community leaders, teachers, parents, and GSA members need to work within their schools and their school districts to ensure that all students have an equal opportunity to learn. These findings help us better understand what that work should entail, and we call upon all school authorities to undertake such measures so that schools may promote better educational outcomes for LGBT students.

≈

JUSTICE ANTHONY KENNEDY
Ruling in *Lawrence v. Texas* (2003)

On September 17, 1998, John Lawrence and Tyron Garner were found having consensual anal sex in Lawrence's apartment in the suburbs of Houston. Harris County sheriff's deputy Joseph Quinn entered the unlocked apartment with his weapon drawn and arrested the two on charges of sodomy. Six years later, the Supreme Court ruled in Lawrence v. Texas *that the antisodomy law in Texas banning male-male sex was unconstitutional, as were all state laws barring particular sex acts between consenting adults. The 6-to-3 ruling found that the intimate, adult consensual conduct at issue here was protected by the Fourteenth Amendment.*

Held: The Texas statute making it a crime for two persons of the same sex to engage in certain intimate sexual conduct violates the Due Process Clause. Pp. 3–18.

(a) Resolution of this case depends on whether petitioners were free as adults to engage in private conduct in the exercise of their liberty under the Due Process Clause. For this inquiry the Court deems it necessary to reconsider its *Bowers* holding. The *Bowers* Court's initial substantive statement—"The issue presented is whether the Federal Constitution confers a fundamental right upon homosexuals to engage in sodomy . . .," 478 U.S., at 190—discloses the Court's failure to appreciate the extent of the liberty at stake. To say that the issue in *Bowers* was simply the right to engage in certain sexual conduct demeans the claim the individual put forward, just as it would demean a married couple were it said that marriage is just about the right to have sexual intercourse. Although the laws involved in *Bowers* and here purport to do not more than prohibit a particular sexual act, their penalties and purposes have more far-reaching consequences, touching upon the most private human conduct, sexual behavior, and in the most private of places, the home. They seek to control a personal relationship that, whether or not entitled to formal recognition in the law, is within the liberty of persons to choose without being punished as criminals. The liberty protected by the Constitution allows homosexual persons the right to choose to enter upon relationships in the confines of their homes and their own private lives and still retain their dignity as free persons. Pp. 3–6.

(b) Having misapprehended the liberty claim presented to it, the *Bowers* Court stated that proscriptions against sodomy have ancient roots. 478 U.S., at 192. It should be noted, however, that there is no longstanding history in this country of laws directed at homosexual conduct as a distinct matter. Early American sodomy laws were not directed at homosexuals as such but instead sought to prohibit nonprocreative sexual activity more generally, whether between men and women or men and men. Moreover, early sodomy laws seem not to have been enforced against consenting adults acting in private. Instead, sodomy prosecutions often involved predatory acts against those who could not or did not consent: relations between men and minor girls or boys, between adults involving force, between adults implicating disparity in status, or between men and animals. The longstanding criminal prohibition of homosexual sodomy upon which *Bowers* placed such reliance is as consistent with a general condemnation of nonprocreative sex as it is with an established tradition of prosecuting acts because of their homosexual character. Far from possessing "ancient roots," *ibid.,* American laws targeting same-sex couples did not develop until the last third of the 20th century. Even now, only nine States have singled out same-sex relations for criminal prosecution. Thus, the historical grounds relied upon in *Bowers* are more complex than the majority opinion and the concurring opinion by Chief Justice Burger there indicated. They are not without doubt and, at the very least, are overstated. The *Bowers* Court was, of course, making the broader point that for centuries there have been powerful voices to condemn homosexual conduct as immoral, but this Court's obligation is to define the liberty of all, not to mandate its own moral code. *Planned Parenthood of Southeastern Pa. v. Casey,* 505 U.S. 833, 850. The Nation's laws and traditions in the past half century are most relevant here. They show an emerging awareness that liberty gives substantial protection to adult persons in deciding how to conduct their private lives in matters pertaining to sex. See *County of Sacramento v. Lewis,* 523 U.S. 833, 857. Pp. 6–12.

8
I Am That Name
AMERICAN QUEER ACTIVISM,
NOW AND THEN

If we take Audre Lorde's call to move from silence to action seriously, then anytime queers take control of language, whenever they name that which they are, they are engaging in activism. As words like "queer" and "dyke" moved from labels meant to demean and isolate to powerful words expressing identities, queers began to claim power over their own lives. Queer activism began the first time someone said, "I am queer" in the face of silence. Some of the earliest forms of overt political activism on behalf of queers happened not in the United States, but in Germany. In fact, what might be called the first "gay rights movement" happened in Berlin in the 1920s, the same city that became the seat of Nazi power.

In the United States, some have argued that activism happens on an everyday level whenever a queer fights back, kisses in public, or has sex that violates social norms. In its broadest understanding, activism is the act of challenging established power structures. Other critics think that the simple expression of desire, a desire that may flaunt convention, is not in and of itself activism. To call something activism, one must have the goal not just of *challenging* power structures (or in more recent forms of self-described activism, becoming part of power structures) but also of *changing* those structures. For two men to have sex in a New York subway toilet in 1920 or for two women to have children and a suburban home in 1990 are not considered activism unless the goal of those actors is to force the police to reexamine a fear of gay sex or to force suburbia to reexamine the definitions of family.

Overt expressions of activism began with one of the earliest examples of a gay rights organization appearing in Chicago in the years after World War I. Using the medicalized language of the time, Henry Gerber petitioned the State of Illinois to issue a charter to the Society for Human Rights, which was officially dedicated to "promote and protect the interests" of people who, because of "mental and physical abnormalities," were hindered in their "pursuit of happiness." Gerber's organization and newspaper were quickly suppressed and the organization disappeared from most history books. But Gerber was not alone. Harlem writers were publishing short stories about same-sex love, and in 1930, Mary Casal published *The Stone Wall,* a book narrating Casal's life as a woman who loved other women. She wrote her book in order "to speak openly of things which, in the modern novel, are represented by asterisk." She speaks openly about, in Oscar Wilde's words, the "love that dare not speak its name." Gerber and Casal took Lorde's sentiment to heart and broke out of silence.

If scholars had to date the beginning of a lasting and effective gay activist movement, most would pick the summer of 1950, when several gay white men met in the Hollywood Hills at the home of Harry Hay, a communist peace activist and homosexual, to found the Mattachine Society. It is not surprising that an era of repression following a wartime era of more sexual freedom elicited an activist response. With the establishment of Mattachine and its newsletter, *One,* a gay rights movement was born in the United States. The Mattachine society desired visibility and a distinctive culture that marked people as queer. The mission statement asked, Who are we? Where are we? What are we? Homosexuals needed to find one another and come together in order to create a social movement. Mattachine spawned the lesbian group Daughters of Bilitis along with other forms of activism on behalf of "androgyns," "homosexuals," "inverts," and others oppressed because of their sexual identity.

In an era of civil rights and feminism, when everyone seemed to be clamoring for space in U.S. society, gays and lesbians too argued that they had a right to be considered Americans. But in 1969, the era of activism as a battle for rights shifted to one of gay liberation. Many mark the dawn of gay liberation with the Stonewall rebellion in New York City, when patrons of a working-class bar called the Stonewall Inn, along with local residents, resisted police oppression publicly and violently for the first time. Stonewall grew out of earlier activism, developed in response to the Vietnam War and the civil rights movements. Without that framework, Stonewall might not have become an event that sparked a social movement. It is also not a coincidence that much of the history of queer activism in the United States is documented almost exclusively by the voices of those who experienced it. An oppressed group that never saw its oppression as part of U.S. history rarely maintained great records about its past. Oral history has proven to be the window to much of this story.

Stonewall and 1960s feminism spawned a reexamination of the way people of different sexualities and genders were, or were not, included in U.S. society. Lesbians who had felt excluded from the feminist movement formed their own social movement—lesbian separatism. They argued that lesbians, because they avoided the constraints of patriarchal relationships, lived a higher form of existence than straight women. Lesbian separatists formed their own spaces, cultures, and politics that rejected mainstream feminism's attempt to gain power in, as the radical separatists saw it, a fundamentally flawed system.

The 1970s split between mainstream feminists and lesbian separatists marked an era when social movements, including the queer movement, struggled with internal differences and internal forms of oppression. Lesbians in the 1970s, especially the group that called itself Radicalesbians, felt excluded from the feminist movement because of its perceived heterosexism and homophobia. But even within a queer social movement, some felt as if their experience of oppression was not addressed or acknowleged. As questions of sexuality became more important in the post-Stonewall world, some saw issues of race and racism moving to the back burner, prompting queer people of color to become active *within* the queer movement. African American women like Audre Lorde and Barbara Smith argued that activism needed to be systemic and not simply "issue oriented." Others, like Marlon Riggs, showed that queer people of color are doubly in need of activism for their racial invisibility in queer community and culture and for their sexual invisibility in black community and culture. Jews too created activism that worked both to change the Jewish world to make space for those of different sexualities and genders and to show the queer movement that it was still driven by a Christian-dominated understanding of U.S. society and culture.

Although gay movements splintered in this way, the activism also became increasingly visible, especially in the late 1970s with the election of Harvey Milk, the first openly gay U.S. politician, to the San Francisco City Council. Queer activists responded publicly to the murder of Harvey Milk and the near acquittal of his murderer, Dan White; to Anita Bryant "Save the Children" campaign, which successfully lobbied Florida voters to ban any form of law that would protect sexual minorities from discrimination; and to California's Briggs Amendment campaigns, which failed to prohibit openly gay teachers from working in California public schools. On top of this, the 1970s gave birth to annual gay pride celebrations marking the anniversary of the Stonewall rebellion. In many ways, Harry Hay's vision of a visible minority with a distinct culture and set of political goals came true in the 1970s. It was also the decade that witnessed the establishment of national queer organizations. The National Gay Task Force, later to become the National Gay and Lesbian Task Force, was founded in 1973 as a grassroots organization fighting for social change. Its first major success was lobbying to have the American Psychiatric Association (APA) remove "homosexuality" from the *Diagnostic and Statistical Manual of Mental Disorders* in 1973.

Many women did not find a home in the 1970s gay movement. Thus, the National Center for Lesbian Rights was founded in 1977 and headquartered in San Francisco. The organization is a national lesbian feminist nonprofit law firm, the mission of which has been to create a world "in which every lesbian can live fully, free from discrimination." In 2002, NCLR served more than 4,000 clients throughout the fifty states. NCLR has won several high-profile cases that have profoundly shaped family law in the United States.

The Human Rights Campaign (HRC) began in 1980 as a small political action group raising money for gay-supportive congressional candidates. The organization emerged as a response to the success of New Right groups like the National Conservative Political Action Committee and the Moral Majority, which helped put conservative Republicans in the White House and U.S. Senate in 1980. By the beginning of the twenty-first century, HRC became the largest, most visible, and most well-funded gay political lobbying organization in the world. Focusing its efforts on national campaigns, HRC has been characterized by some as mainstream, especially because of its explicitly bipartisan approach to U.S. politics and what some consider single-issue politics.

In the 1980s, women were debating whether sex was an acceptable and integral part of lesbian culture and lesbian activism. At the same time, gay men were trying to respond to the AIDS epidemic that forced a fundamental shift in gay culture and gay activism. Gay liberation in the 1970s had been marked by sexual freedom, the claiming of public space, and the celebration of queer life, aspects of queer culture that were challenged by AIDS and the new fear of gay male sex in the 1980s. The silence of government officials in the face of the ever-growing epidemic, the lack of funding for services or research, and the ever-increasing death rates in the gay male community forced a reexamination of what it meant to be a gay community and what it meant to be a liberated gay man. Did it mean the right to have sex in public? Or did it mean the right to expect the U.S. government to treat a plague killing gay men as it would any other plague attacking U.S. citizens?

AIDS generated the largest mobilization of gays and lesbians in history. In urban areas, large institutions like the San Francisco AIDS Foundation and New York's Gay Men's Health Crisis began raising funds, supporting research, educating the public, and lobbying the government on behalf of the gay community. Activists like Larry Kramer called on gays to take responsibility for their own well-being and called for a fundamental change in the gay community. Some more radical activists founded the AIDS Coalition to Unleash Power, known as ACT UP, which sponsored street rallies and other forms of political activism and theater. ACT UP accused the government of conspiring to allow queers to die of AIDS by not considering AIDS a public health crisis and therefore not funding research into prevention and treatment. Did queer culture have to be defined by sex or could it be defined by community support, fundraising, lobbying, and other forms of community building and activism? In many ways, these questions stayed with queer activism into the twenty-first century.

By the 1990s, queer activism had begun the process of collaborating with well-established mainstream organizations to gain political clout. One of the most visible signs of mainstreaming was the interest that nonqueer organizations like the American Civil Liberties Union (ACLU) and even the Anti-Defamation League (ADL) began taking in issues of sexuality. Activism moved from primarily local organizing to large-scale political and legal battles on issues such as job and housing discrimination, the Supreme Court's 1986 *Bowers v. Hardwick* decision to uphold sodomy laws, and the lack of legal recognition for queer relationships and queer families.

In the twenty-first century, queer activism is mature, established, and increasingly asking if combating homophobia and antiqueer violence is the primary goal. Queer Jews, African Americans, Latinos, Asians, youth, seniors, people with disabilities, and others have formed institutions that advocate for their particular constituencies under the rubric of queer activism. Huge fundraisers support some of the largest queer activist organizations, which employ dozens. Queer activism has come a long way since Henry Gerber got arrested for publishing a single broadsheet and since Mary Casal had the strength to utter the love that dare not speak its name.

As queer sexualities become more visible, as queers become a political constituency courted by mainstream political parties and a consumer group courted by large corporations, queer activism has been forced to ask what its goals are. When some queer organizations like the Log Cabin Republicans support political parties dominated by the same right-wing Christians who attempted to bar queers from the teaching profession in the 1970s, and when gay pride parades give more space to product placement than to political activism, some queers are left asking if queer activism is over. At the same time, the very ability for openly gay activists to be visible members of the Republican Party suggests that queer activism has already achieved something—the ability for queers to become part of the power structure. Although as radicals, Harry Hay, the Radicalesbians, and Harvey Milk might not have liked all of the outcomes of their activism, the mainstreaming of queer activism is a sign of the success of the early activists to break the silence, organize, build community, and transform culture.

HENRY GERBER

The Society for Human Rights (1925)

What some scholars consider the first gay rights organization in the United States, the Society for Human Rights, sprang up in Chicago after World War I. Its single-edition newsletter was quickly suppressed and memory of the organization summarily written out of history. Its long-term political efficacy may have been minimal, but its presence in the heartland in the 1920s shows that activism sprang up all over the country and earlier than many people have believed.

On December 24, 1924, the state of Illinois issued a charter to the Society for Human Rights, founded by Henry Gerber, and officially dedicated to "promote and protect the interests" of people who, because of "mental and physical abnormalities," were hindered in the "pursuit of happiness." The Society would also "combat the public prejudices against" such people by the dissemination of "scientific" information.

Gerber and others in the group were arrested on trumped-up charges, jailed, and publicized in a scandal-mongering Chicago newspaper. Though the case was finally dismissed on the grounds that the arrests had occurred without a warrant, that prosecution put an end to the earliest documented homosexual rights organization in the United States.

In 1953, twenty-nine years after the incorporation of the Society for Human Rights, Henry Gerber briefly described the group's fate in a letter, published anonymously in the newly established homosexual emancipation magazine *ONE*. Gerber wrote:

> In 1925 [*sic*—1924], I met several inverts in Chicago and conceived a society on the order of that existing in Germany at that time, Society for Human Rights, and we published a few issues of a paper, called Friendship and Freedom and even had a charter from the State of Illinois.
>
> But one of our members turned out to be a married man (bisexual) and his wife complained to a social worker that he carried on his trade in front of his children and the social worker found a copy of our paper and all of us (4) were arrested without a warrant and dragged to jail.
>
> I managed to get out on bail and hired a good lawyer but the first judge was prejudiced and threatened to give us the limit ($200 fine) but I got a better lawyer who was politically connected and we also got a new judge, who was rumored "to be queer himself" and he dismissed the case and fined the married member $10 and cost.

I was then a postal clerk and a stupid and mean post office inspector brought the case before the Federal commission with an eye to have us indicted for publishing an "obscene paper" although of course, like your paper, no physical references were made. But the commissioner turned it down. However, the post office inspector, even in spite of us being acquitted, arranged my dismissal from the post office. The whole thing cost me all my savings of about $800 and no one helped us, not even the homosexuals of Chicago.

Of course, I see now the faults we committed, we should have had prominent doctors on our side and money on hand for defense, and a good lawyer. . . .

Little is now known of the Society for Human Rights. But evidence indicates that some member, probably Henry Gerber, had sought affiliation with an English sexual reform group, the British Society for the Study of Sex Psychology.

The British Society had been established in 1914, with Edward Carpenter as first president, Laurence Housman as chair, George Ives and Stella Browne among the active members, Havelock Ellis and others as backers. The group was concerned with "sexual psychology" in its "medical, juridical, and sociological aspect," and with educating the public toward greater toleration on sexual matters. Several active members were, as they called themselves, "sexual inverts," or early supporters of invert rights. Ives was the founder of a secret invert emancipation organization of which the socialist-feminist Housman was a member. A special sub-committee of the British Society for the Study of Sex Psychology focused on sexual inversion. Members of the society gave lectures, and the society published seventeen pamphlets between 1915 and 1933.

On June 4, 1925, George Ives's handwritten minutes of the executive committee of the British Society for the Study of Sex Psychology report:

A letter was read from the Society for Human Rights, Chicago, announcing their formation and suggesting cooperation. It was agreed to reply pointing out that the aspect of the subject which appeared to be their particular interest [the rights of "intermediate types"] was only one of the aspects covered by our society, and suggesting membership for any of their members who would care to receive publications as issued.

The executives of the British Society were afraid of any direct affiliation with the American group dedicated specifically to the rights of "intermediates."

On August 6, 1925, the minutes of the British Society record:

Capt. Green read a letter he had received from the Society for Human Rights, Chicago, relating to the prosecution of their officers, to which he promised to reply.

(Neither the letter from Chicago nor Green's reply seems to have been preserved in George Ives's papers.)

In October 1925, the printed "Eleventh Annual Report" of the British Society declared that it had been "in correspondence with" Magnus Hirschfeld's Institute for Sexual Science, Berlin, with another such institute in The Hague, and with "the Society for Human Rights, U.S.A."

A rough draft of this annual report includes a paragraph deleted from the printed version, providing a few more details about the U.S. group, and even a quote from the group's correspondence:

> The Society for Human Rights was formed in Chicago at the beginning of the year with "the ultimate aim of bettering the living conditions of the intermediate type of persons." They started with an ambitious programme which included the publication of a monthly paper entitled "Friendship and Freedom." Unfortunately their offices [*sic*—officers] did not scrutinise the qualifications of intending members with sufficient care, and the Society has been involved in legal proceedings from which it has emerged vindicated, but its resources have been severely strained by the cost of these proceedings.

The annual report of the British Society in October 1925, also mentioned that the group had three honorary members in the United States. Two of these were probably Margaret Sanger and Dr. William Robinson. Whether Henry Gerber was a member of the British group is not known.

❦

MARY CASAL
The Stone Wall (1930)

The autobiography of the pseudonymous Mary Casal fully details the sexual life and relationships of an American lesbian born in rural New England in 1864. Casal's book presents a rarely heard early lesbian voice recounting her own history from just after the Civil War through the first quarter of the twentieth century. The work records her early rebellion against traditional female roles and describes a series of emotional involvements with other women, including various forms of sexual expression. Her relationships with women culminate in her meeting and taking up life with her great love, whom she calls Juno.

If you do not want to hear the truth about things which have been greeted with that most dangerous weapon, "S-s-s-sh," don't read this book, said weapon being to my mind more dangerous to the development of the human mind and soul than the machine gun is to the body of a man placed in front of the firing line.

I believe the time has come when there should be less secrecy about matters which are at the root of many evils of today. Not a new thought. Many are thinking along those lines and many are accepting very frank articles now written on sex problems which bear on the conduct of the youth of today.

Novels are being written dealing in open terms with the so-called normal types of humans, leading one through the various channels of lovemaking and the resultant episodes, leaving nothing to the imagination, but supplying a few asterisks to conform to the ideas of the snooping reformers and self-appointed censors.

This book is not fiction. I am writing of my own life; my actual experiences from my earliest recollection to the age of nearly seventy years.

Many will declare it to have been an abnormal life. I do not believe every woman has been through all the experiences that I have (I certainly hope not for their sakes), but I do believe that every woman has had some of the problems that I have had to face.

Many will deny a knowledge of any of them, afraid to acknowledge even to themselves the whole truth. In judging reactions in a child's mind, I ask the readers of today to remember that I was born in 1864, and also to realize the atmosphere of the home life of that period.

I expect to speak openly of things which, in the modern novel, are represented by asterisks; on the stage by the lowering of the curtain; in the press many times without restriction, but as ordinary "news" to sell the paper; and in conversation by a raising of the eyebrows or a shrug of the shoulders.

It has taken courage to bare the facts of an extraordinary life, but it is done with the sincere hope that it may throw light from a new and different angle on the effort of the parent to understand children, and also to bring out the thought that without truth nothing may be accomplished in this life.

∽

Mattachine Society

Statement of Missions and Purposes (1951)

The Mattachine Society, organized in Los Angeles in 1950 by Harry Hay and seven other gay men, was named after the Mattachines, a medieval troupe of men who went from village to village advocating social justice. The founders modeled Mattachine after the Communist Party, which emphasized secrecy, hierarchical structures, and centralized leadership. In 1951, the group adopted two major purposes: (1) it called for a grassroots effort to challenge antigay discrimination, and (2) it called for building a positive homosexual community and culture. In 1953, with Joseph McCarthy's witch hunts at their peak, an article linking Mattachine to communism shook the group to its foundations. As a result, many in the group began advocating a more moderate, assimilationist, or accommodationist platform and the group distanced itself from its radical roots.

To UNIFY: While there are undoubtedly individual homosexuals who number many of their own people among their friends, thousands of homosexuals live out their lives bewildered, unhappy, alone, isolated from their own kind and unable to adjust to the dominant culture. Even those who have many homosexual friends are still cut off from the deep satisfactions man's gregarious nature can achieve *only* when he is consciously part of a large, unified whole. A major purpose of the Mattachine Society is to provide a consensus of principle around which all of our people can rally and from which they can derive a feeling of "belonging."

To EDUCATE: The total of information available on the subject of homosexuality is woefully meagre and utterly inconclusive. The Society organizes all available material and conducts extensive researches itself—psychological, physiological, anthropological and sociological—for the purpose of informing all interested homosexuals and for the purpose of informing and enlightening the public at large.

The Mattachine Society holds it as possible and desirable that a highly ethical, homosexual culture emerge as a consequence of its work, parallelling the emerging cultures of our fellow-minorities—the Negro, Mexican and Jewish peoples. The Society believes homosexuals can lead well-adjusted, wholesome and socially productive lives once ignorance and prejudice against them are successfully combatted and once homosexuals themselves feel they have a dignified and useful role to play in society. The Society, to these ends, is in the process of developing a homosexual ethic—disciplined, moral and socially responsible.

To LEAD: It is not sufficient for an oppressed minority like the homosexuals merely to be conscious of belonging to a minority collective when, as is the situation at the present time, that collective is neither socially organic nor objective in its directions and activities—although this minimum is, in itself, a great step forward. It is necessary that the more far-seeing and socially conscious homosexuals provide leadership to the whole mass of social deviants if the first two missions (the unification and the education of the homosexual minority) are to be accomplished. Further, once unification and education have progressed it becomes imperative (to consolidate these gains) for the Society to push forward into the realm of political action to erase from our law books the discriminatory and oppressive legislation presently directed against the homosexual minority.

The Society, founded upon the highest ethical and social principles, serves as an example for homosexuals to follow and provides a dignified standard upon which the rest of society can base a more intelligent and accurate picture of the nature of homosexuality than currently obtains in the public mind. The Society provides the instrument necessary to work with civic-minded and socially valuable organizations and supplies the means for the assistance of our people who are victimized daily as a result of our oppression. Only a Society, providing an enlightened leadership, can rouse the homosexuals—one of the largest minorities in America today—to take the actions necessary to elevate themselves from the social ostracism an unsympathetic culture has perpetrated upon them.

(Drafted April, 1951)   (Ratified July 20, 1951)

∿

DAUGHTERS OF BILITIS (DOB)
The Ladder (1956)

Del Martin and Phyllis Lyons founded the Daughters of Bilitis in 1955 in San Francisco. With the support of the Mattachine Society and its newsletter, One, *The Ladder made its debut in October 1956. It became an instant success, letters poured in by the thousands, and the membership of DOB rocketed to such an extent that in January 1957 it became a nonprofit organization under the state law of California.*

October 1956
Volume 1, Number 1
Published monthly in San Francisco, California, by the Daughters of Bilitis

> OFFICERS:
> President—Del Martin
> Vice-President—Tori Fry
> Secretary—Ann Ferguson
> Treasurer—Pat Hamilton
> Trustee—D. Griffin
> STAFF:
> Editor—Ann Ferguson
> Assistant Editor—Tori Fry
> Art Editor—BOB
> Production Manager—Bobbi Deering

We are sending this first issue to you with our compliments in order to acquaint you with our organization and the work we are doing.

However, in order to help defray publishing expenses we are asking for donations of $1.00 for one year of *The Ladder.* If you wish to receive future issues and to help the cause please send in the questionnaire on page 12.

Just one year ago the Daughters of Bilitis was formed. Eight women gathered together with a vague idea that something should be done about the problems of Lesbians, both within their own group and with the public.

The original idea was mainly that of providing an outlet for social activities, but with discussion came broader purposes and the club was formed with a much wider scope than that originally envisioned, as can be seen from the club "Purpose" on page 4.

The eight charter members, with a constitution, by-laws and a name, started out to find more members. And this has been the biggest problem in this first year.

As our President has so aptly pointed out in her message, "the Lesbian is a very elusive creature." Membership has fluctuated from a low of six to the present 15, and only three of the eight charter members remain. But the basic need for, and validity of, such a club continues, and our membership is growing.

This membership is open to all women over 21 who have a genuine interest in the problems of the female homophile and the related problems of other minorities. Initiation fee is $5 for active and $2.50 for associate members, with monthly dues of $1 for the former and 50¢ for the latter.

The name "Daughters of Bilitis" is taken from "Songs of Bilitis," a narrative love poem written by Pierre Louys and published in 1894. Bilitis would seem to have been a contemporary of Sappho on the isle of Lesbos, and the poem is purported to be a translation from the Greek. Although it has been more or less conclusively established that the poem is not authentic, it presents a sensitive and searching picture of Lesbian love.

Our organization is endeavoring to develop a program of interest to all. This includes our monthly public discussion meetings featuring speakers from local business, professional and medical fields; monthly business meetings; and brunches, parties, picnics and beach parties, bowling, horseback riding and other social events.

This newsletter we hope will be a force in uniting the women in working for the common goal of greater personal and social acceptance and understanding. With this first issue we enter a field already ably served by "One" and "Mattachine Review." We offer, however, that so-called "feminine viewpoint" which they have had so much difficulty obtaining. It is to be hoped that our venture will encourage the women to take an ever-increasing part in the steadily-growing fight for understanding of the homophile minority.

Suggestions and constructive criticisms are urgently solicited, as is your support, aid and assistance. Full information may be obtained by writing Post Office Box 2183, San Francisco 26, California.

DAUGHTERS OF BILITIS: PURPOSE

1. Education of the variant, with particular emphasis on the psychological and sociological aspects, to enable her to understand herself and make her adjustment to society in all its social, civic and economic implications by establishing and main-

taining a library of both fiction and nonfiction on the sex deviant theme; by sponsoring public discussions on pertinent subjects to be conducted by leading members of the legal, psychiatric, religious and other professions; by advocating a mode of behaviour and dress acceptable to society.

2. Education of the public through acceptance first of the individual, leading to an eventual breakdown of erroneous conceptions, taboos and prejudices; through public discussion meetings; through dissemination of educational literature on the homosexual theme.

3. Participation in research projects by duly authorized and responsible psychology, sociology and other such experts directed towards further knowledge of the homosexual.

4. Investigation of the penal code as it pertains to the homosexual, proposal of changes to provide an equitable handling of cases involving this minority group, and promotion of these changes through due process of law in the state legislatures.

The Daughters of Bilitis is not now, and never has been, affiliated with any other organization, political, social or otherwise.

CALENDAR OF EVENTS

Sunday, Sept. 30—Picnic at Samuel P. Taylor State Park. $1.00. Transportation and food will be provided. Reservations must be made by Friday night, September 28. Phone PLaza 6-3382.

Thursday, Oct. 11—Business Meeting and election of officers. Members only. 60 Los Olivos, Daly City, at 8 p.m.

Saturday, Oct. 13—Bowling. 7 p.m. at the Sports Center, 30th & Mission. Meet at the coffee counter.

Tuesday, Oct. 23—Panel discussion at 465 Geary St., Studio 51, at 8:15 p.m. Subject will be "What Are You Afraid Of?", the first in a series of discussions on Lesbian fears—both real and imaginary. On the panel will be Pat Hamilton and Del Martin. Dr. Vera Plunkett will act as moderator.

Saturday, Oct. 27—Hallowe'en Party at 651 Duncan St. at 8 p.m. $1.50 per person. Refreshments provided. Phone your reservation (VAlencia 4-2790) by Friday night, Oct. 26.

Guests will be more than welcome to all events except the meeting on Oct. 11. The picnic on Sept. 30 will be an excellent opportunity for newcomers to get acquainted and to learn more about our group. The discussion meeting will be the first of a series to bring FEAR into the open and deal with it. Future speakers will include a lawyer, social worker, psychiatrist, and others.

PRESIDENT'S MESSAGE

Since 1950 there has been a nationwide movement to bring understanding to and about the homosexual minority.

Most of the organizations dedicated to this purpose stem from the Mattachine Society which was founded in Los Angeles at that time. Members of these organizations—The Mattachine Society, One, and National Association for Sexual Research—are predominantly male, although there are a few hardworking women among their ranks.

The Daughters of Bilitis is a women's organization resolved to add the feminine voice and viewpoint to a mutual problem. While women may not have so much difficulty with law enforcement, their problems are none the less real—family, sometimes children, employment, social acceptance.

However, the Lesbian is a very elusive creature. She burrows underground in her fear of identification. She is cautious in her associations. Current modes in hair style and casual attire have enabled her to camouflage her existence. She claims she does not need help. And she will not risk her tight little fist of security to aid those who do.

But surely the ground work has been well laid in the past 5½ years. Homosexuality is not the dirty word it used to be. More and more people, professional and lay, are becoming aware of its meaning and implications. There is no longer so much "risk" in becoming associated with [it].

And why not "belong"? Many heterosexuals do. Membership is open to anyone who is interested in the minority problems of the sexual variant and does not necessarily indicate one's own sex preference.

Women have taken a beating through the centuries. It has been only in this 20th, through the courageous crusade of the Suffragettes and the influx of women into the business world, that woman has become an independent entity, an individual with the right to vote and the right to a job and economic security. But it took women with foresight and determination to attain this heritage which is now ours.

And what will be the lot of the future Lesbian? Fear? Scorn? This need not be—if lethargy is supplanted by an organized constructive program, if cowardice gives way to the solidarity of a cooperative front, if the "let Georgia do it" attitude is replaced by the realization of individual responsibility in thwarting the evils of ignorance, superstition, prejudice, and bigotry.

Nothing was ever accomplished by hiding in a dark corner. Why not discard the hermitage for the heritage that awaits any red-blooded American woman who dares to claim it?

Del Martin, President
Daughters of Bilitis

. . .

RAISING CHILDREN IN A DEVIANT RELATIONSHIP

This heretofore untouched subject has been broached by members of the Daughters of Bilitis in several discussion sessions, one of which was led by Faith Rossiter, psychotherapist. It is surprising to learn how many women are raising children in a deviant relationship (we have also learned of instances where men are undertaking this responsibility too).

To be of any assistance to those who are meeting this problem, we need more data and more research into the various facets of such a relationship. If you are interested or if you can help us in this project, please let us hear from you.

∾

RADICALESBIANS
The Woman Identified Woman (1971)

Just as gay organizing was moving from accommodation to liberation, the women's movement was undergoing its own inner frictions. For many radical lesbians, the women's liberation movement of the 1960s was too bourgeois, too homophobic, and still too focused on how women needed to operate in a man's world. It made women who loved women invisible. In 1970 a group known as the Radicalesbians brought gay liberation and feminism together by arguing that a separatist world was the highest form of feminism and would lead to the complete elimination of patriarchy. For Radicalesbians, lesbianism was not merely a desire or a sexual object choice, but a deliberate rejection of heterosexuality in a patriarchal world.

What is a lesbian? A lesbian is the rage of all women condensed to the point of explosion. She is the woman who, often beginning at an extremely early age, acts in accordance with her inner compulsion to be a more complete and freer human being than her society—perhaps then, but certainly later—cares to allow her. These needs and actions, over a period of years, bring her into painful conflict with people, situations, the accepted ways of thinking, feeling, and behaving, until she is in a state of continual war with everything around her, and usually with herself. She may not be fully conscious of the political implications of what for her began as personal necessity, but on some level she has not been able to accept the limitations and oppression laid on her by the most basic role of her society—the female role. The turmoil she experiences tends to induce guilt proportional to the degree to which she feels she is not meeting social expectations, and/or eventually drives her to question and analyze what the rest of her society more or less accepts. She is forced to evolve her own life pattern, often living much of her life alone, learning usually much earlier than her "straight" (heterosexual) sisters about the essential aloneness of life (which the myth of marriage obscures) and about the reality of illusions. To the extent that she cannot expel the heavy socialization that goes with being female, she can never truly find peace with herself. For she is caught somewhere between accepting society's view of her—in which case she cannot accept herself—and coming to understand what this sexist society has done to her and why it is functional and necessary for it to do so. Those of us who work that through find ourselves on the other side of a tortuous journey through a night that may have been decades long. The perspective gained from that journey, the liberation of self, the inner peace, the real love of self and of all women, is something to be shared with all women—because we are all women.

It should first be understood that lesbianism, like male homosexuality, is a category of behavior possible only in a sexist society characterized by rigid sex roles and dominated by male supremacy. Those sex roles dehumanize women by defining us as a supportive/serving caste *in relation to* the master caste of men, and emotionally cripple men by demanding that they be alienated from their own bodies and emotions in order to perform their economic/political/military functions effectively. Homosexuality is a by-product of a particular way of setting up roles (or approved patterns of behavior) on the basis of sex; as such it is an inauthentic (not consonant with "reality") category. In a society in which men do not oppress women, and sexual expression is allowed to follow feelings, the categories of homosexuality and heterosexuality would disappear.

But lesbianism is also different from male homosexuality, and serves a different function in the society. "Dyke" is a different kind of put-down from "faggot," although both imply you are not playing your socially assigned sex role . . . are not therefore a "real woman" or a "real man." The grudging admiration felt for the tomboy, and the queasiness felt around a sissy boy point to the same thing: the contempt in which women—or those who play a female role—are held. And the investment in keeping women in that contemptuous role is very great. Lesbian is a word, the label, the condition that holds women in line. When a woman hears this word tossed her way, she knows she is stepping out of line. She knows that she has crossed the terrible boundary of her sex role. She recoils, she protests, she reshapes her actions to gain approval. Lesbian is a label invented by the Man to throw at any woman who dares to be his equal, who dares to challenge his prerogatives (including that of all women as part of the exchange medium among men), who dares to assert the primacy of her own needs. To have the label applied to people active in women's liberation is just the most recent instance of a long history; older women will recall that not so long ago, any woman who was successful, independent, not orienting her whole life about a man, would hear this word. For in this sexist society, for a woman to be independent means she *can't be* a woman—she must be a dyke. That in itself should tell us where women are at. It says as clearly as can be said: woman and person are contradictory terms. For a lesbian is not considered a "real woman." And yet, in popular thinking, there is really only one essential difference between a lesbian and other women: that of sexual orientation—which is to say, when you strip off all the packaging, you must finally realize that the essence of being a "woman" is to get fucked by men.

"Lesbian" is one of the sexual categories by which men have divided up humanity. While all women are dehumanized as sex objects, as the objects of men they are given certain compensations: identification with his power, his ego, his status, his protection (from other males), feeling like a "real woman," finding social acceptance by adhering to her role, etc. Should a woman confront herself by confronting another woman, there are fewer rationalizations, fewer buffers by which to avoid the stark horror of her dehumanized condition. Herein we find the overriding fear of many women toward being used as a sexual object by a woman, which not only will bring her no male-connected compensations, but also will reveal the void which is woman's real situation. This dehumanization is expressed when a straight woman learns that a sister is a lesbian; she begins to relate to her lesbian sister as her potential sex object, laying a surrogate male role on the lesbian. This reveals her heterosexual conditioning to make herself into an object when sex is potentially involved in a relationship, and it denies the lesbian her full humanity. For women, especially those in the movement, to perceive their lesbian sisters through this male grid of role definitions is to accept this male cultural conditioning and to oppress their sisters much as they themselves have been oppressed by men. Are we going to continue the male classification system of defining all females in sexual relation to some other category of people? Affixing the label "lesbian" not only to a woman who aspires to be a person, but also to any situation of real love, real solidarity, real primacy among women, is a primary form of divisiveness among women: it is the condition which keeps women within the confines of the feminine role, and it is the debunking/scare term that keeps women from forming any primary attachments, groups, or associations among ourselves.

Women in the movement have in most cases gone to great lengths to avoid discussion and confrontation with the issue of lesbianism. It puts people up-tight. They are hostile, evasive, or try to incorporate it into some "broader issue." They would rather not talk about it. If they have to, they try to dismiss it as a "lavender herring." But it is no side issue. It is absolutely essential to the success and fulfillment of the women's liberation movement that this issue be dealt with. As long as the label "dyke" can be used to frighten a woman into a less militant stand, keep her separate from her sisters, keep her from giving primacy to anything other than men and family—then to that extent she is controlled by the male culture. Until women see in each other the possibility of a primal commitment which includes sexual love, they will be denying themselves the love and value they readily accord to men, thus affirming their second-class status. As long as male acceptability is primary—both to individual women and to the movement as a whole—the term lesbian will be used effectively against women. Insofar as women want only more privileges within the system, they do not want to antagonize male power. They instead seek acceptability for women's liberation, and the most crucial aspect of the acceptability is to deny lesbianism—that is, to deny any fundamental challenge to the basis of the female. It should also be said that some younger, more radical women have honestly begun to discuss lesbianism, but so far it has been primarily as a sexual "alternative" to men. This, however, is still giving primacy to men, both because the idea of relating more completely to women occurs as a negative reaction to men, and because the lesbian relationship is being characterized simply by sex, which is divisive and sexist. On one level, which is both personal and political, women may withdraw emotional and sexual energies from men, and work out various alternatives for those energies in their own lives. On a different political/psychological level, it must be understood that what is crucial is that women begin disengaging from male-defined response patterns. In the privacy of our own psyches, we must cut those cords to the core. For irrespective of where our love and sexual energies flow, if we are male-identified in our heads, we cannot realize our autonomy as human beings.

But why is it that women have related to and through men? By virtue of having been brought up in a male society, we have internalized the male culture's definition of ourselves. That definition consigns us to sexual and family functions, and excludes us from defining and shaping the terms of our lives. In exchange for our psychic servicing and for performing society's non–profit-making functions, the man confers on us just one thing: the slave status which makes us legitimate in the eyes of the society in which we live. This is called "femininity" or "being a real woman" in our cultural lingo. We are authentic, legitimate, real to the extent that we are the property of some man whose name we bear. To be a woman who belongs to no man is to be invisible, pathetic, inauthentic, unreal. He confirms his image of us—of what we have to be in order to be acceptable by him—but not our real selves; he confirms our womanhood—as he defines it, in relation to him—but cannot confirm our personhood, our own selves as absolutes. As long as we are dependent on the male culture for this definition. for this approval, we cannot be free.

The consequence of internalizing this role is an enormous reservoir of self-hate. This is not to say the self-hate is recognized or accepted as such; indeed most women would deny it. It may be experienced as discomfort with her role, as feeling empty, as numbness, as restlessness, as a paralyzing anxiety at the center. Alternatively, it may be expressed in shrill defensiveness of the glory and destiny of her role. But it does exist, often beneath the edge of her consciousness, poisoning her existence, keeping her alienated from herself, her own needs, and rendering her a stranger to other women. They try to escape by identifying with the oppressor, living through him, gaining status and identity from his ego, his power, his accomplishments. And by not identifying with other "empty vessels" like themselves. Women resist relating on all levels to other women who will reflect their own oppression, their own secondary status, their own self-hate. For to confront another woman is finally to confront one's self—the self we have gone to such lengths to avoid. And in that mirror we know we cannot really respect and love that which we have been made to be.

As the source of self-hate and the lack of real self are rooted in our male-given identity, we must create a new sense of self. As long as we cling to the idea of "being a woman," we will sense some conflict with that incipient self, that sense of I, that sense of a whole person. It is very difficult to realize and accept that being "feminine" and being a whole person are irreconcilable. Only women can give to each other a new sense of self. That identity we have to develop with reference to ourselves, and not in relation to men. This consciousness is the revolutionary force from which all else will follow, for ours is an organic revolution. For this we must be available and supportive to one another, give our commitment and our love, give the emotional support necessary to sustain this movement. Our energies must flow toward our sisters, not backward toward our oppressors. As long as women's liberation tries to free women without facing the basic heterosexual structure that binds us in one-to-one relationship with our oppressors, tremendous energies will continue to flow into trying to straighten up each particular relationship with a man, into finding how to get better sex, how to turn his head around—into trying to make the "new man" out of him, in the delusion that this will allow us to be the "new woman." This obviously splits our energies and commitments, leaving us unable to be committed to the construction of the new patterns which will liberate us.

It is the primacy of women relating to women, of women creating a new consciousness of and with each other, which is at the heart of women's liberation, and the basis for the cultural revolution. Together we must find, reinforce, and validate our authentic selves. As we do this, we confirm in each other that struggling, incipient sense of pride and strength, the divisive barriers begin to melt, we feel this growing solidarity with our sisters. We see ourselves as prime, find our centers inside of ourselves. We find receding the sense of alienation, of being cut off, of being behind a locked window, of being unable to get out what we know is inside. We feel a real-ness, feel at last we are coinciding with ourselves. With that real self, with that consciousness, we begin a revolution to end the imposition of all coercive identifications, and to achieve maximum autonomy in human expression.

～

Barbara Smith

Introduction to *Home Girls: A Black Feminist Anthology* (1983)

Since the 1970s, Barbara Smith has consistently written about, advocated for, and mobilized others to create a flourishing movement of African American feminism and women's studies. A cofounder of Kitchen Table: Women of Color Press, Smith has dedicated her working life to exploring the lives and experiences of African American women through her publishing, scholarship, political activism, and essays. In this excerpt, Smith outlines the ways black lesbians have encountered and resisted pernicious forms of homophobia, racism, and sexism.

History verifies that Black women have rejected doormat status, whether racially or sexually imposed, for centuries. Not only is there the documented resistance of Black women during slavery followed by our organizing around specific Black women's issues and in support of women's rights during the nineteenth century, there is also the vast cultural record of our continuously critical stance toward our oppression. For example, in the late nineteenth and early twentieth centuries, poets

Frances E. W. Harper (1825–1911), Angelina Weld Grimké (1880–1958), Alice Dunbar-Nelson (1875–1935), Anne Spencer (1882–1975), and Georgia Douglas Johnson (1886–1966) all addressed themes of sexual as well as racial identity in some of their work. . . .

I have always felt that Black women's ability to function with dignity, independence, and imagination in the face of total adversity—that is, in the face of white America—points to an innate feminist potential. To me the phrase, "Act like you have some sense," probably spoken by at least one Black woman to every Black child who ever lived, is a cryptic warning that says volumes about keeping your feet on the ground and your ass covered. Alice Walker's definition of "womanist" certainly makes the connection between plain common sense and a readiness to fight for change. She writes:

> WOMANIST: (According to Walker) From *womanish*. (Opp. of "girlish," i.e. frivolous, irresponsible, not serious.) A black feminist or feminist of color. From the colloquial expression of mothers to daughters, "You're acting womanish," i.e., like a woman. Usually referring to outrageous, audacious, courageous or *willful* behavior. Wanting to know more and in greater depth than is considered "good" for one. Interested in grown-up doings. Acting grown-up. Being grown-up. Interchangeable with other colloquial expression: "You're trying to be grown." Responsible. In charge. *Serious*. . . .
>
> 2. Also: Herstorically capable, as in "Mama, I'm walking to Canada and I'm taking you and a bunch of other slaves with me." Reply: "It wouldn't be the first time."

Black women as a group have never been fools. We couldn't afford to be. Yet in the last two decades many of us have been deterred from identifying with a liberation struggle which might say significant things to women like ourselves, women who believe that we were put here for a purpose in our own right, women who are usually not afraid to struggle.

Although our involvement has increased considerably in recent years, there are countless reasons why Black and other Third World women have not identified with contemporary feminism in large numbers. The racism of white women in the women's movement has certainly been a major factor. The powers-that-be are also aware that a movement of progressive Third World women in this country would alter life as we know it. As a result there has been a concerted effort to keep women of color from organizing autonomously and from organizing with other women around women's political issues. Third World men, desiring to maintain power over "their women" at all costs, have been among the most willing reinforcers of the fears and myths about the women's movement, attempting to scare us away from figuring things out for ourselves.

It is fascinating to look at various kinds of media from the late 1960s and early 1970s, when feminism was making its great initial impact, in order to see what Black men, Native American men, Asian American men, Latino men, and white men were saying about the irrelevance of "women's lib" to women of color. White men and Third World men, ranging from conservatives to radicals, pointed to the seeming lack of participation of women of color in the movement in order to discredit it and to undermine the efforts of the movement as a whole. All kinds of men were running scared because they knew that if the women in their midst were changing, they were going to have to change too. In 1976 I wrote:

> Feminism is potentially the most threatening of movements to Black and other Third World people because it makes it absolutely essential that we examine the way we live, how we treat each other, and what we believe. It calls into question the most basic assumption about our existence and this is the idea that biological, i.e., sexual identity determines all, that it is the rationale for power relationships as well as for all other levels of human identity and action. An irony is that among Third World people biological determinism is rejected and fought against when it is applied to race, but generally unquestioned when it applies to sex.

In reaction to the "threat" of such change, Black men, with the collaboration of some Black women, developed a set of myths to divert Black women from our own freedom.

MYTHS

Myth 1: The Black woman is already liberated.

This myth confuses liberation with the fact that Black women have had to take on responsibilities that our oppression gives us no choice but to handle. This is an insidious, but widespread myth that many Black women have believed themselves. Heading families, working outside the home, not building lives or expectations dependent on males, seldom being sheltered or pampered as women, Black women have known that their lives in some ways incorporated goals that white middle-class women were striving for, but race and class privilege, of course, reshaped the meaning of those goals profoundly. As W. E. B. DuBois said so long ago about Black women: ". . . our women in black had freedom contemptuously thrust upon them." Of all the people here, women of color generally have the fewest choices about the circumstances of their lives. An ability to cope under the worst conditions is not liberation, although our spiritual capacities have often made it look like a life. Black men didn't say anything about how poverty, unequal pay, no childcare, violence of every kind including battering, rape, and sterilization abuse, translated into "liberation."

Underlying this myth is the assumption that Black women are towers of strength who neither feel nor need what other human beings do, either emotionally or materially. White male social scientists, particularly Daniel P. Moynihan with his "matriarchy theory," further reinforce distortions concerning Black women's actual status. . . .

Myth 2: Racism is the primary (or only) oppression Black women have to confront.
(Once we get that taken care of, then Black women, men, and children will all
flourish. Or as Ms. Luisah Teish writes, we can look forward to being "the property
of powerful men.")

This myth goes hand in hand with the one that the Black woman is already liberated. The notion that struggling against or eliminating racism will completely alle-
viate Black women's problems does not take into account the way that sexual
oppression cuts across all racial, nationality, age, religious, ethnic, and class group-
ings. Afro-Americans are no exception.

It also does not take into account how oppression operates. Every generation
of Black people, up until now, has had to face the reality that no matter how hard
we work we will probably not see the end of racism in our lifetimes. Yet many of us
keep faith and try to do all we can to make change now. If we have to wait for
racism to be obliterated *before* we can begin to address sexism, we will be waiting
for a long time. Denying that sexual oppression exists or requiring that we wait to
bring it up until racism, or in some cases capitalism, is toppled, is a bankrupt position. A Black feminist perspective has no use for ranking oppressions, but instead
demonstrates the simultaneity of oppressions as they affect Third World women's
lives.

Myth 3: Feminism is nothing but man-hating. (And men have never done anything
that would legitimately inspire hatred.)

It is important to make a distinction between attacking institutionalized, systematic
oppression (the goal of any serious progressive movement) and attacking men as
individuals. Unfortunately, some of the most widely distributed writing about Black
women's issues has not made this distinction sufficiently clear. Our issues have not
been concisely defined in these writings, causing much adverse reaction and confusion about what Black feminism really is.

This myth is one of the silliest and at the same time one of the most dangerous. Anti-feminists are incapable of making a distinction between being critically
opposed to sexual oppression and simply hating men. Women's desire for fairness
and safety in our lives does not necessitate hating men. Trying to educate and
inform men about how their feet are planted on our necks doesn't translate into
hatred either. Centuries of anti-racist struggle by various people of color are not
reduced, except by racists, to our merely hating white people. If anything it seems
that the opposite is true. People of color know that white people have abused us
unmercifully and it is only sane for us to try to change that treatment by every
means possible.

Likewise the bodies of murdered women are strewn across the landscape of
this country. Rape is a national pastime, a form of torture visited upon all girls and
women, from babies to the aged. One out of three women in the U.S. will be raped
during her lifetime. Battering and incest, those home-based crimes, are pandemic.
Murder, of course, is men's ultimate violent "solution." And if you're thinking as
you read this that I'm exaggerating, please go get today's newspaper and verify the

facts. If anything is going down here it's woman-hatred, not man-hatred, a war against women. But wanting to end this war still doesn't equal man-hating. The feminist movement and the anti-racist movement have in common trying to ensure decent human life. Opposition to either movement aligns one with the most reactionary elements in American society.

Myth 4: Women's issues are narrow, apolitical concerns. People of color need to deal with the "larger struggle."

This myth once again characterizes women's oppression as not particularly serious, and by no means a matter of life and death. I have often wished I could spread the word that a movement committed to fighting sexual, racial, economic, and heterosexist oppression, not to mention one which opposes imperialism, anti-Semitism, the oppressions visited upon the physically disabled, the old and the young, at the same time that it challenges militarism and imminent nuclear destruction is the very opposite of narrow. All segments of the women's movement have not dealt with all of these issues, but neither have all segments of Black people. This myth is plausible when the women's movement is equated only with its most bourgeois and reformist elements. The most progressive sectors of the feminist movement, which includes some radical white women, have taken the above issues, and many more, quite seriously. Third World women have been the most consistent in defining our politics broadly. Why is it that feminism is considered "whiteminded" and "narrow" while socialism or Marxism, from verifiably white origins, is legitimately embraced by Third World male politicos, without their having their identity credentials questioned for a minute?

Myth 5: Those feminists are nothing but Lesbians.

This may be the most pernicious myth of all and it is essential to understand that the distortion lies in the phrase "nothing but" and not in the identification Lesbian. "Nothing but" reduces Lesbians to a category of beings deserving of only the most violent attack, a category totally alien from "decent" Black folks, i.e., not your sisters, mothers, daughters, aunts, and cousins, but bizarre outsiders like no one you know or *ever* knew.

Many of the most committed and outspoken feminists of color have been and are Lesbians. Since many of us are also radicals, our politics, as indicated by the issues merely outlined above, encompass all people. We're also as Black as we ever were. (I always find it fascinating, for example, that many of the Black Lesbian-feminists I know still wear their hair natural, indicating that for us it was more than a "style.") Black feminism and Black Lesbianism are not interchangeable. Feminism is a political movement and many Lesbians are not feminists. Although it is also true that many Black feminists are not Lesbians, this myth has acted as an accusation and a deterrent to keep non-Lesbian Black feminists from manifesting themselves, for fear it will be hurled against them.

Fortunately this is changing. Personally, I have seen increasing evidence that many Black women of whatever sexual preference are more concerned with exploring and ending our oppression than they are committed to being either homophobic or sexually separatist. Direct historical precedent exists for such commitments. In 1957, Black playwright and activist Lorraine Hansberry wrote the following in a letter to *The Ladder,* an early Lesbian periodical:

> I think it is about time that equipped women began to take on some of the ethical questions which a male-dominated culture has produced and dissect and analyze them quite to pieces in a serious fashion. It is time that "half the human race" had something to say about the nature of its existence. Otherwise—without revised basic thinking—the woman intellectual is likely to find herself trying to draw conclusions—moral conclusions—based on acceptance of a social moral superstructure which has never admitted to the equality of women and is therefore immoral itself. As per marriage, as per sexual practices, as per the rearing of children, etc. In this kind of work there may be women to emerge who will be able to formulate a new and possible concept that homosexual persecution and condemnation has at its roots not only social ignorance, but a philosophically active anti-feminist dogma.

I would like a lot more people to be aware that Lorraine Hansberry, one of our most respected artists and thinkers, was asking in a Lesbian context some of the same questions we are asking today, and for which we have been so maligned.

Black heterosexuals' panic about the existence of both Black Lesbians and Black gay men is a problem that they have to deal with themselves. A first step would be for them to better understand their own heterosexuality, which need not be defined by attacking everybody who is not heterosexual.

AIDS COALITION TO UNLEASH POWER
No More Business as Usual (1987)

Furious at the U.S. government's business-as-usual attitude in the face of the AIDS epidemic, protesters gathered for a morning rush hour demonstration in the heart of New York. That traffic-stopping action on March 24, 1987, which included demands for faster government approval and lower prices for AIDS drugs, launched a new organization that would eventually exercise remarkable influence on AIDS policy in this country and beyond—the AIDS Coalition to Unleash Power (ACT UP). ACT UP, along with the 1987 March on Washington, ushered in several years of heightened grassroots activism and media visibility in which the GLBT movement became larger, more visible, and more politically effective. In 1990 a more radical branch of ACT UP formed

Queer Nation, which staged loud public protests and started "outing campaigns" to force people in power who were living double lives to come out.

MASSIVE AIDS DEMONSTRATION
To demand the following:

1. Immediate release by the Federal Food and Drug Administration of drugs that might help save our lives.

These drugs include: Ribavirin (ICN Pharmaceuticals); Ampligen (HMR Research Co.); Glucan (Tulane University School of Medicine); DTC (Merieux); DDC (Hoffman-LaRoche); AS 101 (National Patent Development Corp.); MTPPE (Ciba-Geigy); AL 721 (Praxis Pharmaceuticals).

2. Immediate abolishment of cruel double-blind studies wherein some get the new drugs and some don't.

3. Immediate release of these drugs to everyone with AIDS or ARC.

4. Immediate availability of these drugs at affordable prices. Curb your greed!

5. Immediate massive public education to stop the spread of AIDS.

6. Immediate policy to prohibit discrimination in AIDS treatment, insurance, employment, and housing.

7. Immediate establishment of a coordinated, comprehensive, and compassionate national policy on AIDS.

President Reagan, nobody is in charge!
AIDS IS THE BIGGEST KILLER IN NEW YORK CITY OF YOUNG MEN AND WOMEN.
Tell your friends. Spread the word. Come protest together.
7 AM, March 24. You must be on time!
AIDS IS EVERYBODY'S BUSINESS NOW.

TRIKONE

Mission Statement (1986)

Founded in 1986 in the San Francisco Bay Area, Trikone is the oldest group of its kind in the world. Through social and political activities, Trikone offers a supportive, empowering, and nonjudgmental environment where queer South Asians can meet and make connections, and proudly promote awareness and acceptance of their sexuality in society. Trikone actively works against all forms of oppression based on race, gender, class, and other identities.

SOUTHERNERS ON NEW GROUND (SONG)
Mission Statement (1993)

SONG's work is rooted in the understanding that there is no liberation in isolation. We focus on local communities in twelve states of the Southeast, providing an important regional infrastructure for building progressive lesbigaytrans organizing in the traditionally conservative, under-resourced south. SONG serves Southern organizers who want to do multi-issue, cross-constituency organizing. We focus on people who want to move within an antiracist, antisexist, antihomophobic, and anticlassist framework, and who seek skills and information on how to do that more effectively.

∽

GENDERPAC
Mission Statement (1995)

The Gender Public Advocacy Coalition (GenderPAC) works to end discrimination and violence caused by gender stereotypes by changing public attitudes, educating elected officials and expanding human rights. GenderPAC also promotes understanding of the connection between discrimination based on gender stereotypes and sex, sexual orientation, age, race, class.

∽

NATIONAL LATINA/O LESBIAN, GAY, BISEXUAL, AND TRANSGENDER ORGANIZATION (LLEGÓ)

Mission Statement (1990)

LLEGÓ, the National Latina/o Lesbian, Gay, Bisexual, and Transgender Organization, is the only national nonprofit organization devoted to representing Latina/o lesbian, gay, bisexual and transgender (LGBT) communities and addressing their growing needs regarding an array of social issues ranging from civil rights and social justice to health and human services. LLEGÓ develops solutions to social, health, and political disparities that exist due to discrimination based on ethnicity, sexual orientation, and gender identity and that affect the lives and well-being of Latina/o LGBT people and their families.

~

MOSAIC: THE NATIONAL JEWISH CENTER FOR SEXUAL AND GENDER DIVERSITY

Mission Statement (2004)

Mosaic partners with Jewish organizations, communities, and individuals of every denomination to create a world where all Jews are fully included in Jewish communal life, regardless of sexual orientation or gender identity. Founded in the summer of 2003, Mosaic is the first and only national Jewish organization dedicated to this structural change.

9
Conclusion
WE'RE HERE, WE'RE QUEER,
NOW WHAT?

We both lead pretty out lives. In 1996, David got married to his partner, Gregg, in a Jewish wedding ceremony attended by 150 of their closest friends and family. At the time, they may not have realized how revolutionary that act was, but also how privileged they were to have the public space to be able to proclaim their love for one another. Caryn has taken a different path to her open, queer self, having been married to a man, only to come out of the closet in her late twenties. *American Queer, Now and Then* has shown that one of the most important changes over the past 100 years in the United States has been the *visibility* of queerness. If, in the early 1900s, queerness was coded, and queers met in separate places, in the new millennium, queerness is being marketed, sold, and broadcast to audiences across the world—and *everyone* (well, maybe not Aunt Barbara, Caryn's aunt in Skokie who had issues with the word "queer") knows it's queer. In the early 1900s there were not many options for queers other than leading double lives, in the words of W. E. B. Du Bois, the famous black intellectual who argued that leading double lives was part and parcel of living the life of an oppressed minority in the United States. For Du Bois, race was his marker of difference, and one that was often difficult to make invisible. Queerness, on the other hand, could almost always be rendered invisible.

Nearly all of the authors included in this book call for some form of visibility, whether through words, activism, entertainment, literature, or art. The idea of "the closet," of being locked up in a place in which people could not see you, became the guiding metaphor over the last two decades of the twentieth century. "Coming out," which used to denote a young queer's coming out into queer culture, now celebrates the process of releasing oneself from the bondage of a dark, gloomy place. As queerness became more visible, people finally had the *choice* of living multiple lives, of keeping identities separate, of maintaining boundaries between private and public, or of integrating one's lives and spaces.

Or at least people thought it was a question of choice. In the late 1980s and early 1990s, the radical queer activist groups ACT UP and Queer Nation began a campaign of "outing" people in public positions who were known to lead a "double life," in the hopes that by forcing powerful people to come out, they would then be more sympathetic to gay political and legal activism. Outing became a popular, and very threatening, political weapon that some queer activists used to accelerate the process of making the invisible visible. Others began to balk that by rendering everything visible, the line between private and public was disappearing. Outing continues into the new century in popular memoirs, on television exposés, and on the cover of the most popular queer magazine, *The Advocate*.

Since the mid-1990s, it seems that queerness is everywhere . . . in courtrooms, newspapers, television shows, movie theaters, classrooms, and every place in between. Those who choose to lead double lives, who may lead a public nonqueer life and a private queer one, are often derided as self-hating, as political opportunists, or at worst, as traitors who perpetuate homophobic social structures. At the same time, others like to remind those critics that early queer activism was about rights, the right to come out, the right to marry, the right to adopt children, but also the right not to do any of those things. In a more global world, as different notions of sexuality and identity come into contact with one another, the seemingly static notions of "out" and "not out" don't necessarily make sense.

If the degree of queer visibility has changed radically, some things have not changed much at all. Race, gender, and class are still three of the most important markers of difference *within* queer communities and continue to shape people's identities in profound ways. In 2005, a popular gay bar in San Francisco was sued for racism and for violating patrons' civil rights by requiring multiple forms of I.D. from queers of color who wanted to come in. And as *Boots of Leather* and *Gay New York* show, class has always been an often insurmountable obstacle in creating broad-based queer communities. Not surprisingly, queer men, queer women, and now the visible category of queer transgender people often remain in separate worlds, with their own politics, culture, and language that mark them as different both from other queers and from the rest of U.S. society.

Another change in the past twenty years is the clash between *being* queer and *studying* queerness, or between the experience of queer America and the theorization of queer America. In its early incarnations, people assumed that one informed the other, that the growth of a field known as queer theory would somehow benefit queer experience in America. But theoreticians and academics are not necessarily activists, and as Josh Gamson shows, the theorizing of queerness, the breaking down of categories like gay and lesbian or the rise of the category "transgender," can make community formation and the activism that often follows much more difficult. If, as some gender theoreticians suggest, the category "woman" has no meaning, then how can future generations fight for "women's rights"? Some activists wonder whether the work of queer theory to break down static categories may have unintended, and not always positive, consequences for those who live their lives in those categories. We hope that this book has brought together these two conflicting ideas—of breaking down categories by making them more fluid across time and space and of the debates about categories, both now and then, moving activism forward.

We argue that the active and visible contests over power among American queers show that queers now occupy an important place in our culture. The fact that queerness, real and performed, is everywhere shows that people have heeded Audre Lorde's call to move from silence to action. We're here, we're queer, but the question remains, if everything becomes "queer," what will the experience of being and thinking queer in America mean in the future?

JOSH GAMSON

Must Identity Movements Self-Destruct? A Queer Dilemma (1995)

Josh Gamson, an associate professor at the University of San Francisco, is one of the fore-most academic scholars in the areas of popular culture and sexualities. In this article, Gamson discusses the dilemma faced by social movements in general, and lesbian and gay politics in particular, that depend on fixed identity categories as a source of collective oppression and mobilization.

Focused passion and vitriol erupt periodically in the letters columns of San Francisco's lesbian and gay newspapers. When the *San Francisco Bay Times* announced to "the community" that the 1993 Freedom Day Parade would be called "The Year of the Queer," missives fired for weeks. The parade was what it always is: a huge empowerment party. But the letters continue to be telling. "Queer" elicits familiar arguments: over assimilation, over generational differences, over who is considered "us" and who gets to decide.

On this level, it resembles similar arguments in ethnic communities in which boundaries, identities, and cultures are negotiated, defined, and produced (Nagel 1994:152). Dig deeper into debates over queerness, however, and something more interesting and significant emerges. Queerness in its most distinctive forms shakes the ground on which gay and lesbian politics has been built, taking apart the ideas of a "sexual minority" and a "gay community," indeed of "gay" and "lesbian" and even "man and "woman."[1] It builds on central difficulties of identity-based organizing: the instability of identities both individual and collective, their made-up yet necessary character. It exaggerates and explodes these troubles, haphazardly attempting to build a politics from the rubble of deconstructed collective categories. This debate, and other related debates in lesbian and gay politics, is not only over the *content* of collective identity (whose definition of "gay" counts?), but over the everyday *viability* and political *usefulness* of sexual identities (is there and should there be such a thing as "gay," "lesbian," "man," "woman"?).

This paper, using internal debates from lesbian and gay politics as illustration, brings to the fore a key dilemma in contemporary identity politics and traces out its implications for social movement theory and research.[2] As I will show in greater detail, in these sorts of debates—which crop up in other communities as well—two different political impulses, and two different forms of organizing, can be seen facing off. The logic and political utility of deconstructing collective categories vie with those of shoring them up; each logic is true, and neither is fully tenable.

On the one hand, lesbians and gay men have made themselves an effective force in this country over the past several decades largely by giving themselves what civil rights movements had: a public collective identity. Gay and lesbian social movements have built a quasi-ethnicity, complete with its own political and cultural institutions, festivals, neighborhoods, even its own flag. Underlying that ethnicity is typically the notion that what gays and lesbians share—the anchor of minority status and minority rights claims—is the same fixed, natural essence, a self with same-sex desires. The shared oppression, these movements have forcefully claimed, is the denial of the freedoms and opportunities to actualize this self. In this *ethnic/essentialist* politic,[3] clear categories of collective identity are necessary for successful resistance and political gain.

Yet this impulse to build a collective identity with distinct group boundaries has been met by a directly opposing logic, often contained in queer activism (and in the newly anointed "queer theory"): to take apart the identity categories and blur group boundaries. This alternative angle, influenced by academic constructionist thinking, holds that sexual identities are historical and social products, not natural or intrapsychic ones. It is socially produced binaries (gay/straight, man/woman) that are the basis of oppression; fluid, unstable experiences of self become fixed primarily in the service of social control. Disrupting those categories, refusing rather than embracing ethnic minority status, is the key to liberation. In this *deconstructionist* politic, clear collective categories are an obstacle to resistance and change.

The challenge for analysts, I argue, is not to determine which position is accurate, but to cope with the fact that both logics make sense. Queerness spotlights a dilemma shared by other identity movements (racial, ethnic, and gender movements, for example):[4] Fixed identity categories are both the basis for oppression and the basis for political power. This raises questions for political strategizing and, more importantly for the purposes here, for social movement analysis. If identities are indeed much more unstable, fluid, and constructed than movements have tended to assume—if one takes the queer challenge seriously, that is—what happens to identity-based social movements such as gay and lesbian rights? Must sociopolitical struggles articulated through identity eventually undermine themselves?

Social movement theory, a logical place to turn for help in working through the impasse between deconstructive cultural strategies and category-supportive political strategies, is hard pressed in its current state to cope with these questions. The case of queerness, I will argue, calls for a more developed theory of collective identity formation and its relationship to both institutions and meanings, an understanding that *includes the impulse to take apart that identity from within.*

In explicating the queer dilemma and its implications for social movement theory, . . . I make use of internal debates, largely as they took place in the letters column of the weekly *San Francisco Bay Times* in 1991, 1992, and 1993. I turn initially to debates within lesbian and gay communities over the use of the word "queer," using them to highlight the emergence of queer activism, its continuities with earlier lesbian and gay activism, and its links with and parallels to queer theory. Next, I take up debates over the inclusion of transgender and bisexual people— the two groups brought in under an expanded queer umbrella—in lesbian and gay politics. Here I point to a distinctive (although not entirely new) element of queerness, a politic of boundary disruption and category deconstruction, and to the resistance to that politic, made especially visible by the gendered nature of these debates. Finally, in drawing out ramifications for social movement theory, I briefly demonstrate affinities between the queer debates and debates over multiracialism in African American politics, arguing that queerness illuminates the core dilemma for identity movements more generally. I conclude by suggesting ways in which social movement literature can be pushed forward by taking seriously, both as theoretical and empirical fact, the predicament of identity movements. . . .

QUEER POLITICS AND QUEER THEORY

Since the late 1980s, "queer" has served to mark first a loose but distinguishable set of political movements and mobilizations, and second a somewhat parallel set of academy-bound intellectual endeavors (now calling itself "queer theory"). Queer politics, although given organized body in the activist group Queer Nation, operates largely through the decentralized, local, and often anti-organizational cultural activism of street postering, parodic and non-conformist self-presentation, and underground alternative magazines ("zines") (Berlant and Freeman 1993; Duggan 1992; Williams 1993);[5] it has defined itself largely against conventional lesbian and gay politics. The emergence of queer politics, although it cannot be treated here in detail, can be traced to the early 1980s backlash against gay and lesbian movement gains, which "punctured illusions of a coming era of tolerance and sexual pluralism"; to the AIDS crisis, which "underscored the limits of a politics of minority rights and inclusion"; and to the eruption of "long-simmering internal differences" around race and sex, and criticism of political organizing as "reflecting a white, middle-class experience or standpoint" (Seidman 1994:172).[6] . . .

My discussion of this and the two debates that follow is based on an analysis of 75 letters in the weekly *San Francisco Bay Times,* supplemented by related editorials from national lesbian and gay publications. The letters were clustered: The debates on the word "queer" ran in the *San Francisco Bay Times* from December 1992 through April 1993; the disputes over bisexuality ran from April 1991 through May 1991; clashes over transsexual inclusion ran from October 1992 through December 1992. Although anecdotal evidence suggests that these disputes are widespread, it should be noted that I use them here not to provide conclusive data, but to provide a grounded means for conceptualizing the queer challenge.

The Controversy over Queerness: Continuities with Existing Lesbian and Gay Activism
In the discussion of the "Year of the Queer" theme for the 1993 lesbian and gay pride celebration, the venom hits first. "All those dumb closeted people who don't like the Q word," the *Bay Times* quotes Peggy Sue suggesting, "can go fuck themselves and go to somebody else's parade." A man named Patrick argues along the same lines, asserting that the men opposing the theme are "not particularly thrilled

with their attraction to other men," are "cranky and upset," yet willing to benefit "from the stuff queer activists do." A few weeks later, a letter writer shoots back that "this new generation assumes we were too busy in the '70s lining up at Macy's to purchase sweaters to find time for the revolution—as if their piercings and tattoos were any cheaper." Another sarcastically asks, "How did you ever miss out on 'Faggot' or 'Cocksucker'?" On this level, the dispute reads like a sibling sandbox spat.

Although the curses fly sometimes within generations, many letter writers frame the differences as generational. The queer linguistic tactic, the attempt to defang, embrace and resignify a stigma term, is loudly rejected by many older gay men and lesbians.[7] "I am sure he isn't old enough to have experienced that feeling of cringing when the word 'queer' was said," says Roy of an earlier letter writer. Another writer asserts that 35 is the age that marks off those accepting the queer label from those rejecting it. Younger people, many point out, can "reclaim" the word only because they have not felt as strongly the sting, ostracism, police batons, and baseball bats that accompanied it one generation earlier. For older people, its oppressive meaning can never be lifted, can never be turned from overpowering to empowering.

Consider "old" as code for "conservative," and the dispute takes on another familiar, overlapping frame: the debate between assimilationists and separatists, with a long history in American homophile, homosexual, lesbian, and gay politics. Internal political struggle over agendas of assimilation (emphasizing sameness) and separation (emphasizing difference) has been present since the inception of these movements, as it has in other movements. The "homophile" movement of the 1950s, for example, began with a Marxist-influenced agenda of sex-class struggle, and was quickly overtaken by accommodationist tactics: gaining expert support; men demonstrating in suits, women in dresses.[8] Queer marks a contemporary anti-assimilationist stance, in opposition to the mainstream inclusionary goals of the dominant gay rights movement.

"They want to work from within," says Peggy Sue elsewhere (Berube and Escoffier 1991), "and I just want to crash in from the outside and say, 'Hey! Hello, I'm queer. I can make out with my girlfriend. Ha ha. Live with it. Deal with it.' That kind of stuff." In a zine called *Rant Rave*, co-editor Miss Rant argues that:

> I don't want to be gay, which means assimilationist, normal, homosexual. . . . I don't want my personality, behavior, beliefs, and desires to be cut up like a pie into neat little categories from which I'm not supposed to stray. (1993:15)

Queer politics, as Michael Warner puts it, "opposes society itself," protesting "not just the normal behavior of the social but the *idea* of normal behavior" (1993:xxvii). It embraces the label of perversity, using it to call attention to the "norm" in "normal," be it hetero or homo.

Queer thus asserts in-your-face difference, with an edge of defiant separatism: "We're here, we're queer, get used to it," goes the chant. We are different, that is, free from convention, odd and out there and proud of it, and your response is either your problem or your wake-up call. Queer does not so much rebel against outsider status as revel in it.[9] Queer confrontational difference, moreover, is scary, writes Alex Chee (1991), and thus politically useful:

> Now that I call myself queer, know myself as a queer, nothing will keep [queer-haters] safe. If I tell them I am queer, they give me room. Politically, I can think of little better. I do not want to be one of them. They only need to give me room.

This goes against the grain of civil rights strategists, of course, for whom at least the appearance of normality is central to gaining political "room." Rights are gained, according to this logic, by demonstrating similarity (to heterosexual people, to other minority groups) in a nonthreatening manner. "We are everywhere," goes the refrain from this camp. We are your sons and daughters and co-workers and soldiers, and once you see that lesbians and gays are just like you, you will recognize the injustices to which we are subject. "I am not queer," writes a letter writer named Tony. "I am normal, and if tomorrow I choose to run down the middle of Market Street in a big floppy hat and skirt I will still be normal." In the national gay weekly *10 Percent*—for which *Rant & Rave* can be seen as a proud evil twin—Eric Marcus (1993:14) writes that "I'd rather emphasize what I have in common with other people than focus on the differences," and "the last thing I want to do is institutionalize that difference by defining myself with a word and a political philosophy that set me outside the mainstream." The point is to be not-different, not-odd, not-scary. "We have a lot going for us," Phyllis Lyon says simply in the *Bay Times*. "Let's not blow it"—blow it, that is, by alienating each other and our straight allies with words like "queer."

Debates over assimilation are hardly new, however; but neither do they exhaust the letters column disputes. The metaphors in queerness are striking. Queer is a "psychic tattoo," says writer Alex Chee, shared by outsiders; those similarly tattooed make up the Queer Nation. "It's the land of lost boys and lost girls," says historian Gerard Koskovich (in Berube and Escoffier 1991:23), "who woke up one day and realized that not to have heterosexual privilege was in fact the highest privilege." A mark on the skin, a land, a nation: These are the metaphors of tribe and family. Queer is being used not just to connote and glorify differentness, but to revise the criteria of membership in the family, "to affirm sameness by defining a common identity on the fringes" (Berube and Escoffier 1991:12; see also Duggan 1992).[10]

In the hands of many letter writers, in fact, queer becomes simply a shorthand for "gay, lesbian, bisexual, and transgender," much like "people of color" becomes an inclusive and difference-erasing shorthand for a long list of ethnic, national, and racial groups. And as some letter writers point out, as a quasi-national shorthand "queer" is just a slight shift in the boundaries of tribal membership with no attendant shifts in power; as some lesbian writers point out, it is as likely to become synonymous with "white gay male" (perhaps now with a nose ring and tattoos) as it is to describe a new community formation. Even in its less nationalist versions, queer can easily be difference without change, can subsume and hide the internal differences it attempts to incorporate. The queer tribe attempts to be a multicultural, multigendered, multisexual hodge-podge of outsiders; as Steven Seidman points out, it ironically ends up

> denying differences by either submerging them in an undifferentiated opposi-
> tional mass or by blocking the development of individual and social differences
> through the disciplining compulsory imperative to remain undifferentiated.
> (1993:133)

Queer as an identity category often restates tensions between sameness and difference in a different language.

Debates over Bisexuality and Transgender: Queer Deconstructionist Politics

Despite the aura of newness, then, not much appears new in recent queerness debate; the fault lines on which they are built are old ones in lesbian and gay (and other identity-based) movements. Yet letter writers agree on one puzzling point: Right now, it matters what we are called and what we call ourselves. That a word takes so prominent a place is a clue that this is more than another in an ongoing series of tired assimilationist-liberationist debates. The controversy of queerness is not just strategic (what works), nor only a power struggle (who gets to call the shots); it is those, but not only those. At their most basic, queer controversies are battles over identity and naming (who I am, who we are). Which words capture us and when do words fail us? Words, and the "us" they name, seem to be in critical flux.

But even identity battles are not especially new. In fact, within lesbian-femi-
nist and gay male organizing, the meanings of "lesbian" and "gay" were contested almost as soon as they began to have political currency as quasi-ethnic statuses. Women of color and sex radicals loudly challenged lesbian feminism of the late 1970s, for example, pointing out that the "womansculture" being advocated (and actively created) was based in white, middle-class experience and promoted a bland, desexualized lesbianism. Working-class lesbians and gay men of color have consistently challenged gay as a term reflecting the middle-class, white homosexual men who established its usage (Stein 1992; Phelan 1993; Seidman 1993, 1994; Clarke 1983; Moraga 1983; Reid-Pharr 1993; Hemphill 1991). They have challenged, that is, the definitions.

The ultimate challenge of queerness, however, is not just the questioning of the content of collective identities, but the *questioning of the unity, stability, viabil-
ity, and political utility of sexual identities*—even as they are used and assumed.[11] The radical provocation from queer politics, one which many pushing queerness seem only remotely aware of, is not to resolve that difficulty, but to exaggerate and build on it. It is an odd endeavor, much like pulling the rug out from under one's own feet, not knowing how and where one will land.

To zero in on the distinctive deconstructionist politics of queerness, turn again to the letters columns. It is no coincidence that two other major *Bay Times* letters column controversies of the early 1990s concerned bisexual and transgender people, the two groups included in the revised queer category. Indeed, in his anti-queer polemic in the magazine *10 Percent* (a title firmly ethnic/essentialist in its reference to a fixed homosexual population), it is precisely these sorts of people, along with some "queer straights,"[12] from whom Eric Marcus seeks to distinguish himself:

> Queer is not my word because it does not define who I am or represent what I believe in. . . . I'm a man who feels sexually attracted to people of the same gender. I don't feel attracted to both genders. I'm not a woman trapped in a man's body, nor a man trapped in a woman's body. I'm not someone who enjoys or feels compelled to dress up in clothing of the opposite gender. And I'm not a "queer straight," a heterosexual who feels confined by the conventions of straight sexual expression. . . . I don't want to be grouped under the all-encompassing umbrella of queer . . . because we have different lives, face different challenges, and don't necessarily share the same aspirations. (1993:14)

The letters columns, written usually from a different political angle (by lesbian separatists, for example), cover similar terrain. "It is not empowering to go to a Queer Nation meeting and see men and women slamming their tongues down each other's throats," says one letter arguing over bisexuals. "Men expect access to women," asserts one from the transgender debate. "Some men decide that they want access to lesbians any way they can and decide they will become lesbians."

Strikingly, nearly all the letters are written by, to, and about women—a point to which I will later return. "A woman's willingness to sleep with men allows her access to jobs, money, power, status," writes one group of women. "This access does not disappear just because a woman sleeps with women 'too' . . . That's not bisexuality, that's compulsory heterosexuality." You are not invited; you will leave and betray us. We are already here, other women respond, and it is you who betray us with your back-stabbing and your silencing. "Why have so many bisexual women felt compelled to call themselves lesbians for so long? Do you think biphobic attitudes like yours might have something to do with it?" asks a woman named Kristen. "It is our community, too; we've worked in it, we've suffered for it, we belong in it. We will not accept the role of the poor relation." Kristen ends her letter tellingly, deploying a familiar phrase: "We're here. We're queer. Get used to it."[13]

The letters run back and forth similarly over transgender issues, in particular over transsexual lesbians who want to participate in lesbian organizing. "'Transsexuals' don't want to just be lesbians," Bev Jo writes, triggering a massive round of letters, "but insist, with all the arrogance and presumption of power that men have, on going where they are not wanted and trying to destroy lesbian gatherings." There are surely easier ways to oppress a woman, other women shoot back, than to risk physical pain and social isolation. You are doing exactly what anti-female and anti-gay oppressors do to us, others add. "Must we all bring our birth certificates and two witnesses to women's events in the future?" asks a woman named Karen. "If you feel threatened by the mere existence of a type of person, and wish to exclude them for your comfort, you are a bigot, by every definition of the term."

These "border skirmishes" over membership conditions and group boundaries have histories preceding the letters (Stein 1992; see also Taylor and Whittier 1992), and also reflect the growing power of transgender and bisexual organizing.[14] Although they are partly battles of position, more fundamentally the debates make concrete the anxiety queerness can provoke. They spotlight the possibility that sexual and gender identities are not the solid political ground they have been thought to be—which perhaps accounts for the particularly frantic tone of the letters.

Many arguing for exclusion write like a besieged border patrol. "Live your lives the way you want and spread your hatred of women while you're at it, if you must," writes a participant in the transgender letter spree, "but the fact is we're here, we're dykes and you're not. Deal with it." The Revolting Lesbians argue similarly in their contribution to the *Bay Times* bisexuality debate: "Bisexuals are not lesbians— they are bisexuals. Why isn't that obvious to everyone? Sleeping with women 'too' does not make you a lesbian. We must hang on to the identity and visibility we've struggled so hard to obtain." A letter from a woman named Caryatis sums up the perceived danger of queerness:

> This whole transsexual/bisexual assault on lesbian identity has only one end, to render lesbians completely invisible and obsolete. If a woman who sleeps with both females and males is a lesbian; and if a man who submits to surgical procedure to bring his body in line with his acceptance of sex role stereotypes is a lesbian; and if a straight woman whose spiritual bonds are with other females is a lesbian, then what is a female-born female who loves only other females? Soon there will be no logical answer to that question.

Exactly: In lesbian (and gay) politics, as in other identity movements, a logical answer is crucial. An inclusive queerness threatens to turn identity to nonsense, messing with the idea that identities (man, woman, gay, straight) are fixed, natural, core phenomena, and therefore solid political ground. Many arguments in the letters columns, in fact, echo the critiques of identity politics found in queer theory. "There is a growing consciousness that a person's sexual identity (and gender identity) need not be etched in stone," write Andy and Selena in the bisexuality debate, "that it can be fluid rather than static, that one has the right to PLAY with whomever one wishes to play with (as long as it is consensual), that the either/or dichotomy ('you're either gay or straight' is only one example of this) is oppressive no matter who's pushing it." Identities are fluid and changing; binary categories (man/woman, gay/straight) are distortions. "Humans are not organized by nature into distinct groups," Cris writes. "We are placed in any number of continuums. Few people are 100 percent gay or straight, or totally masculine or feminine." Differences are not distinct, categories are social and historical rather than natural phenomena, selves are ambiguous. "Perhaps it is time the lesbian community re-examined its criteria of what constitutes a woman (or man)," writes Francis. And does it really matter?" Transsexual performer and writer Kate Bornstein, in a *Bay Times* column triggered by the letters, voices the same basic challenge. Are a woman and a man distinguished by anatomy? "I know several women in San Francisco who have penises," she says. "Many wonderful men in my life have vaginas" (1992:4). Gender chromosomes, she continues, are known to come in more than two sets ("could this mean there are more than two genders?"); testosterone and estrogen don't answer it ("you could buy your gender over the counter"); neither child-bearing nor sperm capacities nail down the difference ("does a necessary hysterectomy equal a sex change?"). Gender is socially assigned; binary categories (man/woman, gay/straight) are inaccurate and oppressive; nature provides no rock-bottom definitions. The opposite sex, Bornstein proposes, is neither.[15]

Indeed, it is no coincidence that bisexuality, transsexualism, and gender crossing are exactly the kind of boundary-disrupting phenomena embraced by much post-structuralist sexual theory. Sandy Stone, for example, argues that "the transsexual currently occupies a position which is nowhere, which is outside the binary oppositions of gendered discourse" (1991:295).[16] Steven Seidman suggests that bisexual critiques challenge "sexual object-choice as a master category of sexual and social identity" (1993:123). Judith Butler argues that butch and femme, far from being "copies" of heterosexual roles, put the "very notion of an original or natural identity" into question (1990:123). Marjorie Garber writes that "the cultural effect of transvestism is to destabilize all such binaries: not only 'male' and 'female,' but also 'gay' and 'straight,' and 'sex' and 'gender.' This is the sense—the radical sense—in which transvestism is a 'third'" (1992:133).

The point, often buried in over-abstracted jargon, is well taken: The presence of visibly transgendered people, people who do not quite fit, potentially subverts the notion of two naturally fixed genders; the presence of people with ambiguous sexual desires potentially subverts the notion of naturally fixed sexual orientations. (I say "potentially" because the more common route has continued to be in the other direction: the reification of bisexuality into a third orientation, or the retention of male-female boundaries through the notion of transgendered people as "trapped in the wrong body," which is then fixed.) Genuine inclusion of transgender and bisexual people can require not simply an expansion of an identity, but a subversion of it. This is the deepest difficulty queerness raises, and the heat behind the letters: If gay (and man) and lesbian (and woman) are unstable categories, "simultaneously possible and impossible" (Fuss 1989:102), what happens to sexuality-based politics?

The question is easily answered by those securely on either side of these debates. On the one side, activists and theorists suggest that collective identities with exclusive and secure boundaries are politically effective. Even those agreeing that identities are mainly fictions may take this position, advocating what Gayatri Spivak has called an "operational essentialism" (cited in Butler 1990b; see also Vance 1988). On the other side, activists and theorists suggest that identity production "is purchased at the price of hierarchy, normalization, and exclusion" and therefore advocate "the deconstruction of a hetero/homo code that structures the 'social text' of daily life" (Seidman 1993:130). . . .

CONCLUSION: COLLECTIVE IDENTITY, SOCIAL MOVEMENT THEORY AND THE QUEER DILEMMA

Buried in the letters column controversies over a queer parade theme, and over bisexual and transsexual involvement in lesbian organizations, are fights not only over who belongs, but over the possibility and desirability of clear criteria of belonging. Sexuality-based politics thus contains a more general predicament of identity politics, whose workings and implications are not well understood: it is as liberating and sensible to demolish a collective identity as it is to establish one.

Honoring both sets of insights from the queer debates is a tall order. It calls for recognizing that undermining identities is politically damaging in the current time and place, and that promoting them furthers the major cultural support for continued damage. It means reconnecting a critique of identity to the embodied political forces that make collective identity necessary and meaningful, and reconnecting a critique of regulatory institutions to the less tangible categories of meaning that maintain and reproduce them.[17]

The neatest and most true to life means for doing so—the theoretical recognition of paradoxes and dialectics—can satisfy intellectually. Certainly a political structure that directs action towards ethnic interest group claims, and requires therefore solid proofs of authentic ethnic membership (the immutability of sexual orientation, for example), creates paradoxical forms of action for stigmatized groups. In the case of lesbians and gays, for example, gender stereotypes used to stigmatize actors (the gay man as woman, the lesbian as man) have been emphasized in order to undermine them; pejorative labels are emphasized in an effort to get rid of them.[18] But the recognition of paradox, while a significant step, is too often a stopping point of analysis. I want to suggest potentially fruitful paths forward, through research and theorizing that take the queer dilemma to heart.

The recent revival of sociological interest in collective identity has brought important challenges to earlier assumptions that identities were either irrational (and irrelevant) or antecedents to action. Yet, even as theorizing has recognized that collective identities are achieved in and through movement activity, the assumption has remained that the impetus to solidify, mobilize and deploy an identity is the only rational one. The suggestion of most social movement theory, sometimes assumed and sometimes explicit, is that secure boundaries and a clear group identity are achievable, and even more importantly, that "if a group fails in [these], it cannot accomplish any collective action" (Klandermans 1992:81); without a solid group identity, no claims can be made. These theories have little to say about the queer impulse to blur, deconstruct, and destabilize group categories. Current theories take hold of only one horn of the dilemma: the political utility of solid collective categories.

Serious consideration of queerness as a logic of action can force important revisions in approaches to collective identity formation and deployment and their relationship to political gains. First, it calls attention to the fact that *secure boundaries and stabilized identities are necessary not in general, but in the specific*—a point current social movement theory largely misses. The link between the two logics, the ways in which the American political environment makes stable collective identities both necessary and damaging, is sorely undertheorized and underexamined.

More importantly, accommodating the complexity of queer activism and theory requires sociology to revisit the claim that social movements are engaged in simply constructing collective identities. Queer movements pose the challenge of a form of organizing in which, far from inhibiting accomplishments, the *destabilization of collective identity is itself a goal and accomplishment of collective action.* When this dynamic is taken into account, new questions arise. The question of how collective identities are negotiated, constructed, and stabilized, for example, becomes transformed into a somewhat livelier one: for whom, when, and how are stable collective identities *necessary* for social action and social change? Do some identity movements in fact avoid the tendency to take themselves apart?

Investigating social movements with the queer predicament in mind, moreover, brings attention to repertoires and forms of action that work with the dilemma in different ways. At the heart of the dilemma is the simultaneity of cultural sources of oppression (which make loosening categories a smart strategy) and institutional sources of oppression (which make tightening categories a smart strategy). Are some movements or movement repertoires more able to work with, rather than against, the simultaneity of these systems of oppression? When and how might deconstructive strategies take aim at institutional forms, and when and how can ethnic strategies take aim at cultural categories? Are there times when the strategies are effectively linked, when an ethnic maneuver loosens cultural categories,[19] or when a deconstructionist tactic simultaneously takes aim at regulatory institutions?[20]

Such questions can point the way towards novel understandings and evaluations of social movements in which collective identity is both pillaged and deployed. These questions are not a path out of the dilemma, but a path in. The fact that the predicament may be inescapable is, after all, the point: first to clearly see the horns of the dilemma, and then to search out ways for understanding political actions taking place poised, and sometimes skewered, on those horns.

NOTES

Thanks to Steven Epstein, William Gamson, Arlene Stein, Verta Taylor, Steven Seidman, Barry Adam, Jeffrey Escoffier, Cathy Cohen, Mark Blasius, Roger Lancaster, Steve Murray, and Matthew Rottnek for comments on an earlier draft of this paper.

1. Although I am discussing them together because of their joint struggle against the "sex/gender system" (Rubin 1975) on the basis of same-sex desire, lesbians and gay men have

long histories of autonomous organizing (Adam 1987; D'Emilio 1983). Gender has been the strongest division historically in movements for gay and lesbian rights and liberation, not surprisingly, given the very different ways in which male homosexuality and lesbianism have been constructed and penalized. This division is taken up explicitly later in the discussion.

2. In this discussion, I am heeding recent calls to bring sociology into contact with queer theory and politics (Seidman 1994). It has taken a bit of time for sociologists and other social scientists to join queer theoretical discussions, which although they emerged primarily from and through humanities scholars, could hardly be "imagined in their present forms, absent the contributions of sociological theory" (Epstein 1994:2). On the relationship between sociology of sexuality and queer theory, see also Stein and Plummer 1994; Namaste 1994.

3. I borrow this term from Seidman (1993).

4. See, for example, Di Stefano (1990), Bordo (1990), and Davis (1991).

5. Queer Nation, formed in 1990, is an offshoot of the AIDS activist organization ACT UP. Queer Nation owes much to ACT UP, in its emergence, its personnel and tactics, which are often to "cross borders, to occupy spaces, and to mime the privileges of normality" (Berlant and Freeman 1993:195). On similar tactics within ACT UP, see J. Gamson (1989). On Queer Nation specifically and queer politics more generally, see Berube and Escoffier (1991); Duggan (1992); Stein (1992); Cunningham (1992); Patton (1993); Browning (1993, especially Chapters 2, 3, and 5).

6. See, for example, Rich (1983); Moraga (1983); Hemphill (1991); Clarke (1983); Reid-Pharr (1993).

7. Although its most familiar recent usage has been as an anti-gay epithet, the word actually has a long and complex history. Along with "fairy," for example, "queer" was one of the most common terms used before World War II, "by 'queer' and 'normal' people alike to refer to 'homosexuals.'" In the 1920s and 1930s, "the men who identified themselves as part of a distinct category of men primarily on the basis of their homosexual interest rather than their womanlike gender status usually called themselves queer" (Chauncey 1994:14, 16). Whether as chosen marker or as epithet, the word has always retained its general connotation of abnormality (Chauncey 1994).

8. On assimilation-separation before Stonewall, see D'Emilio (1983) and Adam (1987). On assimilation-separation after Stonewall, see Epstein (1987).

9. Indeed, the "outlaw" stance may help explain why gender differences are (somewhat) less salient in queer organizing (Duggan 1992). Whereas in ethnic/essentialist lesbian and gay organizations participants are recruited as gay men and lesbian *women*, in queer organizations they are recruited largely as *gender outlaws*.

10. There is no question that part of what has happened with queer activism is simply the construction of a new, if contentious, collective identity: Queer Nation, with its nationalist rhetoric, is one clear example. My point, however (developed here), is not that queer indicates a group with no boundaries, but that it indicates a strategy for identity destabilization. This logic is not confined to a particular group formation; although it is considerably stronger in groups identifying as queer, many of which are loose associations that are very intentionally decentralized (Williams 1993), it is also often present in more mainstream organizing, albeit in more occasional and muted form. Queer is more useful, I am suggesting, as a description of a particular action logic than as a description of an empirically distinguishable movement form.

11. This questioning is not entirely unique to recent queer politics but has historical ties to early gay liberation calls to "liberate the homosexual in everyone" (Epstein 1987).

That the current queer formulations have such affinities with earlier political activity under-lines that queerness is less a new historical development than an action impulse that comes to the fore at certain historical moments. There is certainly a difference in degree, however, between the strength of a queer-style politic now and in earlier decades: With a few excep-tions, earlier lesbian feminist and gay liberationist discourses rarely questioned "the notion of homosexuality as a universal category of the self and sexual identity" (Seidman 1994:170).

12. On "queer straights," self-identifying heterosexuals who seek out and participate in lesbian and gay subcultures, see Powers (1993).

13. For more bisexuality debate, see Wilson (1992) and Queen (1992).

14. For articulations of these young movements see, on bisexual organizing, Hutchins and Kaahumanu (1991), and on transgender organizing, Stone (1991).

15. For a more developed version of these arguments, see Bornstein (1994).

16. See also Shapiro (1991), on the ways in which transsexualism is simultaneously subversive and conservative of sex and gender organization.

17. I am indebted here to Steven Seidman's discussion and critique of queer theory and politics, which make some of the points from different directions (Seidman 1993; see also Patton 1993 and Vance 1988). I want to push the discussion towards the ground, how-ever, to open questions for political action and empirical research.

18. On this dynamic, see Weeks (1985, especially Chapter 8), Epstein (1987), and J. Gamson (1989).

19. The public pursuit of same-sex marriage and parenting may be an example of this. On the one hand, the call for institutions of "family" to include lesbians and gays—as a rec-ognizably separate species—is quite conservative of existing gender and sexual categories. It often appears as mimicry, and its proponents typically appear as close to "normal" as possi-ble: Bob and Rod Jackson-Paris, for example, a former body-builder/model married couple who have been the most publicly available symbol of gay marriage, are both conventionally masculine, "traded vows in a commitment ceremony, share a house in Seattle, and plan to raise children" (Bull 1993:42).

Yet gay families, in attacking the gender requirements of family forms, attack the cul-tural grounding of normality at its heart (as the religious right fully recognizes). If and when family institutions, pushed by ethnic/essentialist identity movements, shift to integrate gays and lesbians, the very markers of gay/straight difference start to disintegrate (see Weston 1991). If bodily erotic desire implies nothing in particular about the use of one's body for reproduction, its usefulness as a basis of social categories is largely gutted. In this, the gay family strategy may also be a queer one. To the degree that it succeeds, to the degree that the institution of the family changes, the categories must also lose much of their sense—and their power. This may not be true of all ethnic/essentialist actions.

20. The AIDS activist group ACT UP provides a promising starting point from this direction. Many of ACT UP's tactics have been discursive: meaning deconstruction, bound-ary crossing, and label disruption (J. Gamson 1989). Yet, for reasons obviously related to the immediacy of AIDS and the visible involvement of medical and state institutions, it has rarely been possible to make the argument that AIDS politics should have as its goal the deconstruction of meanings of sex, sexual identity, and disease. In much queer AIDS activism, the disruption of these meanings takes place through direct targeting of their insti-tutional purveyors: not only media and cultural institutions, but science, medicine, and gov-ernment (Epstein 1991).

For example, interventions into some spaces (medical conferences as opposed to opera houses) put queerness—its sometimes scary confrontation, its refusal to identify itself as a fixed gay or lesbian subject, its disruption of sex and gender boundaries—to use in ways that clearly mark the dangers of institutional control of sexual categories. Refusing the categories for itself, this strategy names and confronts the agents that fix the categories in dangerous, violent, and deadly ways. To the degree that the strategy succeeds, to the degree that cultural categories become frightening and nonsensical, institutional actors—and not just the vague and ubiquitous purveyors of "normality"—must also be called upon to justify their use of the categories.

REFERENCES

Adam, Barry. 1987. *The Rise of a Gay and Lesbian Movement.* Boston: Twayne.

Alba, Richard. 1990. *Ethnic Identity: The Transformation of White America.* New Haven: Yale University Press.

Berlant, Lauren, and Elizabeth Freeman. 1993. "Queer nationality." In *Fear of a Queer Planet,* ed. Michael Warner, 193–229. Minneapolis: University of Minnesota Press.

Berube, Allan, and Jeffrey Escoffier. 1991. "Queer/Nation." *Out/Look* (Winter):12–23.

Bordo, Susan. 1990. "Feminism, postmodernism, and gender-skepticism." In *Feminism/ Postmodernism,* ed. Linda J. Nicholson, 133–156. New York: Routledge.

Bornstein, Kate. 1992. "A plan for peace." *San Francisco Bay Times,* December 3:4.

———. 1994. *Gender Outlaw.* New York: Routledge.

Browning, Frank. 1993. *The Culture of Desire.* New York: Vintage.

Bull, Chris. 1993. "Till death do us part." *Advocate,* November 30:40–47.

Butler, Judith. 1990a. *Gender Trouble: Feminism and the Subversion of Identity.* New York: Routledge.

———. 1990b. "Gender trouble, feminist theory, and psychoanalytic discourse." In *Feminism/Postmodernism,* ed. Linda J. Nicholson, 324–340. New York: Routledge.

———. 1993. "Critically queer." *GLQ* 1:17-32.

Chauncey, George. 1994. *Gay New York.* New York: Basic.

Chee, Alexander. 1991. "A queer nationalism." *Out/Look* (Winter):15–19.

Clarke, Cheryl. 1983. "Lesbianism: An act of resistance." In *This Bridge Called My Back,* eds. Gloria Anzaldua and Cherrie Moraga, 128–137. New York: Kitchen Table Press.

Cohen, Jean. 1985. "Strategy or identity: New theoretical paradigms and contemporary social movements." *Social Research* 52:663–716.

Cunningham, Michael. 1992. "If you're queer and you're not angry in 1992, you're not paying attention." *Mother Jones* (May/June):60–66.

Davis, F. James. 1991. *Who Is Black? One Nation's Definition.* University Park: Pennsylvania State University Press.

de Lauretis, Teresa. 1991. "Queer theory." *differences* 3 (Summer):iii–xviii.

D'Emilio, John. 1983. *Sexual Politics, Sexual Communities: The Making of a Homosexual Minority in the United States, 1940–1970.* Chicago: University of Chicago Press.

Di Stefano, Christine. 1990. "Dilemmas of difference: Feminism, modernity, and postmodernism." In *Feminism/Postmodernism,* ed. Linda J. Nicholson, 63–82. New York: Routledge.

Duggan, Lisa. 1992. "Making it perfectly queer." *Socialist Review* 22:11–32.

Epstein, Steven. 1987. "Gay politics, ethnic identity: The limits of social constructionism." *Socialist Review* 93/94:9–54.

————. 1991. "Democratic science? AIDS activism and the contested construction of knowledge." *Socialist Review* 21:35–64.

————. 1994. "A queer encounter: Sociology and the study of sexuality." *Sociological Theory* 12:188–202.

Espiritu, Yen. 1992. *Asian American Panethnicity: Bridging Institutions and Identities.* Philadelphia: Temple University Press.

Faderman, Lillian. 1981. *Surpassing the Love of Men.* New York: Morrow.

Franzen, Trisha. 1993. "Differences and identities: Feminism in the Albuquerque lesbian community." *Signs* 18:891–906.

Friedman, Debra, and Doug McAdam. 1992. "Collective identity and activism." In *Frontiers in Social Movement Theory*, eds. Aldon Morris and Carol McClurg Mueller, 156–173. New Haven: Yale University Press.

Fuss, Diana. 1989. *Essentially Speaking: Feminism, Nature, and Difference.* New York: Routledge.

————. 1991. *Inside/Out.* New York: Routledge.

Gamson, Josh. 1989. "Silence, death, and the invisible enemy: AIDS activism and social movement 'newness.'" *Social Problems* 36:351–367.

Gamson, William A. 1992. "The social psychology of collective action." In *Frontiers in Social Movement Theory*, eds. Aldon Morris and Carol McClurg Mueller, 53–76. New Haven: Yale University Press.

Garber, Marjorie. 1992. *Vested Interests: Cross-Dressing and Cultural Anxiety.* New York: Routledge.

Hemphill, Essex, ed. 1991. *Brother to Brother.* Boston: Alyson.

Hennessy, Rosemary. 1993. "Queer theory: A review of the differences special issue and Wittig's 'the straight mind.'" *Signs* 18:964–973.

Hutchins, Loraine, and Lani Kaahumanu, eds. 1991. *Bi Any Other Name.* Boston: Alyson.

Ingraham, Chrys. 1994. "The heterosexual imaginary: Feminist sociology and theories of gender." *Sociological Theory* 12:203–219.

Kauffman, L. A. 1990. "The anti-politics of identity." *Socialist Review* 20:67–80.

Klandermans, Bert. 1992. "The social construction of protest and multiorganizational fields." In *Frontiers in Social Movement Theory*, eds. Aldon Morris and Carol McClurg Mueller, 77–103. New Haven: Yale University Press.

Marcus, Eric. 1993. "What's in a name." *10 Percent*:14–15.

Melucci, Alberto. 1989. *Nomads of the Present: Social Movements and Individual Needs in Contemporary Society.* Philadelphia: Temple University Press.

Minkowitz, Donna. 1993. "Trial by science." *Village Voice*, November 30:27–29.

Moraga, Cherrie. 1983. *Loving in the War Years.* Boston: South End Press.

Mueller, Carol McClurg. 1992. "Building social movement theory." In *Frontiers in Social Movement Theory*, eds. Aldon Morris and Carol McClurg Mueller, 3–25. New Haven: Yale University Press.

Nagel, Joane. 1991. "Democratic science? AIDS activism and the contested construction of knowledge." *Socialist Review* 21:35–64.

————. 1994a. "Constructing ethnicity: Creating and recreating ethnic identity and culture." *Social Problems* 41:152–176.

————. 1994b. "'A queer encounter': Sociology and the study of sexuality." *Sociological Theory* 12:188–202.

Namaste, Ki. 1994. "The politics of inside/out: Queer theory, poststructuralism, and a sociological approach to sexuality." *Sociological Theory* 12:220–231.

Nicholson, Linda, ed. 1990. *Feminism/Postmodernism*. New York: Routledge.

Omi, Michael, and Howard Winant. 1986. *Racial Formation in the United States*. New York: Routledge and Kegan Paul.

Padilla, Felix. 1985. *Latino Ethnic Consciousness: The Case of Mexican Americans and Puerto Ricans in Chicago*. Notre Dame: University of Notre Dame Press.

Patton, Cindy. 1993. "Tremble, hetero swine!" In *Fear of a Queer Planet*, ed. Michael Warner, 143–177. Minneapolis: University of Minnesota Press.

Phelan, Shane. 1989. *Identity Politics: Lesbian Feminism and the Limits of Community*. Philadelphia: Temple University Press.

―――. 1993. "(Be)coming out: Lesbian identity and politics." *Signs* 18:765–790.

Powers, Ann. 1993. "Queer in the streets, straight in the sheets: Notes on passing." *Utne Reader* (November/December):74–80.

Queen, Carol. 1992. "Strangers at home: Bisexuals in the queer movement." *Out/Look* (Spring):23, 29–33.

Rant, Miss. 1993. "Queer is not a substitute for gay." *Rant and Rave* 1:15.

Reid-Pharr, Robert. 1993. "The spectacle of blackness." *Radical America* 24:57–66.

Rich, Adrienne. 1980. "Compulsory heterosexuality and lesbian existence." *Signs* 5:631–660.

Rubin, Gayle. 1975. "The traffic in women." In *Toward an Anthropology of Women*, ed. Rayna R. Relter, 157–210. New York: Monthly Review Press.

Schlesinger, Philip. 1987. "On national identity: Some conceptions and misconceptions criticized." *Social Science Information* 26:219–264.

Sedgwick, Eve Kosovsky. 1990. *Epistemology of the Closet*. Berkeley: University of California Press.

Seidman, Steven. 1993. "Identity politics in a 'postmodern' gay culture: Some historical and conceptual notes." In *Fear of a Queer Planet*, ed. Michael Warner, 105–142. Minneapolis: University of Minnesota Press.

―――. 1994. "Symposium: Queer theory/sociology: A dialogue." *Sociological Theory* 12:166–177.

Shapiro, Judith. 1991. "Transsexualism: Reflections on the persistence of gender and the mutability of sex." In *Body Guards*, eds. Julia Epstein and Kristina Straub, 248–279. New York: Routledge.

Stein, Arlene. 1992. "Sisters and queers: The decentering of lesbian feminism." *Socialist Review* 22:33–55.

Stein, Arlene, and Ken Plummer. 1994. "'I can't even think straight': 'Queer' theory and the missing sexual revolution in sociology." *Sociological Theory* 12:178–187.

Stone, Sandy. 1991. "The empire strikes back: A posttranssexual manifesto." In *Body Guards*, eds. Julia Epstein and Kristina Straub, 280–304. New York: Routledge.

Taylor, Verta, and Leila Rupp. 1993. "Women's culture and lesbian feminist activism: A reconsideration of cultural feminism." *Signs* 19:32–61.

DAVID SHNEER AND CARYN AVIV
Heeding Isaiah's Call (2002)

In their book Queer Jews, *from which this essay comes, Shneer and Aviv argue that for the first time in history queer Jews are leaders and activists in their communities both as Jews and as queers. For many of these leaders, there is no ambivalence or tension between their queer and Jewish selves. They also show that liberal Judaism in America is at the forefront of advancing queer empowerment and visibility for all Americans. The contributors explore the conflict between the desire to integrate into established Jewish communities and the comforts of creating separate spaces for queer Jews.*

> *I created you, and appointed you a covenant people, a light of nations—opening eyes deprived of light, rescuing prisoners from confinement.*
> —Isaiah 42:6–7

Who knew that King David and Jonathon were lovers? Or that a queer Jew coined the term *transvestite* and gave birth to the idea of gay rights? Or that the first openly gay Congressional representative was a Jew? Did you know that an official body of Jewish rabbis allowed its clergy to officiate at same-sex weddings way back in 1989? Or that there are over 25 lesbian, gay, bisexual, and transgender (LGBT) synagogues in North America? Did you know that there is a school in San Francisco for the children of queer Jews? Peek inside a recent catalog of the clothing brand Abercrombie and Fitch and you will find a lesbian Jewish wedding as a centerpiece. What other minority within a minority is producing such campy erotica as *Kosher Meat* and *Friday the Rabbi Wore Lace*? Queer Jews are everywhere. Or at least so it seems. At the beginning of the twenty-first century, we are witnessing an increasingly visible, flourishing, and assertive queer Jewish culture.

Jews and queers are a vibrant part of American culture.[1] It is no accident that liberal Judaism is at the forefront of advancing queer empowerment and visibility, as the recent decision of the Central Conference of American Rabbis to sanction queer commitment ceremonies demonstrates. *Queer Jews* explores sexual, ethnic, and religious diversity and their interaction with each other. It challenges the very notion of margins and center, sameness and difference, normative and alternative, assimilation and separatism by looking at the experiences of those who complicate these categories. Queer people's demands for inclusion have created an unprecedented, often contentious dialogue about who we are and where we belong within Judaism and civil society. *Queer Jews* makes that conversation public and broadens our understanding of diverse sexualities, identities, families, and politics. . . .

Queer Jews explores the conflict between the desire to integrate into established Jewish communities, changing them from within, and the comforts of creating and maintaining "separate" spaces for queer Jews. Jonathan Krasner explores questions around separatism and assimilationism by suggesting that, as "queer" and "Jewish" come to inform one another, queer Jews are not as compelled to seek out separate space, but instead create space within established institutions. David Shneer, in his essay on queering Jewish education, shows how one LGBT synagogue is broadening its image away from metaphors of safety and refuge from oppression toward language of progressive leadership within the wider Jewish community, making it an attractive congregation for liberal straight people. Moreover, most LGBT synagogues are affiliated with broader Jewish movements, receive money from general sources of Jewish funding, and are engaged in outreach to diverse populations that include heterosexuals. And more personally, Lesléa Newman struggles with the tension of wanting to be a queer Jewish writer while not having her identity limit how her work is read or how it is marketed. We remain convinced that queer Jews should not be separatists, since as Jews, they always hold a connection to the broader community and historical memory.

Likewise, incremental reform and adaptation, reworking existing social, political, and religious structures, rather than revolutionizing or overturning them, are clearly the preeminent political strategies of this historical moment. The late 1960s marked a transition from an activism that sought equal access to the law, modeling itself on the civil rights movement, to Gay Liberation, which fundamentally criticized basic civil institutions such as marriage and family. Our authors suggest that now those institutions that Gay Liberation rejected have become sites of radical social transformation. . . .

From all edges of Jewish society, queer Jews are accommodating and adapting to Jewish organizations while pushing them to acknowledge our presence with dignity and respect. The number of groups that have the words lesbian, gay, bisexual, transgendered, queer, or questioning and "Jew" in the title is increasing exponentially.[2] There are more synagogues, gay Jewish *havurot* (community groups), queer Jewish conferences, and other means of creating social spaces for ourselves. Moreover, there are now institutions that cater to a diverse queer Jewish community and reflect generational concerns, including parenting classes, educational and camping programs for queer families. There are now groups for gay Jewish youth, aging queer Jews, same-sex interfaith couples, Jews-by-choice, and more recently queer Orthodox Jews. . . .

These trends that are expanding the parameters of both Jewish and queer identity seem to be dialectical. The sheer centrifugal forces at work here, the ever more specific identifiers, suggest that queer Jews as an organized group of people are finding differences within themselves. The solidarity wrought by external oppression of a homophobic and heterosexist society is no longer enough to define these groups. We hope the diversity of voices included in this anthology demonstrates that queer Jews define ourselves with increasing multiplicity and innovation. We are also redefining what it means to be Jewish, and what the role of Jewish institutions is and should be. . . .

But are there unanticipated consequences of the growing inclusion and main-streaming of queers in Jewish organizations? According to Krasner, Temple Israel, the large Reform synagogue in the Boston area, founded a gay and lesbian *havurah*. But in the past few years, its programming has dropped off, because "queers have become so integrated into the temple that there does not seem to be any 'motivation' to create their own programming." We wonder if separate queer Jewish space might dissolve as other Jewish organizations open their doors to queer Jews. Is this what happens to the original institutions designed as a place of refuge when oppressed groups become integrated?

Although the most visible changes are in communal institutions, the most significant reforms are happening within our personal institutions—our families and intimate relationships. Queer Jews are at the forefront of redefining conceptions of family, relationships, and community, and our reformation project has forced everyone to reexamine what it means to be a family. From the calls for legalized marriage, which are finally being heard in some rabbinic institutions, to bringing children into our families, queer Jews have forced Jews and Americans (and apparently Abercrombie and Fitch) alike to reexamine their "family values." For queer Jews, creating family involves both adopting the dominant social paradigms—a monogamous couple with two kids and a picket fence—and moving beyond the mere assimilation of bourgeois definitions by undermining the assumption that family is determined solely via biology. Queer Jews' calls for integration are *transformative* rather than *assimilationist*.

The construction of queer families means making conscious, deliberate choices all along the life course. Queers have irrevocably changed the meaning and discourse of marriage and reproduction, affecting Jewish communities on multiple levels.[3] Most queers marry, because they *want to,* because they want to express their love publicly to their communities, because they want to bring two lives into one. Most queers do not marry for tax breaks or to make parents happy. For Rabbi Jane Litman, queer marriage transformed the institution from what she saw as an empty ritual into a spiritual practice, which has changed her understanding of commitment and *kavannah* (intention). As Inbal Kashtan remarks, most non-queers who attend queer weddings remark on the intensity, the spirituality, the "authenticity" of the ceremony, something often lacking at heterosexual ceremonies. At the same time, this drive toward *transformative integration,* for which our authors overwhelmingly advocate, has pushed liberationists, whose voices are not as prevalent in this anthology, to challenge the new hegemony of queer marriage as ideal by reasserting an anti-marriage platform.[4] . . .

Writing our own literature, history, poetry, and autobiography has been critical to our survival as queers (just as it has been for wider communities of Jews), and has contributed to queer Jewish communities and the emergence of a reading public. Now queer Jews can go to a bookshelf and find several books of fiction, autobiography, poetry, and other material that can help foster the queer Jewish imagined community and further the development of historical memory. We hope that this book is part of the continuing move to action over reaction, toward self-definition, and to an era when queers, Jews, and queer Jews, who have always been social, cultural, and political leaders, will be able to lead *as queers, as Jews, and as queer Jews,* for we are the ones heeding Isaiah's call.

NOTES

1. We define *queer* broadly to include lesbians, gay men, bisexuals, and transgendered people. We also use the adjective "queer" rather than "same-sex" or "same-gender" when describing commitment ceremonies, relationships, and so on, in order to avoid the dichotomy of sameness and difference.

2. Hardly any organization uses the term *queer* in its title, which suggests that the utilitarian use for such a term (to be as all-encompassing as possible) has not yet overridden the negative connotation many people have of the word "queer." Only on the margins of the margins, among radical queer Jewish groups, or within casual community vernacular, is the word "queer" an acceptable identifier. We deliberately chose our title of this anthology to advocate for more visibility and increased acceptance of the word "queer," which reflects the experiences and political leanings of post-Stonewall LGBT people.

3. For example, the *Jewish Bulletin of Northern California* recently covered the roiling debate on same-sex marriages and how many rabbis, particularly in the Conservative movement, craft their personal stances towards officiating these ceremonies. Alexandra J. Wall, "Conservative Rabbis Here Defy Movement's Ban on Gay Nuptials," *Jewish Bulletin of Northern California,* March 30, 2001.

4. There are rabbis at the most left-leaning rabbinic institution, the Reconstructionist Rabbinic College, who question whether queer Jews should struggle for equal access to marriage or should overturn the institution, a call that echoes the 1960s liberationists' debates about rejecting the military rather than aspiring to join it.

REFERENCES

Alpert, Rebecca. *Like Bread on the Seder Plate: Jewish Lesbians and the Transformation of Tradition.* New York: Columbia University Press, 1998.

Alpert, Rebecca T., Sue Levi Elwell, and Shirley Edelson (eds.). *Lesbian Rabbis: The First Generation.* New Brunswick, NJ: Rutgers University Press, 2001.

Balka, Christie, and Andy Rose (eds.). *Twice Blessed: On Being Lesbian, Gay, and Jewish.* Boston: Beacon Press, 1989.

Shokeid, Moshe. *A Gay Synagogue in New York.* New York: Columbia University Press, 1995.

Index

Achilles, Nancy, 59

ACLU. *See* American Civil Liberties Union

Acquired tendency, 8–9

Action, and language, transformation of silence into, xii, 5–7

Activism, 217–221, 246–247, 250, 260n; and African Americans, 219; and AIDS, 220; definition of, 217; and gay rights organizations, 223; goals of, 221; and Jews, 219; LGBT, 79; mainstreaming of, 220, 221; and organizations, 217–218; and power structures, 217; and Republican Party, 221; and visibility, xii, 219

Activist organizations, 94. *See also* Organizations

ACT UP. *See* AIDS Coalition to Unleash Power

Addiction, sex, 112

Addison, Dick, 24

ADL. *See* Anti-Defamation League

Adolescence, powerlessness of, 70

Adoption, 125, 129, 131, 150, 153, 154, 161n2

Adultery, and divorce, 114

The Adventures of Priscilla, Queen of the Desert (film), 149

The Advocate, 246

Affleck, Ben, 120

African American(s): and activism, 219; artists, 169; and feminism, 236, 237–238; and gender expectations, 30–31; literature, 117; and multiple identities, 81; and queer families, 158–159; and queer space, 54; violence against, 70; and women's studies, 236;

writers, 117, 169. *See also* Black men; Black women

Age, and homosexual activity, 14–15

Ageism, 80

AIDS, 94, 157, 169, 174, 200, 220, 241–242, 251, 261n20; and bathhouse sex, 105–110; drugs for, 242; research, 220

AIDS Coalition to Unleash Power (ACT UP), 220, 241–242, 246, 260n, 261n20

Alda, Alan, 31

Alienist, as term for psychiatrist, 57

The Alienist and Neurologist, 9, 54, 57

Allison, Dorothy, 104, 169

All the Rage: The Story of Gay Visibility in America (Walters); prologue from, 176–180

Ally McBeal (television program), 138

Altman, Dennis, 107

Amazon books, 104

American Civil Liberties Union (ACLU), 220

American Couples (Blumstein and Schwartz), 157

An American Family (television show), 168

American Psychiatric Association (APA), 38, 219

America Online (AOL), 118

Angels in America: A Gay Fantasia on America (Kushner), 169; excerpts from, 174–176

Animation, and gay cartoon characters, 167

Anti-Defamation League (ADL), 220

Anti–gay marriage bill, 135

Antigay sentiment, in United States, 150

Credits

"Renegotiating the Social/Sexual Identities of Places," by Wayne Myslik. Copyright © 1997 Routledge. Reprinted by permission from *Body Space,* edited by Nancy Duncan, pp. 156–164, 168–169.

"At the Michigan Womyn's Music Festival," by Bonnie J. Morris. *Gay and Lesbian Review* (September–October, 2003): 16–18.

One of the Children: Gay Black Men in Harlem, by William G. Hawkeswood and Alex W. Costley. Copyright © 1997 University of California Press. Reprinted by permission of the Trustees of the University of California, pp. 125–135.

"Smoke, Lilies, and Jade." In *Black Like Us* by Richard Bruce Nugent. Copyright © 1926, pp. 75–87.

"Opening Pandora's Box," by Christi Cassidy. *On Our Backs* (June–July, 2004): 28–29.

"Mike Goes to the Baths" (previously unpublished) (1984). Copyright © 1998 estate of Michael Callen. Available at http://members.aol.com/sigothinc/bathvis.htm.

"Paradigms Old and New." Copyright © 1998 Dossie Easton and Catherine A Liszt. Reprinted by permission from *The Ethical Slut: A Guide to Infinite Sexual Possibilities,* Greenery Press, pp. 25–37.

"It's a White Man's World." Copyright © 2005 Dwight A. McBride. Reprinted by permission from *Why I Hate Abercrombie and Fitch: Essays on Race and Sexuality,* New York University Press, pp. 110–112, 113–118.

"Younger Brother Dynamics." Copyright © 2000 Dan Savage. Reprinted by permission from *The Kid: What Happened after My Boyfriend and I Decided to Go Get Pregnant,* Plume, pp. 3–8.

"Take My Domestic Partner Please: Gays and Marriage in the Era of the Visible," by Suzanna Danuta Walters. From *Queer Families, Queer Politics,* edited by Mary Bernstein and Renate Reimann. Copyright © 2001 Columbia University Press, pp. 338–357. Reprinted with the permission of the publisher.

"Queer Families Quack Back," by Judith Stacey and Elizabeth Davenport. Copyright © 2002. Reprinted by permission of Sage Publications Ltd. from *Handbook of Lesbian and Gay Studies,* edited by Diane Richardson and Steven Seidman, pp. 355–358, 365–374.

"Weddings/Celebrations, Daniel Gross and Steven Goldstein." *New York Times,* September 1, 2002. Available at http://www.nytimes.com.

"Why I Wrote *The Well of Loneliness.*" Letter by Radclyffe Hall, 1932. Reprinted from Lesbian Herstory Archives.

Angels in America, by Tony Kushner. Copyright © 1992. Reprinted by permission of the Theatre Communications Group, pp. 46–49, 100–103, 146.

"Prologue." Reprinted by permission from *All the Rage: The Story of Gay Visibility in America,* by Suzanna Danuta Walters. Copyright © 2001 University of Chicago Press, pp. xii–xvii, 8–16.